THE LEGAL RECOGNITION OF ANIMAL SENTIENCE

This book explores the movement towards the recognition of animal sentience in the law. It explores some first principles underpinning the recognition of animal sentience, including the nature and scope of sentience provisions, the connection between sentience and empathy, drafting issues, and the relationship between sentience recognition and animal rights. The book highlights the operation of animal sentience provisions in several jurisdictions throughout the world and considers some sector-specific applications and limitations of animal sentience recognition.

The first book of its kind, it draws together different perspectives as to what this novel turn in the law might mean and where it might lead. The chapters provide a full picture of what the recognition of animal sentience might entail for humans, animals, and our environment, as well as the experiences of different legal jurisdictions in pursuing recognition of animal sentience.

This collection is an essential read for both practitioners and academics alike, as well as any group seeking to advance the interests of non-human animals.

The Legal Recognition of Animal Sentience

Principles, Approaches and Applications

Edited by
Jane Kotzmann
and
MB Rodriguez Ferrere

•HART•
OXFORD • LONDON • NEW YORK • NEW DELHI • SYDNEY

HART PUBLISHING

Bloomsbury Publishing Plc

Kemp House, Chawley Park, Cumnor Hill, Oxford, OX2 9PH, UK

1385 Broadway, New York, NY 10018, USA

29 Earlsfort Terrace, Dublin 2, Ireland

HART PUBLISHING, the Hart/Stag logo, BLOOMSBURY and the Diana logo are trademarks of Bloomsbury Publishing Plc

First published in Great Britain 2024

A catalogue record for this book is available from the British Library.

A catalogue record for this book is available from the Library of Congress.

Library of Congress Control Number: 2023952397

ISBN: HB: 978-1-50997-045-2
ePDF: 978-1-50997-047-6
ePub: 978-1-50997-046-9

Typeset by Compuscript Ltd, Shannon

FOREWORD

Scientific, legal and public thinking about the position of humans within the animal world has seen significant changes in recent times. Although some of the changes have been human-centred, in that many people have increased respect and affection for animals known individually to them and concern for the welfare of all animals, the biggest changes have followed increases in scientific knowledge about biological function, in particular that of brain function. These research results emphasise that humans are part of the animal world and not separate from it. There is only one biology and it is very difficult to find any biological process or ability in humans that does not exist to some degree in another animal species.[1] As a consequence, language, attitudes and practices need to be changed.

Those who exploit other animal species, for example for food, work or as companions, have often tried to distance themselves from those animals by asserting that there are great differences between humans and other species. In its extreme form, the assertion may be that the animal is stupid or lacking in some key ability or behaviour. The words 'animal', 'beast', 'pig', 'donkey' and 'bitch' are used in a pejorative way that suggests a great moral and intellectual disparity between humans and said animal. However, people increasingly now know about the high levels of cognitive ability and emotional functioning in non-human animals. The idea that morality has evolved and necessarily exists in many other social species is increasingly understood.[2] Although there remain many people who retain archaic attitudes to non-human animals, and all people are likely to change their attitudes further in the future, some of this attitudinal change is starting to be reflected in laws, and an important aspect of this is the very welcome subject of this book.

Sentience means having the capacity, the level of awareness and cognitive ability, necessary to have feelings, and a number of abilities are a part of sentience. Hence it is now apparent that many animals are sentient.[3] Individual humans are sentient by a certain stage during early development and they remain sentient unless their brain is significantly damaged. The current scientific view is that the same is true for all vertebrate animals and for some invertebrate animals. At present, cephalopod molluscs such as octopus, cuttlefish and squid and decapod crustaceans such

[1] Tarazona, A.M., Ceballos, M.C. and Broom, D.M. 2020. Human relationships with domestic and other animals: one health, one welfare, one biology. Animals, 10, 43; (pp. 23) doi:10.3390/ani10010043.

[2] Broom, D.M. 2003. The Evolution of Morality and Religion (pp.259). Cambridge: Cambridge University Press.

[3] Broom, D.M. 2014. Sentience and Animal Welfare (pp. 200). Wallingford: CABI; Broom, D.M. 2022. Concepts and interrelationships of awareness, consciousness, sentience and welfare. Journal of Consciousness Studies, 29, 129–149. doi.org:10.53765/20512201.29.3.129.

as crabs, lobsters, prawns and shrimps are considered to be sentient. There are many animals that are not sentient, so the word 'animal' has to be qualified when used in relation to sentience in law.

Many changes or potential changes in law associated with the concept of sentience are discussed in this book. There has also been a challenge to philosophers who comment on what practices are ethical so many of these issues are also the subject of discussion. If animal subjects of legal statements are viewed only as objects or possessions the law has different effects from those if they are viewed as sentient individuals with moral value. The content of the chapters is described in the editors' Introduction. Much of the discourse about law is relevant to the improvement of the welfare of animals that are used by people or affected by human actions. The terminology and phraseology used by the public and in laws is an important aspect of this. One of the consequences of the similarity between humans and other species is that it is desirable that words should be used in the same way when pertaining to humans as when pertaining to non-humans.[4]

Emeritus Professor Donald M Broom
St Catharine's College and Department of Veterinary Medicine
University of Cambridge

[4] Broom, D.M. 2022. Broom and Fraser's Domestic Animal Behaviour and Welfare, 6th edn (pp.545). CABI.

ACKNOWLEDGEMENTS

The editors would like to thank each of the contributors to this volume for their thoughtful and engaging work; Roberta Bassi and Verity Stuart at Hart Publishing for their patient and supportive guidance; and Hayden Clift for his excellent administrative assistance.

CONTENTS

LIST OF CONTRIBUTORS

Eva Bernet Kempers is postdoctoral researcher in law at the University of Antwerp in Belgium, and Junior Research Associate at the Cambridge Centre for Animal Rights Law. She specialises in animal law, with a particular focus on the region of continental Europe. Her research interests include the legal theory of animal rights, animals in private law, and the environmental dimensions of animal rights.

Charlotte Blattner is a Senior Lecturer and Researcher at the Institute of Public Law, University of Bern, Switzerland. She specialises in animal law and climate law. She earned her PhD in Law from the University of Basel, Switzerland, and completed postdoctoral fellowships at Queen's University, Canada and Harvard Law School, Cambridge MA. Her books include *Protecting Animals Within and Across Borders* (Oxford University Press, 2019) and *Animal Labour: A New Frontier of Interspecies Justice?* (Oxford University Press,2020, coedited with Will Kymlicka and Kendra Coulter).

Paulien Christiaenssen is a PhD researcher at the faculty of Law of KU Leuven (Belgium) and the faculty of veterinary science of Ghent University (Belgium). Her joint and interdisciplinary PhD forms part of the governmental research project 'Animal welfare, ethics and law', founded and funded by the Flemish Minister of Animal Welfare. As part of her research, Paulien organises an annual multidisciplinary lecture series on animal welfare.

Carlos Andrés Contreras López, a law graduate from Pontifical Xaverian University and the University of the Basque Country, penned the first animal law PhD thesis in Spain, published as a book in 2016. He taught at the Autonomous University of Barcelona, coordinated Master's in Animal Law, and translated Steven Wise's *Rattling the Cage* into Spanish. A licensed attorney since 2010, he founded www.murlacontreras.com, an animal law firm. Currently, he is the President of the Barcelona Bar Association's Animal Rights Commission, and won the Lush Public Awareness Prize in 2022 for combating animal cruelty. He is currently a Visiting Fellow at the Brooks McCormick Jr Animal Law & Policy Program at Harvard Law School.

Rachel Dunn is a Course Director at Leeds Law School, Leeds Beckett University, UK. She oversees all of the pro bono and employability initiatives in the school, and has set up an animal law module. Rachel's research mainly focuses on the effectiveness and enforcement of animal welfare laws.

Hope Ferdowsian is a professor of medicine at the University of New Mexico School of Medicine and president of Phoenix Zones Initiative, a nongovernmental organisation, in the United States. She is a double board-certified internal medicine, preventive medicine, and global public health physician with expertise in research ethics and policy.

Vanessa Gischkow Garbini is a Brazilian scholar specialising in Animal Law, Human Rights and International Law. She was a Visiting Fellow at the Animal Law & Policy Program (ALLP) from Harvard Law School (2022) and the first Brazilian to accomplish the Animal Law LLM Degree from Lewis & Clark College. She also holds a Master's degree in international law from the Federal University of Rio Grande do Sul, Brazil, where she earned her law degree *cum laude*.

Daniel Goldsworthy is an academic at Deakin University, Australia and is an Australian lawyer admitted to the Supreme Court of Victoria. His work focuses on legal theory and jurisprudential methodology, public law and animal welfare law.

Hira Jaleel is a Teaching Fellow & Adjunct Professor at the Center for Animal Law Studies at Lewis & Clark Law School in Portland, OR, USA, where she teaches Food Law and Aquatic Animal Law. Prior to her academic career, Hira practiced animal law in Pakistan for a number of years, where she litigated extensively to protect animal interests. Hira's current research and scholarship focuses on international and comparative animal law issues, and she is especially interested in developing animal law as a field of study in South Asia, with a focus on Pakistan.

Joshua Jowitt is a lecturer in law at the University of Newcastle. He has published widely in the area of contemporary natural law and the rights of nonhuman beings, and is the author of *Agency, Morality and Law* (Bloomsbury, 2023).

Jane Kotzmann is an Alfred Deakin Postdoctoral Research Fellow looking at the legal recognition of animal sentience in the School of Law at Deakin University in Melbourne, Australia.

Michaël Lessard is a Professor of Law at the University of Sherbrooke, Québec, Canada.

Rajesh K Reddy is Assistant Professor at Lewis & Clark Law School, USA, where he directs the Animal Law Program at the Center for Animal Law Studies. He has served as Editor in Chief of the *Animal Law Review* and sits on the boards of Minding Animals International and the International Coalition for Animal Protection.

Ian Robertson is a barrister and solicitor and Principal at Guardianz Animal Law in Auckland, New Zealand. He is also the cofounder and director of the Sentient Animal Law Foundation and has published widely in the field of animal sentience.

Marcelo Rodriguez Ferrere is an associate professor in the Faculty of Law at the University of Otago in Dunedin, New Zealand. He is the co-author of *Wells on Animal Law in New Zealand.*

Morgan Stonebridge is a PhD candidate at Deakin University, Australia where she researches in animal law. Her doctoral research concerns the use of empathy in generating stable support for the principles of animal law reform. Morgan has an undergraduate degree in Law (with Honours) from Deakin University and has published in leadings journals such as the *University of New South Wales Law Journal, Cornell Journal of Law and Public Policy* and *the Columbia Journal of Environmental Law.*

Steven White is a senior lecturer at Griffith Law School, Griffith University, Brisbane, Australia. He teaches and researches in the area of animal law. Steven has published widely in the field, including in the areas of companion, farm and wild animal protection law, and in international developments in the legal protection of animals.

Joe Wills is a lecturer in law at the University of Leicester and a former Leverhulme Research Fellow. He has published widely on the legal status of animals, the legal foundations of animal welfarism, animal legal personhood and non-anthropocentric jurisprudence. He is also working on a Leverhulme-funded monograph on the legal status of animals in Britain.

TABLE OF CASES

TABLE OF STATUTES AND LEGISLATIVE INSTRUMENTS

Introduction

JANE KOTZMANN AND MB RODRIGUEZ FERRERE

I. Defining Sentience

It is intuitively easy to grasp the broad contours of the concept of sentience. The term refers to an individual's capacity to subjectively experience the world around them. A more detailed and concrete scientific understanding of the term, however, is somewhat elusive. What criteria should be applied to determine whether an individual is sentient? Which species fall within the definition of sentience, and which do not? These and other questions help to explain Professor of Animal Behaviour Mark Briffa's assertion that, 'we can recognise components of sentience but the concept itself is stubbornly resistant to pinning down with a single and broadly agreed on definition … at least when discussed by scientists.'[1]

A cursory glance at some of the more detailed scientific definitions of sentience highlight this problem of indeterminacy. The scientific community will often adopt definitions when working at the outer limits of animal sentience. Thus, Jonathan Birch et al's *Review of the Evidence of Sentience in Cephalopod Molluscs and Decapod Crustaceans* defines sentience simply as:

> [T]he capacity to have feelings. Feelings may include, for example, feelings of pain, distress, anxiety, boredom, hunger, thirst, pleasure, warmth, joy, comfort, and excitement. We humans are sentient beings, and we are all familiar with such feelings from our own lives. A sentient being is 'conscious' in the most elemental, basic sense of the word. It need not be able to consciously reflect on its feelings, as we do, or to understand the feelings of others: to be sentient is simply to have feelings.[2]

David Mellor focuses instead consciousness as the key criterion:

> Sentience is defined as having a capacity to perceive by the senses; a capacity to feel or experience subjectively. For something to be perceived or experienced the animal must be conscious. Thus, the words perceive and experience are taken here to mean to consciously perceive and to consciously experience. This means that the animal is aware

[1] Mark Briffa, 'When should we ascribe sentience to animals? A commentary on "Hermit crabs, shells and sentience" (Elwood 2022)' (2022) 25 *Animal Cognition* 1375, 1376.

[2] Jonathan Birch, Charlotte Burn, Alexandra Schnell, Heather Browning and Andrew Crump, Review of the evidence of sentience in cephalopod molluscs and decapod Crustaceans (LSE Consulting Ltd, 2021) 12.

> of sensations, feelings, emotions and other subjective outputs of the neural processing of sensory inputs generated both from within the body and outside it. By this definition, therefore, animals that are sentient must possess a capacity to be conscious.[3]

While consciousness and 'having feelings' also feature within Donald Broom's seminal encapsulation of sentience, his definition goes further by including a range of abilities, meaning that:

> [A] sentient being is one that has some ability: (i) to evaluate the actions of others in relation to itself and third parties; (ii) to remember some of its own actions and their consequences; (iii) to assess risks and benefits; (iv) to have some feelings; and (v) to have some degree of awareness.[4]

As Briffa notes, Broom's definition and his use of the modifier 'some' indicates that he 'views sentience as a continuum rather than a binary distinction'.[5]

The different emphases and understanding represented in the above scientific definitions of sentience can bring about similar ambiguity when the term is included in legislation and thus transformed into a legal term. Legislators have generally pursued the approach advocated by contributors Ian Robertson and Daniel Goldsworthy, that 'a legislative definition of sentience should be consistent with contemporary developments in the science of animal welfare'.[6] Following this approach, however, means that the indeterminacy present in science then becomes incorporated in law. The result is, as Charlotte Blattner presciently noted in a previous work, 'despite the widespread avowal to sentience, the function and operability of the legal recognition of animal sentience are nebulous and lack scholarly conceptualisation'.[7]

Robertson and Goldsworthy themselves advance a definition based on Mellor's Five Domains model, viz: 'Sentience means that an animal experiences negative and positive (physical, mental and emotional) states'.[8] This broad idea returns us to our intuitive idea about animal sentience, helpfully with a little additional texture and more contours. While there might be dissensus within animal welfare science about the limits and depth of animal sentience, there is consensus about its central idea: animals can experience affective emotional states.

Lest we forget, humans are animals who can experience affective emotional states; indeed, discussions about sentience often reveal a deep anthropocentrism that sees those states and human sentience as the benchmark for measuring

[3] David Mellor, 'Welfare-aligned Sentience: Enhanced Capacities to Experience, Interact, Anticipate, Choose and Survive' (2019) 9 *Animals* 440, 444.

[4] Donald M Broom, *Sentience and Animal Welfare* (London, CABI, 2014) 20.

[5] Briffa (n 1) 1376.

[6] Ian Robertson and Daniel Goldsworthy, 'Recognising and Defining Animal Sentience in Legislation: A Framework for Importing Positive Animal Welfare through the Five Domains Model' (2022) 48 *Monash Law Review* 244, 245.

[7] Charlotte E Blattner, 'The Recognition of Animal Sentience by the Law' (2019) 9 *Journal of Animal Ethics* 121, 122.

[8] At 246.

the sentience of other animals. For the avoidance of doubt, however, whenever contributors refer to 'animals', this is simply shorthand for 'non-human animals'.

II. Legal Implications of Sentience Recognition

This collection was motivated by the desire to contribute to filling the gap in scholarship on the legal recognition of animal sentience identified by Blattner. Numerous jurisdictions around the world have enacted legal provisions recognising that animals are sentient. The placement of and language in these provisions differ as between jurisdictions. Drawing on this wealth of experience, the intention of this collection is to explore the theoretical principles that might underpin the legal recognition of animal sentience, the legal implications of sentience recognition, the different experiences of sentience recognition in diverse jurisdictions, and what sentience recognition means for animals that are frequently discriminated against (if anything). This detailed analysis will hopefully serve not only to deepen understanding of this development in the law, but also to provide some insight as to whether legally recognising sentience is a worthy objective for animal advocates, and whether it goes any way towards improving the legal landscape – and thus lived experience – for the animals with whom we share this planet.

Establishing an overarching definition of sentience to apply across this collection would assist clarity for the reader. The different scientific and legal understandings of sentience, however, would make such a definition essentially unworkable for contributors. Moreover, the lack of clarity that frequently accompanies the legal recognition of animal sentience forms the basis of several discussions in this collection. Thus, where relevant, contributors will state their preferred definition of sentience.

III. The Contributions in this Volume

This collection is divided into three parts. Part one features four chapters that address the first principles of sentience recognition. These principles encompass theoretical issues with, and the potential for, the recognition of sentience in the abstract. In the first chapter, Charlotte Blattner seeks to clarify the nature and scope of the legal recognition of sentience. Her analysis explores the relationship between sentience and dominant theories in animal ethics and the motivations underlying the earliest instances of the legal recognition of sentience. Blattner argues that at least nine consequences of this legal development can be identified. More importantly, however, she argues that a consistent approach to sentience recognition should lead to additional consequences, which would be of significantly greater import for the lives of individual animals.

In chapter two, 'Sentience, Empathy, and the Need for Both Justification and Motivation', Morgan Stonebridge focuses on the connection between sentience and empathy, which she conceptualises as the human and animal sides of animal protection. In this respect, she asserts that, 'sentience represents the animal side – it goes to justifying their claims to protection, and empathy represents the human side – it makes that justification *felt*.' Stonebridge argues that legal recognition of sentience may be conceived as a tool for cultivating empathy, which is critical to motivate support for animal protection. Stonebridge's work here joins a recent turn in animal studies scholarship away from a focus on rationality and towards a focus on sentiment.

Daniel Goldsworthy and Ian A Robertson focus on the more practical issue of drafting and interpreting sentience provisions in chapter three. They assert that careful drafting of sentience recognition provisions can effectively incorporate modern animal welfare science into legislation. In this respect, they assert that legislators should recognise and define animal sentience by reference to the negative and positive affective states of animals and consistently with the Five Domains model of animal welfare. Usefully for legislators and policy-makers, they provide suggested objects clauses and definitions for inclusion into principal animal welfare legislation.

In chapter four, 'Sentience Recognition as a Means for Moving Beyond Animal Welfare to Animal Rights', Jane Kotzmann addresses a prominent criticism of the legal recognition of animal sentience – that in itself it will not make any difference to the lives of animals and will not lead to the recognition of animal rights. She contends that while sentience recognition can fairly be criticised, it does have the potential to strengthen public debate in relation to the situation of animals, which must precede any significant change in the legal paradigm governing animals. Moreover, she argues that sentience recognition can provide a theoretical foundation for fundamental animal rights. On balance, then, Kotzmann views sentience recognition as a positive development for animals.

While part one focuses on theoretical aspects of animal sentience recognition, the chapters in part two survey different jurisdictions that have legally recognised animal sentience in some manner. The intent of this part is to provide a survey of the varied and various approaches to recognising animal sentience, as well as provide the reader with an insight into the common themes behind that recognition in both civil law and common law jurisdictions.

In that vein, Eva Bernet Kempers begins chapter five with an analysis of the recognition of animal sentience across the civil law world. She argues that the trend of such jurisdictions needs to go further than simply recognising sentience, but also that averring that 'animals are not things' – the dereification of animals – 'has the potential to further influence the way in which animals are addressed in private law, limiting the powers of animal owners'.

From the common law perspective, Joe Wills in chapter six helpfully provides a primer of common law methodology before examining the many entry points of the common law in the recognition of sentience. This begins with an analysis of the common law's inheritance of Roman law's categorisation of non-human animals as property, before looking at the ways the common law has slowly eroded the hard edges of that classification; in family custody disputes, tort law, and criminal procedure we see common law courts increasingly willing to challenge the status of animals as property. At the same time, Wills also documents judicial reticence to advance that cause, showing that while statutory recognition of animal sentience has the potential to lead to judicial momentum that achieves congruence with the way society commonly views animals, 'even the most well-crafted litigation efforts to extend animal protection through the common law are by no means a guarantee of success'.

Having set the general scene from both the civil law and common law perspectives, this part then examines several jurisdictional experiences of the recognition of sentience. In chapter seven Vanessa Gischkow Garbini considers the experience in Brazil, one of the few countries to give animal protection constitutional status. Gischkow Garbini surveys the country's differing levels of protection for companion animals, and recent developments within Brazil, including the 'Animals Are Not Things Bill', which would continue the trend of dereification in civil law. Hira Jaleel's contribution in chapter eight covers both India and Pakistan, providing a compelling and timely comparative account of the two jurisdictions. While India and Pakistan share some traditions and have similar political and legal systems, there are major differences in the legislative protections they provide to animals. India gives the protection of animals constitutional status, whereas Pakistan still relies on pre-Partition colonial animal cruelty legislation. Jaleel's chapter is a fascinating assessment of the recent advances by courts in both jurisdictions, for instance India's Supreme Court recognition of the inherent dignity of animals in the *Nagaraja* decision,[9] and Islamabad High Court of Pakistan's *Kaavan* decision, which ordered the closure of the city's zoo after holding that animals possess both legal and natural rights.[10]

In chapter nine, Marcelo Rodriguez Ferrere assesses the impact of New Zealand's legislative recognition of animal sentience in 2015, concluding that in the intervening eight years, while there has been some movement in the language used by courts, it has not fomented a revolution in the way that jurisdiction views animals. In contrast, in chapter ten Michaël Lessard looks at the impact of Québec's legislative dereification of animals and recognition of sentience which occurred in the same year as New Zealand's recognition. Lessard notes that the law's further recognition that animals have 'biological needs' potentially has echoes in Martha Nussbaum's capabilities approach. Carlos Andrés Contreras López's analysis of Spain in chapter eleven shows that amendments to that jurisdiction's Civil Code, distinguishing animals from things by recognising them as

[9] *Animal Welfare Board of India v Nagaraja and Ors* 2014 (7) SCC 547, [32].

[10] *Islamabad Wildlife Management Board v Metropolitan Corporation of Islamabad* (2021) PLD (Islamabad) 6 (Pak).

'living beings endowed with sensitivity' and as 'sentient beings' is a major step forward. The recognition led directly to the creation of a General Directorate for Animal Rights, which in turn saw the enactment of both national animal rights and protection legislation and the amendment of the Spanish Criminal Code, showing the recognition of animal sentience has the power to initiate further, substantive changes within the law.

In chapter twelve, Rachel Dunn and Joshua Jowitt provide extensive analysis of the United Kingdom's establishment of the Animal Science Committee following the enactment of that jurisdiction's Animal Welfare (Sentience) Act 2022. This Committee – with the capacity to 'scrutinise all government policy at the pre-legislative stage for the extent to which drafters have paid due regard to any adverse effect their proposals might have on the interests of sentient animals' – is globally unique and the object of much attention, particularly from the common law world. However, as Dunn and Jowitt argue, the wide discretion of the Committee to choose which policy proposals to scrutinise, alongside the narrow expertise of its volunteer membership, should temper any excitement around the novelty of this innovation. Whilst in its infancy, the Committee has the potential to become a highly effective source of protection for animals, but that efficacy is still only hypothetical. Raj Reddy concludes part two by focusing primarily on the experience of Oregon's recognition of animal sentience. While that state jurisdiction is a clear leader within the United States in recognising and protect the interests of animals, the corpus of jurisprudence it has generated following its legislative recognition of sentience also makes it a leader within the common law world. Reddy's analysis – like all the chapters in this part – provides a compelling historical and contextual account of Oregon's approach, whilst looking to the potential of the success of the legislative recognition of animal sentience begetting more success in that jurisdiction and others, such as New York and Oklahoma.

Finally, the volume canvasses some of the sector-specific applications of animal sentience recognition and the likely limitations of this legal development. In chapter fourteen, Steven White investigates how the legal recognition of animal sentience might affect the level of legal protection provided to commercial farm animals. Through an analysis of Australian regulation and international developments, White demonstrates that express recognition of sentience in animal protection law may not materially change the legal status of farm animals. Nevertheless, White maintains that if sentience recognition becomes institutionalised and acknowledged in both law and non-statutory standards, it has potential to contribute to a shared understanding of farm animals as having intrinsic interests worthy of protection.

Paulien Christiaenssen provides a valuable insight into the European Union's recognition of animal sentience as it might apply to invertebrates in chapter fifteen. Drawing from the experience of environmental law's adoption of the precautionary principle, Christiaenssen argues that such a principle could and should apply to policy-making involving species whose sentience does not have a conclusive answer. Her case study into both the legal application of the precautionary principle and studies showing the sentience of invertebrates is a good demonstration of the concomitant relationship between animal welfare science and legal scholarship.

In chapter sixteen, Jane Kotzmann and Hope Ferdowsian investigate whether the legal recognition of animal sentience might impact decisions relating to the use of animals in scientific research. Although animal sentience has been a long-standing principle for the use of animals in research, Kotzmann and Ferdowsian argue that express recognition of sentience carries meanings that could impact the public perception of animals. As a result, they contend that sentience recognition may 'refocus attention away from what constitutes tolerable cruelty by and for humans, towards the impact of research on the subjective experience of animals and resulting ethical and legal implications'.

Finally, in chapter seventeen, Marcelo Rodriguez Ferrere ends the volume by assessing the nature and effect of symbolic legislation. Especially within common law jurisdictions, recognising animal sentience within the preambular sections of legislation is often a strong indication of symbolic intent by legislatures. Coupled with the indeterminacy surrounding such recognition of animal sentience when the term lacks an accompanying legislative definition, there is justification in asking whether such provisions have the potential to lead to any substantive change. Rodriguez Ferrere argues that while there are drawbacks to symbolic legislation, the potential for indirect and direct positive outcomes means that any symbolic recognition of sentience should not be dismissed out of hand.

The three sections of this volume cohere to provide a comprehensive account of recognition of animal sentience in different legal contexts and environments. In this dynamic and burgeoning field, there are many questions surrounding the efficacy and potential of the legal recognition of sentience. Is sentience recognition merely a trend, followed by different jurisdictions to keep up with one another? Or is it the beginning of a paradigm shift that gives legislatures, courts and society a new vocabulary to talk about the importance of protecting the interests and dignity of animals? This volume details the experiences of different jurisdictions, the potential and the pitfalls of the legal recognition of sentience, and it is hoped that that the contributions here represent merely the beginning of an important and exciting conversation.

PART ONE

First Principles of Sentience Recognition

1

The Nature and Scope of the Legal Recognition of Animal Sentience: A Functional Comparative Analysis of the *Lex Lata*, and Critical Remarks on its Future Development

CHARLOTTE E BLATTNER

I. Introduction

Over the past 35 years, we have witnessed a wave of legal reforms across civil and common law jurisdictions to recognise animals as sentient beings. In the last five years alone, media outlets have reported almost monthly on the enactment of such new laws and hailed it as a 'huge milestone'.[1] New laws recognising animal sentience are often backed by political consensus and enjoy broad public support, but they tend to be poorly understood, both in theory and practice. It is regularly unknown, for example, which animals qualify as sentient (and based on which factors) and who defines their sentience (or the lack thereof) or decides on their recognition. Most importantly, the normative consequences of this recognition remain opaque, as highlighted by the debate over Brexit, the lack of recognition of animal sentience in the EU Withdrawal Act 2018, and the question of whether adding such a provision to existing law would materially affect it.[2]

Taking a bird's eye perspective, this chapter aims to contribute to clarifying the nature and scope of the legal recognition of animal sentience. In an introductory fashion, section II locates sentience as a central concept underlying the most dominant theories in animal ethics. Section III explores the earliest sites of the

[1] Margarita Sachkova, 'Huge Milestone! UK Law Now Recognises Animals as Being Sentient' (PETA UK, 28 April 2022).

[2] See Elena Ares, 'Research Briefing "Animal Welfare (Sentience) Bill"' (UK Parliament, House of Commons Library, 3 March 2022).

legal recognition of animal sentience in Austria (1988), Germany (1990), and the Treaty of Amsterdam (1997) to uncover the underlying political and legislative intentions. Section IV offers a functional comparative analysis of the most notable and recent forms of this recognition in common and civil law countries. Building on this, section V argues that there are at least nine effects that have already manifested as a result. Their normative force and transformational potential, however, remain limited. Thinking sentience through more consistently, section VI argues for four more effects that are both urgent and important: (1) equal treatment among and between sentient beings; (2) laws protecting the positive dimensions of animal sentience, including through duties to protect and fulfill; (3) introducing fundamental rights for animals based on sentience; and (4) challenging the 'necessary' use of nonhuman animals. The chapter concludes with tentative remarks on the value of the legal recognition of animal sentience.

II. Sentience in Animal Ethics

Sentience is a somewhat peculiar concept. Although human animals are sentient, too, sentience tends to be discussed mostly in relation to beings whose capacities and qualities to be or experience sentience stand to the test, like nonhuman animals and artificial intelligence.[3] Sentience today is a multifactorial area of research that is informed by a range of disciplines, including animal welfare science, neuroscience, physiology, animal behaviour science, comparative psychology, animal ethics and the law – each with its own methodology, terminology and theories about what sentience encompasses (or ought to encompass).[4]

Among these, it is recognised that sentience comprises far more than the ability to experience nociception, which is a simple response to sensations. In reaction to stimuli, sentient animals learn to associate these sensations physically and emotionally. For example, they seek to avoid negative stimuli and, if they cannot avoid them, they develop anxiety or learned helplessness. The reactions of sentient animals demonstrate their ability to experience negative affective states – such as pain, suffering and anxiety – and positive affective states – such as pleasure, joy, happiness and fulfillment.[5] These states in turn motivate animals to either seek satisfaction (of positive needs) or avoid suffering (by avoiding negative stimuli).[6] In both cases, there is an intrinsic importance of this satisfaction or avoidance to

[3] See for a provoking account of sentience (or lack thereof) across humans, artificial intelligence and nonhuman animals, Marian Stamp Dawkins, 'Unconscious Humans, Autonomous Machines and the Difficulty of Knowing which Animals Are Sentient' (2022) 32 *Animal Sentience* 436.

[4] Helen Proctor, 'Animal Sentience: Where Are We and Where Are We Heading?' (2012) 2 *Animals* 628; Ian JH Duncan, 'The Changing Concept of Animal Sentience' (2006) 100 *Applied Animal Behavior Science* 11.

[5] Donald M Broom, *Sentience and Animal Welfare* (Cabi, 2014) 20.

[6] John Webster, 'Sentience and Animal Protection' in Marc Bekoff and Carron A Meaney (eds), *Encyclopedia of Animal Rights and Animal Welfare*, 2nd edn (ABC-CLIO, 2013) 507, 508.

the animal.[7] As Darwin succinctly put it some 150 years ago: 'A Sentient Animal is one for whom Feelings Matter.'[8] Or in more elaborate words by Francione,

> the observation that animals are sentient is different from saying that they are merely alive. To be sentient means to be the sort of being who is conscious of pain and pleasure; there is an 'I' who has subjective experiences.[9]

Awareness about or intrinsic importance of affective states are the key ingredients, if you will, of sentience that renders it an axiomatic concept across disciplines, which has slowly but surely redirected the earlier emphasis on rationality. In animal ethics, sentience plays a pivotal role from its very beginnings. Building on the late eighteenth-century doctrine of Jeremy Bentham (1748–1832),[10] Peter Singer famously argued that sentience is what determines the status of being a moral subject. Every sentient being – be it human or nonhuman – deserves to have their interests given equal consideration.[11] Also in the deontological tradition, sentience features prominently as the relevant threshold criterion for establishing animal rights, in key writings from Regan,[12] to Francione,[13] Cavalieri,[14]

[7] Some scholars refer to the ability to experience affective states as sentience and to the intrinsic importance of affective states as consciousness. In this view, sentience is a minimal definition or a nuance of consciousness. Most theorists of animal sentience, however, usually use a broad definition that includes both the ability to experience pain and pleasure and the intrinsic importance to the being experiencing those feelings. See, eg, Broom, *Sentience and Animal Welfare* (n 5) 5: 'a sentient being is one that has some ability: (i) to evaluate the actions of others in relation to itself and third parties; (ii) to remember some of its own actions and their consequences; (iii) to assess risks and benefits; (iv) to have some feelings; and (v) to have some degree of awareness.' See also Gary Steiner, *Animals and the Moral Community: Mental Life, Moral Status, and Kinship* (Columbia University Press, 2008) xi–xii: 'Sentience is a capacity shared by all beings for whom the struggle for life and flourishing matters, whether or not the being in question has a reflective sense of which things matter or how they matter.'

[8] Charles Darwin, *The Expression of Emotions in Man and Animals* (John Murray, 1872).

[9] Gary L Francione, *Introduction to Animal Rights: Your Child or the Dog?* (Temple University Press, 2000) 6. See also Steiner (n 7) xi–xii: 'Sentience is a capacity shared by all beings for whom the struggle for life and flourishing matters, whether or not the being in question has a reflective sense of which things matter or how they matter.'

[10] A footnote from Jeremy Bentham is probably the most quoted argument for sentientism: 'It may one day come to be recognised that the number of the legs, the villosity of the skin, or the termination of the os sacrum are reasons equally insufficient for abandoning a sensitive being to the same fate. What else is it that should trace the insuperable line? Is it the faculty of reason or perhaps the faculty of discourse? But a full-grown horse or dog is beyond comparison a more rational, as well as more conversable animal, than an infant of a day or a week or even a month old. But suppose they were otherwise, what would it avail? The question is not, Can they reason?, nor Can they talk? but, *Can they suffer*?' (Jeremy Bentham, *An Introduction to the Principles of Morals and Legislation* (Clarendon, 1781) 310–11 fn 1, emphasis in original).

[11] Peter Singer, *Animal Liberation* (Random House, 1975) 8–11. On the principle of equal consideration, see Peter Singer, *Practical Ethics* (Cambridge University Press, 1993) 21: 'The essence of the principle of equal consideration of interests is that we give equal weight in our moral deliberations to the like interests of all those affected by our actions.' Note that Singer clearly distinguishes between sentient beings who are 'just that' and those that additionally have consciousness (*not* self-consciousness). Only the latter, in his view, have a personal interest in continuing to live.

[12] Tom Regan, *The Case for Animal Rights* (University of California Press, 2004) 81.

[13] eg, Gary L Francione, *Animals as Persons: Essays on the Abolition of Animal Exploitation* (Columbia University Press, 2008) 129 ff.

[14] Paola Cavalieri, *The Animal Question: Why Nonhuman Animals Deserve Rights* (Oxford University Press, 2002) 32.

Dunayer[15] and Steiner.[16] The more recent political turn in animal ethics works toward developing theories of interspecies justice where sentience, too, operates as the baseline upon which animals qualify for inviolable basic rights.[17] As Donaldson and Kymlicka argue, animals are 'selves,' ie 'they have a distinctive subjective experience of their own lives and the world, which demands a specific kind of protection in the form of inviolable rights.'[18] Feminist scholars, too, support the shift in animal ethics away from rationality to sentience, but argue for more expansive criteria that capture features of embodiment, vulnerability and relationality.[19] Nevertheless, sentient beings do clearly qualify for moral status according to feminist theorists.

III. The Emergence of Sentience as a Concept in Law

Given the axiomatic relevance of sentience in animal ethics debates, it is unsurprising that the concept also plays a key role in the emergence of animal laws during the twentieth century. In the United Kingdom (UK), for example, Ruth Harrison's *Animal Machines* prompted politics to hone in on sentience following widespread public outcry; this ultimately culminated in the Brambell Report that changed animal welfare legislation in the UK and beyond, by putting emphasis back on animals and their needs, and further professionalising the legal bases, requirements and institutional arrangements.[20] A majority of states today have in

[15] Joan Dunayer, *Animal Equality: Language and Liberation* (Ryce Publishing, 2001) xvii: 'Sentience entitles nonhuman animals to legal rights.'

[16] Steiner (n 7) 5. See also Gary Steiner, *What We Owe to Nonhuman Animals: The Historical Pretensions of Reason and the Ideal of Felt Kinship* (Routledge, 2023).

[17] eg, Sue Donaldson and Will Kymlicka, *Zoopolis: A Political Theory of Animal Rights* (Oxford University Press, 2011) 24–26; Svenja Ahlhaus and Peter Niesen, 'Animal Politics: A New Research Agenda in Political Theory' (2015) 40 *Historical Social Research* 15; Alasdair Cochrane, *Sentientist Politics: A Theory of Global Inter-Species Justice* (Oxford University Press, 2018) 3.

[18] Donaldson and Kymlicka (n 18) 24–26.

[19] For many, see Maneesha Deckha, *Animals as Legal Beings: Contesting Anthropocentric Legal Orders* (University of Toronto Press, 2021) 145 ff.

[20] Ruth Harrison, *Animal Machines* (Vincent Stuart, 1964). Harrison was motivated by more than 'the fact that these animals were stressed …; it was the fact that they were sentient and could feel stressed.' (Duncan (n 4) 13). While drafting the Brambell Report, the responsible committee said assessing animal welfare depended on acknowledging sentience: 'Welfare is a wide term that embraces both the physical and mental well-being of the animal. Any attempt to evaluate welfare, therefore, must take into account the scientific evidence available concerning the feelings of animals that can be derived from their structure and functions and also from their behaviour.' (FW Rogers Brambell, Report of the Technical Committee to Enquire into the Welfare of Animals Kept under Intensive Livestock Husbandry Systems (Her Majesty's Stationery Office, 1965), command paper 2836). The Brambell Report spurred the Agriculture (Miscellaneous Provisions) Act 1968 (UK) and the UK Farm Animal Welfare Advisory Body, which established the Five Freedoms: freedom from hunger and thirst (animals shall have ready access to fresh water and adequate food); freedom from discomfort (animals shall be given appropriate shelter and comfortable resting area); freedom from pain, injury, and disease (which requires acting preventively, rapidly, and with adequate treatment); freedom to express normal

force acts specifically dedicated to protecting animals or their welfare.[21] Most of these have historically not given an explicit reason for what concept or criterion prompted legislators to enact those laws (Is it animals' sentience? Their proximity to humans? The social relations we share? Compassion?).[22] Rather, these acts consider animals worthy of protection (in whatever form) by the law, mostly in an implicit and self-evident manner.[23]

IV. The Legal Recognition of Animal Sentience

In a somehow peculiar fashion – lagging behind these enactments – in recent decades, we have been witnessing a wave of legal reforms across civil and common law jurisdictions that explicitly or implicitly recognise animals as sentient beings.[24] The earliest site of this recognition is Central Europe. In 1988, the Austrian legislator first began to break with the sacrosanct distinction in property law between legal subjects and legal objects by introducing §285a to the Austrian Civil Code on the basis of sentience, providing, among other things, that 'animals are not things – they are protected by special laws.'[25] The amendment soon met with sharp criticism. Legal scholars remarked that the provision had no normative content,[26] arguing that it merely was an 'act of appeasement'[27] and 'verbal cosmetics'.[28] The criticism seems justified considering that §285a, in the second sentence, clarifies that despite this recognition, 'The provisions applicable to property are only to be applied to animals insofar as no deviating regulations exist.' Any normative force that could, in theory, arise from the recognition of the first sentence, is thus immediately cancelled out by this second sentence. In other

behaviour (animals shall have sufficient space, proper facilities, and be able to maintain social relations); and freedom from fear and distress.

[21] See for an up-to-date assessment, 'Database Legislation: Animal Legislations in the World at National Level' (Global Animal Law (GAL) Association, 2023), available at www.globalanimallaw.org/database/national/index.html.

[22] See for an interesting discussion among a group of philosophers about what basis is most adequate and/or effective for giving chimpanzees rights: Kristin Andrews, Gary Comstock, Crozier GKD, Sue Donaldson, Andrew Fenton, Tyler John, L Syd M Johnson, Robert Jones, Will Kymlicka, Letitia Meynell, Nathan Nobis, David Pena-Guzman and Jeff Sebo, *Chimpanzee Rights: The Philosophers' Brief* (Routledge, 2019).

[23] See Charlotte E Blattner, *Protecting Animals Within and Across Borders: Extraterritorial Jurisdiction and the Challenges of Globalization* (Oxford University Press, 2019) 75.

[24] See generally, Charlotte E Blattner, 'The Recognition of Animal Sentience by the Law' (2019) 9 *Journal of Animal Ethics* 121.

[25] *Allgemeines Bürgerliches Gesetzbuch, BGBl. I No. 43/2016* (AUS), § 285a.

[26] This is still the case today; see Christian Holzner, '§ 285a ABGB' in Peter Rummel and Meinhard Lukas (eds), *Kommentar zu Allgemeinen bürgerlichen Gesetzbuch, Teilband §§ 285–446 ABGB* (Manz, 2016) 1.

[27] Peter Bydlinski, 'Das Tier, (k)eine Sache?' (1988) *RdW* 157, 157.

[28] Monika Gimpel-Hinteregger, 'Das Tier als Sache und Ersatz der Heilungskosten für ein verletztes Tier' (1989) *ÖJZ* 65.

words, law enforcement authorities have no choice but to apply the property law principles to animals – unless there are *leges speciales* in animal law, which would require legislators to become active.[29] Two years after the introduction of this new provision in Austria, the German Civil Code enshrined an almost identical provision with section 90a.[30]

The first reference to animals as sentient beings in EU legislation emerged in 1997.[31] In that year, the Treaty of Amsterdam added a protocol to the EC Treaty,[32] whereby parties, 'Desiring to ensure improved protection and respect for the welfare of animals *as sentient beings*' (emphasis added), committed themselves and the EC to 'pay full regard to the welfare requirements of animals … in formulating and implementing the Community's agricultural, transport, internal market and research policies.'

Similar provisions were enacted in other jurisdictions. In 1999, New Zealand's Animal Welfare Act in its long title provided that it is an act to, amongst other things, 'recognize that animals are sentient'.[33] In 2002, Switzerland newly introduced Article 641*a* of the Swiss Civil Code, which provides that 'Animals are not objects', and as such recognises animals as living and sentient beings.[34] In 2008, Tanzania made explicit mention of sentience in its Animal Welfare Act.[35] In 2009, Chile enacted its Animal Protection Law on the basis of, among others, animal sentience.[36] In 2011, the Netherlands amended its Animals Act to provide in a separate norm that animals' intrinsic value is recognised, stating:

> Recognition of the intrinsic value as referred to in the first paragraph is taken to mean recognition of the inherent value of animals, being sentient beings. When rules are laid down by or pursuant to this Act, and decisions based on those rules are taken, full account is taken of the consequences of these rules or decisions for the intrinsic value of the animal, without prejudice to other legitimate interests.[37]

In 2012, the Czech Civil Code abandoned the definition of animals as 'things' and replaced it with 'living creature with senses'.[38] The same year, Lithuania lay down that it is the purpose of its animal protection act to 'ensure the welfare and

[29] Theresa Bahn, 'Das Tier im Familien- und Erbrecht' (2018) *TiRuP* 63, 64.

[30] *Bürgerliches Gesetzbuch, BGBl. I 42, 2909, 2003 at 738* (GER), § 90a.

[31] Tara Camm and David Bowles, 'Animal Welfare and the Treaty of Rome: A Legal Analysis of the Protocol on Animal Welfare and Welfare Standards in the European Union' (2000) 12 *Journal of Environmental Law* 197, 204.

[32] Hence, the protocol is an integral part of the treaty (as set out in Art 239 EC Treaty). See today, Consolidated Version of the Treaty on the Functioning of the European Union [2012] OJ C 326/47, Art 13.

[33] Animal Welfare Act 1999 (NZ), long title.

[34] The exact German wording is 'Tiere sind keine Sachen' (Civil Code, SR 210 2002 (SWITZ), Art 641*a*, para 1). The recognition of animal sentience is made explicit in the accompanying report: Kommission für Rechtsfragen des Nationalrates, *Bericht Parlamentarische Initiativen 'Tiere keine Sache' und 'Wirbeltiere: Geesetzliche Bestimmungen'* (18 May 1999) 8940.

[35] Animal Welfare Act 2008 (TZ), §§ 3, 4(b)(i).

[36] Law No 20380, Sobre Protección de Animales, 11 September 2009 (CL), Art 2.

[37] Wet dieren 2011 (Animals Act) (NL), Art 1.3(2).

[38] Občanský Zákoník, No 89/2012, 3 February 2012 (CZ), § 494.

protection of animals as sentient beings'.[39] Also in 2012, in *Martinez v Robledo*, the California Court of Appeals held that 'animals are special, sentient beings, because unlike other forms of property, animals feel pain, suffer and die.'[40] One year later, in 2013, Oregon amended its animal cruelty laws to establish that 'animals are sentient beings capable of experiencing pain, stress and fear.'[41] On 16 February 2015, France passed Article 515-14 in the French Civil Code, which now provides that animals are living beings who are able to suffer.[42] In Canada, Minister Paradis introduced a Bill in 2015 to modify the Civil Code of Québec to remove animals from the movable property category. The Code now determines that 'Animals are not things. They are sentient beings and have biological needs.'[43]

In January 2016, then-President Santos of Colombia signed a law introducing Article 655 to Colombia's Civil Code, which recognises animals as sentient beings and penalises crimes against animals with fines up to 11,000 USD and 36 months' imprisonment.[44] Also in 2016, Peru chose to include animal sentience as a principle in its animal welfare and protection legislation.[45] In December 2016, the Portuguese Party for Animals (*Partido Animalista Portugués*) succeeded in convincing Parliament to approve a modification of the Civil Code that provides animals are not legal objects and recognises them as sentient beings.[46] A few months later, in February 2017, the Spanish Congress unanimously voted to reform the Spanish Civil Code to consider animals as 'sentient beings'.[47] Similar provisions emerged in 2018 in Brussels[48] and Sweden,[49] in 2019 in the Australian Capital Territory (ACT),[50] and in 2020 in Denmark.[51] In sum, an impressive number of states today expressly embrace the view that animals are sentient beings.

V. Effects of the Legal Recognition of Animal Sentience *de lege lata*

From a scientific point of view, such a recognition is in essence redundant. Sentience is not something we bestow upon animals (or anyone else) and which

[39] Gyvūnų Gerovės ir Apsaugos Įstatymas, No XI-2271, 20 October 2012, No 122-6216 (LT), Art 1(1).
[40] *Martinez v Robledo*, 210 Cal App 4th 384 (2012) (US). See also *Kimes v Grossnerc*, 195 Cal App 4th 1556 (2011) (US).
[41] Offenses Against General Welfare and Animals, Or Rev Stat 2021 (US), §167.305(1).
[42] Code civil, 19 December 2015 (FR), Art 515-14 (FR): 'Les animaux sont des êtres vivants doués de sensibilité.'
[43] Civil Code of Québec, SQ 1991, c 64 (CAN), Art 898.1.
[44] Ley No 1774 de 2016 (CO), Art 665.
[45] Norma 30407/ Ley de Protección y Bienestar Animal 2016 (PE), Art 1.
[46] Código Civil, No 47344/66, 2016 (Port), Arts 333 and 333bis.
[47] Civil Code of Catalonia (Ley de 2006) (Spain), Art 511-1(3).
[48] Law Relating to the Protection and Welfare of Animals 2018 (Brussels), Art 1.
[49] Government Bill No 2017/18 (SWE), 147.
[50] Animal Welfare Act 1992 (ACT) (AUSTR), s 4A(1)(a).
[51] Animal Welfare Act 2020 (DK), Aart 1.

hence only exists because of our recognition. Rather, as Zuolo explains, sentience is an intrinsic property 'that belong[s] to the individual itself' and 'which does not depend on there being a relation with another individual'.[52] From this point of view, the legal recognition of animal sentience cannot be anything but declaratory and hence appears superfluous.

However, because of the broad grounding of animal sentience in animal ethics, where it is used to argue for a whole range of theories (welfarism, abolitionism, political rights), it comes as no surprise that legal theorists, too, debate what the purpose of such a recognition is and what, if any, legal consequences should flow from it. Is its purpose to provide subsequent justification for animal welfare/protection legislation? If so, does sentience add new normative dimensions to the concept of animal welfare? Have legal practitioners misapplied animal protection laws and neglected animals' interests, and are legislators therefore putting emphasis back on sentience? Ought this recognition, as many argue, give rise to new duties and rights?[53] Or is it, as early Austrian law scholars have observed and scientists seem to suggest, devoid of normative content?[54]

Most commentators on animal sentience bemoan its legal recognition as a political gesture without any direct or indirect effect.[55] This would render it an act of mere symbolism.[56] Others argue that the recognition does in fact serve a purpose and have an effect: namely by 'humane-washing'[57] or 'welfare-washing'[58] our use of animals, leading to complacency with the *status quo* and further legitimising future exploitation of animals.[59] A practical example of this is the Victorian Department of Primary Industries' assertion that 'Failure to recognise sentience in livestock species could result in production losses [and] market access loss'.[60]

We should, however, not lose sight of the more subtle effects of this recognition. Between these two extremes, there are, at present, at least nine different types

[52] Federico Zuolo, 'The Moral Value of Animal Sentience and Agency' in Augusto Vitale and Simone Pollo (eds), *Human/Animal Relationships in Transformation: Scientific, Moral and Legal Perspectives* (Palgrave Macmillan 2022) 47, 50.

[53] For many, see Jane Kotzmann, 'Sentience and Intrinsic Worth as a Pluralist Foundation for Fundamental Animal Rights' (2023) 43 *Oxford Journal of Legal Studies* 405.

[54] See nn 27and 28 above.

[55] Blattner (n 24). See similarly, Camm and Bowles (n 31) 198.

[56] Marcelo Rodriguez Ferrere, 'The (Symbolic) Legislative Recognition of Animal Sentience' (2022) 28 *Animal Law* 117.

[57] Marc Bekoff, 'Time to Stop Pretending We Don't Know Other Animals Are Sentient Beings' (2022) 31 *Animal Sentience* 2.

[58] Gary L Francione, 'Surprise: U.K. Law Recognizes That Sentient Animals Are Sentient' (Medium, 16 May 2021), available at www.gary-francione.medium.com/surprise-u-k-law-recognizes-that-sentient-animals-are-sentient-d1e42c29f777.

[59] Jessica Scott-Reid, '"Humane" Meat, Dairy, and Eggs: How to Decipher Animal Welfare Claims on Food Labels' (Vox, 21 December 2021). A longer report published as part of the Effective Altruism Forum acknowledges that humane-washing represents a significant concern but that it is not overall a net negative development: Max Carpendale, 'Does Sentience Legislation Help Animals?' (Effective Altruism Forum, 9 December 2022).

[60] Mariko Lauber, 'Department of Primary Industries: Animal Welfare for Livestock Producers' (Brochure, 15 November 2007) 2, 6.

of effects that have already manifested. The following section will present each in turn in a functional comparative fashion, without qualifying them as either positive or negative, direct or indirect, and without analysing whether and how they are or can be combined in different jurisdictions.

The first and most obvious effect is that sentience is used as *a shorthand to determine the personal scope of animal protection/welfare acts*. These laws usually define animals, and hence (at least supposed) beneficiaries of their protective functions, with reference to their sentience.[61] An example of this is section 1(1) of the UK Animal Welfare Act, which declares that an animal 'means a vertebrate other than man'.[62] As the explanatory notes clarify, the law's narrow focus on vertebrates is justified by sentience: 'The Act will apply only to vertebrate animals, as these are currently the only demonstrably sentient animals.'[63] The Act can, however, be extended to cover invertebrates if they, too, are shown to be 'capable of experiencing pain or suffering'.[64]

The second effect is closely related to the first: reference to sentience tends to *expand the personal scope of animal laws*. By using sentience as the relevant criterion for their personal scope of jurisdiction, the law uses a science-based, and prima facie objective standard to unfold its protective capacities. In other words, those animals that are sentient are protected, not those we consider particularly cute, useful, attractive, or, more broadly speaking, bear similarities to humans. Having a law in place that determines that sentience alone matters helps to eradicate some of the biggest cognitive biases that shape our subjective social reality as we (aim to) protect other animals.[65] This, in turn, tends to lead to a more expansive protective reach of animal laws.

An apt example in this respect is the legislation in Norway: The Norwegian Animal Welfare Act applies to conditions that affect the welfare of or respect for mammals, birds, reptiles, amphibians, fishes, decapods, squid, octopi and honey bees.[66] The law extends this protection to animals in prenatal stages, with reference to sentience: 'The Act applies equally to the development stages of the animals referred to in cases where the sensory apparatus is equivalent to the developmental level in living animals.'[67] In other jurisdictions, recognition of sentience is enshrined in civil law and, if animal laws remain concerned, eg, with vertebrates only, this may result in a broader scope of the civil law provisions compared to the animal welfare/protection acts.[68] The last point to mention here is that determination of sentience is in many legislations guided by the precautionary principle, such that when it doubt, we should err on the side of considering a species rather

[61] See generally, Blattner (n 24) 124.
[62] Animal Welfare Act (AWA) 2006 (UK), s 1(1).
[63] AWA, Explanatory Notes, section 1, at 11.
[64] ibid.
[65] See further Blattner (n 24) 127 ff.
[66] Animal Welfare Act 2009 (NOR), § 2.
[67] ibid.
[68] That is the case, eg, in Austria and Switzerland.

sentient than insentient.[69] This, too, leads to a more expansive reach of animal protection/welfare acts.

Third, and again related to the first and second points, expansion of the personal scope of animal laws may have a *material effect on the protections these animals receive as a matter of law*. This sounds straightforward, but is not necessarily self-evident considering the idiosyncrasies of animal law. Many animal protection/welfare acts tend to have detailed provisions laying down how nonhuman animals ought to be handled. If the law recognises a species of animal as 'newly' sentient for the first time, eg, octopi, these animals often do not immediately enjoy material 'protections' – that is, until the legislator also lays down the more detailed provisions on how they should be handled. Switzerland, for example, had long recognised the sentience of crustaceans, but only a few years later made international headlines when it became the first country to ban boiling lobsters alive.[70]

The fourth effect relates to the legal status of animals. Legislators, as they recognised and established sentience as a guiding principle of animal law, often have done so in an effort to distinguish animals as sentient beings from inanimate objects (eg a chair or pair of shoes) and animate but mostly insentient objects (eg a sunflower). Consider the amendment of the Swiss Civil Code in 2002, stipulating that 'Animals are not objects.'[71] This was done to meet society's growing concern for animals and to ameliorate the legal status of animals. The traditional conception that animals are things, as the Federal Council stipulated, was seen by society as an ancient relict.[72] As in Austria, the Swiss legislator, too, foresaw that property rules nonetheless apply to animals unless more specific laws suggest otherwise.[73] Despite this, the Swiss and other legislators' decision to distance animals from inanimate/insentient objects linguistically and through the law is increasingly argued to add to the steady dissolution of the seemingly rigid Roman law subject/object division, leading the way to the *gradual establishment of a third form of legal personhood for animals* (legal personhood *sui generis*).[74]

Fifth, recognition and emphasis on animal sentience are argued to be *motivated by concern for 'individual animals* rather than a commercial or conservationist interest in the health of species or of farm stocks.'[75] In this sense, the bill of rights introduced for cats and dogs in California in 2022 explicitly states that 'Dogs and

[69] See the chapter in this book by Paulien Christiannsen.

[70] Animal Welfare Ordinance, SR 455.1 2008 (SWITZ), Art 178, 179a. See Alina Polianskaya, '"No Rationale" Behind UK Law that Allows Lobsters to Be Boiled Alive, Crustacean Expert Says' (*Independent*, 19 February 2018).

[71] n 34.

[72] Parliamentary Initiative, 'Animals in the Swiss Legal System', Report by the Commission to the Council of States for Legal Questions, 25 January 2002, SR 99.467, at 4166 (SWITZ).

[73] Swiss Civil Code (n 34), Art 641a, para 2.

[74] See further, Saskia Stucki, *Grundrechte für Tiere: Eine Kritik des geltenden Tierschutzrechts und rechtstheoretische Grundlegung von Tierrechten im Rahmen einer Neupositionierung des Tieres als Rechtssubjekt* (Nomos, 2016) 302 ff.

[75] Camm and Bowles (n 31) 200 (emphasis added).

cats have the right to be respected as sentient beings that experience complex feelings that are common among living animals while being unique to each individual animal.'[76] And almost a decade before, the Oregon Court of Appeals held in *State v Nix* that '[Oregon's animal welfare law] reflects a broader public interest in protect[ing] individual animals as sentient beings.'[77]

Sixth, and related to the concern of those reforms with individual animals, is the fact that such recognitions are often *grounded in or legitimised with reference to the intrinsic value of animals*. A number of states are expressly committed to this sentientist ethic. For instance, the preamble to the Animal Welfare Act of the Netherlands expresses 'recognition of the intrinsic value of the animal'.[78] Article 3(a) of the Swiss Animal Welfare Act states that 'the inherent worth of the animal that has to be respected'.[79] And the Latvian Animal Protection Law recognises that it is 'the ethical obligation of humankind … to ensure the welfare and protection of all species of animals, because every unique being is in itself of value.'[80] Similar references are made in Australia,[81] Norway,[82] and, at times, by courts in India[83] and the US.[84]

Seventh, recognition of animal sentience, politically speaking, puts concern for animals back on the political agenda and may *prompt decision-makers to draw stricter legal consequences* from this, eg, by pronouncing stronger penalties. For example, when the Colombian civil law reform to recognise animals as sentient beings came into force in 2016, new and stronger penalties for animal abuse were introduced to the Colombian Criminal Code.[85]

The eighth effect of the growing emphasis on animal sentience is that the law may *resort to (seemingly) 'less sentient' animals*. This is the case especially in animal research. Following the 3R principle (refine, reduce, replace), wherever possible, research should be done on animals considered 'less sentient' as opposed to animals whose sentience is clearly established.[86] Researchers should use eg, fruit flies (*Drosophila melanogaster*) and nematodes (*Caenorhabditis elegans*) to study

[76] An Act to add Division 14.6 (commencing with Section 31800) to the Food and Agricultural Code, Relating to Animal Welfare, Cal Stat, Assembly Bill No 1881 (2022).

[77] *State v Nix*, 334 P.3d 437, 439 (OR 2014) (US).

[78] Wet dieren 2011 (Animals Act) (NL), preamble.

[79] Animal Welfare Act, SR 455 2005 (SWITZ), Art 3(a).

[80] Dzīvnieku aizsardzības likums, Latvijas Vēstnesis, 444/445 1999 (LAT) (1999).

[81] Animal Welfare Act 1992 (ACT) (AUSTR), s 4A(1).

[82] Animal Welfare Act 2009 (NOR), § 3.

[83] High Court of Kerala, AIR 2000 KER 340, 6 June 2000 (IND).

[84] *Nonhuman Rights Project (Happy) v Breheny* (19 February 2020) Supreme Court of the State of New York, No 260441/2019, 16 (US).

[85] Law 1774, of January 6, 2016 which modifies the Civil Code, Law 84 of 1989, the Criminal Code, the Criminal Procedure Code and dictates other provisions; Colombian Criminal Code ley 1774, art 5, title XI-A, Art 339A. L 1774, enero 6, 2016, Diario Oficial [DO] (Colom). See further Carlos Andrés Contreras López, 'Sentient Beings Protected by Law: Analysis of Recent Changes in Colombian Animal Welfare Legislation' (2016) 2 *Global Journal of Animal Law* 1.

[86] See also chapter by Kotzmann and Ferdowsian in this volume.

biological processes, rather than, eg, pigs, dogs or cows.[87] This is also known as 'relative replacement' in animal research (law).[88]

Finally, recognition of animal sentience may lead to *institutional and/or procedural reforms*. The most prominent and recent example of this is the newly enacted UK Animal Welfare (Sentience) Act 2022, which established the Animal Sentience Committee (ASC).[89] The ASC has raised hopes of animal protectionists in the UK for significant institutional reforms in favour of animals, but seems to have several shortcomings. The Committee is entitled (not obliged) to examine 'whether, or to what extent, the government is having, or has had, all due regard to the ways in which the policy might have an adverse effect on the welfare of animals as sentient beings.'[90] The aim is to get at policy proposals before they manifest as law in 'all policy areas' but mostly areas of animal welfare, the keeping of animals, farming, and contexts of environmental regulation, by analysing their effects on animals and making recommendations.[91] The resulting reports have to be answered by ministers through a written statement to Parliament within three months.

So, despite what ASC's name might suggest, it is likely to focus much more on the welfare needs of animals in the classic sense of welfarism rather than evaluating government action from the ground up with a view to taking animal sentience seriously. In the latter sense, and similar to environmental impact assessments, the Committee might have been constituted to evaluate in a more or less strategic manner the role of government in either furthering or hampering progress for animals, which may (or may not) result in distinct 'animal impact assessments'.[92]

Per the ASC's (Draft) Terms of Reference, the ASC reports

> should also contain recommendations on the steps the Committee considers the government should take for the purpose of ensuring that, in relation to any further formulation or implementation of the policy, the UK Government has all due regard to the ways in which that policy might have an adverse effect on the welfare of animals as sentient beings.[93]

[87] Matthias Eggel and Hanno Würbel, 'Internal Consistency and Compatibility of the 3Rs and 3Vs Principles for Project Evaluation of Animal Research' (2021) 55 *Laboratory Animals* 202.

[88] Craig Redmond, 'When is an Alternative not an Alternative? Supporting Progress for Absolute Replacement of Animals in Science' in Kathrin Herrmann and Kimberly Jayne (eds) *Animal Experimentation: Working Towards a Paradigm Change* 654 (Brill, 2019) 654.

[89] Animal Welfare (Sentience) Act 2022 (UK).

[90] ibid § 2(2).

[91] Talk by Michael Seals at the SLS Annual Seminar, held at Newcastle University, 22 June 2023.

[92] See for a pre-Act evaluation, Steven P Mulloch, 'Brexit and Animal Welfare Impact Assessment: Analysis of the Opportunities Brexit Presents for Animal Protection in the UK, EU, and Internationally' (2019) 9 *Animals* 877. Further on animal impact assessments, Charlotte E Blattner, 'Animal Impact Assessments: Contesting Denial, Changing the Future?' in Randall S Abate (ed), *What Can Animal Law Learn from Environmental Law?* (ELI Press, 2020) 95.

[93] 'Animal Sentience Committee Terms of Reference' (Department for the Environment Food & Rural Affairs (Defra), 17 November 2021) 7, available at data.parliament.uk/DepositedPapers/Files/DEP2022-0007/Animal_Sentience_Committee_Draft_Terms_of_Reference.pdf.

Adverse effects happen 'where a selected policy might harm or have a negative effect on the welfare of animals as sentient beings, such as animals being deprived of one or more of the five "welfare needs" as set out in the Animal Welfare Act 2006.'[94] And vice versa, there will prospectively not be a review of policy with a view to increasing animal welfare, ie, taking their positive interests into account.[95] The ASC just constituted itself, featuring people with expertise in farming, agricultural economics, veterinary and welfare science.[96] This in and of itself predetermines the aspired scope of the ASC, as neither philosophers, policy experts, nor lawyers were appointed.[97] Additionally, ASC operates with limited resources, and members are appointed for a small percentage of their time, which further points to the limited transformative potential of ASC on policy in the UK.[98] In principle, however, the recent UK Animal Welfare (Sentience) Act 2022 and its move to establish a new committee specifically dedicated to animals' interests, may operate as a prompt for other legislators to initiate (more capacious) institutional reforms in response to the recognition of animal sentience.

Overall, reforms to recognise animals as sentient beings are increasing in number and importance. These effects manifest in a range of jurisdictional, substantive, institutional and procedural contexts, resulting in at times novel legal constructs, like the ASC. The breadth and reach of these reforms are, however, difficult to predict and depend on multiple cultural, societal, economic and political factors, hence, even if potentially net-positive, there is a level of unpredictability and inconsistency that goes with the recognition of animal sentience. On a final note, with a view to existing effects of the recognition, many of the leading organisations evaluating states' performance in protecting animals consider the recognition of animal sentience central to that end. The World Animal Protection (WAP)'s 'Animal Protection Index', for example, treats recognition of animal sentience as one of 11 indicators to rank states according to their level of animal protection.[99] In similar fashion, the Global Animal Law (GAL) association

[94] ibid.

[95] See for a critique of this with a view to sentience more generally, chapter in this book by Ian Robertson.

[96] The ASC has one chair (Michael Seals) and five standing members (Richard Bennett, Richard Cooper, Penny Hawkins, Anna Meredith and Christine Nicol); the ASC reaches out to external experts and stakeholders to review policy decisions.

[97] See further, Mulloch (n 92).

[98] See also Peter Mills, 'Animals as Sentient Beings' (Nuffield Council on Bioethics, 7 March 2022); Conference Document 'Animal Sentience: Science, Policy and "Real World" Application' (2 May 2019), Friends House, Euston, organised by the RSPCA Science & Policy Group, the Uehiro Centre for Practical Ethics and the Wellcome Centre for Ethics and Humanities, University of Oxford, supported by grants from the Open Philanthropy Project and the RSPCA, available at science.rspca.org.uk/documents/1494935/9042554/Workshop+5+Representation+in+government+systems+%28PDF+546KB%29.pdf/5c0f0366-4c8d-1209-cf6e-031905b69ffd?t=1575392076333.

[99] 'Methodology' (World Animal Protection, 2023), available at api.worldanimalprotection.org/methodology.

considers legislation 'giving a new status to animals recognise the sentient nature of animals' as one of eight cases to evaluate them.[100]

VI. *Lex Ferenda*: Towards the Normative

Given the axiomatic importance and the sweeping consequences tied to sentience in animal ethics, the effects observed as a consequence of the recognition of animal sentience in the law appear, relatively speaking, conservative. This is somewhat surprising considering that the acknowledgment that humans are vulnerable as biological beings (rather than smart, autonomous, independent, self-sufficient, etc) has served as a basis for the establishment of some of our most fundamental rights.[101] Since human and nonhuman animals share precisely that vulnerability as sentient beings, the question arises, normatively speaking, whether more sweeping legal consequences should be tied to the recognition of animal sentience. Four such consequences seem both important and urgent.

First, the recognition of sentience as a concept underpinning animal law may imply a *claim to equal treatment of sentient animals*. For example, if it is established that pigs are, scientifically speaking, just as sentient as dogs, and since sentience is seen as the relevant basis for protection, this raises the question of whether pigs should not also come to enjoy the same levels of protection as dogs do. At a minimum, that could, for example, necessitate that painful methods of slaughter for pigs, like CO_2 gassing,[102] are replaced by less painful ones, such as when veterinarians euthanise dogs at old age. Taking this a step further, it would require that we, as for dogs, expand welfare provisions for pigs (spacing, feed, movement, social relations, etc). Even better, and thinking sentience through more consistently, we should stop rearing pigs for (human) consumption just as we (mostly) did with dogs. Along the lines of argument by O'Sullivan, Kotzmann and Nip, equality is

[100] 'Database Legislation' (Global Animal Law (GAL) Association, 2023), available at www.globalanimallaw.org/database/national/index.html.

[101] See for a critique, however, Alexandra Timmer, Moritz Baumgärtel, Louis Kotzé and Lieneke Slingenberg, 'The Potential and Pitfalls of the Vulnerability Concept for Human Rights' (2021) 39 *Netherlands Quarterly of Human Rights* 190.

[102] In 2004 and 2006, the European Food Safety Authority (EFSA) issued reports that drew attention to the most flagrant weaknesses of Directive 93/119/EC (eg, Opinion of the Scientific Panel on Animal Health and Welfare (AHAW) on a Request from the Commission Related to Welfare Aspects of the Main Systems of Stunning and Killing the Main Commercial Species of Animals (EFSA, Parma, 10 October 2004)). It recommended that, in order to ensure proper stunning and the least painful methods of slaughter, the EU must phase out the use of carbon dioxide in pig slaughter and use of water electric current in chicken slaughter. These insights are critically important since they affect most land animals slaughtered for food, but the Commission decided not to implement the EFSA's recommendations because it considered them 'not economically viable at present in the EU' (Council Regulation 1099/2009 [2009] OJ L303/1, 1, 2).

in this sense used to ameliorate protection for animals toward more consistency with a view to sentience.[103] Better still, sentience would operate as a ground for more consistency among and between laws governing human and nonhuman animals.

Second, animal sentience legislation is criticised for unduly focusing on negative dimensions of sentience, although animals also experience positive affective states.[104] Taking the positive dimensions of animal sentience seriously, such as pleasure, joy, happiness, self-fulfillment, participation, etc, could put in motion a new era of animal law.[105] Human rights theory was initially focused on preventing governments from infringing on them (duty to respect), yet states are now also required to protect individuals and groups against human rights abuses (duty to protect) and take positive action to facilitate the enjoyment of basic human rights (duty to fulfill).[106] In similar fashion, emphasising the positive interests animals have as sentient beings might operate as a *normative basis to ground and/or expand government duties to protect them and take all the necessary measures for the realisation of those interests*. That, in turn, would require more solid laws, more government intervention to protect animals from how we treat them, and creating the necessary institutional, procedural and other safeguards (means of enforcement, public attorney for animals, representation in politics, etc) to take the interests of animals as sentient beings more seriously than we do today.

Third, and related to that point, given the near-ubiquitous foundation of moral animal rights on sentience,[107] legal scholars are increasingly demanding that sentience (among others) *grounds legal rights for animals* (ie, fundamental rights such as the right to life and liberty).[108] In line with the prevailing interest theory, as Stucki explains, 'the capacity for having interests … is bound up with sentience – the capacity for conscious and subjective experiences of pain, suffering and pleasure.'[109] Just as humans need their fundamental interests in being alive, and having their bodily and mental integrity be respected, to be recognised

[103] Siobhan O'Sullivan, *Animals, Equality and Democracy* (Palgrave McMillan, 2011); Jane Kotzmann and Gisela Nip, 'Bringing Animal Protection Legislation Into Line With its Purported Purposes: A Proposal for Equality Amongst NonHuman Animals' (2020) 37 *Pace Environmental Law Review* 247.

[104] Ian Robertson and Daniel Goldsworthy, 'To Feel or Not to Feel; That Is the Legal Question' (2017) 1 *New Zealand Law Journal* 10, 10. See also the chapter of Ian Robertson in this collection.

[105] See also David E Cooper, 'Jeremy Bentham on Animal Ethics' (Daily Philosophy, 2023).

[106] eg, UN Human Rights Council, 'Protect, Respect and Remedy: A Framework for Business and Human Rights', Report of the Special Representative of the Secretary-General on the Issue of Human Rights and Transnational Corporations and Other Business Enterprises, John Ruggie, A/HRC/8/5, 7 April 2008.

[107] See above section II.

[108] Kotzmann additionally grounds legal rights for animals in intrinsic worth: Kotzmann (n 54) 405. See also Kotzmann's chapter in this volume.

[109] Saskia Stucki, 'Towards A Theory of Legal Animal Rights: Simple and Fundamental Rights' (2020) 40 *Oxford Journal of Legal Studies* 533, 542–43.

as infringeable, so do animals need robust legal protections *qua* rights to safeguard those very same interests. As Kotzmann insists, 'Locating sentience at the foundation of animal rights aligns with this conception of the core purpose of rights.'[110]

Relatedly, the final effect one would wish for in a normative sense is that either *qua* rights or otherwise, sentience would *operate as a challenge to the expansive (ab)use of animals*, which is often colloquially justified, without closer scrutiny, as '*necessary practices*'. Technically, the necessity test could be a powerful tool to protect animals more robustly. In practice, however, it is rare to find legislators or courts applying the 'necessity' test in this unbiased manner.[111] Because it is us humans who decide on the necessity of animal suffering, this test is uniquely used to favour human interests and, as a consequence, subordinate animal protection to human use.[112] Drawing on Bell's work in the desegregation context, Satz refers to this as the problem of 'interest-convergence':[113] the privileged (humans in this case) protect the disadvantaged (nonhuman animals) only when their interests align, which is the case only when protecting animals is consistent with our use of them. Since we profit enormously from the exploitation of nonhuman animals, our interests and those of nonhuman animals diverge. And '(w)hen this divergence occurs, all protections for animals are placed in jeopardy'.[114] If sentience, *qua* rights or otherwise, was taken seriously, common interests of humans in using animals – such as convenience, tradition and gustatory pleasure – would no longer suffice to qualify as 'necessary' means to compromise, restrict, thwart or otherwise ignore some of the most fundamental interests that animals (and we, too) have as sentient beings, including the interest in leading a good life.

[110] Kotzmann (n 54) 408.

[111] See for an exemplary application of the proportionality/necessity test (and, as such, an outlier among courts), HCJ9232/01 *Noah v Att'y General*, 2002–2003, 215 PD 233–34, 247 (ISR). See further for an analysis of the case, Mariann Sullivan and David J Wolfson, 'What's Good for the Goose … The Israeli Supreme Court, Foie Gras, and the Future of Farmed Animals in the United States' (2007) 70 *Law & Contemporary Problems* 139. Necessity was also used in similarly unbiased (yet less detailed) way in *Western Australia Magistrates Court, Department of Local Government and Regional Development v Emanuel Exports Pty Ltd, Graham Richard Dawes and Michael Anthony Stanton*, 8 February 2008, Magistrate CP Crawford, §§ 97–100 (AUSTLE).

[112] This has led to the continued perception of nonhuman animals as 'property' and valuable by 'human interests': *Stephens v State* 65 Miss 329 (1888) (US); *Saltoon v Lake and Others* [1978] 1 NSWLR 52 (AUSTL). See for an analysis, Will Kymlicka, 'Social Membership: Animal Law beyond the Property/Personhood Impasse' (2017) 40 *Dalhousie Law Journal* 123, 126; Corey Lee Wrenn, 'Abolition Then and Now: Tactical Comparisons Between the Human Rights Movement and the Modern Nonhuman Animal Rights Movement in the United States' (2014) 27 *Journal of Agricultural Environmental Ethics* 177, 192; Maneesha Deckha, 'Welfarist and Imperial: The Contributions of Anticruelty Laws to Civilizational Discourse' (2013) 65 *American Quarterly* 515. For a further analysis of the proportionality test, see Morgan Stonebridge, 'The Legality of Calf Roping in Australia: A Ford v Wiley Proportionality Analysis' (2022) 41 *University of Queensland Law Journal* 59.

[113] Ani B Satz, 'Animals as Vulnerable Subjects: Beyond Interest-Convergence, Hierarchy and Property' (2009) 16 *Animal Law* 65.

[114] ibid.

VII. Concluding Remarks

Animal sentience is slowly but steadily becoming an explicit and central concept underlying modern animal laws across the world. The normative consequences tied to it, and its utility, however, remain opaque. From a scientific standpoint, the recognition of sentience by the law serves little, if any purpose, since sentience can only be descriptively determined and, consequently, its recognition can only be declaratory. However, in line with the dominant theories of animal ethics (utilitarianism, deontology, political theory), lawyers are (rightfully) expecting the recognition of animal sentience by the law to have a certain normative import.[115] This chapter has identified nine effects of the recognition of animal sentience that have already manifested today: (1) sentience can be used as a shorthand to determine the personal scope of animal welfare/protection acts; (2) sentience tends to expand the personal scope of animal laws; (3) said expansion has a material effect on the protections for animals; (4) recognition of sentience challenges the Roman law subject/object divide; (5) emphasis on sentience raises concern for individual animals; (6) it contributes to intrinsic animal protection; (7) and it may yield stricter legal consequences (eg, penalties); (8) in research especially, the recognition of sentience leads to the use of 'less sentient' animals; and (9) more generally, it may prompt institutional/procedural reforms, such as new committees being formed, as seen in the UK with the ASC.

Considering the axiomatic relevance of (animal) sentience in (animal) ethics, the effects of the legal recognition of animal sentience we are observing are still conservative. Going forward, it is to be hoped that through interpretation, strategic litigation, popular vote, or other initiatives, the legal recognition of animal sentience will be systematically invoked to: (1) push for equal treatment among and between sentient beings; (2) push for laws protecting the positive dimensions of animal sentience, including through duties to protect and fulfill; (3) invoke the legal recognition of animal sentience as a basis for fundamental rights for animals; and (4) ultimately, use sentience as a challenge to encroachments of animals' interests, challenging the ubiquitous 'necessary use' of nonhuman animals by human ones.

Evaluating the utility of the legal recognition of animal sentience at this point in time seems premature. Its emergence and continued development should in either case not be dismissed too readily as useless. Instead, creative legal argumentation, strategic litigation and other avenues should be used to exploit its potential to take

[115] See, eg, Ian Robertson and Daniel Goldsworthy, 'Recognising and Defining Animal Sentience in Legislation: A Framework for Importing Positive Animal Welfare Through the Five Domains Model' (2022) 48 *Monash University Law Review* 244, 245; Jane Kotzmann and Morgan Stonebridge, 'There is Value in Stating the Obvious: Why United States Legislatures Should Explicitly Recognize Animal Sentience in Their Laws' (2021) 30 *Cornell Journal of Law and Public Policy* 425, 425.

sentience truly seriously. Finally, as Trøite and Myskja remind us, we should not forget that:

> There is … a well-known socio-psychological effect of pretending to be better than you are. You are influenced by your words and behaviour, even if you use them to give a certain impression and do not care about their truth content. What starts out as bullshit, gradually becomes truth.[116]

[116] Matilde F Trøite and Anne I Myskja, 'Legal Protection of Animal Intrinsic Value – Mere Words?' in Svenja Springer and Herwig Grimm (eds), *Professionals in Food Chains: Ethics, Roles, and Responsibilities* (Wageningen Academic Publishers, 2018) 369, 373.

2

Sentience, Empathy and the Need for Both Justification and Motivation

MORGAN STONEBRIDGE*

I. Introduction

Animal sentience is increasingly being recognised as fundamental to understanding and guiding our relationships with animals.[1] The fact that animals are feeling beings that have subjective experiences has been a relevant factor in questions concerning animal protection for decades.[2] More recently, many countries have begun explicitly recognising that animals are capable of experiencing subjective states in animal protection legislation.[3] Typically, any question about what humans owe to animals – whether in the context of welfare, rights or some other form of

* Many thanks to Jane Kotzmann and Daniel Goldsworthy for their constructive comments on this chapter. This research has been supported by an Australian Government Research Training Program Scholarship.

[1] See generally, Peter Singer, *Animal Liberation*, 40th anniversary edn (Open Road Media, 2009) 38; Jane Kotzmann, 'Sentience and Intrinsic Worth as a Pluralist Foundation for Fundamental Animal Rights' (2023) *Oxford Journal of Legal Studies* 1; Gary L Francione, *Introduction to Animal Rights: Your Child or the Dog* (Temple University Press, 2000) 4–7. For legislative examples, see Protocol annexed to the Treaty of the European Community – Protocol on Protection and Welfare of Animals [1997] OJ C340/110; Animal Welfare Act 1999 (NZ), long title; Animal Welfare Act 2008 (TZ), ss 3, 4(b)(i); Animal Welfare Act 1992 (ACT), s 4A(1)(a).

[2] See, for instance, the discussion on the approach towards the first anti-cruelty legislation in Jane Spencer, *Writing About Animals in the Age of Revolution* (Oxford University Press, 2020) ch 7.

[3] Protocol annexed to the Treaty of the European Community – Protocol on Protection and Welfare of Animals [1997] OJ C340/110; Consolidated Version on the Treaty on the Functioning of the European Union [2012] OJ C326/01, Art 13; Animal Welfare Act 2008 (Tanzania), ss 3 and 4(b)(i); OR Rev Stat §167.305 (2021) (Oregon); Animal Welfare and Safety Act, CQLR 2016, c B-3.1, preamble (Canada); Ley No 1774 de 2016 (Colombia), Art 1, 665; Ley 20.380, 2009 (Chile), Art 2; Ley No 30407, 2015 (Peru), art 14; Wet dieren 2011 (Animals Act) (Netherlands), Art 1.3; Gyvūnų Gerovės ir Apsaugos Įstatymas (Law on Welfare and Protection of Animals) No XI-2271, Valstybės Žinios, 20 October 2012 No 122-6216 (Lithuania) (2012), Art 1(a); Code Civil (Civil Code) (France), Art 515-14; Animal Welfare Act 2018 (Sweden); Government Bill (Sweden) No 2017/18, 147; Law Relating to the Protection and Welfare of Animals 2018 (Brussels), Art 1; Animal Welfare Act 2020 (Denmark), Art 1; Civil Code of Catalonia (Ley de 2006) (Spain), art 511-1 (3); Animal Welfare Act 1999 (New Zealand), long title; Animal Welfare Act 1992 (ACT), s 4A(1)(a); Animal Welfare Sentience Act 2022 (United Kingdom), ss 1–2.

animal protection – is answered by reference to their sentience. It appears, then, that animal sentience plays an important role in justifying animal protection.

This chapter does not seek to define this role or examine how it should operate in the law. Rather, acknowledging the prevalence of sentience as a justification for protection here is designed to elucidate the motivating sentiment it brings into play – empathy. The fact that animals are sentient means they have experiences enough like our own to give rise to empathy. This connection provides the link between the animal and human sides of animal protection. That is, sentience represents the animal side – it goes to justifying their claims to protection, and empathy represents the human side – it makes that justification *felt*.

Making the justification felt is important because arguments for animal protection are clearly (and rightly) directed at improving the lives of animals, as opposed to benefiting humans directly. This means that such arguments require the support of those that are not the primary beneficiary of them and who, in fact, may experience some level of initial sacrifice if those arguments are successful. Thus, connecting the justification for protection with some factor that will motivate support for that justification is vital in ensuring the realisation of animal protection principles. This chapter argues that empathy is the relevant link.

Accordingly, there is a need for a detailed conceptualisation of the role empathy plays in generating stable support for the principles of animal protection and how this role may be furthered.[4] This chapter seeks to contribute to this need at a foundational level. It does so by explaining why sentience and empathy must be understood as interdependent and by framing legal sentience recognition itself as a potential cultivation tool for empathy. Understanding the legal recognition of sentience as contributing to furthering the human side of animal protection may, in turn, provide for more targeted legal recognitions in the future and may assist in developing the appropriate next steps for cultivating empathy towards animals.

Section II of this chapter begins by establishing sentience as a justificatory element of animal protection. Section III then makes the claim that empathy is a vital part of motivating human action and generating support for the principles of animal protection. It also defines empathy and demonstrates its validity when directed at the animal case. In section IV, the need for sentience to connect with empathy is explained, with examples from the human rights case. With this link established, it argues that efforts towards cultivating empathy are necessary to generate support for animal protection principles. Finally, section V explains how the legal recognition of animal sentience represents one such empathy-producing effort.

[4] 'Stable' in this context refers to the concept of stability: see John Rawls, *A Theory of Justice*, revised edn (The Belknap Press of Harvard University Press, 1999) 397–505; John Rawls, *Political Liberalism* (Columbia University Press, 2005) 385–95. For the principles of animal protection to be implemented in the first instance, and for this level of protection to be sustained or increased, support for those principles must be stable and reaffirming.

II. Animal Sentience as a Justification for Protection

Sentience has taken a front seat in animal protection. It must be noted that 'protection' as used here is to be understood broadly. It refers to a diverse range of approaches that aim to ensure the interests of animals, either through regulation or radical reform. Animal protection as employed by this chapter therefore bridges the welfare-rights dichotomy commonly drawn in animal law arguments – protection captures all such approaches, and those that cannot be neatly categorised as rights or welfare, but still seek to protect and ensure animal interests.

Within this broad approach, there has been increasing emphasis on the subjective states of animals appearing in welfarist regulations, rights arguments, and those protectionist positions in between. On the welfare side, the emphasis on animal sentience is occurring in the form of legislative recognition. While animal sentience could be understood as an implicit purpose for animal protection legislation, its role is increasingly being made explicit.[5] On the rights side, arguments for both moral and legal animal rights typically rely on animal sentience as the core capacity underpinning an award of rights. For instance, Tom Regan utilises animal sentience in arguing that all animals satisfying the 'subjects-of-a-life' criterion have a moral value that ought to be protected through inviolable rights.[6] In the legal rights case, sentience is also a key player given its natural association with the interest theory of rights.[7] Here, animal sentience allows for animals to have interests, which in turn provides that animals may have certain interests that are sufficient for grounding a duty in others.[8] Even in protectionist arguments that focus on relationship as opposed to capacity, sentience still typically underpins the purpose of protection. For example, care ethics as applied to the animal case involves 'listening … to the "voice" of animals, hearing their standpoint vis-à-vis a system that oppresses them'.[9] The animal standpoint relies on the subjective experience of animals, and thus again emphasises the importance of sentience.

Sentience is clearly a prominent justificatory feature in each of the above arguments for animal protection. It is at least commonly accepted across interested groups that an animal's sentience means they are owed some kind of protection over and above what is awarded to other forms of legal property.[10] This is

[5] See n 3.

[6] Tom Regan, *The Case for Animal Rights* (Routledge & Kegan Paul, 1983) 243–48, 279–80, 295–97. Regan uses an enhanced form of animal sentience, requiring levels of subjectivity and experience that exceed the typical definition of sentience.

[7] Saskia Stucki, 'Towards a Theory of Legal Animal Rights: Simple and Fundamental Rights' (2020) 40 *Oxford Journal of Legal Studies* 533.

[8] Joseph Raz, *The Morality of Freedom* (Clarendon Press, 1986) 9–14.

[9] Josephine Donovan, *Animals, Mind, and Matter: The inside Story* (Michigan State University Press, 2022).

[10] Even in the context of industry groups. For instance, the executive summary of the Australian Government's Australian Animal Welfare Strategy, which guided the development of animal welfare law in Australia and was developed in consultation with animal agricultural industry groups, states that the strategy 'covers all sentient animals – that is, those with a capacity to experience suffering

an important point given the significant variations and disputes between (and in) welfarist animal protection efforts and rights-based arguments.[11] While there may be disagreements between welfare and rights advocates on the extent of protection required, or between rights advocates on the foundation and scope of proposed rights, there is broad agreement that animal sentience is an important part of an animal's claim for protection.[12] Sentience therefore presents a uniting feature in arguments for animal protection – a common ground to build from. This makes sentience an ideal justification for arguments for increased protection given that it begins from a point of consensus.

This is enhanced by the fact that sentience is a concept that can be scientifically affirmed. While further development is required, scientific research concerning animal sentience has been increasing over previous decades, culminating in the Cambridge Declaration on Consciousness in 2012.[13] Many animals are now recognised as sentient, including those most commonly used in production for human benefit such as poultry, pigs and cattle.[14] This sets a justificatory standard that is able to be scientifically defined and confirmed.[15] This should in turn increase the ability for sentience to act as a broad point of consensus, given that interested parties should be able to accept the concept from within their own perspectives, which are informed by their personal beliefs and values.[16]

This is, however, not to discount the controversies surrounding animal sentience. It is important to note that sentience is, in some respects, a contested ground. For instance, while industry groups acknowledge the importance of sentience in some contexts, many vehemently disagree with its use in animal protection legislation. In the Australian state of Victoria, for example, where community

and pleasure. *Sentience is the reason that welfare matters*' (italics added): see Australian Government Department of Agriculture, Fisheries and Forestry, 'Australian Animal Welfare Strategy (AAWS) and National Implementation Plan 2010–14' (2011) Executive summary.

[11] For instance, each of the following accounts offer a broadly rights-based approach but feature significant departure points: Robert Garner, *A Theory of Justice for Animals: Animal Rights in a Nonideal World* (Oxford University Press, 2013); Gary L Francione, *Animals, Property, and the Law* (Temple University Press, 1995); David Favre, 'Animals as Living Property' in Linda Kalof (ed), *The Oxford Handbook of Animal Studies* (Oxford University Press, 2017); Maneesha Deckha, *Animals as Legal Beings: Contesting Anthropocentric Legal Orders* (University of Toronto Press, 2021).

[12] For example, sentience features prominently in each of the above accounts despite the variations in rights theories. See Garner (n 11) ch 8; Francione (n 11) ch 1, in which animal interests feature heavily in the discussion; Favre (n 11) 74–79; Deckha (n 11) ch 4, 145–46, 152–53, in which sentience provides opportunities for the embodied vulnerability and relationality that gives rise to Deckha's beingness model.

[13] Philip Low, 'The Cambridge Declaration on Consciousness' (Francis Crick Memorial Conference on Consciousness in Human and Non-Human Animals, Cambridge, 7 July 2012).

[14] Donald M Broom, 'Considering Animals' Feelings' (2016) 5 *Animal Sentience* 8.

[15] Although there are difficulties associated with establishing that animals are sentient, which can have negative implications for those animals whose sentience status is unclear due to a lack of positive evidence (as opposed to clear evidence against a sentience finding). See ch 17 of this collection for further discussion. Further, it is important to note that science is not always objective and free from bias, which can impact sentience recognition. See Charlotte E Blattner, 'The Recognition of Animal Sentience by the Law' (2019) 9 *Journal of Animal Ethics* 121, 129–30.

[16] Or from within their own comprehensive doctrines: Rawls, *Political Liberalism* (n 4).

engagement was recently undertaken as to the possibility of explicitly recognising animal sentience in new animal welfare legislation, 'nearly all agricultural organisations that provided feedback … did not support explicitly recognising animal sentience'.[17] This is despite animal sentience long featuring in industry arguments regarding animal well-being that equate profit with animal welfare, in that negative welfare results in negative returns.[18] The Victorian Department of Primary Industries, for example, recognised in 2007 that 'Failure to recognise sentience in livestock species could result in production losses, market access loss and breaches of [the Prevention of Cruelty to Animals Act 1986] POCTA'.[19] Thus, while animal sentience as an important welfare factor may be broadly agreeable, there is opposition to some uses of sentience.[20]

Despite certain points of contention, the continued reference to animal sentience in questions concerning the treatment of animals suggests that it plays an important role in justifying actions that concern animal well-being. While considerable room remains to make this role explicit, it suffices for this discussion to recognise the importance of sentience as a justification for all approaches to animal protection, including both welfare and rights.

III. Empathy: A Condition for Caring about Sentience

Sentience, then, can be considered a justificatory element of animal protection. Sentience as a justification represents the animal side of the animal protection movement. That is, sentience in this context underpins an animal's claim as to what they are owed. However, this represents just one side of animal protection. While animals are, and should clearly be, the central concern in questions concerning animal well-being, it is also important to recognise and pay attention to the human side of animal protection.

Any arguments relating to increasing animal protection necessarily demand changes in human behaviour. The consequences of these arguments, if accepted and implemented, would not only impact the intended beneficiaries. They would

[17] Victoria State Government, 'A New Animal Welfare Act for Victoria' (Engagement Summary Report, April 2021) 8.

[18] Jed Goodfellow, 'Animal Welfare Regulation in the Australian Agricultural Sector: A Legitimacy Maximising Analysis' (PhD Thesis, Macquarie University, September 2015) 44–47.

[19] Mariko Lauber, Department of Primary Industries, 'Animal Welfare for Livestock Producers' (Brochure, 15 November 2007) 2, 6.

[20] It is relevant to note that this opposition in some instances is driven by fear of the consequences of sentience recognition. For instance, in relation to the Victorian legislative recognition of sentience, one opponent stated 'the idea of sentience goes too far and gives certain groups the ability to attempt to shut down hobbies', and an agricultural organisation stated, 'Despite this clear and scientific definition [of sentience], animal sentience as a concept has been used as a weapon against livestock producers'. See Victoria State Government (n 17) 8–9. Charlotte Blattner details further concerns surrounding sentience, including the refusal from some states to recognise sentience and cognitive biases in society and science. See Blattner (n 14) 126–30.

also demand some level of sacrifice from the humans that benefit from current systems of animal use. Increased welfare conducive to animal sentience would impact, for instance, current food production systems that would likely have to adapt to reduced stocking densities or free-range systems.[21] Rights arguments would likely result in the prohibition of such systems, clearly demanding a significant change in human behaviour.[22] Thus, the principles of increased welfare, animal rights or some other form of protection over and above the current situation are inherently other-regarding. This means that such principles do not exist for the direct purpose of the politically active.[23] It is, however, humans as the makers of laws and political principles that must come to give their support to the principles and legal frameworks captured by these approaches if implementation is to be successful and stable.

The other-regarding nature of animal protection therefore brings about a question of human motivation. The changes that would flow from increased protection are unlikely to be supported entirely out of self-interest, given that the approaches are not designed directly for the benefit of humans and demand some initial sacrifice. This means that something else is required to generate the kind of support necessary to improve animal well-being. The justificatory element on the animal side of animal protection provides some guidance here. If animal sentience underpins animal protection claims, the side of animal protection reliant on human motivation should be connected to and work with that justification. In this respect, empathy is a natural candidate. As will be demonstrated in the following sections, if animal sentience answers questions about what animals are owed, empathy motivates human support for those claims. Empathy and sentience are intertwined, in that sentience provides a core experience for humans to empathise with. It is this

[21] See generally, Goodfellow (n 18) 48–54, which discusses intensive confinement and associated welfare concerns.

[22] For instance, Gary Francione takes an abolitionist rights-based approach, which involves recognising that animals have the right not to be treated as property. Such an approach prevents all human uses of animals on the basis that animals should not be treated as resources. See Gary L Francione and Anna E Charlton, 'Animal Rights' in Linda Kalof (ed), *The Oxford Handbook of Animal Studies* (Oxford University Press, 2015) 34–39. Maneesha Deckha, who takes a relational approach, argues that animals should be granted the legal status of 'beingness' and states that such a status is incompatible with slaughter and consumption. See Deckha (n 11) 156.

[23] They may benefit this group in the long term. For example, changes resulting from animal rights arguments may benefit population health. However, the animals are the intended beneficiaries of these laws, and other practical consequences are incidental: Essi Päivärinta et al, 'Replacing Animal-Based Proteins with Plant-Based Proteins Changes the Composition of a Whole Nordic Diet – A Randomised Clinical Trial in Healthy Finnish Adults' (2020) 12 *Nutrients* 943; Tao Huang et al, 'Cardiovascular Disease Mortality and Cancer Incidence in Vegetarians: A Meta-Analysis and Systematic Review' (2012) 60 *Annals of Nutrition & Metabolism* 233; Jane Kotzmann and Morgan Stonebridge, 'Preventing Another Pandemic: How Changing the Legal Paradigm Governing Intensive Animal Agriculture Will Reduce the Risk of Future Zoonoses' (2022) 47 *Columbia Journal of Environmental Law* 458; Charlotte E Blattner, 'Just Transition for Agriculture? A Critical Step in Tackling Climate Change' (2020) 9 *Journal of Agriculture, Food Systems, and Community Development* 53; Helen Harwatt, 'Including Animal to Plant Protein Shifts in Climate Change Mitigation Policy: A Proposed Three-Step Strategy' (2019) 19 *Climate Policy* 533.

emotional experience that motivates human support for other-regarding principles by identifying animals as the appropriate subjects of consideration.

A. What is Empathy?

Before developing this claim further, it is important to make clear what is meant by empathy, particularly in the context of human empathy directed towards animals. There are various ways of understanding empathy, including the common idea of placing oneself in the shoes of another. This conception of empathy is evident in the description of sympathy (which accords with what we now know as empathy) offered by Adam Smith, a forefather of liberalism who also explored empathy at length in *The Theory of Moral Sentiments*.[24] Smith captures the notion of feeling an emotional stir at another's experience in stating:

> By the imagination we place ourselves in his situation, we conceive ourselves enduring all the same torments, we enter as it were into his body, and become in some measure the same person with him, and thence form some idea of his sensations, and even feel something, though weaker in degree, is not all together unlike them.[25]

This description provides a clear overview of empathy as an imaginative experience, designed to generate an understanding of another's feeling. This can involve imagining how the other feels, or how the self would feel if in the position of the other.[26] In the context of animal-directed empathy, such an imaginative experience could involve picturing what it would be like to live as an animal in an intensive farming operation. It could also involve imagining what it would be like for oneself to live in an intensive farming operation. There is a clear risk in both instances here, though most notably in the latter. In imagining oneself in the position of an animal, there is likely to be a significant lack of consideration of the animal other. That is, the human empathising is at risk of ignoring the animal experience, focusing instead on their own imagined experience, and subsequently losing animal specificities.[27] It flows, then, that there is a risk of anthropomorphism, such that the animal target of the empathetic experience is blurred through the imposition of human standards.

This is, however, just one understanding of empathy. More generally, empathy captures 'a broader range of feelings, expressions, and behaviours that enable individuals to recognize, to perceive, and to respond appropriately to the emotional

[24] The word 'empathy' is relatively recent and there was previously no distinction between 'sympathy' and what is now known as 'empathy'. Thus, writers such as Adam Smith and David Hume described what is typically known as empathy via the term 'sympathy'.

[25] Adam Smith, *The Theory of Moral Sentiments* (Penguin, 2009).

[26] For further discussion on this distinction, and the importance of self-directed projection transitioning into other-directed simulation, see Elisa Aaltola, *Varieties of Empathy: Moral Psychology and Animal Ethics* (Rowman and Littlefield International, 2018) ch 2.

[27] ibid 31.

states of others'.[28] Importantly, empathy involves both affective and cognitive elements.[29] Elisa Aaltola describes cognitive empathy as a situation where 'one forms a representation of the mental state of another individual, which again can be based on perception (facilitated by instantaneous mental processing), inference and ultimately a theory of mind.'[30] Affective empathy, according to Aaltola, is where 'one resonates with the phenomenal aspects of another individual's mental states; her suffering or joy stirs responses with similar emotive content in the observer.'[31]

This chapter captures each of these elements in defining empathy as the ability to recognise another's emotional experience and feel an appropriate emotion in response to that experience.[32] The recognition of one's emotional experience is most aligned with cognitive empathy, in that it requires the empathiser to perceive and represent the mental state of the relevant individual. The requirement that the empathiser feel an apt emotional response captures affective empathy, given that it operates at the felt level and differentiates the feelings of the empathiser from the individual being empathised with.

B. Empathy for Animals

The definition of empathy does not change depending on the subject, whether they be nonhuman or human animal. However, it is important to note that further attention may be required when directing empathy towards an animal subject.[33] This is to avoid the imposition of human experiences described above – failure to provide the requisite level of attention to the specificity of animal experience can risk substituting the particular experiences of animals with those familiar to the human doing the empathising. However, despite the challenges that might arise in directing empathy towards an animal subject, research affirms that it is

[28] Sue Carter, James Harris and Stephen W Porges, 'Neural and Evolutionary Perspectives on Empathy' in Jean Decety and William Ickes (eds), *The Social Neuroscience of Empathy* (MIT Press, 2009) 169.

[29] While captured broadly under the term 'empathy' here and across the literature, it is important to note that cognitive and affective empathy are distinct phenomena. As Abigail A Marsh explains, 'The brain regions that subserve cognitive empathy overlap minimally, if at all, with those that subserve emotional empathy': Abigail A Marsh, 'Extraordinary Altruism: A Cognitive Neuroscience Perspective' in Joshua D Greene, India Morrison and Martin EP Seligman (eds), *Positive Neuroscience* (Oxford University Press, 2016) 145.

[30] Elisa Aaltola, 'Affective Empathy as Core Moral Agency: Psychopathy, Autism and Reason Revisited' (2014) 17 *Philosophical Explorations* 76.

[31] ibid.

[32] Note also that this definition captures the fact that empathy is not itself a feeling. This definition includes the capacity to 'feel an appropriate emotion' and thus the impact of understanding another's emotional state produces in us an apt emotional response. This emotional response is not the feeling of empathy itself but a feeling of (for instance) sympathy, embarrassment or anger resulting from the process of empathising.

[33] See generally, Lori Gruen, *Entangled Empathy: An Alternative Ethic for Our Relationships with Animals* (Lantern Books, 2015) ch 3.

in fact possible for human empathy to extend to animals.[34] For example, Decety and Cowell explain that 'Humans can feel empathic concern for a wide range of "others", including for nonhuman animals, such as pets (in the Western culture) or tamagotchi (in Japan). This is especially the case when signs of vulnerability and need are noticeable.'[35]

Similarly, Mattiassi et al found that a subject's lack of control can result in greater human empathy, given that the subject is perceived as lacking agency and is thus particularly vulnerable to victimisation.[36] Thus, in this study, a cat, which is 'considered high in experience and low in agency', was more readily empathised with than a robot, which is 'perceived to be high in agency and low in experience'.[37] Angantyr and co-authors have also found that 'a child, a baby and a puppy elicited approximately the same levels of empathy' in participants, with a suggestion that certain animals may provoke empathy in humans partly due to a perception that they are not responsible for the situation bringing about their need.[38]

Further, human empathy directed at animals has some link to human–human empathy. For instance, empathy has been found to be an 'underlying common factor' in attitudes regarding well-being in human–human relationships and in human–animal relationships.[39] Participants in a study undertaken by Anna Stone 'showed some consistency between their attitudes to the rights and welfare of other humans and their attitudes to the rights and welfare of animals' with empathy partly responsible for that consistency.[40] Taylor and Signal have similarly found that participants who scored higher in empathic concern (feelings of warmth towards others) had 'a more welfare-orientated attitude to animals'.[41] Thus, according to Taylor and Signal, when empathy is understood 'as a specific construct, rather than subsumed within general personality, there is a substantive link between it and attitudes to animals'.[42] Further, according to Bastian and co-authors, drawing out similarities between humans and animals can result

[34] Malin Angantyr, Jakob Eklund and Eric M Hansen, 'A Comparison of Empathy for Humans and Empathy for Animals' (2011) 24 *Anthrozoös* 369.

[35] Jean Decety and Jason M Cowell, 'The Complex Relation between Morality and Empathy' (2014) 18 *Trends in Cognitive Sciences* 337. There is considerable commentary surrounding the idea of empathiszing with distant others. This chapter suggests that animals are the appropriate object of empathetic feeling as they feel pain and can suffer. The capacity for suffering is necessarily tied to the ability to experience, which allows a core interest to empathise with without undue projection. In anchoring empathy to sentience, this chapter is suggesting that empathy is not the appropriate response to the non-sentient world. Thus, in approaching the question of generating support for an environmental regime (for instance) utilising empathy would likely not be the most attractive approach.

[36] Alan DA Mattiassi et al, 'What Do Humans Feel with Mistreated Humans, Animals, Robots, and Objects? Exploring the Role of Cognitive Empathy' (2021) 45 *Motivation and Emotion* 543.

[37] ibid 546.

[38] Malin Angantyr, Jakob Eklund and Eric M Hansen, 'A Comparison of Empathy for Humans and Empathy for Animals' (2011) 24 *Anthrozoös* 369, 375.

[39] Anna Stone, 'The Relationship between Attitudes to Human Rights and to Animal Rights is Partially Mediated by Empathy' (2023) 163 *Journal of Social Psychology* 367.

[40] ibid 375.

[41] N Taylor and TD Signal, 'Empathy and Attitudes to Animals' (2005) 18 *Anthrozoös* 18, 23.

[42] ibid 23–24.

in the 'expanding [of] moral concern, not only to animals but also to human outgroups'.[43]

There are also variables that can impact the relative strength of human–animal empathy. Key amongst these is pet ownership. For instance, Angantyr et al found more empathy for a puppy subject amongst those who owned dogs than those that did not.[44] Similarly, in Taylor and Signal's study into the connection between empathy and attitudes to animals, participants that were currently living with a pet scored significantly higher on the Animal Attitude Scale than those that were not.[45] This connection between companion animal ownership and human–animal empathy has also been affirmed by Rothgerber and Mican, who identified pet ownership as being 'associated with greater connections to living animals' with those who owned a pet as a child conveying greater empathy for animals.[46] However, this does not always translate into certain expected behaviours, with Rothgerber and Mican finding that 'these affections for living animals did not transfer to decisions about whether to eat them'.[47]

C. Empathy and Motivation

There is, in addition to the cognitive and affective components of empathy, a further important third category – empathic concern.[48] This represents the translation of empathy into action and can be the outcome of the empathetic process.[49] Here, empathy is the impetus behind prosocial or altruistic behaviour, which is generally induced where the target being empathised with is in a situation of vulnerability or need.[50] As Abigail A Marsh explains, empathic concern involves

[43] Brock Bastian et al, 'When Closing the Human–Animal Divide Expands Moral Concern: The Importance of Framing' (2012) 3 *Social Psychological and Personality Science* 421, 427.

[44] Angantyr, Eklund and Hansen (n 38) 375.

[45] Taylor and Signal (n 41) 24.

[46] Hank Rothgerber and Frances Mican, 'Childhood Pet Ownership, Attachment to Pets, and Subsequent Meat Avoidance: The Mediating Role of Empathy Toward Animals' (2014) 79 *Appetite* 11, 15.

[47] ibid 15.

[48] While often captured under the term 'empathy' (see for instance, Jean Decety and Philip L Jackson, 'The Functional Architecture of Human Empathy' (2004) 3 *Behavioural and Cognitive Neuroscience Reviews* 71, 73) there is some division in the literature as to whether pro-social behaviour (captured here as empathic concern) is better defined as 'compassion or sympathy, as opposed to empathy. See generally, Tania Singer, 'The Neuronal Basis and Ontogeny of Empathy and Mind Reading: Review of Literature and Implications for Future Research' (2006) 30 *Neuroscience and Biobehavioral Reviews* 855, 859–60; Francis Stevens and Katherine Taber, 'The Neuroscience of Empathy and Compassion in Pro-Social Behavior' (2021) 159 *Neuropsychologia* 107925.

[49] Marsh (n 29) 145: 'emotional empathy, at least some forms of it, appears to be critical for experiencing empathic concern'.

[50] Nancy Eisenberg and Paul A Miller, 'The Relation of Empathy to Prosocial and Related Behaviors' (1987) 101 *Psychological Bulletin* 91; Shaun Nichols, 'Mindreading and the Cognitive Architecture Underlying Altruistic Motivation' (2001) 16 *Mind and Language* 425; Abigail A Marsh, Megan N Kozak and Nalini Ambady, 'Accurate Identification of Fear Facial Expressions Predicts Prosocial Behavior' (2007) 7 *Emotion* 239.

'feeling for them – wishing, in the case of another's distressed emotional state, that it were better and desiring to make it so'.[51] The link between empathy and pro-social behaviour has been explored in depth by C Daniel Batson through his empathy–altruism hypothesis.[52] Batson's claim is that 'empathic concern produces altruistic motivation'.[53] Here, altruistic motivation captures 'a motivational state with the ultimate goal of increasing another's welfare'.[54] Importantly, the altruistic motivation must be for the ultimate goal of increasing the welfare of the person in need, as opposed to some egotistical motive directed at reducing the arousal of unpleasant feelings in oneself.[55] A review of the empathy–altruism research undertaken in 1990 found support for 'the view that true altruism – acting with the goal of benefitting another – does exist and is part of human nature'.[56] Similarly, in 2014, Batson et al concluded 'It is time to accept – at least as a working hypothesis – the proposition that empathic concern produces altruistic motivation'.[57]

When discussed alongside the motivation to act, empathy is closely linked to compassion. However, while the terms do overlap, they are not synonymous.[58] As Singer and Klimecki explain, 'In contrast to empathy, compassion does not mean sharing the suffering of the other'.[59] Altruistic behaviour can be considered an act of compassion grounded in empathy. However, compassion is not necessarily rooted in empathy – compassion can operate without the requirement for shared experience. While empathy and compassion can exist independently, this chapter takes the view that both are more robust when considered together. For instance, compassion devoid of empathy can increase the risk of inappropriate helping behaviour. As Segal et al explain, 'When we do not put ourselves in the place of others, we run the risk of misinterpreting the other and considering what would alleviate our own suffering, not what works for the other.'[60] Thus, this chapter takes a wide understanding of empathy *that includes empathic concern and altruistic motivation*. Capturing the many facets of empathy – cognitive, affective

[51] Marsh (n 29) 145.

[52] See, C Daniel Batson, 'The Empathy-Altruism Hypothesis: What and So What?' in Emma M Seppälä et al (eds), *The Oxford Handbook of Compassion Science* (Oxford University Press, 2017); C Daniel Batson, *Altruism in Humans* (Oxford University Press, 2010); C Daniel Batson, *A Scientific Search for Altruism: Do We Only Care About Ourselves?* (Oxford University Press, 2017); Miho Toi and C Daniel Batson, 'More Evidence That Empathy is a Source of Altruistic Motivation' (1982) 43 *Journal of Personality and Social Psychology* 281.

[53] C Daniel Batson, David A Lishner and Eric L Stocks, 'The Empathy-Altruism Hypothesis' in David A Schroeder and William G Graziano (eds), *The Oxford Handbook of Prosocial Behavior* (Oxford University Press, 2014) 260.

[54] ibid 275.

[55] ibid 259.

[56] Jane Allyn Piliavin and Hong-Wen Charng, 'Altruism: A Review of Recent Theory and Research' (1990) 16 *Annual Review of Sociology* 27, 27.

[57] Batson, Lishner, and Stocks (n 53) 271. In relation to animals, see Jamie Berenguer, 'The Effect of Empathy in Proenvironmental Attitudes and Behaviors' (2007) 39 *Environment and Behavior* 269.

[58] Francis Stevens and Katherine Taber, 'The Neuroscience of Empathy and Compassion in Pro-Social Behavior' (2021) 159 *Neuropsychologia* 107925.

[59] Tania Singer and Olga M Klimecki, 'Empathy and Compassion' (2014) 24 *Current Biology* 875, 875.

[60] Elizabeth A Segal et al, *Assessing Empathy* (Columbia University Press, 2017) 69.

and altruistic – in the definition employed here helps to represent the concept in its entirety, and in alignment with its common use.[61]

Understood in such a way, empathy is the connection between animal sentience and human action. Sentience provides the necessary condition for the extension of human empathy, and this empathic experience can translate into the motivated behaviour necessary to bring about the changes demanded by animal protection arguments. It is important to acknowledge, however, that empathy does not guarantee action. While altruistic behaviour can be motivated by empathic concern, the experience of empathy can also produce an alternative to direct helping behaviour or a lack of action altogether.[62] This is, however, not detrimental to the claim of this chapter, which concerns the use of empathy in generating human support for other-regarding principles. While certainly beneficial, the key here is not that the process of empathy results in immediate helping behaviour directed at animals. Rather, the focus is on empathy combining with sentience to identify animals as the *proper subjects of consideration*. It is this process, captured predominantly by the cognitive and affective elements of empathy, that will be most useful in generating long-term, stable support for the principles of animal protection.

IV. Connecting the Animal and Human Sides of Animal Protection

The importance of sentience as a particularly salient attribute in questions of animal protection has been established in this chapter, along with the idea that sentience therefore constitutes the animal side of animal protection. This chapter has argued that empathy should accordingly constitute the human side. This section is concerned with the importance of connecting these sides – that is, connecting the justificatory basis for animal protection with the motivating basis that will contribute to generating support from the human side and ensuring that this remains stable over time.

The key argument here is that the principles of animal protection require emotional support to ensure their stability given that they are inherently other-regarding. Of course, the importance of connecting a *justification* for certain behaviour to that which *motivates* that behaviour is not exclusive to animal

[61] For a discussion on definitional issues relating to empathy, see Benjamin MP Cuff et al, 'Empathy: A Review of the Concept' (2014) 8 *Emotion Review* 144. For support in relation to the wide definition used in this chapter, see Douglas F Watt and Jaak Panksepp, *Psychology and Neurobiology of Empathy* (Nova Science Publishers, 2016) 7–8, where the authors state: 'Such ultrafine semantic distinctions may promote conceptual confusion and may not, in the end, prove useful scientifically. More importantly, it may be troublesome for the field at large to argue for such finely nuanced distinctions between empathy, sympathy and compassion, when many textbook definitions and virtually all major dictionary references use them as rough synonyms and often define them in terms of one another.'

[62] Batson, Lishner, and Stocks (n 53) 263; C Daniel Batson, *Altruism in Humans* (Oxford University Press, 2010) ch 5.

protection. As Sharon Krause explains, 'the norms governing us should reflect motives that naturally animate us. The considerations that make something the right thing to do should also be considerations about which we care enough to act'.[63] In the present context, this means that the various approaches to animal protection, brought together by the respective importance they place on sentience, should all be concerned with the cultivation of empathy.

Outside of animal protection efforts, the importance of empathy as a motivator towards the norms governing us is reflected in human rights. Historian Lynn Hunt has argued that empathy was central to the recognition of contemporary human rights norms.[64] Richard Rorty, a well-known proponent of the importance of sentiment, sought to explain how emotion can further human rights culture through what he called a 'sentimental education'.[65] Rorty critiqued the philosophical grounding of human rights in some special status, such as the human condition, human nature or dignity.[66] He did not believe that the validity of rights could be found in the grounds of rights.[67] Rather, Rorty proposed that the focus in furthering rights should be on questions such as 'Why should I care about a stranger, a person who is no kin to me, a person whose habits I find disgusting?'[68] He argued that stories of sentiments provide a better answer to this question than traditional responses based on a search for the metaphysical grounds of human rights.

Similarly, András Sajó argues that 'Empathy helps to explain the acceptance and endorsement of rights that concern and benefit people other than ourselves.'[69] In linking empathy to the abolition of slavery, Sajó claims that 'rational arguments and considerations might have worked where there was no major social or economic price to be paid' but 'The abolition of slavery is tied to a public sentiment that found slavery emotionally unacceptable.'[70] In the same tone as Rorty's 'sentimental education', Sajó explains that the subjective experiences of slaves featured prominently in antislavery movements.[71] He emphasises, however, that the power of sentiment is connected to and limited by the conditions of the world and the ability for private emotions to translate into public emotions.[72] In respect of the latter, Sajó outlines that motivating sentiments must be extended past those particular groups that have emotionally driven personal dedication.[73] The key to

[63] Sharon R Krause, *Civil Passions: Moral Sentiment and Democratic Deliberation* (Princeton University Press, 2008) 202.

[64] Lynn Hunt, *Inventing Human Rights: A History* (WW Norton & Co, 2007); Peter Cumper and Tom Lewis 'Empathy in Human Rights: The Case of Religious Dress' (2018) 18 *Human Rights Law Review* 61, 66.

[65] Richard Rorty, *Truth and Progress: Philosophical Papers* Vol 3 (Cambridge University Press, 1991) 176.

[66] ibid 171.

[67] ibid 170–71.

[68] ibid 185.

[69] András Sajó, *Constitutional Sentiments* (Yale University Press, 2011) 157.

[70] ibid 160.

[71] ibid ch 4.

[72] ibid 178.

[73] ibid 182–94.

mobilising large groups, according to Sajó, was 'generating empathy primarily by making suffering *visible*'.[74]

These accounts of the importance of emotions – and empathy, in particular – in the context of human rights demonstrate the validity of empathy in the context of animal rights. Key in Sajó's account specifically is that empathy is not offered as the sole justification for the rights themselves. Rather, empathy was important in the 'acceptance and endorsement' of other-regarding rights. This is in recognition of the fact that moral truth itself may not be sufficient to motivate a group to act – rational arguments directed at identifying this truth may require sentiment to make that truth felt. Thus, in the context of animal protection, empathy is not designed to *replace* sentience in the development of animal protection norms. The connection of the animal and human sides of animal protection is instead targeted towards ensuring those norms have robust justifications that can generate and sustain the necessary support.[75]

V. Animal Sentience Recognition: Building Empathy, Building Motivation

Having established the importance of empathy in ensuring stable support for the principles of animal protection, the question now turns to how empathy may best be utilised to achieve this goal. Utilising empathy in this way is likely to involve something akin to what Rorty called a 'sentimental education'. That is, it demands that structures be built (or removed) to allow for the cultivation of empathy for animals to generate support for animal protection principles. While this presents a myriad of possible approaches, the focus of this section is on the role of sentience recognition specifically as a fundamental first step in cultivating empathy towards animals.

Sentience as part of a sentimental education as proposed here is not isolated – it must be consciously connected to the human side of animal protection. This is represented by the fact that scientific research concerning animal sentience has been prevalent since the Brambell Report was initiated in 1965,[76] giving rise to the Five Freedoms of Animal Welfare.[77] If recognition of animal sentience itself was enough to change human behaviour, the increase in scientific research affirming

[74] ibid 180.

[75] It is important to note that it need not be the case that sentiment is involved only in a motivational respect, with reason the sole factor in norm justification. The fact of the motivating sentiment is connected to norm justification. See Krause (n 63) ch 1.

[76] Rogers Brambell, 'Report of the Technical Committee to Enquire into the Welfare of Animals kept under Intensive Livestock Husbandry Systems' (Her Majesty's Stationery Office, 1965), available at edepot.wur.nl/134379.

[77] Melissa Elischer, 'The Five Freedoms: A History Lesson in Animal Care and Welfare' (Michigan State University, 6 September 2019), available at www.canr.msu.edu/news/an_animal_welfare_history_lesson_on_the_five_freedoms.

animal sentience would assumedly have produced a visible downward trend in the number of animals used for food.[78] This has not been the case.[79] There are, of course, various potential reasons why sentience alone has not produced the behaviour changes petitioned for in animal protection arguments. However, as Marc Bekoff and Jessica Pierce explain, much of this relates to the framing of animal sentience as operating from within the status quo.[80] Bekoff and Pierce state, 'Welfare science is predicated on the fact that animals have subjective experiences, yet many in the field downplay these very same subjective feelings when it comes to implementing welfare guidelines or drawing moral conclusions from their work.'[81] They further outline that 'science cannot help improve the lot of animals as long as it remains wedded to industry, because there is no internal motivation to translate knowledge about what animals need into significant changes in how we treat them.'[82]

Thus, while scientific research recognising animal sentience has been increasing, this has so far occurred largely in the context of industries such as intensive animal agriculture that do not seek to eliminate animal suffering altogether.[83] In fact, these industries entail structures that obscure subjective animal experience and therefore hinder the forming of empathic relationships with animals. In Western countries, for instance, the first and only contact with animals that are commonly consumed, such as chickens, cows and pigs, typically occurs at the grocery store once the animal has been reduced to flesh and packaged. This means that citizens are unlikely to have had a relationship with the animals they eat outside of the realm of preparation and consumption. This introduces a significant disconnect between human and animal that hinders the forming of any empathetic feeling. Further, animal sentience is typically mobilised in a way that amplifies positive experience and conceals negative experience. For example, if consumers are reminded of the origin of meat in marketing, the experience of the animal is presented positively.[84]

In this respect, Martha Nussbaum argues that 'tragic spectatorship' provides a powerful means of fostering compassion amongst citizens.[85] This is because it 'emphasises common human vulnerability' and 'generates a valuable dialogue

[78] Marc Bekoff and Jessica Pierce, *The Animals' Agenda: Freedom, Compassion, and Coexistence in the Human Age* (Beacon Press, 2017) ch 2.

[79] ibid 18–21.

[80] ibid ch 2.

[81] ibid 30.

[82] ibid 33.

[83] Rather, what constitutes acceptable suffering is subject to a productivity analysis. Some level of animal suffering is inherent in animal-use industries, particularly those industries that produce animals for consumption.

[84] Jane Kotzmann and Morgan Stonebridge, 'There is Value in Stating the Obvious: Why United States Legislatures Should Explicitly Recognize Animal Sentience in Their Laws' (2021) 30 *Cornell Journal of Law and Public Policy* 425, 470; Ben Grossblatt, 'Suicide Food' (Blog, 2011), available at suicidefood.blogspot.com. Specifically, Grossblatt defines 'suicide food' in his blog's sidebar.

[85] Martha Craven Nussbaum, *Political Emotions: Why Love Matters for Justice* (The Belknap Press of Harvard University Press, 2013) 257–66.

about fault and social change'.[86] Applied to animal protection, tragic spectatorship can also be understood as a way to make animal suffering visible. As Sajó explained, making suffering visible is key to generating empathy and mobilising larger groups of citizens. If animal suffering is invisible, so too is the fundamental capacity with which humans can empathise. It is therefore likely that initial efforts to foster empathy in individuals will need to focus on removing structures that hide subjective animal experience.[87]

This is the primary place of *legal* recognition of animal sentience in the context of an animal-centred sentimental education. Legal recognition of animal sentience centralises animal experience and contributes to the view that animals are the appropriate subjects of empathy. It represents a fundamental step in making animal suffering *visible*. This connects with what Kate McClellan refers to as the 'legibility and knowability of animal others'.[88] McClellan states that 'in order to be empathized with, an animal first has to be understood in emotional and cognitive terms'.[89] Legally recognising animal sentience signals to citizens that animals *can* be understood emotionally and cognitively, that they *can* be empathised with, and that such an understanding is an important part of answering questions about their welfare.

Further, legal recognition of animal sentience often represents a form of recognition that is not intended for industry alone. This is evidenced in the Australian Capital Territory, for instance, where recognition of animal sentience occurs in a legislative instrument that does not regulate the welfare of farmed animals.[90] If, as Bekoff and Pierce suggest, sentience recognition as tied to industry has suffered from a motivational deficit in generating significant behaviour changes, the emphasising of animal sentience before the general public may produce that motivation by presenting animals as appropriate beings to empathise with. The Victorian consultation mentioned in section III indicates that this may at least be an industry concern. As noted above, most agricultural organisations who participated in the consultation did not support explicitly recognising sentience in the Victorian animal welfare legislation,[91] with one stating that 'animal sentience as a concept has been used as a weapon against livestock producers to attempt to de-legitimise or shut down the practice of raising livestock'.[92] Thus, explicitly

[86] ibid 257–65.

[87] On the other hand, obstacles to empathy are likely less effective where empathy towards animals has been cultivated. That is, the relationship between structures that prevent empathy and empathy itself is self-perpetuating. High empathy may result in fewer obstacles, or less effective obstacles, and thus the cultivation of empathy could be utilised to remove these obstacles and to prevent their reappearance. Thank you to Leo Bromberg for this point.

[88] Kate McClellan, 'Becoming Animal People: Empathy Pedagogies and the Contested Politics of Care in Jordanian Animal Welfare Work' (2019) 92 *Anthropological Quarterly* 787, 800.

[89] ibid 800.

[90] Animal Welfare Act 1992 (ACT) s 4A(1)(a), pt 3.

[91] Victoria State Government (n 17) 8.

[92] ibid 9.

recognising animal sentience in legislation that applies to and concerns the general population may bring to the forefront the notion that animals in industries involving animal use have subjective experiences – it may present the first step in making animal suffering *visible*.

VI. Conclusion

This chapter has not sought to address whether legal recognition of animal sentience has moral value, or whether it brings about legal duties. It is not concerned with the operation of sentience itself in law. Rather, the focus here has been on acknowledging the prevalence of sentience as a justification in questions about what animals are owed and connecting this justification to what it is that makes humans *care* about animal sentience.

This second step – linking the justification to the motivation – is necessary to generate support for the principles of animal protection. This is because those principles do not exist to benefit humans directly. They are targeted at improving the lives of animal others and, while they may offer some benefit to humans, they demand significant behavioural changes and some level of sacrifice in the first instance. Generating support for other-directed laws and policies therefore requires something more than moral truth alone, and some motivator other than self-interest to buttress this truth.

This chapter has argued that empathy is a prime candidate in this respect. Empathy clearly aligns with the justification offered for animal protection – it makes the *fact* of animal sentience *felt*. While empathy faces some challenges when directed at animals as opposed to humans, research demonstrates that humans can feel cognitive and emotional empathy towards animals and can be moved to empathic responding when confronted with animal suffering. Further, the ability for empathy to generate support for other-regarding laws and principles has been established in the human rights case. It is therefore clear that empathy has a role to play in ensuring that animal protection principles can generate stable and sufficient support for themselves.

Legal recognition of animal sentience is a key area that may contribute to cultivating empathy in the manner proposed in this chapter. Legally recognising animal sentience highlights the fact that animals are feeling beings with experiences of their own. While this fact is likely considered common sense to most humans, the sentience of animals involved in animal-use industries is often made opaque by various structures that prevent the recognition of subjective experience in those animals. Consequently, bringing animal sentience to the forefront in legislation may represent a fundamental first step in removing those barriers because it makes explicit the fact that animals are the appropriate subjects of empathy.

This is not to suggest that legal recognition of animal sentience alone is enough to constitute a sentimental education of the type discussed here, or that all legal recognition may have the same impact. It forms just one important step of a broader effort to cultivate empathy towards animals and different approaches to legislative recognition may be more successful in this respect than others. However, understanding legal recognition of sentience as part of an animal-centred sentimental education may help to guide the phrasing of future legal recognitions and the development of next steps.

3

Drafting and Interpreting Sentience Provisions: Incorporating Modern Science in Animal Welfare Law as a Legislative Requirement

DANIEL GOLDSWORTHY AND IAN ROBERTSON

I. Introduction

This chapter explores how modern science in animal welfare may be integrated as a legislative requirement within animal welfare statutes to improve welfare outcomes for sentient animals and, as a consequence of the inseparable human–animal–environmental relationship, for people and our shared planet. Drafting legislative provisions to explicitly recognise and define animal sentience, by reference to their negative and positive states, facilitates outcomes that pragmatically address contemporary societal expectations and issues involving animal welfare regulation. First, we clarify what sentience is and why a definition of sentience referring to negative and positive states is the pathway to improving animal welfare outcomes, and why legislative reform and statutory interpretation are keys to advancing these outcomes. We advocate for a dual approach to legislative reform. The first argues for: (a) an explicit recognition of animals as sentient in law, and, crucial to effective implementation of change in real-world practic; and (b) defining sentience in a manner that is consistent with the Five Domains model of animal welfare, thereby extending current legal responsibilities focused solely on the animal's negative states to include obligations regarding the animal's positive affective states.[1] Second, the chapter addresses how to draft and properly interpret sentience provisions in existing animal welfare laws by reference to the contemporary (or 'modern') approach to statutory interpretation that Parliaments

[1] This is in addition to negative affective states which have historically been the concern of animal protection legislation.

typically require (*statutory* approach(es) to statutory interpretation).[2] In light of modern science in animal welfare,[3] and drawing on legislative examples from various jurisdictions, we then offer suggestions for articulating crucial welfare concepts effectively within new legislative provisions that recognise and define animal sentience.

II. What is Sentience and why does it Matter?

Before examining how 'sentience' may be best incorporated into law, we must first establish what is meant by the term and how the definition is significant to animals, people and to wider global issues. The word 'sentience' derives from the Latin word *sensus*, meaning 'feeling'.[4] It is generally defined as the ability to 'see or feel things through the senses'[5] and the 'capacity for sensation or feeling'.[6] Animal welfare scientist David Mellor defines sentience as a capacity 'to consciously perceive by the senses; to consciously feel or experience subjectively'.[7] UK animal welfare scientist Donald Broom argues that sentience implies a range of particular abilities:

> A sentient being is one that has some ability: (i) to evaluate the actions of others in relation to itself and third parties; (ii) to remember some of its own actions and their consequences; (iii) to assess risks and benefits; (iv) to have some feelings; and (v) to have some degree of awareness.[8]

Referencing the recent science and terminology of the Five Domains, a comprehensive and succinct definition that is suitable for legislative purposes and which incorporates the concept of positive animal welfare in order to align 'modern' animal law with 'modern' science, 'sentience' means that 'animals experience negative and positive (physical, mental and behavioural) states'.

[2] The focus here is on the approaches to statutory interpretation primarily used in Australia, New Zealand, and the UK, though the purposive approach (ie the common law approach) to statutory interpretation is also adopted in the United States and Canada, as well as other jurisdictions based on the common law tradition.

[3] Mike Radford, UK animal law expert, helpfully identifies the importance of science in understanding welfare and relevant legislation in stating: 'Familiarity with the scientific background is therefore necessary in order to appreciate the basis of legislative provisions. It is also a prerequisite if one is to understand the concept of welfare, for it is in the scientific literature not in the law that this is to be found: although the is used extensively in legislation, nowhere is it defined'. Mike Radford, *Animal Welfare Law in Britain* (Oxford University Press, 2001) 7.

[4] 'sentient' (*Online Etymology Dictionary*, Douglas Harper, 2023), available at www.etymonline.com/word/sentient#etymonline_v_23225.

[5] 'sentient' (*Oxford Leaner's Dictionary*, Oxford University Press, 2023), available at www.oxfordlearnersdictionaries.com/definition/english/sentient?q=sentient.

[6] 'sentience' (*Macquarie Dictionary*, Macmillan Publishers Australia, 2023).

[7] David J Mellor, 'Welfare-Aligned Sentience: Enhanced Capacities to Experience, Interact, Anticipate, Choose and Survive' (2019) 9 *Animals* 440, 449–50.

[8] Donald M Broom, *Sentience and Animal Welfare* (Cambridge University Press, 2014) 5.

Philosophical debates about who or what should be worthy of *moral* status are many and varied, as are jurisprudential debates about who or what should be conferred *legal* status.[9] Sentience may be considered a determinative criterion for ascribing moral status and, possibly, legal status,[10] *because* things matter only to sentient beings. As Sebo says, when we speak of moral status 'Typically we mean to be asking whether this being matters morally for their own sake'.[11] Sebo sketches eight different theories based on features which may be used to justify the moral status of some being or thing.[12] Relevant to this proposed extension of legal responsibility, 'sentientism' is the view that to have moral status is to possess certain interests, specifically to have 'interests in the capacity for positive and negative conscious experience'.[13]

As Stancioli argues, sentient beings perceive the world in a valanced way, and 'Only sentient beings have a true stake in the world around them because they have their own purposes and objectives and, thus, behave accordingly'.[14] Although moral status is largely conceptually different from legal status, having moral status has also been considered an appropriate basis to generate kinds of legal or political statuses. For example, despite identifying as a Kantian, Korsgaard distinguishes her position from Kant's,[15] saying that 'we are not the only beings for whom things can be good

[9] See, eg David Fagundes, 'What We Talk About When We Talk About Persons: The Language of a Legal Fiction' (2001) 114 *Harvard Law Review* 1768; Ngaire Naffine, 'Who Are Law's Persons? From Cheshire Cats to Responsible Subjects' (2003) 66 *Modern Law Review* 346; Jessica Berg, 'Of Elephants and Embryos: A Proposed Framework for Legal Personhood' (2007) 59 *Hastings Law Journal* 370; Ngaire Naffine, *Law's Meaning of Life: Philosophy, Religion, Darwin, and the Legal Person* (Hart Publishing, 2009); SM Solaiman, 'Legal Personality of Robots, Corporations, Idols and Chimpanzees: A Quest for Legitimacy' (2017) 25 *Artificial Intelligence and Law* 155; Visa A Kurki, *A Theory of Personhood* (Oxford University Press, 2019). Philosophical debates about who or what should be worthy of *moral* status are many and varied, see, eg Matan Mazor et al, 'The scientific study of consciousness cannot and should not be morally neutral' (2023) 18 *Perspectives on Psychological Science* 535; Luke McGuire et al, 'The development of speciesism: Age-related differences in the moral view of animals' (2023) 14 *Social Psychological and Personality Science* 228; David Degrazia, 'Human-Animal Chimeras, "Human" Cognitive Capacities, and Moral Status' (2019) 49 *Hastings Center Report* 33; Harry R Lloyd, 'Moral status, luck, and modal capacities: debating Shelly Kagan' (2021) 38 *Journal of Applied Philosophy* 273.

[10] Some view this idea as controversial. See, eg Kenneth E Goodpaster, 'On Being Morally Considerable' (1978) 75 *Journal of Philosophy* 308. See also Christopher Stone, 'Should Trees Have Standing? Towards Legal. Rights for Natural Objects' (1972) 45 *Southern California Law Review* 450. For more contemporary pieces, see Ali Ladak, 'What would qualify an artificial intelligence for moral standing?' (2023) *AI and Ethics* 1; Angela K Martin, 'Animal vulnerability and its ethical implications: An exploration' (2021) 38 *Journal of Applied Philosophy* 196. For more pieces in favour of this proposition, see Leonard Dung, 'Why the epistemic objection against using sentience as criterion of moral status is flawed' (2022) 28 *Science and Engineering Ethics* 51.

[11] Jeff Sebo, 'Moral Circle Explosion' in David Copp et al (eds), *The Oxford Handbook of Normative Ethics* (Oxford University Press, forthcoming) 4.

[12] ibid 5–8. These include: 'speciesism', 'rationalism', 'sentientism', 'biocentrism', 'ecocentrism', 'contextualism', 'pluralism' and 'elimitavism'.

[13] ibid 6. Two major proponents of this view include Peter Singer, *Animal Liberation: A New Ethics for Our Treatment of Animals* (New York Avon, 1975); Tom Regan, *The Case for Animal Rights* (University of California Press, 1983).

[14] Brunello Stancioli, 'A Bundle of Rights and Pachamama: Visa Kurki's Theory of Legal Personhood' (2021) 44 *Revus* 16, available at journals.openedition.org/revus/6893.

[15] Writing in the 18th century, Kant argued that humans should avoid cruelty to nonhuman animals primarily so that humans may avoid a desensitisation to cruelty: 'for a person who already displays

or bad; other animals are no different from us in that respect. So we are committed to regarding all animals as ends in themselves.'[16] If we ought to be committed, as Korsgaard argues we should be, to regarding animals as ends in themselves for whom things can be good or bad, how should the law deal with such a commitment?

One possible answer to this question lies in the interest theory of rights. This theory supposes that an individual's wellbeing and *interests* are sufficient to generate legal rights (that is, legally protected interests). The confines of this approach are aptly summarised by Stucki: 'the interest theory does little conceptual filtering beyond requiring that right holders be capable of having interests.'[17] Stucki goes on to say that 'the fairly modest and potentially over-inclusive conceptual criterion of "having interests" is typically complemented by the additional, more restrictive moral criterion of "having moral status"'.[18]

Relatedly, Cochrane argues that *only* sentient beings have interests of their own. Although both non-sentient (non-phenomenally) and sentient beings (phenomenally) may be the subjects of benefits or harms the quality of sentience that sentient beings possess implicates the value of that phenomenal experience: that is, in the form of corresponding *positive* or *negative* physical and affective states.[19] Similar to Korsgaard in this respect, Cochrane argues that the vast majority of sentient beings possess autonomy, an intrinsically valuable interest, and that, further, they can exercise agency to make choices and pursue desires that effect their phenomenal experience.[20] In the case of non-human animals, Cochrane draws a very interesting line: he views most sentient animals as lacking the characteristics or capacities that he characterises as necessary for possessing autonomy (in a philosophical more than legal sense here), namely, the abilities to 'frame, revise and review their own particular conceptions of the good'.[21] The thrust of Cochrane's position is captured in the following statement:

such cruelty to animals is no less hardened towards men.' (Immanuel Kant, *Lectures on ethics* Vol 2 (Cambridge University Press, 2001) 212. For further insight into Kant's position on nonhuman animals, see Patrick Kain, 'Kant on animals' in Peter Adamson and G Fay Edwards (eds), *Animals: A History (Oxford Philosophical Concepts)* (Oxford University Press, 2018) 211.

[16] Christine M Korsgaard, *Fellow Creatures: Our Obligations to the Other Animals* (Oxford University Press, 2018) 38–44.

[17] Saskia Stucki, 'Towards a Theory of Animal Rights: Simple and Fundamental Rights' (2020) 40 *Oxford Journal of Legal Studies* 533, 542. See also Joel Feinberg, 'The Rights of Animals and Unborn Generations' in Joel Feinberg, *Rights, Justice, and the Bounds of Liberty: Essays in Social Philosophy* (Princeton University Press, 1980) 167.

[18] Stucki (n 17) 542. See also Matthew H Kramer, 'Do Animals and Dead People Have Legal Rights?' (2001) 14 *Canadian Journal of Law and Jurisprudence* 29.

[19] See Alasdair Cochrane, *Sentientist Politics. A Theory of Global Inter-Species Justice* (Oxford University Press, 2018). To further explore the complexity of phenomenal consciousness, and its implications for sentience, see: François Kammerer, 'Ethics Without Sentience: Facing Up to the Probable Insignificance of Phenomenal Consciousness' (2022) 29 *Journal of Consciousness Studies* 180.

[20] Alasdair Cochrane, 'Labour Rights for Animals' in Robert Garner and Siobhan O'Sullivan (eds), *The Political Turn in Animal Ethics* (Rowman and Littlefield, 2016) 20.

[21] ibid; Alasdair Cochrane, 'Do Animals Have an Interest in Liberty?' (2009) 57 *Political Studies* 660; David Miller, 'Political Philosophy for Earthlings' in David Leopold and Marc Stears (eds), *Political Theory: Methods and Approaches* (Oxford University Press, 2008) 29.

> [B]ecause sentient animals seemingly lack the capacity to *reflect* upon their choices and desires – to decide for themselves the kinds of goals and goods they want to pursue – subjecting an external will on them, say through directing them to the performance of certain kinds of labour, is not intrinsically problematic in the way that it is for persons.[22]

If one can accept that sentient beings possess and exercise agency *at least* (that is, an interest in their own phenomenal experiences) even if they lack other capacities usually associated with personhood, then it follows for Cochrane, that there may be justification for using sentient beings in certain contexts.

The position of UK animal law expert Mike Radford appears consistent with these philosophical views, and also helpfully points out that the current legal paradigm is based on mankind's dominion over other non-human animals, and so law applies legal responsibilities to people regarding the use and treatment of animals.[23] So Cochrane's use-need is qualified by animal laws that have regard to the experience of sentient animals *as a consequence of* their sentience. These restrictions should, in order to give effect to the consideration of this moral status, be represented in law.

Recognising the ability of animals to subjectively feel and experience is implicit in existing anti-cruelty laws which protect animals from experiencing suffering that society generally identifies as morally, and therefore legally, unnecessary. It follows that since sentience does matter, both morally and legally, then the core question is not 'if' animals are sentient, but how broadly should legal responsibilities regarding animals' experiences be applied. Specifically, in addition to the existing duty of care prohibiting unnecessary suffering ('negative states') what are the contrasting arguments for also applying legal responsibility for animals' positive states?

Explicitly recognising and defining sentience in animal welfare legislation by reference to the animal's negative and positive states is crucial to adequately securing the interests of sentient animals and the well-being of people whose lives and livelihoods depend on animals. Legislative recognition and definition, properly interpreted and applied, can extend peoples' legal duties to include not just prevention of unnecessary and unreasonable negative states, but also the promotion of opportunities for positive states.

III. Recognition of Animal Sentience in Law

Before exploring the interpretation of animal welfare statutes, and how scientific best practice may be effectively integrated within these texts, it is important to have clarity regarding the relationship between animal welfare *science* and animal welfare *law*. Though science often informs the development of law, it is not the sole

[22] Cochrane (n 19) 20.
[23] See Radford (n 3) 9–10.

determinant regarding the development of law governing the human–animal relationship. Indeed, historically, animal protection and welfare laws have traditionally been slow, or even resistant, to implementing best practice standards identified by animal welfare science. This point is made clearer when one briefly considers the contrasting rate of progress between animal welfare science and animal law.

A. Models of Animal Welfare: From the Five Freedoms to the Five Domains

The Five Freedoms model of animal welfare frames welfare outcomes in terms of five freedoms: freedom from thirst and hunger; freedom from discomfort; freedom from pain, injury and disease; freedom to express most normal behaviour; and freedom from fear and distress.[24] The principles of the Five Freedoms still underpin animal welfare law in most jurisdictions, informing enforcement powers to act not only when an animal has suffered, but also when an animal is deemed *likely* to suffer.[25] Although groundbreaking in the 1960s,[26] Mellor comprehensively establishes that the Five Freedoms model has now been scientifically superseded by the Five Domains as advancements in scientific knowledge of animal welfare have progressed.[27]

The Five Domains model of animal welfare is a framework for organising and collating scientifically derived evidence of what animals may be feeling in a particular context, and is predicated on scientific validation of what those particular animals are capable of experiencing.[28] The Five Domains framework provides a systematic model for identifying and assessing welfare impacts across four physical or functional and one mental domain.[29] The five interconnected domains are: nutrition, environment, health, behaviour and mental state. The Five Domains

[24] For a critical appraisal of this model, see, eg David J Mellor, 'Updating Animal Welfare Thinking: Moving beyond the "Five Freedoms" towards "a Life Worth Living"' (2016) 6 *Animals* 21; Steven P McCulloch, 'A Critique of FAWC's Five Freedoms as a Framework for the Analysis of Animal Welfare' (2013) 26 *Journal of Agricultural and Environmental Ethics* 959, 961, quoting The Farm Animal Welfare Council, 'Annual Review 2009–2010' (Report, 2010) 4, available at web.archive.org/web/20101008080300/http://www.fawc.org.uk/pdf/annualreview09-10.pdf.

[25] See, eg Animal Welfare Act 1999 (NZ), s 130(1); Animal Welfare Act 1992 (ACT), s 6A.

[26] The Five Freedoms as expressed in the seminal 'Report of the Technical Committee to Enquire into the Welfare of Animals Kept under Intensive Livestock Husbandry Systems' (or Brambell Report), released in 1965 by the UK Government, had a profound impact on the public perception of animal welfare at the time, and was influential in shaping subsequent legislation and guidelines for the treatment of farm animals in the UK. See generally McCulloch (n 24).

[27] See especially Mellor (n 24); David J Mellor, 'Operational Details of the Five Domains Model and Its Key Applications to the Assessment and Management of Animal Welfare' (2017) 7 *Animals* 60; DJ Mellor and NJ Beausoleil, 'Extending the "Five Domains" Model for Animal Welfare Assessment to Incorporate Positive Welfare States' (2015) 24 *Animal Welfare* 241.

[28] See, eg David J Mellor et al., 'The 2020 Five Domains Model: Including Human-Animal Interactions in Assessments of Animal Welfare' (2020) 10 *Animals* 1870; Mellor (n 24); Mellor and Beausoleil (n 27).

[29] Mellor (n 24); Mellor (n 27) 63; Mellor and Beausoleil (n 27) 242; Ian Robertson and Daniel Goldsworthy, 'To Feel or Not to Feel: That Is the Legal Question' [2017] 1 *New Zealand Law Journal* 10, 13.

framework is focused on promoting welfare enhancement (positive states), which differentiates it from the Five Freedoms model, which focuses on avoiding welfare compromise (negative states).

It is necessary to appreciate that animal welfare science, as a broad discipline, largely seeks to assess an animals' subjective internal experience, by reference to the animals' responses to external conditions.[30] What the welfare scientist is observing and measuring are the responses to applied causes and manifestations affecting the animal's experiences.[31] The Five Domains model is 'a valuable reference for the courts and lawyers in implementing credible, scientific and objective measures within an already multifactorial, potentially complicated, and subjective field'.[32] Variances in individual responses of animals and interpretations of animal research observers are just a few of the many variables resulting in debate and disagreement between animal scientists and wider experts on what those experiences may be. In animal welfare cases, for example, the experts consulted may be experts in animal health but not necessarily animal welfare or the welfare assessment criteria established by law. Furthermore, different disciplines demonstrate different perspectives regarding the meaning of animal welfare, which has implications for interpreting related evidence. Indeed, even within a cohort who agrees on affective state orientation to understand animal welfare, what one is trying to understand or demonstrate is predicated on unobservable/unmeasurable factors which can only be inferred.[33] These common sources of disagreement demonstrate why there is a need for more concrete and widely recognised guidance on how the exercise of scientifically appreciating an animals' subjective experience needs to be conducted.

B. Animal Welfare Law: From Anti-Cruelty to Positive Animal Welfare

From the outset, animal welfare laws frequently fall short of fully replicating best scientific practice in animal welfare. The starting point at law, which necessarily informs most animal welfare law debates, is that animals are not legal persons (like human beings or corporations) but are almost universally classified as a

[30] We acknowledge that direct observation and measurement of animal 'states' may inform subsequent hypotheses about what those 'states' may mean for the international experience of animals. For further information on using animal welfare scientific methods to measure animal 'states': Donald M Broom and Richard D Kirkden, 'Welfare, stress, behaviour and pathophysiology' in Robert H Dunlop and Charles-Henri Malbert (eds), *Veterinary pathophysiology* (Blackwell Publishing, 2004) 337–69, 341.

[31] Professor Ngaio Beausoleil, Phone call with Dr Ian Robertson, 16 May 2023. Also, Professor Ngaio Beausoleil, Legalwise Seminars 'The Concept and Practice of Modern Animal 'Welfare' (12 September 2022), available at legalwiseseminars.arlo.co/w/nz/events/2454-animal-law-essentials.

[32] Robertson and Goldsworthy (n 29) 13.

[33] Beausoleil, Phone call (n 31). Also, Beausoleil, Legalwise Seminars (n 31).

type of property. More specifically, animals occupy an unusual conceptual space as *property* that possess unique animate qualities. Animal anti-cruelty law which prohibits acts or omissions that result in an animal experiencing unnecessary suffering implicitly and foundationally relies upon recognition of the animal's sentience. Consequently, it is possible to talk about the protection or *welfare* of animals in the law in ways that is distinguishable from other inanimate property.

This conceptual designation has been questioned on moral grounds, by those asking is it moral to classify animals as property? As Radford points out, debates about the legal classification of animals as animate property arguably 'miss the point' about the realities of human dominion over non-human animals and the legal protections of animals' experiences via legal responsibilities (duties of care).[34] To be clear, the argument is not that animals deserve to be treated well because society, via its laws, has long ago decided that question in the affirmative. Rather, the question is about the standards to be applied by animal law in order to meet the needs and expectations of a modern society.

Differing perspectives are observable in terms of what standards are necessary, and how to see them implemented. Views vary from advocating for *evolution* (change achieved within the current property paradigm) through to *revolution* (upending the current paradigm). Both approaches have their respective advocates, arguments and shortcomings. It is not necessarily the case that pursuing a chosen path to evolve the law will result in a targeted ideal. However, historically, it is possible to identify that law predominantly progress via a process of legal evolution rather than revolution. The process of research, public consultation and political debates is often frustrating for those wanting a quicker process, concerning for those that want to retain the certainty of a status quo, and a very real challenge for those with the responsibility of appropriately balancing and prioritising the interests, agendas and multiple worldviews of society.

For example, some have suggested that there is a 'conceptual incoherence' for a legal system to recognise corporations as legal persons and animate animals as legal property,[35] To perceived dilemmas such as these, the concepts of 'positive animal law' and 'sentient animate property'[36] offers a pragmatic solution which is consistent with the framework and evolves the legal paradigm in a manner that is

[34] Radford (n 3) 10.

[35] For an illuminating discussion on the debate about who or what should be conferred legal personhood, see Ngaire Naffine, *Law's Meaning of Life: Philosophy, Religion, Darwin, and the Legal Person* (Hart Publishing, 2009) ch 2; Kurki (n 9); Joanna J Bryson et al, 'Of, for, and by the people: the legal lacuna of synthetic persons' (2017) 25 *Artificial Intelligence Law* 273; Jason P Kight and TS Johnson, 'Legal Personhood: An Analysis of the Legal Rights of Corporations and Their Relation to Animal Ethics' (2022) 12 *Journal of Animal Ethics* 23; Jiahong Chen and Paul W Burgess, 'The boundaries of legal personhood: how spontaneous intelligence can problematise differences between humans, artificial intelligence, companies and animals' (2018) 27 *Artificial Intelligence Law* 73.

[36] For similar proposals, see, eg Angela Fernandez, *Animals as Property, quasi-property or quasi-person* (Brooks U Animal Law Fundamentals, 2021); David Favre, 'Living property: A New Status for Animals Within the Legal System' (2010) 93 *Marquette Law Review* 1021.

consistent with the modern science of the Five Domains, delivers on the needs of a modern society, and enables governors to implement modern animal law.

While the sentience of animals is implicit in any anti-cruelty law, the move to explicitly recognising animal sentience is observable in a number of legal instruments and jurisdictions. evolving in certain jurisdictions already. The Treaty on the Functioning of the European Union (TFEU) is widely regarded as the first legal instrument to *explicitly* state that 'animals are sentient beings'.[37] Since then, various national animal welfare frameworks are increasingly recognising animal sentience explicitly in legislation;[38] for example, Germany,[39] Austria,[40] Switzerland,[41] New Zealand[42] and France[43] have incorporated legislative provisions that recognise animals as sentient.[44] The explicit recognition has not been accompanied by a definition that evolves legal standards beyond anticruelty law, however these examples demonstrate leading jurisdictions that have sought to provide clarity to their existing animal laws.

Implicit in existing law protecting animals from unnecessary or unreasonable negative states of pain, distress, or suffering (legally defined as 'cruelty'), and moves to extend that duty of care to include providing them with opportunities to experience positive states, is endorsement that sentient animals are not like other inanimate legal property. The fact that society has existing anti-cruelty law demonstrates that it matters to society how we treat them *because* they are sentient.

The early nineteenth century saw the first enactment of anti-cruelty law prohibiting specific acts of cruelty ('animal protection'). In many, though not all, jurisdictions, that standard has evolved from the concept of animal 'protection' to animal 'welfare'. Welfare law is generally distinguishable from protection law because by the fact that animal protection law's focus on punishing cruel acts once committed,[45] welfare law also prohibits acts deemed *likely* to cause an animal to suffer at some future point.

[37] Consolidated Version of the Treaty on the Functioning of the European Union [2016] OJ C202/54, Art 13.

[38] See generally Charlotte Blattner, 'The Recognition of Animal Sentience by the Law' (2019) 9 *Journal of Animal Ethics* 121.

[39] Civil Code (*Bürgerliches Gesetzbuch*) (Germany) § 90a.

[40] General Civil Code *(Allgemeines Bürgerliches Gesetzbuch*) (Austria) § 285a.

[41] Swiss Civil Code (Switzerland) Art 641a(1).

[42] Animal Welfare Act 1999 (NZ).

[43] French Civil Code (France) Art 515-14; *Loi* n° 76-629 du 10 juillet 1976 [Law No 76-629 of 10 July 1976] (France) Art 9.

[44] For recent discussions on legislative recognition of animal sentience, see Jane Kotzmann, 'A Typology of Australian Animal Sentience Recognition Provisions – Enacted and Proposed' (2023) 51 *Federal Law Review* 157; Jane Kotzmann, 'Sentience and Intrinsic Worth as a Pluralist Foundation for Fundamental Animal Rights' (2023) 43 *Oxford Journal of Legal Studies* 405; Ian Robertson and Daniel Goldsworthy, 'Recognising and Defining Animal Sentience in Legislation: A Framework for Importing Positive Animal Welfare Through the Five Domains Model (2022) 48 *Monash University Law Review* 244; Jane Kotzmann, 'Recognising the Sentience of Animals in Law: A Justification and Framework for Australian States and Territories' (2020) 42 *Sydney Law Review* 281.

[45] See, eg Cruel Treatment of Cattle Act 1822, 3 Geo 4. Cruel acts were typically understood to include prohibiting treatment that causes an animal to suffer and criminalising blatant acts of cruelty.

Since the Five Domains model of animal welfare assessment has endorsed the commonly accepted view that animals experience not just negative but also positive states, one of the challenges for those wishing to implement genuinely modern animal law is how to also legislatively account for an animal's *positive* experiences and affective states. For example, how can legislation provide the clarity needed for compliance and enforcement purposes, to mandate that animals must be provided with opportunities to experience positive states such as comfort, contentment and pleasure?

IV. Drafting Sentience Provisions

Blattner states that, 'When legislators refer to sentience … they usually use a broad definition that includes both the ability to experience pain and pleasure and the intrinsic importance to the being experiencing those feelings'.[46] So how does modern society draft legislation incorporating positive animal welfare standards?

A. The Modern Approach to Statutory Interpretation: What is the Law's Purpose?

New Zealand's Animal Welfare Act provides a clear reference to how the law, in theory, is expected to reference science and additional criteria when assessing what standards of animal care are acceptable. Section 10 addresses the obligations in relation to physical, health and behavioural needs of animals in stating:

> The owner of an animal, and every person in charge of an animal, must ensure that the physical, health, and behavioural needs of the animal are met in a manner that is in accordance with both (a) good practice; and (b) scientific knowledge.[47]

Of course, if a matter proceeds to a defended hearing, it is the courts who decide what practices and knowledge are relevant, applicable and sufficiently weighty in interpreting what is 'appropriate to the species, environment, and circumstances of the animal'.[48]

There are various approaches to statutory interpretation in common law jurisdictions, including how parliaments require that statutes be interpreted (statutory approaches to statutory interpretation) and how the courts have traditionally

[46] Blattner (n 38) 125.
[47] Animal Welfare Act 1999 (NZ), s 10.
[48] Animal Welfare Act 1999 (NZ), s 4.

developed approaches to interpreting ambiguous statutes (common law approaches to statutory interpretation).[49]

The modern approach (or the purposive approach) to statutory interpretation has been adopted in many common law jurisdictions and requires that courts interpret legislation by focusing on the underlying purpose or intention of the law rather than relying on the literal meaning of the words.[50] As such, the purposive approach aims to give effect to legislative intent and promote the objectives and policies underlying the law.

In Australia, two seminal cases that adopt the modern approach to statutory interpretation are *CIC Insurance v Bankstown Football Club Ltd*[51] and *Project Blue Sky Inc v Australian Broadcasting Authority*.[52] In *CIC Insurance*, the High Court outlined the modern approach to statutory interpretation in following terms:

> [T]he modem approach to statutory interpretation (a) insists that the context be considered in the first instance, not merely at some later stage when ambiguity might be thought to arise, and (b) uses 'context' in its widest sense to include such things as the existing state of the law and the mischief which, by legitimate means such as [reference to reports of law reform bodies], may discern the statute was intended to remedy ...[53]

The major theme of this account of the purposive approach to statutory interpretation is *context*. Context is to 'be considered in the first instance, not merely at some later stage when ambiguity might be thought to arise' and 'in its widest sense'.[21] Echoing the sentiments of the High Court in *CIC Insurance*, the modern approach to statutory interpretation was reiterated and confirmed in *Project Blue Sky*:

> [T]he duty of a court is to give the words of a statutory provision the meaning that the legislature is taken to have intended them to have. Ordinarily, that meaning (the legal meaning) will correspond with the grammatical meaning of the provision. But not always. The context of the words, the consequences of a literal or grammatical construction, the purpose of the statute or the canons of construction may require the words of a legislative provision to be read in a way that does not correspond with the literal or grammatical meaning.[54]

[49] The focus will be on Australia, New Zealand,and the UK, but the principles generally hold, particularly for legal systems informed by the common law tradition.

[50] For example, in Australia see Acts Interpretation Act 1901 (Cth), s 15AA; Legislation Act 2001 (ACT), s 139; Interpretation Act 1987 (NSW), s 33; Interpretation Act 1978 (NT), s 62A; Acts Interpretation Act 1954 (Qld), s 14A; Legislation Interpretation Act 2021 (SA), s 14; Acts Interpretation Act 1931 (Tas), s 8A; Interpretation of Legislation Act 1984 (Vic), s 35(a); Interpretation Act 1984 (WA), s 18. In New Zealand, see Interpretation Act 1999 (NZ), s 5(1). In the UK, see *Jones v Wrotham Park Estate Co Ltd* [1981] AC 74; *Pepper (Inspector of Taxes) v Hart* [1993] AC 593; *R (ex parte Quintavalle) v Secretary of State for Health* [2003] UKHL 13; *R (Jackson) v Attorney General* [2005] UKHL 56.

[51] *CIC Insurance v Bankstown Football Club Ltd* (1997) 187 CLR 384 ('*CIC Insurance*').

[52] *Project Blue Sky Inc v Australian Broadcasting Authority* (1998) 194 CLR 355 ('*Project Blue Sky*').

[53] *CIC Insurance Ltd*, at 408 (Brennan CJ, Dawson, Toohey, and Gummow JJ) (citations omitted). See also Jacinta Dharmananda, 'Outside the Text: Inside the Use of Extrinsic Materials in Statutory Interpretation' (2014) 42 *Federal Law Review* 333.

[54] *Project Blue Sky*, at 384 (McHugh, Gummow, Kirby, and Hayne JJ).

The modern approach to statutory interpretation has been legislated for in Australia at the Commonwealth level and in every state and territory,[55] as well as in New Zealand.[56] The Interpretation Act 1978 (UK) does not explicitly mention the purposive approach. However, the approach is recognised by the courts as a legitimate method of statutory interpretation to give effect to the underlying object and purpose of legislation.[57]

Legislatively recognising animals as sentient in animal welfare laws would require courts to consider *in the first instance* the purpose of the Act and the intention of the legislature. However, as excited as animal advocates may initially feel about statutory obligations to consider the purpose of the Act, that excitement is tempered by remembering that anti-cruelty law implicitly recognises that animals are capable of feeling and experiencing ('sentient') so simply explicitly stating what is already implicitly recognised does not shift or extend the existing duty of care. Consequently, just recognising animals as sentient changes little to nothing in practice.

In contrast, explicit recognition that is accompanied with a legislative definition based not just on negative states but also on animals' positive states, rendering it consistent with the modern Five Domains model, would, by virtue of the modern approach to statutory interpretation, evolve standards and, in practice, require that animals be provided with opportunities to experience positive affective states.[58]

B. Statutory Provisions in Context

There are two common legislative drafting approaches that would allow for an extension of the current anti-cruelty duties of care towards positive animal welfare law, namely integration into: (1) the objects section of Act; or (2) the definition section of an Act. An example of this first approach in Australia is the first (and at the time of writing this, the only) jurisdiction to explicitly recognise animals as sentient in its legislation together with a definition in the accompanying explanatory notes: the Australian Capital Territory.[59] The difference between defining sentience in the objects and defining sentience in the definition section of the Act is important.

[55] Acts Interpretation Act 1901 (Cth), s 15AA; Legislation Act 2001 (ACT), s 139; Interpretation Act 1987 (NSW), s 33; Interpretation Act 1978 (NT), s 62A; Acts Interpretation Act 1954 (Qld), s 14A; Legislation Interpretation Act 2021 (SA), s 14; Acts Interpretation Act 1931 (Tas), s 8A; Interpretation of Legislation Act 1984 (Vic), s 35(a); Interpretation Act 1984 (WA), s 18.

[56] See Interpretation Act 1999 (NZ), s 5(1). This provision provides that the 'meaning of an enactment must be ascertained from its text and in light of its purpose'.

[57] Seminal cases in the UK regarding the purposive approach include *Jones v Wrotham Park Estate Co Ltd* [1981] AC 74; *Pepper (Inspector of Taxes) v Hart* [1993] AC 593; *R (ex parte Quintavalle) v Secretary of State for Health* [2003] UKHL 13; *R (Jackson) v Attorney General* [2005] UKHL 56.

[58] Robertson and Goldsworthy (n 44).

[59] See Animal Welfare Act 1992 (ACT), s 4A(1) which states under its Objects: '(1) The main objects of this Act are to recognise that – (a) animals are sentient beings that are able to subjectively feel and perceive the world around them'.

i. Object Clauses

Given that the modern approach to statutory interpretation is legislatively prescribed in Australia, the objects of an Act directs interpreters to explicitly take parliamentary intent into account. As the modern approach to statutory interpretation requires courts to give effect to the words, phrases, or provision of the Act, objects are influential and guide interpretation. The means of implementing positive animal welfare law by way of an objects clause which may be integrated into existing animal welfare Acts is as follow:

> i. Suggested Objects clauses for Animal Welfare Acts
>
> *that* people have a duty of care to ensure the physical and mental welfare of animals under their care or control, to avoid exposing animals to or causing them causing them unnecessary negative states of pain, suffering or distress, and to provide opportunities for the animals to feel or experience positive states of comfort, interest, or pleasure.
>
> *that* provisions of this Act and associated legislative instruments are to be interpreted consistently with best scientific practice in animal welfare.[60]

Objects clauses, however, determine meaning in the same way that legislative definitions do, so let us now consider an alternative proposal for new definitions which may be integrated into existing animal welfare Acts.

ii. Definitions

Where Parliament has sought to legislatively define a word or phrase in the Act's definition section, the definition will be determinative. One is under no allusion that the word may mean something other than how it has been legislatively defined. As Kotzmann says, 'Defining the animals covered by animal welfare legislation by reference to the concept of sentience expressly makes sentience a prerequisite to legislative protection.'[61] For example, defining what 'animal' means for the purpose of animal welfare legislation is crucial for knowing which animals come within the scope of legislative protection, and grounding that definition in sentience is the key to extending legal duties of care beyond the current duty to avoid acts which cause negative affective states and beyond the current species currently covered in animal welfare statutes.

The scientific advances of the 1960s that generated the Five Freedoms have been superseded by modern scientific research, leading to the more holistic, systematic and practical Five Domains model for welfare assessment.[62] Understanding the

[60] At the time of writing, the Five Domains model is widely regarded as best scientific practice. The Five Domains model should not be directly referenced in legislation to allow for future (and possibly better) iterations of best scientific practice in animal welfare.

[61] Kotzmann (n 44) 177.

[62] It is important to note that, at the time of writing, most common law animal welfare statutes still use the Five Freedoms as the benchmark for informing legally enforceable animal welfare standards.

Five Domains model of animal welfare is key to understanding what evidence is necessary to demonstrate compliance with animal welfare laws that are grounded in current best practice. To that end, the following legislative definition provides specificity and clarity to orient progressive law reform in a manner that is consistent with the Five Domains, yet flexible enough to adapt to scientific advancements in animal welfare: 'Sentience means that animals experience negative and positive (physical, mental, and behavioural) states.' For legislative purposes, the word 'physical' covers domains of nutrition, environment and physical aspects of health. 'Mental' states are distinguished as a separate category to 'behavioural' states.[63] The definition provided moves beyond the status quo scope of contemporary anticruelty legislation, which often focuses primarily on criminalising acts or omissions that do, or are likely to, result in an animal experiencing negative states that, under the law, are assessed as unreasonable or unnecessary.

Introducing the following definitions into existing animal welfare Acts adds further certainty and clarity that supports the intent to extend the duty of care to include responsibility for both the negative, and positive, states that animals experience.

i. Suggested Definitions for inclusion into principal Animal Welfare Acts

Define **'sentience'** as follows: sentience means that animals experience negative and positive (physical, mental, and behavioural) states.

Define **'scientific practice'** as follows: scientific practice refers to principles of animal welfare means that the physical, emotional, and mental needs of the animal are addressed in a manner that conforms to both standards of good practice and contemporary scientific knowledge.

Define **'negative state**s' as follows: negative states means an animal's feeling or experience of pain, distress, or suffering.

Define '**positive states'** as follows: positive states means an animal's feeling or experience of comfort, interest, or pleasure.

Define 'cruelty' as follows: cruelty, to an animal, includes an act or omission that causes, or is likely to cause, the animal to feel or experience a negative state of pain or distress that is either unreasonable or unnecessary.

Define 'pain' as follows: an aversive sensory experience caused by actual or potential injury that elicits protective or withdrawal responses.[64]

[63] Whether and to what extent they are distinguishable is another question. For example, is there a clear distinction between the mental experience of pain and the behaviour of crying? We may infer mental states from physical manifestations we *take to be representative* of mental states, but direct access to the subjective experiences and mental states of animals is likely to remain beyond the scope of welfare assessment which must rely on inferential reasoning.

[64] This definition is consistent with Zimmerman's (1986) definition: see M Zimmerman, 'Physiological mechanisms of pain and its treatment' (1986) 32 *Klinische Anäesthesiol Intensivtherapie* 1, 2. Sneddon (2009) refined this definition suggesting that animals in pain should 'quickly learn to avoid the noxious stimulus and demonstrate sustained changes in behaviour that have a protective function to reduce further injury and pain, prevent the injury from recurring, and promote healing and recovery.' See

Define **'unnecessary'** to include various considerations,[65] such as is provided for in section 4(3) of Animal Welfare Act 2006 (UK).[66]

These definitions direct and assist those who have a duty to comply with the law, as well as those whose responsibility it is to interpret, apply and enforce the law. Moreover, these definitions allow for the application of an extended duty of care that reflects modern expectations, standards of good practice, and contemporary scientific knowledge.

V. Conclusion

This chapter demonstrates how genuinely modern animal welfare law can apply legal responsibilities for providing lives for animals that are enjoyed rather than just endured. A key to advancing beyond simply not being cruel to animals lies in not restating what is already implicit in existing anti-cruelty law. Explicit recognition is laudable, but to secure pragmatic changes in practice it is critical to legislatively define sentience by reference to animals' negative and positive states.

Positive animal welfare law is entirely consistent with the existing legal paradigm that is based on responsibilities rather than rights and which also reflects the contemporary science of the Five Domains which have superseded the Five Freedoms model. Moreover, elevating standards of animal welfare to incorporate a legislative requirement for positive animal welfare has significance that extends well beyond sentimental concerns about animals. This is because, as a result of the inseparable human–animal–environmental relationship, keeping animal welfare law up to date with modern science provides a pragmatic, realistic and replicable way of addressing many wider issues involving animals, the global society and our shared environment, within critical timeframes.

Lynne U Sneddon, 'Pain perception in fish: indicators and endpoints' (2009) 50 *ILAR Journal* 338, 338. These definitions inform the criteria by which possible pain experience might be judged.

[65] Section 4(3) reads as follows: (3) The considerations to which it is relevant to have regard when determining for the purposes of this section whether suffering is unnecessary include – (a) whether the suffering could reasonably have been avoided or reduced;(b) whether the conduct which caused the suffering was in compliance with any relevant enactment or any relevant provisions of a licence or code of practice issued under an enactment; (c) whether the conduct which caused the suffering was for a legitimate purpose, such as – (i) the purpose of benefiting the animal, or (ii) the purpose of protecting a person, property or another animal; (d) whether the suffering was proportionate to the purpose of the conduct concerned; (e) whether the conduct concerned was in all the circumstances that of a reasonably competent and humane person.

[66] Opting for a provision such as this directs courts and others to that which is relevant to have regard to. It provides legislative direction, and a degree of clarity for courts, parties to a dispute, and more generally to interested stakeholders.

4

Sentience Recognition as a Means for Moving Beyond Animal Welfare to Animal Rights

JANE KOTZMANN*

I. Introduction

Arguments for the attribution of fundamental legal rights to animals have gained importance over recent decades.[1] Lori Marino, a neuroscientist and expert in animal behaviour, intelligence and self-awareness, contends that *legal* rights for animals are required because they 'are the only kind of protections that ensure animals are shielded from the self-indulgence and caprices of humans'.[2] Similarly, legal scholar Charlotte Blattner argues that 'The demand for fundamental rights for animals is neither utopian nor far-fetched; it is the only option available to move away from our prevailing perfunctory consideration of animals'.[3] Within this discourse, several scholars have asserted that animal sentience should provide the foundation for animal rights.[4] Not surprisingly, then, the legal recognition

* Many thanks to Morgan Stonebridge and Jessica Tselepy for their outstanding research assistance that contributed to this chapter.

[1] References to animal rights in this article refer to fundamental legal animal rights in the sense described by Saskia Stucki unless otherwise stated: '[F]undamental animal rights are strong legal rights along the lines of human rights that are characterised by the cumulative features of substantive fundamentality and normative robustness due to their reduced infringeability … such as the right to life, bodily integrity, liberty and freedom from torture': Saskia Stucki, 'Towards a Theory of Legal Animal Rights: Simple and Fundamental Rights' (2020) 40 *Oxford Journal of Legal Studies* 533, 552.

[2] Lori Marino, 'Commentary: A Belmont Report for Animals? Rights or Welfare?' (2020) 29 *Cambridge Quarterly of Healthcare Ethics* 67, 68.

[3] Charlotte Blattner, 'Rethinking the 3Rs: From Whitewashing to Rights' in Kathrin Herrmann and Kimberley Jayne (eds), *Animal Experimentation: Towards Paradigm Change* (Brill, 2019) 168, 180.

[4] Gary L Francione, *Introduction to Animal Rights: Your Child or the Dog?* (Temple University Press, 2000) xxvi. See also, Gary L Francione, 'Taking Sentience Seriously' (2006) 1 *Journal of Animal Law and Ethics* 1, 17; Alasdair Cochrane, 'From Human Rights to Sentient Rights' (2013) 16 *Critical Review of International Social and Political Philosophy* 655, 657; Michael L Woodruff, 'Sentience is the Foundation of Animal Rights' (2019) 23 *Animal Sentience*; Jane Kotzmann, 'Sentience and Intrinsic Worth as a Pluralist Foundation for Fundamental Animal Rights' (2023) 43 *Oxford Journal of Legal Studies* 405, 405.

of animal sentience has been broadly popular amongst animal law scholars and animal advocates.[5]

The legal trend towards recognising animal sentience has also been criticised, however, including by prominent legal scholar and philosopher Gary L Francione. Francione argues that animal sentience recognition is meaningless because although sentience has been recognised as important since the first iterations of animal welfare legislation, it has failed to prevent animal exploitation.[6] Moreover, he argues that recognition of animal sentience not only lacks meaning in this sense, but more ominously is being used by governments and animal welfare charities as welfare-washing for political and financial purposes.[7]

This context raises the question explored in this chapter of whether the legal recognition of animal sentience can provide a means for moving beyond a legal paradigm of animal welfare to one of animal rights. In pursuing this question, this chapter seeks to respond to the call from Jessica Eisen to shift beyond the rights-welfare debate and to consider the 'dynamics of legal change in democratic states'.[8] In this respect, it considers the extent to which legal recognition of animal sentience can 'support the public deliberation that will necessarily precede any substantial change in legal relationships with other animals'.[9] The chapter argues that legal recognition of animal sentience holds the potential to strengthen public debate in relation to animals as it calls attention to the subjective, embodied experience of animals and provides an agreed language that can be used to hold governments and industry to account. Moreover, sentience recognition may usefully serve as a theoretical basis for fundamental animal rights. While many animal studies scholars would welcome an animal rights revolution, history and academic commentary suggest that animal rights are more likely to be achieved incrementally.

Thus, this chapter contends that while criticism can fairly be levelled at laws that recognise animal sentience, they are not meaningless. Rather, such laws have the potential to contribute to moving democratic societies beyond a legal welfare paradigm to one of legal rights for animals. Section II of this chapter outlines the increasing prominence of animal rights in scholarship, legal practice and politics

[5] See Ian Robertson and Daniel Goldsworthy, 'Recognising and Defining Animal Sentience in Legislation: A Framework for Importing Positive Animal Welfare Through the Five Domains Model' (2022) 48 *Monash University Law Review* 244, 245; Jane Kotzmann and Morgan Stonebridge, 'There is Value in Stating the Obvious: Why United States Legislatures Should Explicitly Recognize Animal Sentience in Their Laws' (2021) 30 *Cornell Journal of Law and Public Policy* 425, 425; Charlotte Blattner, 'The Recognition of Animal Sentience by the Law' (2019) 9 *Journal of Animal Ethics* 121, 121; Craig Herbst, 'Reform the Animal Welfare Act: Recognize Animal Sentience and Protect all Animals Who Think, Feel, and Suffer' (2023) 62 *Washburn Law Journal* 61, 62. In contrast, see Marcelo Rodriguez Ferrere, 'The (Symbolic) Legislative Recognition of Animal Sentience (2022) 28 *Animal Law* 117, 117.

[6] Gary L Francione, 'Surprise: U.K. Law Recognizes That Sentient Animals Are Sentient' (Medium, 16 May 2021), available at www.gary-francione.medium.com/surprise-u-k-law-recognizes-that-sentient-animals-are-sentient-d1e42c29f777.

[7] ibid.

[8] Jessica Eisen, 'Beyond Rights and Welfare: Democracy, Dialogue, and the Animal Welfare Act' (2018) 51 *University of Michigan Journal of Law Reform* 469, 469.

[9] ibid 495.

by way of context for the discussion. Section III outlines and responds to criticism levelled at sentience recognition. Section IV explores the potentiality of sentience recognition as a means for achieving animal rights in the future.

II. The Increasing Prominence of Animal Rights and Sentience Recognition

A. Animal Rights Scholarship and Sentience

While Peter Singer's seminal 1975 text *Animal Liberation* prompted a renewal of academic interest in animal ethics,[10] his arguments are based on a utilitarian rather than a rights ethic.[11] Following Singer, however, animal rights scholarship has gained prominence and support. Animal rights literature must nevertheless be approached with caution as terms like 'protection', 'welfare' and 'rights' have been used loosely. In this respect, this chapter is interested in whether sentience can lead to *fundamental legal* rights for animals,[12] which aligns with Francione's concern that sentience recognition cannot achieve this type of protection.[13] Fundamental legal rights here refers to

> strong legal rights along the lines of human rights that are characterised by the cumulative features of substantive fundamentality and normative robustness due to their reduced infringeability … such as the right to life, bodily integrity, liberty and freedom from torture.[14]

Scholars have paid increasing attention to the question of fundamental moral and/or legal rights for animals. In his text *The Case for Animal Rights*, Tom Regan argues that animals have *moral* rights because they are the subjects of a life.[15] Paola Cavalieri and Saskia Stucki advocate for an 'expanded theory of human rights' which includes animals.[16] Francione asserts that animals require only one right, being the *legal* right not to be the property of humans.[17] More recent times have

[10] See Jane Kotzmann, 'Recognising the Sentience of Animals in Law: A Justification and Framework for Australian States and Territories' (2020) 42 *Sydney Law Review* 281, 284; Jane Kotzmann and Nick Pendergrast, 'Animal Rights: Time to Start Unpacking What Rights and For Whom' (2019) 46 *Mitchell Hamline Law Review* 157, 158.

[11] Paul Waldau, *Animal Rights: What Everyone Needs to Know* (Oxford University Press, 2011) 177–78.

[12] Stucki (n 1) 552.

[13] Francione (n 6).

[14] Stucki (n 1) 552.

[15] Tom Regan, *The Case for Animal Rights* (Routledge & Kegan Paul, 1983) 243–48.

[16] Paola Cavalieri, *The Animal Question: Why Nonhuman Animals Deserve Human Rights* (Catherine Woollard trans, Oxford University Press, 2001) 137–41; Saskia Stucki, *One Rights: Human and Animal Rights in the Anthropocene* (Springer, 2023) 9.

[17] Francione, 'Taking Sentience Seriously' (n 4) 18. See also, Francione, *Introduction to Animal Rights* (n 4) xxix–xxxi.

seen an increase in scholarship in relation to prospective animal rights, including in relation to their foundations,[18] their substantive content,[19] and their relationship to human rights.[20]

Within this context, sentience has been put forward as the justification for animals' moral status and for prospective legal animal rights. For example, Francione argues that the shared sentience of humans and animals means that the principle of equal consideration should be applied, and animals should be recognised as having 'a basic right not to be treated as things'.[21] Alasdair Cochrane asserts that 'all sentient creatures, as possessors of interests, are possessors of rights'.[22] The author of this chapter has proposed sentience and intrinsic worth as a two-level foundation for fundamental animal rights.[23]

B. Animal Rights Legal Practice and Politics

At the same time, animal rights have gained traction in politics and legal practice. Political parties dedicated to improving the legal status of animals have gained support in jurisdictions including Australia (the Animal Justice Party),[24] the Netherlands (Partij voor de Dieren),[25] Germany (Partei Mensch Umwelt Tierschutz)[26] and France (Animalist Party).[27] Notably, a citizens' initiative was commenced in 2016 in Basel-Stadt, Switzerland.[28] The initiative sought legal recognition of rights to bodily and mental integrity and life for nonhuman primates.[29] In a legal challenge to the initiative, the Constitutional Court of Basel-Stadt held that cantons may 'expand the circle of rights holders beyond the

[18] Kotzmann (n 4).

[19] Alasdair Cochrane, *Should Animals Have Political Rights?* (Polity Press, 2020); James Rachels, 'Why Animals Have a Right to Liberty' in Claire Palmer (ed), *Animal Rights* (Routledge, 2008) 58; Bernd Ladwig, 'Do Animals Have Rights?' (2023) 13 *Animals* 1220.

[20] Tom Regan, The Case for Animal Rights' in MW Fox and LD Mickley (eds), *Advances in Animal Welfare Science 1986/87* (The Humane Society of the United States) 179, 187–88; Cochrane (n 4) 655; Stucki (n 16) 94–95.

[21] Francione, *Introduction to Animal Rights* (n 4) xxvi. See also, Francione, 'Taking Sentience Seriously' (n 4) 17.

[22] Cochrane (n 4) 657.

[23] Kotzmann (n 4).

[24] 'Save Animal Through Political Action' (Animal Justice Party), available at www.animaljusticeparty.org/.

[25] 'Party for the Animals: International Movement' (Party for the Animals), available at www.partyfortheanimals.com.

[26] 'Partei Mensch Umwelt Tierschutz' (*Tierschutzpartei* (Animal Welfare Party)), available at www.tierschutzpartei.de.

[27] 'Les animaux comptent, votre voix aussi' (Parti Animaliste (Animalist Party), 2023), available at www.parti-animaliste.fr.

[28] Charlotte E Blattner and Raffael Fasel, 'The Swiss Primate Case: How Courts Have Paved the Way for the First Direct Democratic Vote on Animal Rights' (2022) 11 *Transnational Environmental Law* 201, 201.

[29] ibid 201.

anthropological barrier',[30] a ruling upheld by the Swiss Federal Supreme Court.[31] The initiative was ultimately put to a vote by the people of Basel-Stadt, in the first direct democratic vote on whether fundamental legal rights should be accorded to (some) nonhuman animals.[32]

Attempts have also been made in various jurisdictions to gain legal recognition of animal rights via habeas corpus proceedings. For example, the Nonhuman Rights Project, based in the United States, has initiated litigation on behalf of chimpanzees and elephants.[33] In these cases, the NhRP has sought the release of their clients from what they contend is illegal detention. While the cases have not yet found success, some judgments have provided hope that change may come.[34] They have also inspired similar litigation in other jurisdictions, which has been more successful. In Argentina, a case was brought on behalf of the chimpanzee Cecilia seeking her release from detention in the Mendoza Zoo. The court held in 2016 that Cecilia was a living being with rights and ordered the defendants to release her to the Great Ape Project Sanctuary in Brazil.[35] In Ecuador, a case was filed on behalf of a woolly monkey called Estrellita seeking her release from a zoo. Although Estrellita tragically died while in captivity, the Constitutional Court of Ecuador ordered the preparation of a bill on animal rights which must be debated and approved by the National Assembly within two years of a draft bill.[36]

Animals have also gained legal prominence in other jurisdictions. In this respect, Indian courts have shown themselves amenable to animal rights in theory if not

[30] Constitutional Court of Basel-Stadt, 15 January 2019, VG.2018.1, para 3.7.3 trans in Blattner and Fasel, 'The Swiss Primate Case' (n 28) 202.

[31] Blattner and Fasel (n 27) 202.

[32] ibid. The vote ultimately failed, see John Revill, 'Swiss Reject Ban on Animal Testing in Referendum' (Reuters, 14 February 2022), available at www.reuters.com/world/europe/switzerland-vote-becoming-first-nation-ban-animal-testing-2022-02-13.

[33] 'A Unique and Vital Mission: Who We Are and What We Do' (Nonhuman Rights Project, 2023), available at www.nonhumanrights.org.

[34] For example, in *Nonhuman Rights Project Inc v Lavery*, 124 AD 3d 148 (NY, 2014) at 7, Fahey J stated that 'The issue whether a nonhuman animal has a fundamental right to liberty protected by the writ of habeas corpus is profound and far-reaching. It speaks to our relationship with all the life around us. Ultimately, we will not be able to ignore it. While it may be arguable that a chimpanzee is not a 'person', there is no doubt that it is not merely a thing'. See also judgment of Tuitt J in *The Nonhuman Rights Project Inc v Breheny* (NY Sup Ct, No 260441/19, 18 February 2020) 10.

[35] *Re Cecilia* (Tercer Juzgado de Garantías, File No P-72.254/15, 3 November 2016) [Third Court of Guarantees, Argentina]; Macarena Montes Franceschini, 'Animal Personhood: The Quest for Recognition' (2021) 17 *Animal and Natural Resource Law Review* 93, 124.

[36] Corte Constitucional del Ecuador [Constitutional Court of Ecuador], *Rights of Nature and Animals as Subject of Rights, 'Estrellita Monkey' Case*, No 253-20-JH/22, 27 January 2022, available at www.animal.law.harvard.edu/wp-content/uploads/Final-Judgment-Estrellita-w-Translation-Certification.pdf; 'A Landmark Ruling for Animal Rights in Ecuador' (Nonhuman Rights, 23 March 2022), available at www.nonhumanrights.org/blog/landmark-ruling-animal-rights-ecuador; 'Historic Milestone in Ecuador: Constitutional Court Recognizes Individual Animals as Subjects of Rights Protected by the Rights of Nature' (World Lawyers' Pledge on Climate Action, 8 May 2022), available at www.lawyersclimatepledge.org/historic-milestone-in-ecuador-constitutional-court-recognizes-individual-animals-as-subjects-of-rights-protected-by-the-rights-of-nature.

in practice.[37] The High Court of Uttarakhand recognised animals 'as legal entities having a distinct persona with corresponding rights, duties and liabilities of a living person' in 2018.[38] The Punjab and Haryana High Court of India in 2019 recognised that animals have the 'rights, duties, and liabilities of a living person'.[39] Similarly, in Pakistan the Islamabad High Court held in 2020 that animals have legal rights[40] and accordingly ordered that the elephant Kaavan be released from Marghazar Zoo.[41]

C. Express Legal Recognition of Animal Sentience

As discussed in this collection, recent decades have seen numerous jurisdictions pass legal provisions expressly recognising that animals are sentient. These jurisdictions include the European Union,[42] Tanzania,[43] Chile,[44] the Netherlands,[45] Lithuania,[46] Oregon in the United States,[47] France,[48] Quebec in Canada,[49] New Zealand,[50] Peru,[51] Colombia,[52] Sweden,[53] Brussels in Belgium,[54] the Australian Capital Territory,[55] Denmark,[56] Spain[57] and the United Kingdom.[58] Broadly,

[37] The decisions have been criticised for seeking to enforce animal welfare laws rather than create animal rights: Franceschini (n 35) 143.

[38] *Narayan Dutt Bhatt v Union of India* (UHC, PIL No 43/2018, 4 July 2018) [99A] (Sharma J).

[39] *Karnail Singh v State of Haryana* (PHHC, CRR-533-2013, 31 May 2019) [29] (Sharma J).

[40] *Islamabad Wildlife Management Board* (WP no 1155/2019, 21 May 2020) at 57–59 (Minallah CJ).

[41] ibid 62.

[42] Protocol annexed to the Treaty of the European Community – Protocol on Protection and Welfare of Animals [1997] OJ C340/110.

[43] Animal Welfare Act 2008 (TZ), ss 3 and 4(b)(i).

[44] Ley 20.380, 2009 (CL), Art 2.

[45] Wet dieren 2011 (Animals Act) (NL), Art 1.3.

[46] *Gyvūnų Gerovės ir Apsaugos Įstatymas* (Law on Welfare and Protection of Animals) No XI-2271, Valstybės Žinios, 20 October 2012 No 122-6216 (LT) (2012), Art 1(a).

[47] OR Rev Stat §167.305 (2021). See generally Jessica Park, 'Yes, Chickens Have Feelings Too. The Recognition of Animal Sentience Will Address Outdated Animal Protection Laws for Chickens and Other Poultry in the United States' (2021) 22 *San Diego International Law Journal* 335.

[48] Code Civil (Civil Code) (FR), Art 515-14. See generally Jean-Marc Neumann, 'The Legal Status of Animals in the French Civil Code' (2015) 1 *Global Journal of Animal Law* 1.

[49] Animal Welfare and Safety Act, CQLR 2016, c B-3.1, preamble. For commentary in relation to this enactment, see Michael Lessard, 'Can Sentience Recognition Protect Animals? Lessons from Quebec's Animal Law Reform' (2021) 27 *Animal Law* 57.

[50] Animal Welfare Act 1999 (NZ), long title.

[51] *Norma 30407/ Ley de Protección y Bienestar Animal 2016* (Animal Protection and Welfare Law 30407) (PE), art 1.

[52] *Ley No 1774 de 2016* (CO), Art 1, 665; Carlos Andrés Contreras López, 'Sentient Beings Protected by Law: Analysis of Recent Changes in Colombian Animal Welfare Legislation' (2016) 2 *Global Journal of Animal Law* 1, 3.

[53] Animal Welfare Act 2018 (SE); Government Bill (SE) No 2017/18, 147.

[54] Law Relating to the Protection and Welfare of Animals 2018 (Brussels), Art 1.

[55] Animal Welfare Act 1992 (ACT), s 4A(1)(a).

[56] Animal Welfare Act 2020 (DK), Art 1.

[57] Civil Code of Catalonia (Ley de 2006), Art 511-1 (3). In relation to Spain, see Marita Gimenez-Candela, 'The De-objectification of Animals in the Spanish Civil Code' (2018) XV *Journal of Animal & Natural Resource Law* 145.

[58] Animal Welfare Sentience Act 2022 (GB), ss 1–2.

animal law scholars have welcomed these legal developments.[59] While many scholars have noted the shortcomings of animal sentience laws, they also recognise the potential of such provisions.[60]

III. Criticism of Sentience Recognition

A. Sentience already Underpins Animal Welfare Laws

Within the context of an increasing prominence of animal rights and a positioning of sentience as important to animal rights, some scholars have nevertheless been highly critical of legal amendments that recognise animal sentience. Francione, the most prominent of these critics, argues that the law has long recognised animal sentience and yet has failed to adequately protect animals, and concludes that sentience recognition will therefore not lead to animal rights.[61] Certainly, it can be persuasively argued that animal welfare legislation – particularly contemporary legislation – is based, to some extent, on an implied recognition of animal sentience.[62] Animal welfare law tries to prevent humans inflicting unnecessary pain and suffering on animals.[63] If animals were not sentient such laws would make little sense.

It should, however, be recognised that animal welfare law also protects human interests and that therefore animal sentience is not necessarily the main motivator of such laws. For example, it could be argued that the law tries to prevent cruelty to animals on the basis that it offends public (human) morals more broadly,[64] or that it protects human property interests.[65] Similarly, research shows a clear link between animal abuse and domestic violence,[66] which could suggest that laws preventing animal abuse are also directed at the prevention of domestic violence.

[59] See Robertson and Goldsworthy (n 5) 245; Kotzmann and Stonebridge (n 5) 425; Blattner (n 5) 121; Herbst (n 5) 62. In contrast, see Rodriguez Ferrere (n 5) 117.

[60] Kotzmann (n 10) 131–32; Bailey Soderberg, 'Reassessing Animals and Potential Legal Personhood: Do Animals Have Rights or Duties?' (2022) 24 *Vermont Journal of Environmental Law* 171, 184; Pablo Lerner, 'Animals are Not Objects But Are Not Yet Subjects: Developments in the Proprietary Status of Animals' (2022) XVIII *Animal & Natural Resource Law Review* 267, 289.

[61] Francione (n 6).

[62] Kotzmann (n 4) 410.

[63] Kotzmann (n 10) 288.

[64] See, for example, discussion in *State v Nix*, 334 P 3d 437, 448 (Or, 2014) at 796–97.

[65] Paulina Siemieniec, 'Centering Animality in Law and Liberation: The Zoopolitics of Reclaiming the Animal in Personhood' (2023) 26 *Between the Species* 93, 95.

[66] LJ Tong, 'Fracture Characteristics to Distinguish between Accidental Injury and Non-Accidental Injury in Dogs' (2014) 199 *Veterinary Journal* 392, 398. See Frank R Ascione et al, 'Battered Pets and Domestic Violence: Animal Abuse Reported by Women Experiencing Intimate Violence and by Nonabused Women' (2007) 13 *Violence Against Women* 354, 355; Piers Beirne, 'From Animal Abuse to Interhuman Violence? A Critical Review of the Progression Thesis' (2004) 12 *Society and Animals* 39, 41–42; Michelle Newberry, 'Pets in Danger: Exploring the Link between Domestic Violence and Animal Abuse' (2017) 34 *Aggression and Violent Behavior* 273, 273.

Further, animal agriculture clearly benefits from the legal legitimisation of industry procedures that may be perceived as constituting an unnecessary infliction of pain and suffering on animals.[67] If these multiple purposes are accepted as underpinning animal welfare laws, it does not mean that the laws do not implicitly recognise animal sentience. They might broadly suggest, however, that there are many reasons human society seeks to prevent cruelty to animals and that concern for the animals themselves may not be the main objective.

On this interpretation of the law, the express legal recognition of animal sentience may take the law beyond the traditional legal approach to animal welfare. This is because such provisions often highlight that animal sentience is the *main* reason that animal welfare matters.[68] In other words, what the explicit recognition of sentience may do is also make explicit the motivation for the law. It can elevate sentience above the other drivers of animal welfare legislation as the *main reason*. This revised focus, together with recent developments in scientific knowledge about animal sentience and capacities,[69] suggest an increasing human concern with and responsibility for the subjective states of other animals.

B. Legal Sentience Recognition Constitutes Welfare-Washing

On the basis that the legal recognition of animal sentience has not led (and will not lead) to animal rights, Francione contends that the development amounts to welfare-washing. Governments, he says, support legal sentience recognition because it gives them the appearance of working to improve animal welfare without having any impact on the operation of animal industries. Animal charities can use sentience recognition in their campaigns to seek financial donations from the public.[70]

This interpretation of motive, while it may be true of some parliamentarians and animal advocates, is unfair to others. For example, analysis of the legislative background to sentience recognition provisions in the Australian Capital Territory suggests that parliamentarians considered the amendments to constitute an important change.[71] Similarly, the historical background to the founding of Compassion in World Farming, the organisation that first advocated for the Treaty of Rome (and later Treaty of Lisbon) to recognise animal sentience, indicates that

[67] Kotzmann (n 10) 308.

[68] See, for example, Animal Welfare Act 1992 (ACT), s 4A(1)(a) which states that 'The *main* objects of this Act are to recognise that – (a) animals are sentient beings' (emphasis added); Victoria State Government Department of Economic Development, Jobs, Transport and Resources, 'Animal Welfare Action Plan' (December 2017) 14.

[69] See, eg, Jaak Panksepp, 'Affective Consciousness: Core Emotional Feelings in Animals and Humans' (2005) 14 *Consciousness and Cognition* 30, 43–56; Helen Proctor, 'Animal Sentience: Where are We and Where are We Heading?' (2012) 2 *Animals* 628, 632–34; Jacky Turner, *Stop – Look – Listen: Recognising the Sentience of Farm Animals* (Report, Compassion in World Farming Trust, 2006) 11–26.

[70] Francione (n 6).

[71] Kotzmann (n 10) 290–92.

its primary concern is with ending intensive animal agriculture.[72] The organisation sees sentience recognition as important in that it changes '*the ground* on which campaigners could lobby for change' because government representatives 'could no longer say that animal welfare did not matter'.[73] While seeking this objective does not necessarily entail recognition of animal rights, it does appear to be based on a concern for the subjective experience of animals in intensive agricultural operations.

IV. Potentiality of Sentience Recognition from an Animal Rights Perspective

A. Rights Through Incremental Legal Change

The increasing prominence of animal rights, proliferation of legal provisions recognising animal sentience and criticism of such provisions elicit the question of whether animal sentience recognition can lead to fundamental legal animal rights and even whether there is a connection between the two. These questions in turn raise the issue of how legal reform to recognise new rights comes about. Does 'real' reform require a rights revolution, or can incremental legal change ultimately lead to fundamental legal rights? If it is concluded that incremental legal changes are required as a transition to animal rights, can sentience recognition play a role in this transition? It is difficult, if not impossible, to isolate the importance of various elements that lead to legal rights protections for groups that have been traditionally discriminated against. With this in mind, this section looks at rights development in other contexts for signs as to how it might work in this one and identifies some general trends on this basis.

i. Scholars Generally Endorse an Incremental Approach

Most animal studies scholars that are in favour of animal rights support a gradual approach to their achievement. Their disagreement relates to the nature of the incremental changes required rather than whether incremental as opposed to revolutionary change is more effective. Philosopher Bernard Rollin, for example, argued that animal rights reform must follow an incremental approach based on animal welfarism, because this allows for changing public values and relationships with animals.[74] Similarly, political scientist Robert Garner appears to

[72] Andrew N Rowan et al 'Animal Sentience: History, Science, and Politics' (2021) 31 *Animal Sentience* 9–10. See also 'About Compassion in World Farming' (Compassion in World Farming, 2023), available at www.ciwf.org.uk/about-us.

[73] Rowan et al (n 72).

[74] Bernard E Rollin, *Animal Rights and Human Morality*, rev edn (Prometheus Books, 1981) 83–85.

support efforts to end the suffering of animals as a more practical means of achieving greater protection for animals compared with seeking the abolition of animal use.[75] While Francione is highly critical of animal *welfare* reforms, he advocates for incremental legal reforms to remove the property status of animals.[76] More recently, legal scholar Eva Bernet Kempers has advocated for a gradual transition to legal personhood for animals.[77]

ii. History seems to Support an Incremental Approach

Further, the history of children's rights and the rights of persons with disabilities reveal an incremental approach to rights recognition.[78] Children, like animals in contemporary society, were once considered to be property.[79] Their transition from property to rights-holders is reflected in the International Convention on the Rights of the Child 1989,[80] which is the contemporary international expression of children's rights. At the international level this document was preceded by the League of Nations' Geneva Declaration on the Rights of the Child 1924,[81] Article 25(2) of the Universal Declaration of Human Rights 1948,[82] the UN General Assembly's Declaration of the Rights of the Child 1959,[83] Art 10(3) of the International Covenant on Economic, Social and Cultural Rights 1966,[84] Art 24 of the International Covenants on Civil and Political Rights 1966,[85] the International Labour Organization's Convention 138 of 1973,[86] the General Assembly's Declaration on the Protection of Women and Children in Emergency and Armed Conflict 1974[87] and the United Nations' Standard Minimum Rules

[75] Robert Garner, 'In Defence of Animal Sentience: A Critique of Cochrane's Liberty Thesis' (2011) 59 *Political Studies* 175, 183–84.

[76] Gary L Francione, *Rain Without Thunder: The Ideology of the Animal Rights Movement* (Temple University Press, 1996) 190–219.

[77] Eva Bernet Kempers, 'Transition Rather Than Revolution: The Gradual Road Towards Animal Legal Personhood Through the Legislature' (2022) 11 *Transnational Environmental Law* 581, 581.

[78] See also David P Forsythe, 'The UN and Human Rights at Fifty: An Incremental but Incomplete Revolution' (1995) 1 *Global Governance* 297 in relation to the incremental shift from rights being a matter for domestic jurisdictions to being an issue of international concern.

[79] Clark Butler, 'Children's Rights: An Historical and Conceptual Analysis' in Clark Butler (ed), *Child Rights: The Movement, International Law, and Opposition* (Purdue University Press, 2012) 13, 13.

[80] Convention on the Rights of the Child (adopted 20 November 1989, entered into force 2 September 1990) 1577 UNTS 3.

[81] Geneva Declaration on the Rights of the Child, LNOJ 1924, Special Supplement No 21, 43.

[82] Universal Declaration of Human Rights (adopted 10 December 1948 UNGA Res 217 A(III) (UDHR), which entitles children to 'special care and assistance' and 'social protection'.

[83] UNGA Res 1386 (XIV) (20 November 1959) A/RES/14/1386.

[84] International Covenant on Economic, Social and Cultural Rights (adopted 16 December 1966, entered into force 3 January 1976) 993 UNTS 3.

[85] International Covenant on Civil and Political Rights (adopted 16 December 1966, entered into force 23 March 1976) 999 UNTS 171.

[86] ILO, Convention Concerning Minimum Age for Admission to Employment (adopted 26 June 1973, entered into force 19 June 1976) C138.

[87] Declaration on the Protection of Women and Children in Emergency and Armed Conflict, UNGA Res A/RES/3318(XXIX) (14 December 1973).

for the Administration of Juvenile Justice 1985.[88] Moreover, as with legal change generally, these and other laws relating to the changing legal status of children were accompanied by societal changes.[89]

Similarly, several legal reforms led to international recognition of the rights of people with disabilities through the United Nations' Convention on the Rights of Persons with Disabilities 2007.[90] These included the Declaration on the Rights of Mentally Retarded Persons 1971,[91] and the General Assembly's Resolution 48/96 Standard Rules on the Equalization of Opportunities for Persons with Disabilities.[92] Legal reform was arrived at gradually, reflecting shifts in public consensus.[93]

iii. Rights Through (the Right) Increments

This brief analysis reveals that animal rights are likely to come about by way of legal increment rather than revolution. Even so, the disagreement between animal studies scholars on what reforms to seek and support is important. Some legal reforms may (intentionally or otherwise) operate to reinforce a welfare paradigm within which animals are the property of humans. Such reforms not only fail to make progress towards rights for animals but can also be used by governments and industry to 'humane wash' cruel practices and mislead the public to believe that animals are well treated, further hampering reform towards animal rights.[94] In light of this real danger, the remaining parts of this chapter consider whether sentience recognition can play a meaningful role in a transition to animal rights.

B. Facilitation of Public Discussion

In democratic states public discussion will ordinarily precede legal change, whether that change is revolutionary or incremental. This is because lawmakers are elected to represent their constituents and must, to some degree, reflect the

[88] UNGA Res 33 (29 November 1985) A/RES/40/33.

[89] See Megan Mitchell, 'Children's Rights in a Changing World' (Australian Human Rights Commission), available at www.humanrights.gov.au/about/news/speeches/childrens-rights-changing-world.

[90] Convention on the Rights of Persons with Disabilities (adopted 13 December 2006, entered into force 3 May 2008) 2515 UNTS 3.

[91] Declaration on the Rights of Mentally Retarded Persons, UNGA Res 2856 (XXVI) (20 December 1971).

[92] Standard Rules on the Equalization of Opportunities for Persons with Disabilities, UNGA Res A/RES/48/96 (20 December 1993). See generally Yanghee Lee, 'Expanding Human Rights to Persons with Disabilities: Laying the Groundwork for a Twenty-First Century Movement' (2009) 18 *Pacific Rim Law & Policy Journal* 283, 284–85.

[93] See generally Fred Pelka, *What We Have Done: An Oral History of the Disability Rights Movement* (University of Massachusetts Press, 2011) 19–29. This brief overview also gives rise to the secondary question of the extent to which international law leads to substantive change in domestic law. Many thanks to Marcelo Rodriguez Ferrere for pointing this out.

[94] See Brian Martin, 'Reform – When Is It Worthwhile?' (2012) 20 *Anarchist Studies* 55, 55.

views of that section of the public or face the prospect of being voted out at the next election. Thus, Eisen's call to shift animal law scholarship beyond the rights-welfare debate and to consider the 'dynamics of legal change in democratic states'[95] is apposite. This section of the chapter will thus consider the extent to which the legal recognition of animal sentience might foster public deliberation in relation to the legal situation of animals.

i. Sentience and the Subjective, Embodied Experience of Animals

Recognising that another individual is sentient, and thus capable of experiencing positive and negative feelings like joy and suffering, should draw attention to the subjective, embodied experience of that individual. If animals are recognised as experiencing the world subjectively, this then invites consideration of what feelings animals might experience in the various contexts in which they live. Further, recognising animals as having their own subjective lives provokes contemplation of the ways that human interactions with animals might lead animals to experience various positive and negative states. In turn, such awareness should encourage human empathy with animals[96] and instigate public discussion of the ways that the law facilitates and permits human cruelty to animals.

Public reflection on the subjective experience of animals should also operate to highlight the inherent vulnerability of animals.[97] Vulnerability can be conceived of in different ways. Like humans, animal vulnerability can be found in their physical embodiment, through which animals can experience pain and suffering.[98] Some animals are made more vulnerable, however, through human action. Domestic animals, for example, are vulnerable because of their dependence on humans.[99] Public conceptions of animals as vulnerable may lead to consideration and discussion of the ethical obligations that humans have towards animals and the extent to which laws ensure or fail to ensure that those obligations are met.

The extent to which the public can reflect on the lived experiences of animals and their connection to law is, however, limited by the availability of information about animal lives. In this respect, the insidiousness of laws that seek to keep this information away from public consideration becomes evident. In the context of animal agriculture, for example, 'ag-gag' laws that operate to prevent animal protection advocates from recording or publishing recordings of animal experiences in commercial animal farms significantly limit the extent to which the public

[95] Eisen (n 8) 469.

[96] For further discussion in relation to empathy with animals see ch 2 of this collection.

[97] For further discussion in relation to animal vulnerability see ch 17 section IV.A of this collection.

[98] Ani B Satz, 'Animals as Vulnerable Subjects: Beyond Interest-Convergence, Hierarchy, and Property' (2010) 16 *Animal Law* 65, 79–80. See also Angela K Martin, 'Animal Vulnerability and its Ethical Implications: An Exploration' (2021) 38 *Journal of Applied Philosophy* 196, 197; Jane Johnson, 'Vulnerable Subjects? The Case of Nonhuman Animals in Experimentation' (2013) 10 *Bioethical Inquiry* 497, 499.

[99] Satz (n 98) 79–80.

can debate the ethics of sentient animal use in these settings.[100] Thus, while legal recognition of animal sentience can assist in encouraging public deliberation of animal law issues, further legal changes will also be required.

ii. *Shared Language and Accountability*

Legal recognition of animal sentience also functions to provide an agreed language that can be used to talk about the experience of animals and hold governments and industry to account. This is a similar explanation to that provided by Rowan et al for the importance of legal sentience recognition: the legal development means that advocates can employ the language of sentience to advocate for animals as governments and industry are unable to claim that the subjective states of animals are unimportant.[101] Sentience recognition can perform this function in different contexts. Advocates can use sentience terminology when lobbying governments. For example, in the United Kingdom advocates were successful in having cephalopod molluscs and decapod crustaceans included in the Animal Welfare (Sentience) Bill on the basis that a commissioned scientific report found them to be sentient.[102] Sentience recognition may also have legal consequences. For example, some courts in the United States have drawn on the legal recognition of animal sentience to find that individual animals can constitute separate 'victims' of crime.[103] Further, sentience terminology can assist efforts to educate the public about other animals and the ethics of human relationships with them.

Sentience also provides a (broadly) objective, scientific lens through which humans can view other animals.[104] This is important because it provides a ground for challenging human use typologies and associated discrimination that is entrenched in most contemporary animal welfare legislation. For example, if sentience is the main reason that animal welfare matters then why do dogs that are used as human companion animals enjoy greater legal protection than dogs used in scientific research? Similarly, if pigs and dogs are both sentient, why do most dogs enjoy the highest available levels of legal protection while pigs are frequently able to be confined in farrowing crates, subjected to painful husbandry procedures such as tail docking, and ultimately be eaten by humans? While legal sentience

[100] See generally Jodi Lazare, 'Animal Rights Activism and the Constitution: Are Ag-Gag Laws Justifiable Limits?' (2022) 59 *Osgoode Hall Law Journal* 667, 668; Jodi Lazare, 'Ag-Gag Laws, Animal Rights Activism, and the Constitution: What is Protected Speech?' (2020) 58 *Alberta Law Review* 83, 83.

[101] Rowan et al (n 72).

[102] 'Lobsters, octopus and crabs recognised as sentient beings' (UK Government, 19 November 2021), available at www.gov.uk/government/news/lobsters-octopus-and-crabs-recognised-as-sentient-beings?utm_medium=email&utm_campaign=govuk-notifications&utm_source=994c7ffd-9c00-4347-9563-bc9a0754ecad&utm_content=immediately.

[103] See *State v Nix*, 334 P 3d 437, 448 (Or, 2014) vacated by *State v Nix*, 345 P 3d 416 (Or, 2015); *State v Crow*, 429 P 3d 1053, 1054 (Or Ct App, 2018); Jessica Rubin, 'Desmond's Law: A Novel Approach to Animal Advocacy' (2018) 24 *Animal Law* 243, 275.

[104] Blattner (n 5) 125.

recognition does not remove this type of legal discrimination, it can be used to highlight the cognitive biases which underpin it.[105]

C. Potential Theoretical Basis for Fundamental Animal Rights

Legal recognition of animal sentience provides a suitable theoretical foundation for the construction of animal rights. Foundation here refers to the reason why animal rights should be recognised and respected. To propose sentience as a foundation for animal rights therefore amounts to asserting that animals should have rights that are recognised and respected because they have their own subjective lives and can experience positive and negative feelings that matter to them.

There are three broad reasons that make sentience an appropriate foundation for animal rights. The first is that the legal proliferation of sentience recognition provisions means that it is now a known legal concept.[106] As a legal concept, animal sentience recognition reflects a public consensus that animals experience life subjectively, and that their lives have moral value. This is important because, as this author has previously stated, 'the existing logic that animals are sentient and thus deserving of legal protection is already found in the law *and provides a ready springboard* for the construction of animal rights'.[107]

The second reason that sentience is an appropriate foundation for animal rights is that it has strong connections to the interest theory of rights.[108] According to the interest theory, to have rights an individual must have interests. For an interest to constitute a right, it must also be important enough to impose an obligation on another individual.[109] Recognition that animals are sentient may be interpreted as a recognition that they also have interests because 'Typically … the capacity for having interests … is bound up with sentience'.[110] Individuals that can experience pain and suffering, for example, have an interest in avoiding pain and suffering. Further, the existence of animal welfare legislation which proscribes human behaviour that would cause unnecessary pain and suffering to animals suggests that many animal interests are of sufficient importance to impose duties on humans.

Third, the legal recognition of animal sentience is appropriate as a basis for animal rights because of its clear connection to states of pain and suffering.[111] In this context, pain and suffering are states that can be experienced only by sentient

[105] ibid 127–29.
[106] Kotzmann (n 4) 416.
[107] ibid (emphasis added).
[108] ibid 417.
[109] Alasdair Cochrane, *Animal Rights without Liberation: Applied Ethics and Human Obligations* (Columbia University Press, 2012) 42. See also Joseph Raz, *The Morality of Freedom* (Oxford University Press, 1986) 335.
[110] Stucki (n 1) 542–43.
[111] Kotzmann (n 4) 419.

beings. Pursuant to some human rights theories, the main objective of human rights is to stop human pain and suffering.[112] If human rights operate for this purpose, it seems reasonable to argue that animal rights would similarly be appropriate to stop animal pain and suffering. This connection is also useful in that it highlights the fundamental similarities between humans and other animals; all are sentient beings capable of positive and negative feelings. This basic similarity also indicates that human rights and animal rights 'are part of the same normative enterprise'[113] and suggests that animal rights are a 'logical extension of the doctrine of human rights'.[114]

V. Conclusion

Legally recognising animal sentience does not mean that animals have rights, or even that they will be accorded rights in the future. While sentience recognition statements may have some impact on the interpretation of other (generally animal welfare) legal provisions through processes of statutory interpretation,[115] such impacts would almost certainly fall short of animal rights. Why, then, are so many provisions of this type being passed and why are many animal advocates broadly in support of them?

Animal rights are an important goal for many in the animal protection movement. As Blattner identifies:

> The fact that certain interests are legally recognized either as rights or as protections, establishes a disparate and unequal footing for the affected parties. Protections are effectively undermined when confronted with rights in a balance of interests, because they are a weaker legal tool. Consequently, protections only take effect where the rights of humans leave room for them.[116]

History, however, suggests that the recognition of new fundamental rights is likely to be achieved through incremental legal reform rather than by revolution. To contribute to the ultimate realisation of rights, legal reforms must establish a basis for further change rather than simply reinforce the system. This is where sentience recognition provides some hope. While sentience recognition may be used by governments and industry to humane wash commercial uses of animals, it may also be used to initiate public discussion regarding the situation of animals. In this case, the terminology of sentience itself may draw attention to the embodied,

[112] Stephen Wheatley, *The Idea of International Human Rights Law* (Oxford University Press, 2019) 25; Costas Douzinas, *The End of Human Rights: Critical Legal Thought at the Turn of the Century* (Hart Publishing, 2000) 351; Upendra Baxi, 'Voices of Suffering and the Future of Human Rights' (1998) 8 *Transnational Law & Contemporary Problems* 125, 127.

[113] Cochrane (n 4) 656.

[114] Sue Donaldson and Will Kymlicka, *Zoopolis: A Political Theory of Animal Rights* (Oxford University Press, 2011) 44.

[115] Kotzmann (n 10) 298–302.

[116] Charlotte Blattner (n 3) 177. See also Stucki (n 1) 554.

subjective, and vulnerable state of animals and be used as a shared language to hold humans accountable. Further, sentience recognition provides a good theoretical basis on which to build animal rights.

Sentience recognition is not a panacea for the pain and suffering of the billions of animals in contemporary society. It may, however, help bring societies to a recognition of animal rights, which would constitute a 'legal infrastructure for moving from a non-ideal reality towards more ideal social conditions in which animal rights can be respected.'[117] In short, legal recognition of animal sentience is a step in the right direction towards animal rights, rather than welfare washing.

[117] Stucki (n 1) 558.

PART TWO

Regional and National Approaches to Legal Recognition

5

Owning Sentient Beings: The Potential of Sentience Recognition in Continental Law

EVA BERNET KEMPERS

I. Introduction

Much of the existing animal law literature starts with the assertion that the law regards animals as merely legal things, property of the legal person.[1] Albeit catchy, this assertion no longer holds true for the region of continental Europe. Over the last 10 years, an increasing number of continental jurisdictions have introduced provisions in their Civil Code that distinguish between animals and legal things, at times (but not always) recognising explicitly that animals are living sentient beings with biological needs.[2] The precise manifestation of this development differs across jurisdictions, but its defining feature is the distinction between 'animals' on the one hand and 'legal things' or 'goods' on the other hand. Hence, animals (specifically 'companion animals') may now be better characterised as 'quasi-things'.[3] At the same time, however, it is clear that this new Civil Code provision does not invest animals with a form of legal personhood. Therefore, animals are sometimes regarded as occupying a third category of neither persons nor things.[4]

Among legal scholars, opinions differ on the question of whether this development, sometimes called 'dereification', has any tangible consequences, or whether we should regard it as a merely symbolic change.[5] As the provision defining

[1] Steven M Wise, 'The Legal Thinghood of Nonhuman Animals' (1996) 23 *Boston College Environmental Affairs Law Review* 471.

[2] Such as is the case in Belgium, Art 3.39 BW.

[3] Johan Van de Voorde, 'Dieren Als Quasi-Goederen. Beschouwingen over de Juridisch-Technische Wenselijkheid van Een Bijzonder Statuut Voor Dieren Tussen Goederen En Rechtssubjecten' (2016) 138 *Rechtskundig Weekblad* 203.

[4] Eva Bernet Kempers, 'Neither Persons nor Things: The Changing Status of Animals in Private Law' (2021) 29 *European Review of Private Law* 39.

[5] Eva Schumann, '"Tiere Sind Keine Sachen" – Zur Personifizierung von Tieren Im Mittelalterlichen Recht' in Lars Kreye, Carsten Stühring and Tanja Zwingelberg (eds), *Natur als Grenzerfahrung*

animals usually contains a sentence asserting that, in some way or another, the provisions applying to things still apply to animals, the main purpose of its introduction seems to have been to align the law with a natural feeling that animals are not things, without changing anything substantive about their legal status.[6] Indeed, it is clear that animals can still be bought and sold, owned by humans, and killed for reasons that can be considered trivial. Therefore, on a pessimistic reading, the provision recognising the special nature of animals as non-things is useless and rid of actual legal effects, merely a symbolic development that incorrectly suggests that animals' legal status is now different from inanimate objects.[7]

On a more optimistic reading, however, the provision can in fact have implications that go beyond its symbolic value, influencing the way in which private law is applied to animals. Such optimistic reading is, at times, confirmed in case law when judges take the provision defining animals as a starting point to depart from property law, taking animal interests into account in their decision, or attach greater weight to the welfare of animals than to the rights of owners. Based on a study of sentience recognition in Québec, Michael Lessard concludes that judges do invest the Civil Code provision with normative force, using it to ground their differential treatment of animals versus other types of property.[8] Something similar seems to occur in Europe, where animals are treated differently from things in the context of family law, but also in liability law (when their value is estimated far above their actual economic value).[9] Indirectly, the development may thus also influence ownership of animals, limiting the powers of owners over their property.

This chapter will consider the way that dereification – including those instances in which animals are recognised as 'sentient beings', as well as those instances where they are merely distinguished from things – influences ownership over animals in a private law context, focusing on its manifestation in continental Europe.[10] As the development has proven most applicable to animals kept for companion, that group will also be the focus of this article. In particular, I will discuss the way in which the distinction with things influences how ownership over animals should be understood. The main argument is that, rather than symbolic change, the Civil Code distinction between animals and things contributes to a de-objectification of animals in private law, giving rise to a separate kind of ownership regime that is grounded in the special nature of animals. By highlighting a number of legal cases involving animals, I will show how judges are increasingly treating animals

(Universitätsverlag Göttingen, 2009); Jelle Eric Jansen, 'Over de Ontzakelijking van Dieren En de Grenzen van Het Zaaksbegrip' (2011) 5 *Rechtsgeleerd Magazijn Themis* 187.

[6] As suggested by the Supreme Court of the Netherlands, Dutch Supreme Court (15 May 2018), Arrest Hoge Raad, ECLI:NL:HR:2018:996.

[7] Such critical perspective is taken, for instance, by Janneke Vink, see Janneke Vink, *The Open Society and Its Animals* (Springer Nature Switzerland, 2020).

[8] Michael Lessard, 'Can Sentience Recognition Protect Animals? Lessons from Québec's Animal Law Reform' (2021) 27 *Animal Law* 58.

[9] Bernet Kempers (n 4).

[10] It should be noted that this shortcut is not 100% correct, as different forms of dereification exist of which not all explicitly recognize the sentience of animals. This will be further discussed in section II.

differently from legal things, sometimes even overruling the rights of the owner in this regard. Finally, I will suggest that this trend may culminate in recognising a form of 'guardianship' rather than ownership over animals. Hence, this chapter will nuance the dogmatic notion that animals, for law, are just things in continental legal systems.[11]

II. Animals as Non-Things: Different Forms of Dereification

The first jurisdiction in continental Europe to distinguish between animals and things was Austria. In 1988, the Austrian Civil Code was adjusted to incorporate a reference that animals are not things.[12] Several other jurisdictions followed, which included Germany in 1990;[13] Switzerland in 2002;[14] Moldova in 2002;[15] Czech Republic in 2012;[16] France in 2015;[17] The Netherlands in 2016;[18] Belgium in 2021;[19] and finally Spain in 2022.[20] However, where some jurisdictions recognised animals as 'sentient', others did not go as far, and just stated that animals 'are not things'. The precise way in which the development has manifested itself, thus differs substantively.[21] We can distinguish four different forms of 'dereification'.

First, in a number of jurisdictions, animals are distinguished from things in a negative manner. This is for instance the case in the Netherlands, where Article 3:2a simply notes that 'animals are not things', without giving any definition of what animals are.[22] After that, it is stated that, even though they are not things, the regulations applying to things still apply to animals. Arguably, as the Animal Protection Act already recognizsed sentience and intrinsic worth, it was not regarded as necessary to repeat this recognition in the Civil Code. The main aim of this type of dereification seems to simply be to make a distinction, and nothing more: the property regime is still understood to apply to animals.

Second, a number of jurisdictions not only distinguish between animals and things, but also add a positive definition of animals, recognizing their sentient nature. This is the case in, for instance, Belgium, where animals are defined as

[11] See also Tomasz Pietrzykowski, *Foundations of Animal Law; Concepts, Principles, Dilemmas* (Katowice, Uniwersytet Śląski, 2023).
[12] Austria, s 285a Allgemeines Bürgerliches Gesetzbuch (ABGB).
[13] Germany, s 90a Bürgerliches Gesetzbuch (BGB).
[14] Switzerland, Art 641a Zivilgesetzbuch (ZGB).
[15] Moldova, Art 458 Codul Civil (CC).
[16] Czech Republic, Art 494 Občanský Zákoník (OZ).
[17] France, Arts 515–14 Code Civil (CC).
[18] The Netherlands, Art 3(2a) Burgerlijk Wetboek (BW).
[19] Belgium, Art 3(38)–(39) Burgerlijk Wetboek (BW).
[20] Spain, Art 333bis Código Civil (CC).
[21] Bernet Kempers (n 4). Poland is left out of this list, as the dereification provision is not found in the Civil Code, but in its animal protection legislation.
[22] Dutch Civil Code, Art 3:2a *Burgerlijk Wetboek*.

'sentient beings with biological needs'.[23] According to the preparatory works, the provision translates the fact that in light of the current scientific knowledge, animals 'can be classified neither as objects, nor as subjects of law'.[24] Even though, in this case as well, the recognition is weakened by the second sentence of the provision (which states that the provisions applying to goods still also apply to animals), the change is somewhat more profound, as such provision arguably enables judges to take more freedom when deciding cases that involve animals.[25] This form of dereification may be regarded as 'sentience-recognition' in private law.

Third, some jurisdictions did not only add a definition of animals as sentient beings, but also amended several other articles of the Civil Code that could potentially apply to animals. This is, for instance, the case in Germany:[26] apart from redefining animals as non-things, the Article on the determination of compensation was amended to formulate an exception to the compensation for animals as potentially exceeding their market value. Another Article now states that with ownership over animals, the powers of the owner are limited.[27] The same is true for Switzerland, where Article 651 concerning the division of property in case of divorce now makes reference to the importance of taking account of animal welfare for courts in the decision where to place an animal.[28] The effect of such Civil Code change is even more substantial, as more aspects of the private law approach to animals are being impacted upon, such as the determination of compensation.

Fourth, some jurisdictions (most notably Spain), take an even more radical approach. Apart from differentiating between animals and things, the relevant provision states that 'The legal regime of goods and things shall apply to animals only to the extent that it is compatible with their nature or with the provisions for their protection.'[29] Hence, in theory such a provision makes it possible to exempt animals from the regime of goods whenever applying the law would conflict with their nature. Moreover, in Spain a large number of provisions was altered to change the private law statute of animals, adjusting the way compensation can be claimed for animals when they are injured by a third party. This form of dereification can be considered as the most profound kind of change in animals' legal status in a private law context.

[23] Belgian Civil Code, Art 3.39 *Burgerlijk Wetboek*.

[24] Proposal concerning the Book on Property Law in the new Civil Code [Wetsvoorstel houdende invoeging van boek 3 'Goederen' in het nieuw BurgerlijkWetboek], Kamer, 16 July 2019, Doc 55 0173/001, 97.

[25] Lessard (n 8).

[26] This more comprehensive change to the status of animals was made through the Act for Improvement of the Status of Animals in Private Law (1990), *TierVerbG, Gesetz zur Verbesserung der Rechtsstellung des Tieres im bürgerlichen Recht vom 20. August 1990, BGBl. I S. 1762.*

[27] See German Civil Code §903 *BGB* 'The owner of an animal must, when exercising his powers, take into account the special provisions for the protection of animals.'

[28] Art 651, Swiss Civil Code, *BGB*. See for a discussion Margot Michel and Eveline Schneider Kayasseh, 'The Legal Situation of Animals in Switzerland: Two Steps Forward, One Step Back-Many Steps to Go' (2010) 7 *Journal of Animal Law* 1.

[29] Spanish Civil Code, Art 333bis *Codigo Civil*.

As an illustration of the way in which these provisions came about, we can zoom in on the case of the Netherlands. It becomes clear that, in parliamentary debates on the amendment, the differentiation between animals and things is first of all framed as the result of the recognition of intrinsic value of animals in public law.[30] The idea was that, as animals' intrinsic value was recognised in the 2011 Animal Protection Act, this would also have implications for the status of animals: they had to be distinguished from legal things that do not have intrinsic value.[31] Consequently, together with the Animal Protection Act, the Civil Code was amended to include such a reference. The provision concerning the extraction of animals from the category of things [*zaken*] is introduced as Article 2a under Title 1 (general provisions), section 1 (definitional provisions) of the Book on the Law of Goods. After defining 'things' as all physical objects that are susceptible to human control, the provision regarding animals now reads as follows: '(1). Animals are not things. (2) Provisions relating to things are applicable to animals, with due observance of the limitations, obligations and legal principles based on statutory rules and rules of unwritten law, as well as of public order and public morality.'[32] Interesting in this respect is the emphasis on unwritten law, which is unique to the Dutch approach. Apart from that, the provision does not exclude animals from the broader category of objects of ownership, which is defined as consisting of, apart from 'things', also 'patrimonial rights'. Furthermore, no positive definition is provided for: animals are simply defined as 'non-things'.

In the explanatory note to the amendment, the reason to introduce provision 2a is primarily the fact that equating animals with things 'is not in line with the natural legal feeling' and follows logically from the broader recognition of intrinsic value.[33] The aim of the Civil Code provision is to make clear that 'it is not just the use-value for humans but also the intrinsic value of the animal that determines the acceptability of behaviour of humans towards animals.'[34] In a 2018 case, the Supreme Court of the Netherlands discussed the special status of animals at length, emphasizing that the aim is to 'subject human treatment of animals to adapted norms but not to bring the animal outside of property law'; if that were the aim, the Court notes, animals should have been recognized as subjects of law.[35] According to the Attorney General, the provision should therefore be seen as nothing more than 'a symbolic deed of political correctness'.[36] This is also the way in which the provision has been interpreted in legal doctrine. Legal scholar and professor of Animal Law Janneke Vink, for instance, remains quite sceptical

[30] See Dutch Parliamentary Debates, *Kamerstukken II* (2009–2010), 31 389, nr. 68 (37).

[31] See for a critical view, HJ Snijders, 'Bij de Beesten Af' (2010) 5 *Nederlands Tijdschrift voor Burgerlijk Recht* 20.

[32] Dutch Civil Code, Art 3:2a *BW*.

[33] Explanatory Note to the Dutch Act Animals. *Memorie van Toelichting Wet Dieren*, Tweede Kamer (2007–2008), 31389 nr 3.

[34] Parliamentary Debates, *Kamerstukken I* (2010–2011), 31 389, nr E, 2.

[35] Dutch Supreme Court (15 May 2018), *Arrest Hoge Raad*, ECLI:NL:HR:2018:996.

[36] ibid, §3.6.

about the Civil Code change, and argues that it does not alter the legal approach towards animals in any substantial way and is only meant to superficially recognise that animals are not things in a literal sense.[37] A similar interpretation is present in other jurisdictions.

But is dereification – whichever of the four forms it takes – really merely symbolic? I suggest that, albeit not the direct intention of the legislator, the recognition of animals' special nature as non-things can have further implications when it is interpreted and used by the judiciary in cases concerning animals.[38] In the next section, I will zoom in on such possible implications, showing how judges increasingly treat animals differently from inanimate things in their case law.

III. Merely Symbolic? Potential Implications of Sentience Recognition

As hinted towards in the introduction, this chapter suggests that sentience recognition has potential implications that go beyond a mere symbolic value. The best way to make sense of the development is, as Favre states, that '[d]ereified animals – treated *like* things but not anymore *as* things – are now more than pure objects but less than full persons.'[39] The nuance can be found in the difference between 'like' and 'as'. The fact that animals are not things, makes it possible to, in some specific instances, treat animals in a special manner, different from legal things that are merely objects of law. Indeed, as Pietrzykowski states, dereification 'precludes the treatment of animals as things in the entire legal order'.[40] In this section, I will focus on such special treatment, especially in cases in which (a) courts take account of animal interests, (b) decide on compensation for animals, and (c) apply family law to animals.

A. Taking Account of Animal Interests

Sentience-recognition can firstly constitute a legal ground for courts to take animal interests into account in their decisions. In particular, judgments concerning the placement of animals in divorce cases now increasingly take the interests of animals into account.[41] In Belgium, for instance, in a case of 2021 concerning a

[37] Vink (n 7).

[38] See also: Bernet Kempers (n 4).

[39] Brian Favre, 'Is There a Need for a New, an Ecological, Understanding of Legal Animal Rights?' (2020) 11 *Journal of Human Rights and the Environment* 297, 307.

[40] Pietrzykowski (n 11) 102.

[41] See for an elaborate discussion: Paulien Christiaenssen, 'Het Gezelschapsdier na Relatiebreuk: Naar een Symbiose tussen Menselijke en Dierlijke Belangen' (2021) 9–10 *Tijdschrift van de Vrederechters* 445.

conflict about which of two former partners could have the dog after they divorced, the Court of Appeal in Brussels noted that the changing position of animals in society required a different approach to animals. Therefore, taking into account 'not only the affective bound between humans and animals – *in casu* both parties – but also the interests of the dog itself should be taken into consideration.'[42] Before the Court of Appeal in Antwerp, the interests of the dog were again explicitly taken into account in the decision, and it was emphasised that animals can no longer be treated equally to things, and should be better regarded 'quasi-things'.[43] The Court stated that the acquisition of a pet in the context of a family or partner relationship, is a transaction that gives rise to certain rights and obligations, independent from the property rights. This involves not only the duty to care for the animal, but also to tolerate that the other partner has a duty of care towards it, even when the relationship ends. This means that an animal who has two owners creates a legal relationship with both owners, which continues to exist even after the relationship breaks down. The classic division of property in which the right of ownership over the animal is assigned to one owner cannot prevent the exercise of this duty of care, and may in some instance give rise to a 'right to contact' on part of the owners.

Similar cases have appeared in other continental jurisdictions. In a 2011 case before the court of Versailles (France) concerning the placement of a dog, the judge noted that 'the current living conditions [of the husband], who lives in a house with a garden, are more in line with the needs of this animal.'[44] This was the first time that the interest of the animal was not only expressly mentioned, but also constituted, explicitly, the decisive criterion for the attribution of the animal during a divorce procedure. Fabien Marchadier characterised the judgment as 'a remarkable and unprecedented development' and argued that the interpretation of the judge should be construed as

> contributing to the consistency of the legal system. Because, taking into account the needs of the animal, the judges reconcile two prescriptions which operate in two quite different fields, [family law and general provisions of animal protection law], the duties which weigh on the owner of an animal due to the explicit recognition of the sensitivity of the latter. … It does not seem incongruous that this general provision should be observed in all circumstances.[45]

Attention for the interest of animals was repeated in later cases, and the capacity of the parties to take care of the animal was taken into account, for instance in a 2014

[42] Court of Appeal Brussels (22 June 2021) No 2021/FA/177, para 2.1 (translation by the author).
[43] Court of Appeal of Antwerp (29 April 2019) RW 2019, 659-661, note G. De Geest, para 8.
[44] France, Court of Versailles (13 January 2011) ch. 2, sect 1, nr 10/00572.
[45] *Fabien Marchadier, 'Chroniques de Jurisprudence: Droit Civil des Personnes et de la Famille' (2011) 1 Revue Semestrielle de Droit Animalier* 43. See also Fabien Marchadier, 'L'animal du Point de Vue du Droit Civil des Personnes et de La Famille après l'article 515-14 du Code Civil' (2015) 1 *Revue Semestrielle de Droit Animalier* 433 (translation by the author).

case, in which the fact that the wife was a veterinarian was mentioned as a reason why the animal was placed with her.[46]

Dereification makes differential treatment easier and may in some cases even lead to a limitation of the rights of owners. In a recent case before the Supreme Court in Belgium, we see how this trend continues beyond the boundaries of family law towards a criminal and property law context.[47] This case concerned the theft of a number of cats, possibly prompted by the owner's failure to care for them properly (which she herself disputed). The thieves were identified and prosecuted, after which the owner claimed the return of her stolen property – the cats. To this end, she invoked compensation in kind under the relevant Civil Code Article. Indeed, the victim of a wrongdoing is entitled to compensation in kind, unless it is impossible to do so or constitutes an abuse of law. Without any clear legal basis, the Court of Cassation ruled the restitution of the cats was contrary to their interests, and therefore an abuse of law. This is a remarkable ruling: abuse of law can thus exist when the exercise of a subjective right would harm animals, even if no humans are harmed. The subjective interests of animals are not only taken into account, but are even a decisive factor. This is another example of how the increasing recognition that animals are sentient beings to which an owner has a duty of care, may influence the exercise of property rights over them.

B. Claiming Compensation for Animals

As we have seen, Germany, Spain and Switzerland have taken dereification still one step further, which also increases the freedom of judges to treat animals differently. Apart from the distinction between animals and things, the regulations on compensation for animals have been altered in order to give rise to a special regime for animals. In Germany, §251 II-2 BGB now states that 'The expenses resulting from the healing treatment of an injured animal are not disproportionate if they significantly exceed its value.'[48] Whereas legal things can only be compensated up to their market value, animals take a special position: compensation can be claimed that far exceeds the market value of an animal. In a case before the Federal Court of Justice, this addition has been further clarified as follows:

> In the event of an animal being injured, §251 II-2 of the German Civil Code (BGB) stipulates that the legal treatment of animals … means that the expenses incurred in the medical treatment of animals are not disproportionate when they significantly exceed its value. Based on the responsibility of humans for animals as 'fellow creatures' and the fact that it is a pain-sensitive living being, the relevant provision prohibits a strictly

[46] France, Court of Appeal Bastia (15 January 2014) nr 12/00848.

[47] Belgium, Court of Cassation (26 November 2021) nr C.20.0578.F. See Eva Bernet Kempers and Johan Van de Voorde, 'Belangen van Dieren schaden kan Rechtsmisbruik uitmaken', *Juristenkrant* (6 April 2022) 2.

[48] German Civil Code, §251 II-2 *BGB*.

> economic approach when assessing damage to animals. Provided that treatment was actually carried out, § 251 II-2 BGB requires that the interests of the injuring party not only consists in the value of the animal, but also the intangible interest in restoring its health and physical integrity, resulting from the responsibility for the animal.[49]

This quote eloquently shows how the German legal perspective on animals is a comprehensive approach that is closely connected to the provisions of public law concerning animals. Animals are clearly distinguished from things that are objects of ownership: interests of the owner encompass more than only the value of the animal and include an interest in restoring its health and integrity, which, according to this court, is rooted in 'the responsibility for the animal'. Interesting here is that a seemingly public law responsibility (rooted in animal protection law) is taken as the starting point for a private law claim. In this way, sentience recognition may be understood as providing a kind of bridge through which public law animal protections are incorporated in the private law understanding of ownership.[50]

In Spain, sentience recognition has influenced the way in which and degree to which owners can claim compensation when their animal is injured. This even more exceptional development is the situation in which compensation can be claimed *from* the owner in name of the companion animal, for instance when the owner has caused the injury him or herself. A famous case in the US context is the case of Justice the Horse, in which a similar claim stood central: the Animal Legal Defence Fund claimed compensation 'on behalf of' Justice against her former owner.[51] In continental Europe, a few civil law jurisdictions have amended their civil codes in order to provide for mechanisms which ensure that claiming compensation is possible in such case. Since 2022, Article 333*bis* (3) of the Spanish Civil Code states that:

> Expenses for the cure and care of an injured or abandoned animal are recoverable by the person who has paid them through the exercise of an action for recovery against the owner of the animal or, as the case may be, against the person to whom the care has been attributed, insofar as the costs have been proportionate, but even if they have been greater than the economic value of the animal.[52]

Hence, when organisations or individuals pay for the medical costs for an animal that has been injured by its owner, they can recover those costs from the owner by instituting an action for recovery. The injury they suffer at the hands of a human being, is recoverable from the owner. The distinction between animals and legal

[49] German Federal Court of Justice (27 October 2015) Urteil vom 27. Oktober 2015 – VI ZR 23/15 §12.

[50] Jansen (n 5).

[51] See *Justice, an American Quarter Horse, by and through his Guardian, Kim Mosiman, Plaintiff-Appellant, v Gwendolyn Vercher.* Court of Appeals of the State of Oregon (US), 4 September 2018, Case No 18CV17601, and the latest ruling *Justice v Vercher*, 321 Or App 439 (2022).

[52] Spanish Civil Code, Art 333bis (3) *Codigo Civil.* See also Rodrigo Bercovitz Rodríguez-cano, 'Cosas, Bienes y Animales' (2022) 2 *Cuadernos de Derecho Privado* 2.

things (for which such action would be hard to imagine) becomes particularly tangible here.

C. Applying Family Law to Animals

Sometimes, courts even go one step further: they interpret the distinction between animals and legal things as bringing animals within the scope of family law. In the earlier mentioned case of 2019 in Antwerp, Belgium, family court on appeal noted that the two dogs concerned 'were also part of the de facto family that the parties then formed'.[53] Therefore, it found that both parties had a right to contact to the dogs, giving rise to a kind of visitation rights between the parties that resembles those in relation to children. From this wording it appears that the companion animal is considered a member of the family. In Spain as well, on 27 May 2019, a court in Valladolid granted shared custody of a dog, ordering that he should spend six months with one party and six months with the other, allowing visitations on weekends.[54] As Montes Franceschini states, 'the consideration of some animals as family members has pushed judges to apply family law to animals, acknowledging that their legal status as property is unsuitable for solving these types of cases.'[55]

The fact that animals sometimes are granted a status that seems to lie close to that of a family member than to that of property, is also illustrated by the aforementioned amendment to the Spanish Civil Code, in which it is now stipulated that in case of injury or death of a companion animal as result of a third party, not only the owner, but also 'those living with the animal are entitled to compensation, including compensation for the non-material damage caused'.[56] The fact that living with an animal gives rise to a claim to compensation when the animal is injured is remarkable, and seems to be analogous to the way in which family members have rights based on their affective relationships with each other. It should be noted that this development may have followed rather than preceded the case law in which animals were, to some extent, already treated as family members by courts, even in the absence of dereification provisions.[57] Hence, it looks like the law was already taking this path, even before the dereification provisions were introduced. Nevertheless, the dereification provisions do

[53] Court of Appeal of Antwerp (29 April 2019) RW 2019, 659-661, note G De Geest, (recital 8, first paragraph).

[54] Juzgado de Primera Instancia 9 de Valladolid [Court of First Instance 9 of Valladolid], 27/5/2019,[Expte. Nro.] 1068-2018 (Spain) 1.

[55] Macarena Montes Franceschini, 'Traditional Conceptions of the Legal Person and Nonhuman Animals' (2022) 12 *Animals* 3.

[56] Court of Appeal of Antwerp (29 April 2019), Note E Verniers and G Verschelden.

[57] Miryam Olivera Oliva, 'Crisis de Pareja de Hecho y Animales de Compañía. Sentencias En Cataluña, Anteriores a La Propuesta de Reforma Del Código Civil de 20 de Abril de 2021' (2021) 12 *Derecho Animal. Forum of Animal Law Studies* 190.

provide an explicit ground on which to base a special regime of ownership applying to animals as non-things.

IV. Reconceptualising Ownership: De-objectification of Animals in Civil Law[58]

Even though the distinction between animals and things may, by the legislator, have been intended as a merely symbolic change, there is some evidence that it involves a broader change to the status of animals as being increasingly less like things. Especially in the case of Spain, companion animals are not merely distinguished from things, but rather granted a status that resembles that of human family members. This also means that animals are, to some degree, transferred from property law to family law; rights of owners are being limited; and interests of animals as sentient beings taken into account. It is clear that ownership over animals is no longer comparable to ownership over inanimate things, and rights of owners are curtailed by the special nature of animals as sentient beings. In this section, I will further zoom in on the way in which this development can be interpreted as a trend of de-objectification of animals in continental law. However, this seems to be primarily the case with companion animals; albeit dereification *in theory* includes all animals, we see that *in practice* it is mostly companion animals that benefit from this change.

It should be noted here that in the civil law tradition, the Civil Code categorises 'things' or 'goods' as objects of property and shapes the relations between persons with regard to things through the concept of ownership (or absence of ownership). In contrast to common law, the category of 'things' is not a synonym of 'property', as categories of things exist that are not owned by anyone (*res nullius*), or cannot be owned at all (*res communes, res extra commercium*). Things only become objects of property when they are appropriated by a person; if not appropriated, they remain things that are owned by no one. The recognition of their sentience in the concerned Civil Code provisions could potentially be regarded a means through which a special regime of ownership is introduced: a form of ownership that takes account of animals' sentience (which also grounds their public law protections) and thereby their (partial) subjectivity. That animals are no longer in the same category as 'things' makes it possible for the powers of animal owners to be limited gradually (as we have seen in the previous section) without limiting their powers over other property. Essentially, this means that a new regime of ownership is created for animals. When animal interests overrule the rights of

[58] See also Eva Bernet Kempers 'The Special Status of Companion Animals' in A Peters, S Stucki and K Stilt (eds), *The Oxford Handbook of Global Animal Law* (Oxford University Press, 2023, forthcoming).

owners, and third parties are able to claim damages on behalf of the animal from the owner, or represent animals directly in court against their owner (as is the case in some jurisdictions already), the comparison with legal things that are defined by their status as property becomes particularly weak, and we may better speak of a form of guardianship.[59] Such transition is visualised in Figure 5.1.[60]

Figure 5.1 Transition from thing to family member

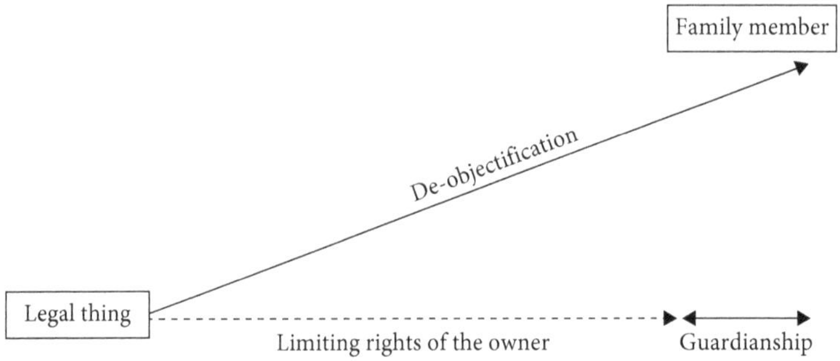

Figure 5.1 illustrates the overall trend of de-objectification that takes place when powers and rights of owners are curtailed 'on behalf of' animals, or as a direct consequence of the recognition of their sentience and interests. We can see this as de-objectification because it essentially means that animals are less and less defined by their status as objects, and treated as partial subjects whose interests matter for law in and of themselves. Dereification in Civil Codes is an aspect of this trend, which can be regarded as providing a ground for the differential regime of ownership that applies to animals in the law. This separate regime of ownership is characterised by its attention for the special nature and interests of owned animals as an important factor in the relation between owner and owned. The process of de-objectification is incremental, as the increasing limits put on animal owners' rights and powers further stir the status of animals in an upward direction.

Some continental civil law jurisdictions have introduced specific laws that make the curtailment of rights of owner over companion animals even more explicit. Such laws make clear that not everyone can own animals: they specify conditions with which an animal owner has to comply. In Wallonia (the French part of Belgium), animal owners are considered to have a virtual permit for keeping companion animals, which can be taken away when they fail to provide adequate care for their animals: Article D6-1 now states that 'A permit is required to keep an animal'.[61] In a similar manner, the new French Animal Protection Act that came into force in 2022 will also include the requirement

[59] This may also be true, to some extent, for the common law context, where property is often understood as a 'bundle of rights', thus making it possible to imagine different degrees of property.
[60] This figure is also published in Bernet Kempers (n 58).
[61] Walloon Animal Welfare Code, Art D6-1 Code Wallon du Bien-Etre Animal, 2018.

for a permit of the owner.[62] In most jurisdictions, ownership can be forcefully ended when an owner is not treating their animal well. Dereification, then, essentially incorporates the increasing public law protection of animals' interests *into* the private law concept of 'ownership', transforming it into a separate regime of ownership that applies to animals, based on their special nature as beings whose interests have intrinsic legal relevance. Animal ownership is, in this way, becoming conditional on the behaviour of owners; animals are no longer defined by their status as objects of property rights and at some point, it may be more adequate to reconceptualise the legal relation between owners and animals as a form of guardianship. As Cochrane notes, the suggestion here is 'that some forms of ownership need not stand in the way of achieving justice for animals'.[63] In the future, this trend could culminate in the redefinition of companion animals as members of families *de lege ferenda*. The concept of the 'multispecies family' aptly catches the differential relations between humans and other species within one family.[64]

The idea that animals can be intrinsically relevant individuals in the context of family law as members of multi-species families, fits well with the existing trend in which a broader diversity of families is being legally accepted across the world. New combinations of persons that were historically placed outside the legal definition of the family, such as single-parent, homo-affective relationships and poly-affective families, are now being incorporated into family law.[65] In a number of jurisdictions, the concept of 'family' is thus being opened to accommodate the modern forms in which people are living together. This means that, instead of being based upon some kind of biological or marital bound, the concept of family is based upon the affection that its members have for each other; it is an understanding of the concept of family that is increasingly less defined by genes and biology. In this evolving understanding, it does not seem too far-fetched to imagine that non-human members may also someday acquire their place in the definition. As Valéria Silva and others state, animals could then possibly be regarded as subjects of rights for purposes of family law, whilst their Civil Code status would not necessarily have to be changed to that of 'person'.[66] Rather, it would mean that they

[62] French Animal Protection Act, Loi n° 2021-1539 du 30 novembre 2021 visant à lutter contre la maltraitance animale et conforter le lien entre les animaux et les hommes. The act states (in Art 1(1), modifying Art Art L 211-10-1 of the Code Rural): 'Any person selling a pet animal or giving one away free of charge shall ensure' that the purchaser signs a 'certificate of commitment and knowledge of the specific needs of the species'. However, it should be noted that this requirement only applies to people buying a dog, cat, rabbit or ferret.

[63] Alasdair Cochrane, 'Ownership and Justice for Animals' (2009) 21 *Utilitas* 424, 426.

[64] Eben Kirksey, 'Multispecies Families, Capitalism, and the Law' in Irus Braverman (ed), *Animals, Biopolitics, Law: Lively Legalities* (Routledge, 2016).

[65] Mariano Croce and Frederik Swennen, 'Cont(r)Actualisation: A Politics of Transformative Legal Recognition of Adult Unions' (2021) 30 *Social and Legal Studies* 230.

[66] Valéria Silva, Galdino Cardin and Tereza Rodrigues Vieira, 'On Multi-Species Families: Pets as Subject of Rights in Cases of Marital Dissolution' [2017] Revista do Programa de Pós-Graduação em Direito da UFBA 195.

would have some incidents of personhood;[67] be 'quasi-persons', in the terminology of Fernandez.[68] The concept of the 'multi-species family' seems well-suited in this regard, making it possible to include all members of the family, regardless of their species, in the legal definition. In the context of Latin America, some courts have already employed this concept to describe the variety of families existing today.[69]

The process of de-objectification may however take place differently for different animals in different jurisdictions. Companion animals constitute the group of animals for whom de-objectification has taken place to the most substantial extent, whereas for other animals the effects have remained very limited or even absent. Production animals, for instance, are still primarily defined by their status as objects of property rights; their interests remain largely invisible for courts. Therefore, the upward path of companion animals in the graph depicted in Figure 5.1 may form an example for the legal situation of other animals, for whom de-objectification may have a different outcome.[70] We can imagine that, with regard to production animals, if the rights of owners would be limited in the future, that may transform their status from a 'unit of production' to a status that, to some degree, could resemble that of human workers. For instance, laws that require animals to have 'resting periods' or 'maternity leave' for racehorses, or even a form of 'retirement' for service dogs, may be regarded as the kind of legislation that, in the case of production animals, deobjectifies them in a similar movement to the graph in Figure 5.1, albeit with a different end-result.

V. Conclusion

This chapter has argued that dereification and sentience-recognition in Civil Codes of continental European jurisdictions has possible implications for the way in which ownership of animals should be understood. Where it used to be regarded a form of 'dominion' over animals, the rights of owners are increasingly curtailed; a process that is accelerated through the recognition that animals are sentient beings in the Civil Code. We have seen how, in case law, animal interests are now more often taken into account, and in some jurisdictions anyone can claim compensation on the animals' behalf. This means that owning animals does no longer equal owning things: the recognition of the relevance of their sentience in a private law context may as well be regarded as grounding a separate regime

[67] Visa AJ Kurki, *A Theory of Legal Personhood* (Oxford University Press, 2019).

[68] Angela Fernandez, 'Not Quite Property, Not Quite Persons: A Quasi Approach for Nonhuman Animals' (2019) 5 *Canadian Journal of Comparative and Contemporary Law* 1.

[69] Myriam Acero Aguilar, 'Esa Relación tan Especial con los Perros y con los Gatos: La Familia Multiespecie y sus Metáforas' [2019] *Tabula rasa* 157. See for the discusión of a Colombian case: Lina Cespedes (2020) Los Animales son Miembros de Familia, *El Malpensante*, 225.

[70] See for a discussion eg Charlotte E Blattner, Kendra Coulter and Will Kymlicka (eds), *Animal Labour: A New Frontier of Interspecies Justice?* (Oxford University Press, 2019).

of ownership over animals, that is rooted in the inherent responsibility of owners for their animals as sentient beings. Essentially, dereification thus incorporates the increasing public law protection of animals *into* the private law concept of 'ownership'. At some point, this would mean that, instead of 'ownership', we may better speak of a form of guardianship over animals that is conditional upon the behaviour of the owner.

6

Common Sense: Animal Sentience and the Common Law

JOE WILLS*

I. Introduction

Over the last two centuries animal protection laws have implicitly recognised the moral and legal significance of animal sentience. In recent decades, this implicit recognition has been made explicit, with legislatures around the world legally enshrining animal sentience as the basis for animal protection.[1] As this edited volume attests, the 'animal sentience' turn in law now attracts significant academic, legal and policy discussion and analysis. However, little attention has been paid to how judges across the common law world have incorporated consideration for animal sentience into the interpretation and development of judicial doctrines.

This chapter will examine how questions concerning animal sentience have appeared before common law judges in myriad contexts. In the next section I will briefly clarify what is meant by the 'common law'. Following that, I will document the traditional common law status of animals as 'mere property' and consider the extent to which this status has and should be legally reimagined in light of statutory recognition of animal sentience and welfare interests. Next, the chapter will contemplate why sentience might be normatively salient to the interpretation and development of common law doctrines. The chapter will then identify areas of the common law where animal sentience has been used to challenge the traditional common law status of animals as mere property. These areas include animal custody disputes, damage claims for death and injury inflicted on animals, criminal procedure rules in cases involving animals and efforts to achieve animal legal standing and personhood. Finally, judicial reasons for accepting or rejecting the salience of animal sentience in common law adjudication are identified and

* I'd like to thank Jane Kotzmann, Marcelo Rodriguez Ferrere, Vanessa Garbini and Eva Bernet Kempers for their feedback on earlier drafts of this chapter. The standard disclaimer applies.

[1] See Charlotte Blattner, 'Nature and Scope of the Legal Recognition of Animal Sentience' in this volume.

discussed. The chapter concludes that the success of common law-based efforts to pursue greater protections for animals hinges significantly on judicial discretion and preference.

II. The Common Law

Before considering the legal status of nonhuman animals I will set out how 'common law' is understood in this chapter. A useful entry point is the distinction between a 'civil law system' and a 'common law system'. Crudely put, civil law systems – such as those in continental Europe and South America – are predominantly based on codified sources of law.[2] By contrast, common law systems – such as those of Britain and its former colonies – use a mixture of codified legislation and 'rules and principles which are judge-made, rather than contained in statutes'.[3] This latter body of law can be called 'the common law'.

Although judges have the power to make law in common law systems, this power is typically exercised within certain parameters. First, the common law is standardly subordinate to legislation.[4] While common law rules can be superseded or replaced by statutes, the common law cannot similarly displace statutory rules. Second, judges are constrained by a system of precedent known as the doctrine of *stare decisis* ('to stand by things decided').[5] In most cases, judges are bound to follow decisions previously made in similar cases. The common law is not, however, completely static. For a start, senior courts in many common law systems have the power to overrule earlier decisions, either when they were made in error or where they are no longer appropriate due to societal changes.[6] Moreover, lower courts frequently encounter novel disputes and must apply existing precedent to unique situations. So, in theory at least, the common law is meant to be orderly whilst having a certain degree of flexibility.

The phrase 'common law' can refer to two discrete areas of judicial law-making. The first is the so-called 'pure common law' which describes those legal doctrines, rules and principles that are exclusively judicial in origin, without the aid of any legislation. Areas of English law like contract, negligence and property are mostly based on this pure common law. Secondly, there is 'interstitial common law', which involves courts clarifying and 'filling in the gaps' of statutory law, for example

[2] James G Apple and Robert P Deyling, *A Primer on the Civil-law System* (Federal Judicial Center, 1995) 1.

[3] John Bell, 'Sources of Law' in Andrew Burrows (ed), *English Private Law* (Oxford University Press, 2013) 10.

[4] While courts in eg the USA or India may be empowered to strike down unconstitutional legislation, this is a power vested to them by the constitution, not the common law.

[5] William O Douglas, 'Stare Decisis' (1949) 49 *Columbia Law Review* 735.

[6] See eg Lord Gardiner LC, 'Practice Statement (Judicial Precedent)' [1966] 1 *Weekly Law Reports* 1234 (allowing the UK House of Lords, and subsequently Supreme Court, to depart from previous decisions 'when it appears right to do so').

providing legal tests and definitions for undefined terms within statutes.[7] For the purposes of this article, 'common law' is used to cover both senses of the term.

III. The Property Status of Animals at Common Law

Before the advent of statutory animal protection laws, the treatment of animals in common law jurisdictions was governed entirely by judicially established doctrines. The English common law inherited the Roman law classification of animals as 'things' (*res*) who were further subdivided into domesticated (*domitae/mansuetae naturae*) and wild (*ferae naturae*) animals.[8] Whereas animals *domitae naturae* can be subject to absolute ownership like other chattels, only qualified or possessory property in animals *ferae naturae* is possible.[9]

Whilst the common law recognised the property rights of animal owners and imposed liabilities on them for harms their animals caused to others, it did not provide any direct forms of legal protection for animals themselves.[10] An owner could bring a claim against a third party for injuring or harming one of their animals on the basis that the animal's economic value was diminished, but there were no legal mechanisms to prevent an owner from committing or authorising harm to their animal. Wild animals in whom no permanent property interests were held lacked even indirect protections from the law.[11]

IV. Animal Protection Law and the Common Law

Beginning in 1822 with the passing of 'Martin's Act' by the British Parliament,[12] legislatures across the common law world have enacted animal anti-cruelty laws

[7] Natalie Coates, 'The recognition of tikanga in the common law of New Zealand' (2015) 1 *New Zealand Law Review* 1, 27.

[8] Steven M Wise, 'The Legal Thinghood of Nonhuman Animals' (1996) *23 Boston College Environmental Affairs. Law Review* 471, 492–505.

[9] See eg *The Case of the Swans* [1572] 7 Co REP.17 b, 438 (England); *R v Diversified Holdings* (1982), 35 BCLR 349 (SC) [17]–[18] (British Colombia); *Yanner v Eaton* (1999) 201 CLR 351 [80] (Australia); *Borwick Development Solutions Ltd v Clear Water Fisheries Ltd* [2020] EWCA Civ 578 [14] (England & Wales).

[10] Prominent English jurist and one-time chief justice Sir Matthew Hale once commented extrajudicially that he thought it an 'unlawful thing to destroy … creatures for Recreation-sake' at a time when there were no statutory provisions outlawing such treatment. Cited in Henry Mares, 'Cockfighting as a common law crime under Charles II' (2022) 5 *Criminal Law Review* 377, 384. This indicates there were some interpretations of the common law that extended protection to animals, but there is little historical evidence of this view being operationalised in judicial practice.

[11] Mike Radford, *Animal Welfare Law in Britain: Regulation and Responsibility* (Oxford University Press, 2001) 101.

[12] The Cruel Treatment of Cattle Act 1822. There were a few limited legislative provisions prior to this. See eg Body of Liberties 92 (Massachusetts Bay Colony 1641) (prohibiting 'Tyranny or Crueltie towards any bruite Creature which are usually kept for man's use') cited in Jerrold Tannenbaum, 'Animals and

or what are often referred to today as 'animal welfare laws'. These laws do not overturn the common law property status of animals, but they have supplemented and modified that status by placing certain positive and negative duties on animal owners and third parties to protect animal health and well-being.

There are two possible interpretations of the legal status of animals in the aftermath of the enactment of animal welfare laws. The first I call *the dualist view*. On this view, animals are legally protected 'against the backdrop of the common law's traditional principles, and wherever these are not superseded by legislation, they continue to apply'.[13] In other words, in the absence of any provisions protecting animal welfare and interests, courts will continue to treat animals as mere property with no legally cognisable interests of their own. This draws on a perspective that identifies a strict division of labour between legislative and judicial law-making; 'statutes and common law flow next to but separately from each other in their separate streams'.[14] Judicial and statutory law are like 'oil and water' within this framework; there can be no intermingling between them.

The alternative approach can be called *the convergence view*. On this view, 'Legislation and the common law are not separate and independent sources of law; the one the concern of parliaments, and the other the concern of courts. They exist in a symbiotic relationship.'[15] Because common law and statutory law not only operate within the same legal order, but sometimes address similar legal claims, it is desirable that appropriate cross-fertilisation and dialogue exists between these bodies of law. For example, many statutes codify the common law whilst courts frequently develop the common law 'by analogy to statute'.[16] We shall explore this more below, but for now it will suffice to note that, on the convergence view, common law doctrines relating to animals can, and perhaps in some instances should, be adapted to mirror the express and implied moral and legal salience attributed to animal sentience in statutory law.

V. The Normative Significance of Animal Sentience

It is worth pausing briefly to reflect on *why* animal sentience does and ought to matter when considering animal legal status. There are, I submit, two important normative dimensions to sentience – what we can call the 'internal' and 'external' dimensions. The internal dimension relates to the inner subjectivity of a sentient

the Law: Property, Cruelty, Rights' (1995) 62 *Social Research* 540, 565; An Act against Plowing by the Tayle, and pulling the Wooll off living Sheep 1635 (Ireland, repealed 1828).

[13] Radford (n 11) 102.

[14] Jack Beatson, 'Has the Common Law a Future?' (1997) 56 *Cambridge Law Journal* 291, 300.

[15] *Brodie v Singleton Shire Council* [2001] HCA 29, [31] (Australia).

[16] Andrew Burrows, *Thinking About Statutes: Interpretation, Interaction, Improvement* (Cambridge University Press, 2018) 50–54.

being; their own first-person 'window to the world' and capacity for felt experiences. Critically, sentient beings have what psychologists call *valanced* experiences, in other words, experiences that are felt as positive (eg, pleasure, satisfaction) or negative (eg, suffering, frustration). It is this vulnerability that forms the basis for animal welfare and anti-cruelty laws.[17] As the Court of Appeal of Alberta recently put it, because animals are 'sentient beings that experience pain and suffering' they must 'be treated as living victims and not chattels'.[18]

In addition to having their own morally salient inner life worlds, sentient beings are the subjects of deep emotional relationships and connections with other animals, including human beings. This is the external element of sentience. Sadly, the human–animal relationship is all too often characterised not by relations of care and affection but rather by brutal exploitation and indifference, as paradigmatically illustrated by industrial agriculture and animal experimentation. Nonetheless, there remain some human–animal relations that are rooted in reciprocal bonds of affection. The relationship between humans and companion animals – though often highly problematic – provides an example of this and presents several ways that companion animals are distinct from other forms of property. First, the primary external value of companion animals is typically not their productive or economic value but rather their companionship and emotional or sentimental value.[19] Accordingly, companion animals are not typically regarded by the general public as fungible. Rather they possess a unique, irreplaceable value that cannot be adequately compensated for by mere payment for their market value.[20] This is not to deny that individuals can have rich, meaningful connections to insentient objects like a family heirloom, a 1,000-year-old oak tree or a beautiful work of art. But this involves only a one-way emotional connection to an object. The type of emotional relationship that humans and animals can experience with their nonhuman companion can be *reciprocal*, placing it in a *sui generis* category from other forms of property. This type of relationship is relevant to the analysis of animal legal status. As Andell J noted in the Texan case of *Bueckner v Hamel*:

> The law should reflect society's recognition that animals are sentient and emotive beings that are capable of providing companionship to the humans with whom they live. In doing so, courts should not hesitate to acknowledge that a great number of people in

[17] Jane Kotzmann, 'Sentience and Intrinsic Worth as a Pluralist Foundation for Fundamental Animal Rights' (2023) 43 *Oxford Journal of Legal Studies* 1, 6–11.

[18] *R v Chen*, 2021 ABCA 382 [27] (Canada).

[19] For example, a 2015 poll of the UK public found that 95% of pet owners believe owning a pet provides 'invaluable companionship' and 75% believed owning a pet made them physically or mentally healthier. 73% bought their pet a birthday or Christmas present. See www.statista.com/statistics/579416/public-oppinion-concerning-pet-ownership-in-the-united-kingdom-uk. In response to a recent petition calling for making dog theft a separate offence, the UK Government acknowledged 'the emotional trauma which the theft of a much-loved dog can cause.' See petition.parliament.uk/petitions/560216.

[20] See section VI.B below.

this country today treat their pets as family members. Indeed, for many people, pets are the only family members they have.[21]

VI. Common Law Disputes Concerning Animal Sentience

I will now explore how courts adjudicating common law disputes have both vindicated and refused to vindicate the normative salience of animal sentience outlined in the previous section. The topics explored are animal custody disputes, emotional damages for harm to animals, criminal procedure rules in cases relating to animals and animal legal standing and personhood.

A. Animal Custody Disputes

Conflicts over who should get custody of a companion animal frequently appear before the courts, usually in the context of divorce proceedings. In the United States, the traditional approach adopted by judges was to treat such conflicts like any other dispute concerning property, and to determine them by recourse to strict ownership analysis.[22] Because animals are regarded as mere chattels, courts have refused to authorise post-divorce visitation orders,[23] even when they have been agreed to by both parties.[24] Shared custody of companion animals has been ruled out as such an arrangement would be 'analogous, in law, to (custody of) a table or a lamp'.[25]

Canadian courts have been even more strident than their US counterparts in refusing to grant shared joint custody of companion animals[26] or consider animal interests in determining who gets to keep them. As a Nova Scotia court bluntly put it: 'the "best interest of the dog" is not a concept any more relevant to the law than would be the best interest of the motorcycle in a dispute over a Harley-Davidson.'[27] Accordingly, the courts have affirmed that possession of animals is determined exclusively in terms of conventional property ownership.[28] Analogies

[21] *Bueckner v Hamel* 886 S.W.2d 368, 377–78 (Tex App 1994).(per Andell J, concurring).

[22] *CRS v TKS* 192 Misc.2d 547, 746 NYS.2d 568 [Sup Ct, NY County 2002], 550 ('The determination of the final distributive award of the dog will be made at trial. A credit for any proven value of the dog could be made at that time').

[23] *Bennett v Bennett* 655 So.2d 109 (Fla App 1 Dist, 1995) 110.

[24] *Nuzzaci v Nuzzaci* 1995 WL 783006 (Del Fam Ct 19 April 1995) (unpublished opinion).

[25] *Desanctis v Pritchard*, 803 A.2d 230, [Pa Super Ct 2002] 232.

[26] See eg *Warnica v Gering*, 2004 CanLII 50065; *Almaas v Wheeler*, 2020 CarswellBC 784 (BC Prov Ct).

[27] *Savoie v Dowell*, 2009 NSSM 5, para 8, In a similar vein see also *Hawes v Redmond*, 2014 NSSM 57, para 26 (in determining who gets custody of a dog, 'The analysis is no different than it would be if we were talking about a bicycle').

[28] *Gardiner-Simpson v Cross*, 2008 NSSM 78, paras 4–5.

with principles governing child custody or family law more broadly have been repeatedly shunned.[29] The Australian judiciary has been equally unwilling to depart from conventional property analysis.[30]

While some jurisdictions have held fast to this traditional property view of animals, courts in some countries are beginning to reject this 'reductionist and utilitarian' framework.[31] Nowhere has this shift been more apparent than in the US. A recent survey of pet custody disputes concludes that various US courts and legislatures have moved 'away from a legal standard that defines animals as personal property to one concerned with the best interests or care of companion animals and the strong emotional attachments of individuals to them'.[32] While judicial rulings reflecting this shift may not expressly allude to 'sentience', as Rook notes, they implicitly recognise 'the status of pets as sentient beings who are valued companions and family members rather than mere items of property'.[33] In line with this emerging approach, evidence of mistreatment or neglect of animals by a divorcing party has been used to find in favour of custody being awarding to the other partner.[34] Courts have noted the 'cherished status accorded to pets in our society',[35] and determined companion animal custody disputes by considering what is in 'the best interests'[36] of the companion animal, or alternatively, what is 'best for all concerned'.[37]

The US is not alone in abandoning pure property analysis in respect of animal custody disputes. Since the late 1970s in New Zealand 'the welfare and best interests of the pet' have been 'primary considerations' in separation proceedings.[38] For example, in *Pence v Pence*, the Christchurch court considered which partner of the divorcing couple their two Chihuahuas should live with. One partner argued that they should have custody of one Chihuahua each. The judge rejected this claim. Instead, applying 'principles applicable to the custody of children' they

[29] See eg *Warnica v Gering* (n 26), para 6 (Ont Sup Ct J): *Gardiner-Simpson v Cross* (ibid), paras 4–5; *Ireland v Ireland*, 2010 SKQB 454, para 1; *Coulthard v Lawrence*, 2011 CarswellOnt 15952, paras 29–30; *Henderson v Henderson*, 2016 SKQB 282, para 21.

[30] See eg *Jarvis and Weston* [2007] FamCA 1339; *Walmsley and Walmsley* [2009] FamCA 1209; *Downey & Beale* [2017] FCCA 316; *Gaynor & Tseh* [2018] FamCA 164.

[31] *Travis v Murray* 977 NYS.2d 621 (Sup Ct 2013), 624.

[32] Marion C Willetts, 'An Exploratory Investigation of Companion Animal Custody Disputes following Divorce' (2020) 62 *Journal of Divorce & Remarriage* 1, 1.

[33] Deborah Rook, 'Who Gets Charlie? The Emergence of Pet Custody Disputes in Family Law: Adapting Theoretical Tools from Child Law' (2014) 28 *International Journal of Law, Policy and Family* 177, 191.

[34] *Pratt v Pratt* 1988 WL 120251 (Minn Ct App 15 November 1998) (unpublished opinion), para 3; In *re the Marriage of Stewart* 356 NW.2d 611 (Iowa Ct App 1984); *Houseman v Dare* 966 A.2d 24 (NJ Super Ct App Div. 2009).

[35] *Raymond v Lachmann* 695 NYS.2d 308 (NY App Div 1999) 308.

[36] *Juelfs v Gough* 41 P.3d 593 (Alaska 2002) 597; *Placey v Placey* 51 So.3d 374 [Ala Ct Civ App 2010] 379. See also *Zovko v Gregory*, N. CH 97-544 (Arlington County (V.) Circuit Court, 17 October 1997 (holding that a cat's 'happiness' took priority over ownership rights between two former roommates).

[37] *Raymond v Lachmann* (n 36) 309; *Travis v Murray* (n 31) 629.

[38] *Kondratyeva v Royal New Zealand Society for the Prevention of Cruelty to Animals* (SPCA) [2022] NZHC 449 [53].

found it would be in the best interests of the Chihuahuas to live with one another. Moreover, four large dogs frequently visited one of the partners' homes, and they would not make appropriate company for the smaller Chihuahuas. The courts duly awarded custody of the Chihuahuas to the other partner.[39] This 'best interests' approach has been followed in subsequent rulings.[40]

Likewise, although the prevalent approach in Canada has been to discard the interests of animals there have been some mould-breaking exceptions.[41] In *Brown v Larochelle*[42] the claimant sought possession or joint custody of a dog named Luna, or compensation for her share of the dog. Luna had been jointly acquired by the claimant and defendant. Taking this into account, Cowling J argued that the parties' acquisition of Luna might be characterised as a partnership or joint venture.[43] From this Cowling J concluded that 'the best interests' of Luna should determine who gets custody of her using the following chain of reasoning:

> Partnership law requires that partners deal with each other fairly and equitably. One of the maxims of the law of equity is: 'Equity presumes that to be done which ought to have been done'. In the context of this case, and having seen and heard the parties, I can assume that if they had directed their minds at the time they acquired Luna or during their joint care of her to what would happen if they split-up they would have agreed that this decision would take into account the best interests of Luna and her humane treatment.[44]

Taking Luna's best interests into account, Cowling J determined that the defendant should get possession of her, given the special bond Luna had formed with him.[45]

B. Damages for Harm to Animals

Where a companion animal has been wrongfully injured or killed, courts have had to grapple with the appropriate method for calculating the monetary damages to compensate the harm. Historically, companion animals have been viewed by

[39] See *Pence v Pence* (1978) 2 MPC 146 (SC), 5.

[40] See eg *O'Brien v Tuer* DC Waitakere FP090/327/03, 9 September 2003; *Sydney v Sydney* [2012] NZFC 2685; *Casey v Lyttle* [2013] NZFC 9109. New Zealand Law Commission, 'Dividing relationship property – time for change' (October 2017, Wellington, ISSUE PAPER 41), 291, available at www.lawcom.govt.nz/sites/default/files/publicationAttachments/PRA%20Issues%20Paper%20IP41.pdf.

[41] See eg *Watson v Hayward* 2002 BCPC 259 (CanLII). This case involved an 'interim custody' dispute between an owner and breeder over a miniature Dachshund. The judge determined that 'Unlike claims over inanimate property, competing claims over domestic animals may take into account a broader range of factors' and applied a 'best interests' standard to resolve the dispute (paras.33, 36, 37). See also *Gandy v Robinson*, [1990] NBJ No 565; *Vallance v Naaykens*, [2001] BCJ No 959.

[42] 2017 BCPC 115 (CanLII), 2017 BCPC.

[43] ibid, para 17.

[44] ibid, para 18.

[45] ibid, para 20. See also the partial dissent from Hoegg JA in *Baker v Harmina*, 2018 NLCA 15 (CanLII) which, although it does not depart from strict property analysis, does problematise it somewhat.

US courts as mere personal property, with recovery limited to the loss of their fair market value.[46] Damages relating to the intrinsic value of the animal, the emotional distress of the owner, and the loss of companionship, let alone the harm experienced by the animal themselves, have been repeatedly rejected.[47] In other words, courts have historically declined to normatively recognise what I termed the 'external element of sentience' in section V, ie the importance of emotional bonds sentient beings form with others.

Judges have nonetheless expressed unease about the gap between the unique value and companionship of animals on the one hand and 'the law's cold characterization' of companion animals 'as mere "property"' on the other.[48] In determining that only replacement value was available for the wrongful death of a dog, the Supreme Court of Vermont nonetheless noted that in 'holding with the traditional view that the law recognizes animals as a type of property, we are not blind to the special place they hold in our lives'.[49]

Justice Andell of the First District Court of Appeals of Texas provides one of the clearest judicial articulations of the problems raised by relying on market value for determining negligent harm to animals in his aforementioned concurring judgment in *Bueckner v Hamel*.[50] He points out that pure property analysis fails to take account of 'the value of the dogs as companions and as beloved pets'.[51] Because companion animals typically have a much higher value to their 'human family' than their economic worth, people 'who love and care for animals should not be forced to accept as compensation for their loss the amount that the animal would bring in the market'.[52] Pointedly, for this chapter, he emphasised, that the 'law should reflect society's recognition that animals are sentient and emotive beings'.[53] Likewise, the Court of Appeals for the second district in California ruled in favour of permitting damage awards beyond market value for injuries experienced by pets on the basis that 'the Legislature has recognized since 1872 that animals are special, sentient beings, because unlike other forms of property, animals feel pain, suffer and die'.[54]

The recognition of animals as a unique form of property has led to a growing number of US courts allowing recovery for non-pecuniary damages that include consequential losses (eg veterinary expenses),[55] recovery for the 'intrinsic value' of

[46] For an overview see Phil Goldberg, 'Courts and Legislatures Have Kept the Proper Leash on Pet Injury Lawsuits: Why Rejecting Emotion-Based Damages Promotes the Rule of Law, Modern Values, and Animal Welfare' (2013) 6 *Stanford Journal of Animal Law and Policy* 30.

[47] ibid.

[48] *Rabideau v City of Racine*, 243 Wis 2d 486, 490 (Wis 2001).

[49] *Scheele v Dustin*, 998 A.2d 697 (Vt 2010).

[50] See n 21.

[51] ibid 373.

[52] ibid 374.

[53] ibid 378.

[54] *Martinez v Robledo* 147 Cal Rptr 3d 921, 926 (Cal Ct App 2012).

[55] See eg *Zager v Dimilia*, 524 NY.Y2d 968, 970 (NY Vill Justice Ct 1988); *Hyland v Borras*, 719 A.2d 662, 663 (NJ Super Ct App Div 1998).

the animal,[56] sentimental loss arising from wrongful death,[57] and for the mental suffering of the animal's owner.[58]

Some Canadian Courts have also adopted a more flexible approach to damages, moving away from the 'coldly unemotional' attitude towards companion animals as 'just another consumer product'.[59] In *Ferguson v Birchmount Boarding Kennels Ltd*,[60] Chapnik J of the Ontario Superior Court of Justice held that the characterisation of a companion animal as just like any other consumer product 'as a general proposition is incorrect in law'.[61] Accordingly, she upheld an award for mental distress damages against the defendants for their negligent failure to look after a dog. Similarly, in *Arnold v Bekkers Pet Care Inc*,[62] the court confirmed that while dogs may be chattels, the profound relationship that a dog can have with a human means that damages for the loss of a dog may well exceed what in commercial terms would be characterised as replacement cost. In particular, damages for mental distress may arise.[63] As Lazare notes, these decisions recognise that 'companion animals are distinct from other types of property' and that the damages awarded reflect 'the unique relationship between the plaintiff and the individual animal'.[64]

C. Criminal Procedure

In common law jurisdictions, all criminal offences relating to animal welfare have a statutory basis. Nevertheless, the purpose of these statutes has been fiercely

[56] See eg *Small Dog Rescue v McKenney*, SOM-L864-04 (NJ Sup 2004); *Stephens v Target Corp.*, 482 F.Supp.2d 1234 (9th Cir 2007); *Sherman v Kissinger*, 146 Wash App 855, 862, 195 P.3d 539, 543 (Wash Ct App 2008); *Brinton v Codoni*, 148 Wash App 1034 (Wash Ct App 2009) (unpublished opinion).

[57] *Laporte v Associated Independent's, Inc*, 163 So 2d 267, 269 (Fla 1964); *Jankoski v Preiser Animal Hosp, Ltd*, 510 NE 2d 1084, 1087 (Ill App Ct 1987).

[58] See eg *Fredeen v Stride*, 269 Or 369, 375, 525 P.2d 166 1974; *Corso v Crawford Dog & Cat Hosp*, Inc, 97 Misc 2d 530, 531 [Civ Ct, Queens County 1979; *Henning v Nicklow*, No 1:08–CV–180, 2009 WL 3642739, 2009; *City of Garland v White*, 368 SW.2d 12, 13–14 (Tex Civ App-Eastland 1963); *Knowles Animal Hosp v Wills*, 360 So.2d 37, 38 (Fla Dist Ct App.3d Dist.1978); *Rex Campbell v Animal Quarantine Station of the State of Hawaii* 632 P.2d 1066 (Hawaii, 1981); *LaPorte v Associated Independents* (ibid); *Johnson v Wander* 592 So 2d 1225 (Fla Dist Ct App 1992).

[59] *Pezzente v McClain*, 2005 BCPC 352 (CanLII), para 4. For examples of cases that have abandoned mere property analysis see eg *Crichton v Noon* [2005] OJ No 4230 (QL) (Sm Claims); *Brown* v *Edwards*, [2005] OJ No 1800 (QL) (Sm.Claims); *Nevelson* v *Murgaski*, [2006] OJ No 3132 (QL) (Sm Claims).

[60] (2006), 79 OR (3d) 681 (Div Ct).

[61] ibid, para 20.

[62] [2010] OJ No 2153.

[63] Quoted in A. Buckley, 'Why we should Keep the Doggie-Door Closed on Emotional Damages' (CanLII Connects, 14 March 2016), available at canliiconnects.org/en/commentaries/41219.

[64] J Lazare, '"Who Gets the Dog?" A Family Law Approach (2020) 45 *Queens Law Journal* 287, 315. New Zealand courts have also ordered convicted defendants to pay 'emotional reparation' to the human companions of animals they had killed. *NZ Police v Spittle* unreported, District Court (Queenstown, NZ), 3 June 2008; NZ *Police v Dingshan Xiao*, unreported, District Court (Christchurch, NZ), 27 August 2008. See Ian A Robinson, *Animals, Welfare and the Law: Fundamental Principles for Critical Assessment* (Routledge, 2015) 172.

contested. There are broadly two perspectives on this matter: the 'direct duty'; and the 'indirect duty' views. According to the direct duty view, the statutes exist to protect animals for their own sake. The indirect duty view[65] holds that animal protection laws are ultimately not concerned with the animals themselves, but protect animal interests only as a means to promoting public morality or other human interests.[66] For example, brutal treatment of animals may offend the sensibilities of others or have a corrupting effect on the perpetrator.[67] As we will see, which of these views one adopts has significant implications for both substantive and procedural criminal law norms.

The indirect duty view once held significant influence over judges. The jurisprudence of apartheid South Africa provides a clear illustration of this tendency. In *R v Moato* Van den Heever J stated that 'the object of the (animal cruelty) legislation was not to confer legal rights upon animals and this prohibition is not intended to provide them with protection.' Instead, 'the aim is obviously to prohibit a person from being so cruel to an animal as to give offence to the finer feelings and sensibilities of other persons.'[68] Likewise, in the Canadian case of *R. v Menard*, Lamer J exclaimed that 'the hierarchy of our planet' does not 'give rights to the animal' but it does prompt humans 'to impose on ourselves behaviour which will reflect in our relations with [animals] those virtues we seek to promote in our relations among humans.'[69]

In recent decades, this 'indirect duty' view has fallen from favour amongst the judiciary. The South African Constitutional Court, for example, has observed that 'the rationale behind protecting animal welfare has shifted from merely safeguarding the moral status of humans to placing intrinsic value on animals as individuals.'[70] In arriving at this conclusion, the Constitutional Court embraced a previous minority judgment by Cameron JA that found the normative basis of South Africa's animal protection laws was that animals 'are sentient beings that are capable of suffering and of experiencing pain.'[71]

[65] Tom Regan, *The Case for Animal Rights* (University of California Press, 2004) 150; Gary L Francione, *Animals, Property and the Law* (Temple University Press, 1995) 122–24.

[66] A number of older English jurisprudence textbooks hold this view; see Graham BJ *Hughes, Jurisprudence* (Butterworths, 1955) 442; Patrick J Fitzgerald, *Salmond on Jurisprudence*, 10th edn (Sweet & Maxwell, 1966) 300–01; George W Paton and David P Derham, *A Textbook of Jurisprudence by George Whitecross Paton*, 4th edn (Clarendon Press, 1972) 294–95.

[67] In the UK context, see eg *Ford v Wiley* (1889) 23 QBD 203 (per Hawkins J) ('Constant familiarity with unnecessary torture to and abuse of dumb animals cannot fail by degrees to brutalize and harden all who are concerned in or witness the miseries of the sufferers'); *In re Wedgwood* [1915] 1 Ch.113, 117 (per Lord Cozens-Hardy MR) (determined that a trust for the protection and benefit of animals was valid on the grounds that such a trust had a good charitable purpose of promoting 'public morality by checking the innate tendency to cruelty').

[68] *R v Moato* 1947 (1) SA 490 (O). See also *S v Edmunds* 1968 (2) PH H398 (N).

[69] *R v Menard* (1978) 43 CCC (2d) 458 (Que CA), [49].

[70] *National Society for the Prevention of Cruelty to Animals v Minister of Justice and Constitutional Development and Another* (CCT1/16) [2016] ZACC 46; 2017 (1) SACR 284 (CC); 2017 (4) BCLR 517 (CC) (8 December 2016).

[71] ibid [57]. See also *Bool Smuts and Another v Herman Botha* (887/20) [2022] ZASCA 3 (10 January 2022) [24].

Canadian courts have likewise recognised that 'society … long ago moved forward from the notion of animals as mere property'[72] and that 'animals, sentient beings that experience pain and suffering, must be treated as living victims and not chattels'.[73]

This shift to a direct duties view has also impacted the common law in some instances. Three cases from the US state of Oregon illustrate this. Importantly, all three of these cases come in the wake of the Oregon legislature enshrining recognition of animals as 'sentient beings' who 'should be cared for in ways that minimize pain, stress, fear and suffering',[74] and all three decisions expressly cite this provision. In *State v Nix*,[75] the defendant was indicted on multiple counts of first- and second-degree animal neglect after dozens of emaciated animals, mostly horses and goats, and several animal carcasses were found on his farm. The State argued that, under Oregon law, a defendant is to be charged with a separate offence for every victim his crime has. The defendant argued that he had only committed one offence because the victim in animal neglect cases is either the public at large or the owner of the animal. The Oregon Supreme Court rejected this argument and found, under the relevant Oregon legislation in dispute animals are properly understood as the victims of crimes. The Court noted:

> Although early animal cruelty legislation may have been directed at protecting animals as property of their owners or as a means of promoting public morality, Oregon's animal cruelty laws have been rooted – for nearly a century – in a different legislative tradition of protecting individual animals themselves from suffering.[76]

Animals, accordingly, were found to be 'victims' of crime, at least for the purposes of identifying how many punishable offences a defendant ought to be indicted for.

Next came *State v Fessenden*.[77] In this case a law enforcement officer entered a private residence and seized a starving horse after a tip-off from a concerned neighbour. Two of the occupants of the property were subsequently convicted of criminal animal neglect. They appealed against their convictions on the basis that the police officer's search and seizure was warrantless and therefore amounted to an unreasonable search under Oregon's constitution. Generally, a search or seizure done without a warrant is considered unreasonable (and hence unconstitutional), but there are a few established exceptions in the common law. One of those is known as the 'emergency aid exception' which allows warrantless searches where they are 'necessary to … render immediate aid to persons'.[78] The State argued the emergency aid exception applied to rescuing animals, notwithstanding the fact

[72] *R v Munroe*, 2010 ONCJ 226, para 23.
[73] *R v Chen* (n 18) [27]. See also *R v Munroe*, 2010 ONCJ 226 [23]; *R v Alcorn*, 2015 ABCA 182 [41] ('Sentient animals are not objects').
[74] ORS 167.305(1)–(2).
[75] 355 Or 777 (Or 2014).
[76] ibid, 796–97.
[77] 258 Or App.639, (Or Ct App 2013).
[78] *State v Baker*, 350 Or 641, 649, 260 P.3d 476 (2011).

that it referred to 'persons'. The Oregon Court of Appeals agreed, holding that 'the societal interest in protecting nonhuman animals … can justify – at least in some circumstances – a warrantless search or seizure aimed at preventing or alleviating (their) suffering'.[79]

In *State v Newcomb*,[80] a police officer took custody of the defendant's dog Juno, who was found in a near-emaciated condition. A vet later took a blood sample which found that Juno had no underlying condition explaining his emaciated state except malnutrition. Newcomb was subsequently charged with second-degree animal neglect and moved to suppress the evidence on the ground that, inter alia, the blood sample was an unreasonable Fourth Amendment search. He claimed that since Juno is mere property in the law 'no different than a folder or a stereo or a vehicle or a boot'[81] the warrantless search (ie the taking of a blood sample) violated Newcomb's expectation of privacy.

The Oregon Supreme Court rejected Newcomb's Fourth Amendment challenge and affirmed his conviction. While granting that animals can be owned as property, the court noted that they are property of a special sort, protected by laws acknowledging that 'animals are sentient beings capable of experiencing pain, stress, or fear'.[82] The protection of animals constitutes a legitimate interest to justify such 'warrantless searches':

> The obligation to provide that minimum care falls on any person who has custody and control of a dog or other animal. A dog owner simply has no cognizable *right*, in the name of her privacy, to countermand that obligation.[83]

Fessenden and *Newcomb* illustrate how different framings of the nature and purpose of animal cruelty legislation can impact judicial doctrines governing the rights of animals. Had the horse and Juno been regarded as mere property, their rescues and medical examinations respectively would have been treated as mere interferences with property and privacy interests. Because, however, weight was attached to their sentience, the judiciary granted more leeway to state authorities to intervene in their interests.

D. Personhood and Legal Standing

So far, the examples provided in this section have been instances where courts have had the opportunity to give weight to animal interests in their determination of common law disputes. A further, bolder step would be to recognise that animals

[79] *State v Fessenden* (n 77) 649. This ruling was affirmed on alternate grounds by the Oregon Supreme Court in *State v Fessenden / Dicke*, 355 Or 759 (2014).
[80] 359 Or 756 (2016).
[81] ibid 761.
[82] ibid 767.
[83] ibid 771.

themselves have the right to initiate common law suits and be recognised under the common law as 'persons'.

In India, several courts have recognised animals as 'persons' by virtue of their protected status under the Indian constitution and national animal welfare legislation.[84] Accordingly, in the Indian context, animal sentience and animal personhood have been closely connected.[85] These decisions have emphasised Indian state governments' duties to enforce India's anti-cruelty laws, establish societies for prevention of cruelty to animals, create infirmaries to treat animals injured in violation of the law and raise animal welfare regulations to levels required by state and national law.[86] Though these decisions have recognised that courts have duties under the *parens patriae* ('father of the people') doctrine to take care of the rights of animals and that humans are their *loco parentis* (legal guardians), they do not provide any basis for animal legal standing or any other direct measures of legal redress.

In the US there have been multiple efforts to get animals recognised as 'persons' or as having legal standing under various statutes. Such efforts have thus far failed, with the courts indicating that, in the absence of any express legislative intent to the contrary, animals will be presumed to have no standing to sue under any statute.[87] To get around this, animal advocates have sought to assert animal personhood and legal standing under common law causes of action, which courts have the power to alter and expand in light of changing social circumstances.[88] Below, we will discuss two common law causes of action US animal advocates have pursued on behalf of animal clients: negligence per se and *habeas corpus*.

In *Justice v Vercher*,[89] the plaintiff in the proceedings was an adult male Quarter Horse and the defendant his former owner. Justice had suffered severe injuries at the hands of Vercher (for which she pled to guilty to first-degree animal neglect) and required life-long special care as a result. The owner of a horse rescue sanctuary where Justice now resides sued on his behalf, arguing that Vercher was liable to pay damages for Justice's ongoing care under the common law doctrine of negligence per se. Rather than having to demonstrate the breach of an objective duty of care – as is required in a standard English negligence action – negligence per se claims are triggered by harm arising from the breach of a statutory obligation. Justice's lawyers argued that he was entitled to sue for the cost of his care on the basis that he had suffered harm because of Vercher's violation of anti-cruelty law and that he 'belongs to the class of persons meant to be protected by the

[84] See *Narayan Dutt Bhatt vs Union Of India And Others* 2018 SCC OnLine Utt 645; *Karnail Singh and others v State of Haryana* 2019 SCC OnLine P&H 704.

[85] *Narayan Dutt Bhatt*, ibid [74] and [91]; *Karnail Singh*, ibid [69] and [87].

[86] *Narayan Dutt Bhatt* (n 84) [99]; *Karnail Singh* (n 84) [95].

[87] See eg *Citizens to End Animal Suffering & Exploitation, Inc v New England Aquarium*, 836 F Supp 45 (D Mass. 1993); *Cetacean Cmty v Bush*, 386 F.3d 1169 (9th Cir 2004); *Naruto v Slater*, 888 F.3d 418 (9th Cir 2018).

[88] See section VII below.

[89] 321 Or App 439 (2022).

statute'.[90] This personhood, the petitioner's argued, is connected to Justice's status as sentient being entitled to welfare protections:

> [A]nimals – as sentient beings with legally protected interests – already have rights, such as the right established by Oregon statutes to be free from cruelty. As such, animals are a limited form of legal persons (sic) with the ability to vindicate their legal interests.[91]

The Oregon Court of Appeals unanimously rejected Justice's appeal for three main reasons. First, they said that in Oregon law the concept of a legal person had always been limited to either natural persons (human beings) or artificial persons (eg corporate entities), not nonhuman animals.[92] Second, they argued that, although animals are protected by anti-cruelty laws, they do not have any rights under Oregon law.[93] Third, they said that 'a procedural mechanism does not appear to exist under Oregon law for a person to sue on behalf of an animal'.[94] They expressed doubt that a court could make informed determinations about whether a self-appointed guardian *ad litem* or next friend was really acting in the best interests of the animal, or even to determine what those best interests are.[95]

The other high-profile effort to get animals recognised as persons under the common law in the US comes from the Nonhuman Rights Project (NhRP), which seeks judicial recognition of *habeas corpus* rights for chimpanzees and elephants. The writ of *habeas corpus* is a legal remedy for challenging unlawful detention. The crux of the NhRP's campaign is that *habeas corpus* exists to protect liberty, which is an interest possessed by all autonomous beings, including nonhuman autonomous beings. The NhRP urges courts to use the flexibility of the common law to bring the writ of *habeas corpus*'s protective mandate in line with contemporary scientific understanding of animal cognition and shifting ethical norms in relation to animals' moral status.[96] Thus far, no court has granted *habeas* relief to any of the NhRP's clients. Courts have variously argued that nonhuman animals cannot be persons because they are not 'members of the human community',[97] lack the capacity to bear legal duties[98] or cannot exercise the type of liberty needed to secure freedom from captivity under *habeas corpus*.[99]

[90] *Scheffel v Oregon Beta Chapter of Phi Kappa Psi*, 273 Or App 390, 415, 359 P3d 436 (2015).
[91] Matthew Liebman et al, 'Petition for Review of Decision of Court of Appeals Affirming Judgement of Cricuit Court for Washington County' (5 December 2022).
[92] *Justice v Vercher* (n 89) 451.
[93] ibid 454.
[94] ibid 445.
[95] This author, alongside Saskia Stucki and Visa A J Kurki and numerous co-amici have challenged these rationales. See *Brief of Amici Curiae Legal Scholars with Expertise in Legal Personhood and Rights* (2023) available at https://www.mpil.de/files/pdf6/justice-v.-vercher_amici-curiae-brief-of-legal-scholars.pdf.
[96] See generally, Steven M Wise, 'Legal Personhood and the Nonhuman Rights Project' (2010) 17 *Animal Law Review* 1.
[97] *Matter of Nonhuman Rights Project, Inc v Lavery* 152 AD.3d 73 (1st Dep't 2017).
[98] *People ex rel Nonhuman Rights Project, Inc v Lavery*, 124 AD.3d 148, 152 (3d Dep't 2014).
[99] *Matter of Nonhuman Rights Project, Inc v Presti*, 124 AD.3d 1334, 1334 (4th Dep't 2015).

Notably, however, in the recent case of *Matter of Nonhuman Rights Project, Inc v Breheny*,[100] two judges issued dissenting judgments in the NhRP's favour. The case concerned an aging Asian elephant called Happy living alone in the Bronx Zoo in New York. The NhRP requested her transfer to an elephant sanctuary using the writ of *habeas*. Judge Wilson's dissent offered a wide-ranging and detailed exposition on the historic role of *habeas corpus*, the purpose of common law adjudication and the evolving place of nonhuman animals in ethics and law. He found that 'Happy has very substantial cognitive, emotional and social needs and abilities, and … those qualities coupled with the circumstances of her particular confinement establish a prima facie case that her present confinement is unjust."[101] Judge Rivera would also have allowed Happy's petition because holding a 'self-determinative, autonomous elephant' in captivity is 'inherently unjust and inhumane'.[102] Although the NhRP's claims of animal personhood are rooted in their animal clients' capacities for autonomy rather than their sentience, animal sentience was relevant to the reasoning of the dissenting judges in *Nonhuman Rights Project, Inc v Breheny*. Judge Wilson, for example, makes reference to animal sentience on six occasions to emphasise that legal doctrines – including common law doctrines – need to approach the legal status of animals differently from insentient chattel.[103] Judge Rivera would have recognised Happy's *habeas corpus* rights on the basis that she is 'a sentient being, who feels and understands, who has the capacity, if not the opportunity, for self-determination'.[104]

VII. Judicial Reasons for Recognising the Significance of Animal Sentience

Having identified some instances of courts grappling with animal sentience and the legal status of animals, we will now consider some reasons courts have given in favour of affording a special status to animals in common law disputes.

A. Social Congruence

'Social congruence' refers to the degree to which legal rules comport with societal standards. Achieving an appropriate fit between legal rules and social practices and values has long been an important objective of the common law:

> For centuries judges have been charged with the responsibility of keeping this law abreast of current social conditions and expectations … Had the judges not discharged

[100] 2022 NY Slip Op 3859 (NY 2022).
[101] ibid 69–70 (Wilson J dissenting).
[102] ibid 21 (Rivera J dissenting).
[103] ibid 42–44, 46 (Wilson J dissenting).
[104] ibid 4 (Rivera J dissenting).

> this responsibility, the common law would be the same now as it was in the reign of King Henry II.[105]

The common law accordingly evolves with shifting moral norms, policy considerations and scientific knowledge.[106]

There are two primary reasons why it is desirable for the common law to reflect societal standards. The first relates to functionality. The law provides the framework within which members of society operate. If it falls behind the times, it cannot perform these functions properly.[107] As the former Chief Justice of Canada observes, where the law becomes completely out of touch 'it falls into desuetude [disuse], and is ignored'.[108] The second reason relates to legitimacy. Unlike the legislature, courts are not representative institutions and are not accountable to the citizenry on an ongoing basis. Whereas the legitimacy of the legislature rests on its accountability and representative nature, the legitimacy of the common law derives from its ability to resolve disputes in a manner that commands the broad support of society, and this legitimacy cannot be achieved if legal norms are completely unmoored from social standards.[109]

The common law classification of animals as 'property' and 'things' is rooted in Roman law and affirmed through medieval and early modern legal treatises. It is trite to observe that the moral and social status of animals has changed dramatically since those times. Whilst animals are still legally classified as property, the view that they can be treated as mere resources with no consideration for their feelings has been firmly rejected by both legislatures and the public at large. As the common law ought to be a flexible and practical instrument to resolve societal disputes fairly, some judges have suggested that courts must reject anachronistic views of animals in common law disputes. As Andell J notes in his concurring judgment in the aforementioned Texan case of *Bueckner v Hamel*:

> The law must be informed by evolving knowledge and attitudes. Otherwise, it risks becoming irrelevant as a means of resolving conflicts. Society has long since moved beyond the untenable Cartesian view that animals are unfeeling automatons and, hence, mere property … The law should reflect society's recognition that animals are sentient and emotive beings.[110]

In *Matter of Nonhuman Rights Project, Inc v Breheny*, Judge Wilson – who would have allowed Happy the elephant's *habeas corpus* petition to proceed – noted the 'long and distinguished history of adapting the common law to reflect new knowledge, changed beliefs and economic and social transformations'.[111] 'Society's

[105] *National Westminster Bank v Spectrum Plus* [2005] 2 AC 680, [32]–[33] (per Lord Nicholls).

[106] Melvin Aron Eisenberg, *The Nature of the Common Law* (Harvard University Press, 1988) 14.

[107] See eg Lord Dyson, 'Where the Common Law Fears to Tread'; *Pettitt v Pettitt* [1970] AC 777, 794; *Kleinwort Benson Ltd v Lincoln City Council* [1999] 2 AC 349, 377; Eisenberg (ibid) 9.

[108] Beverly McLachlin, PC, 'Preface' in Mary Arden, *Common Law and Modern Society: Keeping Pace with Change* (Oxford University Press, 2015) 8.

[109] Eisenberg (n 105) 10.

[110] *Bueckner v Hamel* (n 21) 377.

[111] *Matter of Nonhuman Rights Project, Inc v Breheny* (n 99) 56 (Wilson J dissenting).

determination' he continued, 'as to whether elephants have a right to be free of oppressive confinement … is not likely to be the same today as it was 100 years ago.'[112] In recognising Happy's right to seek *habeas* relief, Judge Wilson was attentive to changing social conditions, noting shifting 'social norms concerning human treatment of animals' and better scientific understanding of 'elephant cognition, social organization, behaviors and needs' as key reasons to expand the writ of *habeas corpus* to at least elephants.[113]

B. Legal Coherence

Legal coherence is a contested and somewhat fuzzy concept.[114] Broadly speaking, coherence denotes how legal phenomena figuratively 'hang together' in a rational way.[115] For our purposes we can focus on what Neil MacCormick calls 'normative coherence'. According to MacCormick, the coherence of a set of legal norms is a matter of their 'making sense' by being rationally connected as a set.[116] This concept goes beyond mere absence of inconsistency between substantive or procedural rules and seeks congruence between the underlying rationales of these rules as well.[117]

In interpreting legislation or the scope of common law doctrine, coherence constitutes an important desideratum because 'the discipline of preserving the logic and symmetry of the law is both a spur to and an important restraint on judicial law-making'.[118] Indeed, abundant evidence shows courts giving primacy to considerations of coherence in determining the shape of common law doctrine. Where legal rules exist to pursue similar principles or values, coherence entails greater convergence in the interpretation and application of those rules.[119]

It goes without saying that coherence has implications for the interplay between the judge-made law and legislation. It entails moving beyond what we called the

[112] ibid 16.

[113] ibid 37.

[114] Stefano Bertea, 'Looking for Coherence within the European Community' (2005) 11 *European Law Journal* 154, 156.

[115] ibid.

[116] Neil MacCormick, *Rhetoric and the Rule of Law* (Oxford University Press, 2005) 193.

[117] See eg Lord Toulson's justification for the common law doctrine of illegality in *Patel v Mirza* [2016] UKSC 42 (UK) ('the law should be coherent and not self-defeating, condoning illegality by giving with the left-hand what it takes with the right hand.'), [99].

[118] Lord Hodge, 'The scope of judicial law-making in the common law tradition' (28 October 2019) Max Planck Institute of Comparative and International Private Law, Hamburg, Germany, 2 available at www.supremecourt.uk/docs/speech-191028.pdf.

[119] See eg *Ivey v Genting Casinos* [2017] UKSC 67 [57(4)] (per Lord Hughes) (UK) (criticising the 'unprincipled divergence between the test for dishonesty in criminal proceedings and the test of the same concept when it arises in the context of a civil action'); *Campbell v MGN* [2004] 2 AC 457 [17] (per Lord Nicholls) (UK) (concerning the relationship between the tort of breach of confidence and the European Convention of Human Rights: 'The values embodied in articles 8 and 10 are as much applicable in disputes between individuals or between an individual and a non-governmental body such as a newspaper as they are in disputes between individuals and a public authority').

'oil and water' view in section V, which sees common law and statute as separate, non-interacting sources of law. Instead, the common law ought to be interpreted and applied, so far as possible, to form part of a coherent system of law.

There are various reasons to think coherence is desirable in a legal system. First, there may simply be inherent value in avoiding normatively incoherent legal systems.[120] Coherence is also linked to the legitimacy of a legal system, for the more a legal order embeds irreconcilable principles and values, the less rationality the law exhibits.[121] Furthermore, coherence in a legal system strengthens rule of law norms such as the principle of treating like cases alike.[122] It also bolsters legal certainty – especially where legal rules are indeterminate – by providing a conceptual adhesive that allows greater predictability about how those rules will be interpreted and applied.[123]

The value of coherence is evident in some judicial interpretations of the common law relating to animals. In *Martinez v Robledo*,[124] the respondent shot and injured the plaintiff's dog and was sued for damages. The trial court limited those damages to the market value of the dog. The plaintiff appealed, arguing that the measure of damages should go beyond market value to cover the reasonable costs of the dog's treatment. The California Court of Appeal agreed. Drawing on both California's civil code and penal code, the Court argued that given 'the Legislature's historical solicitude for the proper care and treatment of animals … the usual standard of recovery for damaged personal property – market value – is inadequate when applied to injured pets.'[125] In other words, the Court did not consider what the appropriate remedy for damages in a common law negligence dispute was in isolation. Instead, it looked to how damages should be determined by reference to California's broader legislative framework relating to animals and its underlying policy rationales. As allowing reasonable costs for veterinary treatment better comported with broader legislative animal protection objectives, the Court said it was 'a rational and appropriate measure of damages'.[126] This is a paradigmatic example of coherence-based legal reasoning.[127]

In short, when determining questions concerning the status and treatment of animals at common law, the principles governing those determinations should not

[120] Joseph Raz, 'The Relevance of Coherence' (1992) 72 *Boston University Law Review* 273, 276.

[121] Ronald Dworkin, *Law's Empire* (Fontana, 1986) 166.

[122] Stephen Perry, 'Associative Obligations and the Obligation to Obey the Law' in Scott Hershovitz (ed), *Exploring Law's Empire: The Jurisprudence of Ronald Dworkin* (Oxford University Press, 2006) 198–99. See also Burrows (n 16) 54 ('coherence dictates that, as far as possible, like cases should be treated alike across common law and statute').

[123] John McGarry, 'The Possibility and Value of Coherence' (2013) 34 *Liverpool Law Review* 17, 23.

[124] See n 54.

[125] ibid 927.

[126] ibid.

[127] See also *Feger v Warwick Animal Shelter* 2008 NY Slip Op 10122 [59 AD3d 68], 69 ('Recognizing companion animals as a special category of property is consistent with the laws of the State').

be completely divorced from those governing the statutory protection of animals. There ought to be some coherent fit between different domains of law, ensuring that animal welfare considerations are not arbitrarily excluded from any domain of the common law where they are relevant to the dispute at hand.

C. Justice

Appeals to 'justice' can also form the basis for judges recognising the special status of animals at common law. To be sure, such appeals have been relatively rare in animal protection cases. This is likely because, to the extent judges appeal to morality in common law disputes, they tend to favour appeal towards a *community standard* of morality as discussed above in section VII.A above.[128] However, occasionally judges make substantive moral appeals, especially to norms closely connected to legal doctrines. This has been especially noticeable in US cases involving the NhRP. In *Nonhuman Rights Project v Lavery* Judge Fahey, whilst concurring that NhRP's motion for leave to appeal should be denied on a procedural technicality, was heavily critical of the lower courts' failure to engage what he called the 'deep dilemma of ethics and policy' raised by the confinement of chimpanzees.[129] Such a dereliction, he said, 'amounts to a refusal to confront a manifest injustice'.[130]

Likewise, in *Nonhuman Rights Project v Breheny* the two dissenting judges who recognised the availability of *habeas corpus* relief for Happy the elephant leaned heavily on the rhetoric of justice. Judge Wilson asserted that

> we should recognize Happy's right to petition for her liberty not just because she is a wild animal who is not meant to be caged and displayed, but because the rights we confer on others define who we are as a society.[131]

To deny animals rights, he argued, 'denigrates the human capacity for understanding, empathy and compassion'.[132] Judge Rivera similarly would have allowed Happy's appeal on the basis, inter alia, that her 'captivity is inherently unjust and inhumane'.[133] Moreover, it is 'an affront to a civilized society, and every day she remains a captive – a spectacle for humans – we, too, are diminished'.[134]

[128] As Benjamin N Cardozo put it, 'A judge is to give effect in general not to his own scale of values, but to the scale of values revealed to him in his readings of the social mind.' Benjamin N Cardozo, *The Paradoxes of Legal Science* (Columbia University Press, 1928) 55.

[129] *Nonhuman Rights Project, Inc ex rel Tommy v Lavery*, 100 NE.3d 846, 848 (NY 2018).

[130] ibid.

[131] *Matter of Nonhuman Rights Project, Inc v Breheny* (n 100) 70 (Wilson J dissenting).

[132] ibid.

[133] ibid 21 (Rivera J dissenting).

[134] ibid.

VIII. Judicial Reasons against Recognising the Significance of Animal Sentience

In the previous section we identified three reasons why judges may interpret common law doctrines in ways that treat animals as more than mere property. In this section we examine some of the reasons the judiciary offer for refusing to do so.

A. Doctrinal Stability

Doctrinal stability requires, as the name suggests, stability of doctrine over time. This means avoiding altering established common law doctrines too quickly or in an erratic manner. Even in instances where courts are not bound by precedent, they are seldom keen on developing the common law in ways that radically alter existing doctrine. Where courts do develop common law doctrine, either by departing from prior precedent or developing the law in response to novel claims, they tend to opt for 'incremental' change rather than 'giant and sudden leaps forward'.[135]

There are various considerations that courts appeal to in defence of a conservative approach to precedent. Doctrinal stability enhances 'certainty, consistency and uniformity' in the law, thereby advancing a core rule of law principle that the law should be 'accessible and so far as possible intelligible, clear and predictable'.[136] Moreover, the more settled the law is, the less likely parties will be to resolve their disputes by recourse to litigation, meaning that 'a system of precedent prevents the legal apparatus from becoming clogged by a myriad of single instances'.[137] Continuity of doctrine also limits 'retrospective' judicial determination, because 'judge-made law is always retrospective'.[138]

Courts have expressed reticence about departing from 'time honoured' principles of English common law, including 'settled' classifications of animals.[139] In the recent English case of *Borwick Development Solutions v Clear* Water, Sir Timothy Lloyd went so far as to state that 'It is not open to the court to alter the long-established classification of animals … Any change to that would have to be a matter for legislation.'[140] In dismissing a horse's ability to sue, the Oregon Court of

[135] Andrew Burrows, 'Common Law Retrospectivity' in Andrew Burrows, David Johnston and Reinhard Zimmermann (eds), *Judge and Jurist, Essays in Memory of Lord Rodger of Earlsferry* (Oxford University Press, 2013) 453, 545.

[136] Lord Bingham, 'The Rule of Law' (2007) 66 *Cambridge Law Journal* 67, 69.

[137] Lord Mackay, 'Can Judges Change the Law?' (1987) *Proceedings of the British Academy* LXXIII 285, 289.

[138] Lord Reid, 'The Judge as Law Maker' (1972) 12 *Journal of the Society of Public Teachers of Law* 22, 23.

[139] *Buckle v Holmes* [1925] All ER Rep 676, 677 (per Shearman J).

[140] [2020] EWCA Civ 578, [12].

Appeals asserted that 'we see no reason to depart from the well-settled common-law doctrine regarding who is a person with the capacity to sue'.[141] Similarly, the New York Court of Appeals acknowledged that the common law may develop by 'slow process of decisional accretion' but recognising that an animal can be a person would amount to a 'sweeping pronouncement' beyond the court's ambit.[142]

B. Policy Considerations

Judges may also elect to treat animals as mere property in common law disputes for policy considerations such as resource and time constraints of the court. This worry was raised by the District Court of Appeal of Florida in its refusal to uphold the award of visitation rights to a dog for a former wife. The ruling stated that 'Our courts are overwhelmed with the supervision of custody, visitation, and support matters related to the protection of our children. We cannot undertake the same responsibility as to animals.'[143] Likewise, family barrister Tom Wilson suggests that English Courts are 'highly unlikely' to heed calls to give consideration to the best interests of companion animals in divorce proceedings because 'our family courts are already overworked and arguments over what is in an animal's "best interests" are likely to require both time and money that the court, and most separating couples, don't have.'[144]

Courts have also expressed consternation about the broader effects of extending protections to animals via the common law. The New York Court of Appeals stressed that extending personhood rights to animals could 'have significant implications … including risking the disruption of property rights, the agricultural industry (among others), and medical research efforts.'[145] They also worried that such moves by the courts would judicially displace 'a carefully crafted state and federal statutory and regulatory legal framework governing animals'.[146] Similarly, the Oregon Court of Appeals cautioned that recognising animals' 'capacity to sue for damages in tort would have profound implications'.[147]

C. Institutional Legitimacy

Some judges see animal protective measures as the proper responsibility of the legislature, not the courts. As Radford notes:

[141] *Justice v Vercher* (n 89) 457.
[142] *Matter of Nonhuman Rights Project, Inc. v Breheny* (n 100) 17 (Majority Opinion).
[143] *Bennett v Bennett*, 655 So. 2d 109, 110–11 (Fla Dist Ct App 1995).
[144] Tom Wilson, 'Pets on Divorce – What are the Rules?' (hanne.co.uk, 18 July, 2014), available at www.hanne.co.uk/pets-on-divorce.
[145] *Matter of Nonhuman Rights Project, Inc. v Breheny* (n 100) 12 (Majority Opinion).
[146] ibid 17 (fn 2).
[147] *Justice v Vercher* (n 89) 458.

> [B]ecause there already exists a substantial body of animal protection legislation … judges would most likely conclude that the territory has been occupied by Parliament and it would therefore be proper to leave it to that institution to take the initiative in deciding whether it should be further examined.[148]

This perspective is on display in several common law decisions relating to animals. In *Shera v NC State Univ Veterinary Teaching Hosp*,[149] the North Carolina Court of Appeals rejected the claim that damages could be awarded for the 'intrinsic value' of a dog who was negligently killed. The 'numerous policy considerations' raised by that proposal makes it 'more appropriately addressed to our Legislature'.[150] Other courts have also dismissed emotional damage claims for companion animals on the basis that such a determination should not 'be undertaken outside of the legislative arena'[151] and that the matter is 'properly left to legislative consideration'.[152] Likewise, the New York First Department of the Appellate Division noted that whilst efforts to get fundamental legal rights to animals are 'certainly laudable' it is 'an issue better suited to the legislative process'.[153]

IX. Conclusion

This chapter has considered the role that common law processes can play in acknowledging the moral and legal salience of animal sentience. It has demonstrated that there are broad swathes of the common law where animal sentience can, and on occasion does, shape the normative content of legal rules. Questions concerning animal sentience have appeared before judges in myriad contexts including custody disputes, negligence claims, contractual disputes, criminal procedure and civil rights. In some instances, courts have recognised that treating animals as mere property rather than as sentient beings would be inappropriate and unjust. This chapter has demonstrated several principles and modes of common law reasoning that support the recognition of animal sentience in common law disputes: the need to develop the common law in line with societal norms; the need to ensure that the common law compliments, rather than contradicts, the values and principles underpinning statutory law, and the need to ensure that the common law accords with principles of justice.

On the other hand, the article has documented instances of judicial reticence to advancing animal protection through the common law. Animal protective measures are often viewed as the appropriate purview of the legislature and courts are reluctant to tread in that terrain for reasons of doctrinal stability and public policy.

[148] Radford (n 11) 104.
[149] 723 SE.2d 352 (NC Ct App 2012).
[150] ibid 358.
[151] *Goodby v Vetpharm, Inc*, 2009 Vt 52, 69 (Vt 2009).
[152] *Kondaurov v Kerdasha*, 271 Va 646, 648–49 (Va 2006).
[153] *Matter of Nonhuman Rights Project, Inc v Breheny* 189 AD.3d 583, 583 (1st Dep't 2020).

Common law doctrine is prone to multiple, often contradictory, readings. In many respects the common law is a Janus-faced phenomenon, concerned both with preserving precedent and evolving with societal norms, maintaining social order and correcting injustice, complementing statutory norms but also remaining discrete from them. Within the constellation of modes of legal reasoning available to judges through the common law there are both tools to extend protections to animals and maintain their status as 'things' with little or no protections. Animal lawyers seeking to advance animal protection through common law litigation should take care to emphasise factors judges find amenable to modifying the common law whilst assuaging concerns about doctrinal stability, public policy and institutional competence to the greatest extent possible. There is, however, no magic bullet for success. As Liebman has noted, 'ideological and non-legal factors influence the adjudication process in animal law cases'.[154] Accordingly, even the most well-crafted litigation efforts to extend animal protection through the common law are by no means a guarantee of success.

[154] Matthew Liebman, 'Who the Judge Ate for Breakfast: The Limits of Creativity in Animal Law and the Redeeming Power of Powerlessness' (2011) 18 *Animal Law* 133, 133.

7

All Roads Lead to Sentience: The Past, Present and Future of Animal Legal Protection in Brazil

VANESSA GISCHKOW GARBINI

I. Introduction

As a country that follows the civil law tradition, Brazil's legal system develops mainly through codification. Any matter intended to be brought before a court needs to be either included in one of the many existing legal codes or framed as its own individual written statute. In other words, in order to be assimilated and binding, new social relationships in Brazil will almost necessarily, at one point, be solidified into law.

Human–animal interactions are one example of an ever-changing relation that constantly presents novelties to Brazil's – and the whole world's – legal order. Animal law itself, as its own legal field, is still in an incipient stage when compared with other traditional areas of legal studies. And one of the most pressing issues of the new field of animal law is promoting the concept of animals being sentient, ie capable of experiencing positive and negative affective states.[1] Given the civil law system's functioning, attempts to grant legal protection to animals – including the recognition of animal sentience – have to observe the code- or statute-based rule.

Thus, the aim of this chapter is to consider how close to recognising animal sentience the Brazilian legal order is. It will be demonstrated that legal recognition of animal sentience not only exists, but is as old as Brazil's animal law and is developing as such field of law evolves. Particularly, this chapter will show that sentience is a constant in the past, present and future of animal law in the country.

For that purpose, section II will analyse the existing rules that intend to advance animal protection and how they came to be (the past). The role of one of those rules, the constitutional rule against animal cruelty, will be emphasised in

[1] Ian JH Duncan, 'The changing concept of animal sentience' (2006) 100 *Applied Animal Behaviour Science* 11.

section III, which will examine how civil law judges have been contributing to the consolidation of such commandment through the creation of jurisprudence (the present). Finally, section IV will investigate existing bills that intend to reinforce sentience thereby enhancing animal protection in Brazil (the future).

II. Sentience as the Fundamentals of Brazil's Legal Protection of Animals

Only a handful of countries have provided constitutional status to animal protection within their territory, and Brazil is one of them.[2] The current 1988 Constitution is also known as Citizen Constitution ('Constituição Cidadã') or Democratic Constitution ('Constituição Democrática') as it emerged as an attempt to recover the country after over two decades of military dictatorship. It is therefore not a coincidence that the Article on fundamental rights and guarantees, Article 5, is also its longest one, presenting a thorough list of individual and collective rights.

Another remarkable characteristic of the 1988 Constitution is its appreciation for the environment and its preservation. Some scholars consider that it established the Socio-environmental Rule of Law ('Estado Socioambiental de Direito'), where the protection of human dignity is still the main but not the only duty of the society and encompasses life as a whole, including non-human life.[3] For that reason, Article 225, §1, VII entrusts the Government with the role of protecting the fauna and flora, as well as prohibiting practices that jeopardise their ecological function or cause the extinction of species.

Up until that point, it is a general environmental rule to safeguard nature as a collective. However, its last part goes above and beyond by prohibiting practices that submit animals to cruelty.[4] Without such animal cruelty prohibition clause, inserted at the very end of the legal text, it would have been a general environmental protection rule. Nonetheless, its inclusion enshrined a sentience-based animal law in Brazil.

On the one hand, by recognising the necessity of safeguarding the fauna, the Brazilian Constitution adopts a broad approach, directed to the preservation of

[2] 'Article 225. All have the right to an ecologically balanced environment, which is an asset of common use and essential to a healthy quality of life, and both the Government and the community shall have the duty to defend and preserve it for present and future generations. Paragraph 1. In order to ensure the effectiveness of this right, it is incumbent upon the Government to: … VII – protect the fauna and the flora, with prohibition, in the manner prescribed by law, of all practices which represent a risk to their ecological function, cause the extinction of species or subject animals to cruelty.' (Constitution of the Federative Republic of Brazil 1988, Art 225, §1, VII, available at www2.senado.leg.br/bdsf/bitstream/handle/id/243334/Constitution_2013.pdf?sequence=11&isAllowed=y).

[3] Ingo Wolfgang Sarlet and Tiago Fensterseifer, 'Algumas Notas Sobre a Dimensão Ecológica Da Dignidade Da Pessoa Humana e Sobre a Dignidade Da Vida Em Geral' (2007) 2 *Revista Brasileira de Direito Animal* 69, 72.

[4] Constitution of the Federative Republic of Brazil 1988, Art 225, §1, VII.

whole species (instead of individuals). That represents an ecological outlook, and is related to environmental law. On the other hand, the specific prohibition of cruelty against animals discloses an intention of detaching animals from the general concept of fauna. It is a gateway for shielding other individual, subjective interests animals have. By prohibiting animal cruelty, the Constitution acknowledges that animals may endure such negative emotions as pain and suffering. Thereby, it also implicitly acknowledges their capacity for feeling other emotions, including positive ones.

Thus, it may be argued that the Brazilian *Magna Carta* recognises that animals are able to experience a wide range of emotions, ie are sentient. Sentience, according to Vicente de Paula Ataíde Junior, is the foundation of animal dignity,[5] which is the touchstone of the constitutional rule against animal cruelty.[6] In summary, sentience is implicitly recognised by the Brazilian Constitution.[7]

The 1988 Constitution is therefore the starting point of animal law in Brazil. Yet, a Decree had already recognised animal sentience and afforded legal value to it long before. Because its proposal is establishing protective measures for animals, apparently for their own sake and interest primarily, Decree 24.645 of 1934 is completely ahead of its time. It defines animal mistreatment in a thorough list of 31 prohibited practices, which include force-feeding birds[8] and killing animals at late stages of pregnancy.[9] The words 'suffering', 'abuse', 'cruelty', 'punishment' and 'disturb', all of which demonstrate and acknowledge animals' feeling capacity, also appear several times in the scope of specific acts that are not allowed.

Due to its withdrawal, Decree 24.645 (especially its definitions of 'mistreatment') is currently used as an interpretative resource to the criminal law offences enshrined in Article 32 of Law 9.605 of 1998 (Environmental Crimes Act), considered its legal successor. Said Article criminalised abusing, mistreating, injuring, or mutilating wild, domestic (or domesticated), native or exotic animals.[10] Due to an addition to Article 32 made in 2020, it now sets a higher penalty when crimes are committed specifically against dogs or cats.[11] In that case, the perpetrator might even face incarceration. There is a clear inconsistency in this distinction, because harming is not inherently more hurtful when committed to dogs and cats than to other species of animals. Behind the change in the law there is the socio-cultural higher appreciation of humans for companion animals, most common of which

[5] Human dignity, enshrined in Art 1, III, is the touchstone of all fundamental rights established by the Brazilian Constitution.

[6] Vicente Ataide Junior, 'Introdução ao Direito Brasileiro' (2018) 13 *Revista Brasileira de Direito Animal* 48, 51.

[7] Vicente Ataide Junior, 'Princípios do Direito Animal' (2020) 30 *Revista Brasileira de Direito Animal* 106, 115.

[8] Decree No 24.645, Establishes measures to protect animals, 10 July 1934, Art 3, XXV.

[9] ibid VII.

[10] Law No 9.605, Environmental Crimes Act, 12 February 1998, Art 32.

[11] Above, Art 32, §1-A.

in Brazil are cats and dogs. Thus, while Article 32 got its inspiration from animal sentience, by affording higher protection to those animals, it reveals speciesist human concerns.

One of the main values in recognising sentience, animal dignity and animal law in Brazil's Constitution is its potential to update the legal treatment of animals in other areas of law, all of which are bound by the Constitution. The Brazilian Civil Code is an example of a statute that needs to be reinterpreted under the light of animal law. In Brazilian civil law, animals are still considered 'goods susceptible of own movement',[12] a very inaccurate and outdated definition, especially since causing suffering to animals is considered a crime, as seen above.

Since the 1988 Constitution determines that states and municipalities are also responsible for legislating on fauna,[13] state statutes on animal protection have been created. In 2003, the Animal Protection Code of the State of Santa Catarina entered into force.[14] Despite its name, the code focuses on reconciling socio-economic development with environmental preservation. Nonetheless, Article 34-A recognises cats and dogs as 'sentient beings, subjects of rights, who feel pain and anguish' and acknowledges 'their specificity and characteristics compared to other living beings'.[15] While the explicit reference to sentience is remarkable, a distinction has been made, once again, in favour of some species without any justification. Also, dogs and cats are not the only animals capable of feeling pain or anguish. Thus, it is unclear what the legal text is referring to when it mentions their 'specificities' or 'characteristics'.

Such a dividing line among species is not present in the 2018 Animal Welfare Code of the State of Paraíba, which confers a series of rights to all animals, without distinctions.[16] According to this law, considered the first Brazilian law to expressly catalogue fundamental rights to animals,[17] 'animals are sentient and born equal'.[18] Among a broad list of terms and meanings, sentience is defined as the 'animal capacity of suffering, feeling pain, pleasure or happiness'.[19] Despite being a state law, since it concretises a national constitutional command – that of establishing fundamental rights to animals – it may be argued that its application encompasses all animals in Brazil, not only to those within the State of Paraíba.[20]

Two other legal initiatives of states in favour of animals are worth mentioning. The first is the 2017 Animal Protection Code of the State of Sergipe, where animal

[12] Law No 10.406, Brazilian Civil Code, 10 January 2002, Art 82.

[13] Constitution of the Federative Republic of Brazil 1988, Art 24, VI.

[14] State law No 12.854/SC, Institutes the State Code for the Protection of Animals, 22 December 2003.

[15] ibid Art 34-A. Horses used to be included in this Article, but were excluded by Law 17.526 in 2018.

[16] State law No 11.140/PB, Establishes the Code of Law and Animal Welfare of the State of Paraíba, 8 June 2018.

[17] Ataíde Junior (n 16).

[18] State law No 11.140/PB, Establishes the Code of Law and Animal Welfare of the State of Paraíba, 8 June 2018, Art 2.

[19] ibid Art 7, §1, XXVII.

[20] Ataíde Junior (n 7) 116.

sentience is recognised by Article 2.[21] Animals are divided into categories of wild and domestic animals, and animals used for experiments. Interestingly, besides dogs and cats, farmed animals and animals used in entertainment were placed in the domestic category, with no further reference to species.

The second is the Environmental Code of the State of Rio Grande do Sul of 2020, which affords a special legal regime to domestic animals, recognising their 'biological and emotional nature as sentient beings, capable of consciously experience sensations and feelings'.[22] The apparent attempt to explain the distinction between domestic and wild animals, expressed by the words 'consciously experience', is unsatisfactory, there being no indication that other animals besides domestic animals experience emotions 'unconsciously'.

Municipal laws have also recognised animal sentience. Law 5.291/2017[23] of the city of Rio Claro, São Paulo, and Law 136/2019[24] of the city of Tefé, Amazonas, are only two examples. The fact that most of the animal-related codifications are relatively recent demonstrate that the prohibition against cruelty enshrined in the Constitution is indeed being progressively enforced the more animal law develops in the country. Sentience is the foundation of all these legal developments and it has been serving as an inspiration to judges, as will be seen in the next section.

III. The Value of Sentience to Judges: A Jurisprudential Analysis

The Brazilian Supreme Court analysed and debated animal ethics for the first time in the 2016 case of prohibition of *vaquejadas*,[25] a sport and cultural practice in the State of Ceará that involves submitting animals to the dominance and control of cowboys. The Office of Federal Prosecution challenged the the law, arguing that it violated the animal cruelty prohibition rule stated in Article 225, §1, VII of the 1988 Constitution.

Despite the defendant's denial of cruelty, the opposing part proved otherwise. The public prosecutor demonstrated that in a *vaquejada*, two cowboys riding different horses try to knock down a bull by pulling it by the tail into a delimited area, resulting in a series of injuries to the animal's tail, including tearing it off.

The significance of this case in Brazilian animal jurisprudence lies in the vote of Judge Luís Roberto Barroso, who referenced eminent scholars and animal

[21] State Law No 8.366/SE, Institutes the Animal Protection Code of the State of Sergipe and provides related measures, 20 December 2017, Art 2.

[22] State Law No 15.434/RS, Institutes the State Environmental Code of the State of Rio Grande do Sul, 9 January 2020, Art 16.

[23] Municipal Law No 5.291, Rio Claro/SP, Institutes the Code of Defense and Protection of Animals, 11 June 2019.

[24] Municipal Law No 136, Tefé/AM, Deals with the ethical and humanitarian control of dog and cat populations in the Municipality of Tefé and other measures, 12 June 2019.

[25] ADI No 4.983, Rapporteur: Marco Aurélio, Full Court, Decision Date: 6 October 2016.

advocates such as Peter Singer, Tom Regan and Gary Francione. Barroso argued that Article 225, §1, VII recognises animals as sentient beings with an interest in avoiding suffering and that the prohibition of animal cruelty is a separate rule distinct from the general protection of the environment.[26]

Another remarkable excerpt in this case, also referring to the same constitutional Article, is Judge Rosa Weber's recognition of animal dignity.[27] As mentioned, this marked the Supreme Court's first in-depth exploration of the ethics of human–animal relations and established a historical distinction between animal law and environmental law in Brazil.

However, this openly pro-animal ruling did not go unnoticed by the ruralist bench of the National Congress. After the case received significant attention by the media, defenders of *vaquejadas* rallied in support of the practice and the constitutionality of the state law. Approximately eight months after the Supreme Court ruling, the National Congress approved an amendment to the Constitution (EC 96), adding section 7 to Article 225. This amendment stated that sport practices that use animals deemed cultural manifestations are not considered cruel.[28]

The inclusion of this new section in Article 225, driven by political pressure, is deemed unconstitutional by animal law scholars.[29] A cruel act does not cease to be cruel just because a rule declares it so. Moreover, the animal cruelty prohibition rule is clear and objective, leaving no room for exceptions. However, in spite of its blatant unconstitutionality, this new paragraph, clearly a backlash, remains in effect.

While other Supreme Court cases involving animal law might not explicitly mention sentience, the concept is implicitly present in any reference to the Article 225, §1, VII, which is indispensable in all animal-related cases in Brazil. The prohibition of *rinhas de galo*[30] (cockfighting) and *farra do boi*[31] (the release of an ox into a delimited place where he is attacked and provoked, so that he chases after the people participating in the practice) are two examples.

The Superior Court of Justice, the second highest court in Brazil, also affirmed animal sentience in a case involving pet custody after a divorce. Judge Luis Felipe Salomão stated that addressing this issue is not a waste of time or futile as it involves not only human affection towards animals but also the observance of the rule stated in Article 225, §1, VII of the Constitution. He further emphasised that

[26] Barroso J, Vote in ADI No. 4.983/CE, STF, 2 June 2016.

[27] Weber J, Vote in ADI No. 4.983/CE, STF, 2 June 2016.

[28] Constitutional Amendment No 96, Adds § 7 to Art. 225 of the Federal Constitution to determine that sports practices that use animals are not considered cruel under specified conditions, 6 June 2017.

[29] Vicente de Paula Ataíde Júnior, 'Principles of the Brazilian Animal Law' (2020) 30 *Journal of Postgraduate Studies of UFBA* 106.

[30] ADI No 1.856, Rapporteur: Celso de Mello, Full Court, Decision Date: 14 October 2011.

[31] RE No 153.531-8/SC, Rapporteur: Marco Aurélio, Second Chamber, Decision Date: 3 June 1997.

property law is insufficient for solving family disputes involving pets, since it is not merely property or possessions that are under discussion. In his view, companion animals have a 'special nature' as sentient beings and deserve to have their well-being considered.[32]

While judges and legislators do not provide a detailed explanation of the 'special' characteristic of companion animals, they freely use this undefined attribute as a justification for granting them a higher level of protection. From an animal law perspective, differentiating companion animals from mere property is undoubtedly a step forward, particularly since Brazilian civil law still treats them as such. However, it is concerning that the recognition of sentience often follows these statements, as it may lead to a misconception that only companion animals can experience pain and emotions.

Fortunately, there are cases where sentience is acknowledged in animals beyond cats and dogs. In an interesting case involving animal law and tax law, sentience played a role in differentiating elephants from goods. This distinction allowed for their transportation from Chile to an elephant sanctuary in Brazil, exempting them from import taxes.[33] Once again, the 'special' characteristic emerges as an explanation for their unique protection compared to 'other kinds of goods'[34] and as a justification for not treating them as mere objects.

Farmed animals were acknowledged as sentient by a widely discussed[35] ruling of April 2023 that has banned the export of live cattle from all of the country's ports due to animal welfare concerns. It all started in 2017, when a large cargo transport ship docked at the port of Santos, a city of the state of São Paulo. According to information provided by Mercy for Animals Brazil, the ship was supposed to load 27,000 animals and head to Turkey.[36] Concerned with the well-being of the huge amount of animals, which arrived at the dock piled up in trucks coming from farms, the animal protection non-profit National Forum for the Protection and Defense of Animals (Forum) obtained legal authorisation to send an expert to investigate the scenario onboard the ship.

What investigators witnessed was an appalling situation. Animals were kept in deplorable conditions, surrounded by enough urine and excrements to form a layer of muddy waste. Breathing was difficult due to the ammonia odour, and there

[32] REsp No. 1.713.167/SP, Rapporteur: Luis Felipe Salomão, Fourth Chamber, Decision Date: 19 June 2018.

[33] *Elephant Sanctuary Association v Brazil*, Case No 5013639-32.2019.4.03.6105, 4th Federal Court of Campinas, 12 August 2020.

[34] ibid, at 4.

[35] Ana Mano, 'Brazil court bans live cattle exports over animal welfare concerns' Reuters (São Paulo, 21 March 2021), available at www.reuters.com/business/sustainable-business/brazil-court-bans-live-cattle-exports-over-animal-welfare-concerns-2023-04-27/?utm_campaign=later-linkinbio-calsanimallaw&utm_content=later-34799138&utm_medium=social&utm_source=linkin.bio.

[36] Aline Baroni, 'Confira fotos do laudo feito por veterinária no navio que exportaria 27 mil animais' Mercy for Animals Brazil (São Paulo, 3 February 2018), available at mercyforanimals.org.br/blog/confira-fotos-navio-santos.

was almost no room to move.[37] Forum then filed a lawsuit asking for the suspension of the exportation and for the animals to be unloaded from the ship. After an initial victory, the decision was reversed by the Court of Appeals, and the animals were sent to Turkey.[38]

After a long judicial battle, during which Forum requested the suspension of all export of live animals in Brazil, the trial court ruled in favour of the non-profit. In the ruling, which is a landmark for Brazilian animal law jurisprudence, federal judge Djalma Gomes stated that 'animals are not things. They are sentient living beings, that is, individuals who feel hunger, thirst, pain, cold, anguish, fear.'[39] Without distinguishing species, she makes use of national laws (Article 225 of the Constitution and Law 9.605 of 1998, both analysed above), international legal sources (the Universal Declaration for Animal Rights and WOAH's Terrestrial Animal Health Code), and even comparative law (Colombian and Australian animal protection laws) to support the view that animals are subjects of rights and worthy of a dignified treatment.[40]

However, despite its undeniable relevance, this ruling has not yet sealed the fate of animals destined to be exported from Brazil. As Carolina Maciel wrote for World Federation for Animals (WFA), the ruling may still be reversed by the Third Regional Federal Court (TRF), which is not unlikely since that same Court of Appeals overturned the lower Court decision of suspending exports, allowing the export to Turkey to proceed.[41] If that happens, Maciel explains, there is still hope for a positive outcome through the Supreme Court, due to its record on ruling in favour of animals,[42] as seen above.

It might take a long time until Brazil has a final decision on the case of live export of animals. Yet, the more animal protection is under debate before the Brazilian courts, the more developed animal law becomes, and more opportunities to reaffirm animal sentience exist. And while the animal protection jurisprudence develops, other promising legal steps are being taken through one of the most important tools of a civil law country, one that might define the direction Brazil is heading in the future in terms of animal law: codes and statutes. The current most relevant bills involving animal protection will be analysed below.

[37] ibid.

[38] Forum Animal de Proteção e Defesa Animal, 'Fim da exportação de animais vivos no Brasil' (São Paulo, 26 April 2023), available at forumanimal.org/site/2023/04/26/hoje-se-reconhece-o-obvio-que-o-animal-nao-e-coisa-e-sim-um-ser-vivo-senciente-com-direitos-fundamentais-e-dignidademp-sp-laerte-fernando-levai.

[39] *National Forum for the Protection and Defense of Animals v Brazil*, Case No 5000325-94.2017.4.03.6135, 25th Federal Civil Court of São Paulo, 25 April 2023, at 26.

[40] ibid at 26 and 27.

[41] Carolina Maciel, 'Brazil's court order to shut down live export: a significant but not yet final win for animal welfare' World Federation for Animals (25 April 2023), available at wfa.org/brazils-court-order-to-shut-down-live-export-a-significant-but-not-yet-final-win-for-animal-welfare.

[42] ibid.

IV. An Everlasting Guideline: Sentience and Animal Protection Bills in Brazil

Brazil has a highly legalistic culture. In other words, there is a strong societal emphasis upon having relevant social relations regulated by comprehensive legislation, in the format of laws, statutes or codes. Since the role of judges in civil law systems is to objectively and formalistically interpret and apply legal texts, the role of written rules is essential. Thus, in order to advance in the Brazilian legal order, animal welfare commandments must be incorporated into law.

For that reason, the number of animal protection-related bills under debate is a direct reflex of the country's interest in a higher and stronger animal law. Hereafter, some relevant federal bills that aim at increasing animal welfare in Brazil will be scrutinised, with a special focus on the role played by the concept of sentience.

A. Animals are not Things (PL 6.054/2019)[43]

This bill, intended to be the country's first Statute for Animals, caught the media's attention and had the Brazilian animal protection movement divided. It hit the news and became known by the name 'animals-are-not-things bill' (*PL animais não são coisas*) because of its goal of acknowledging animal sentience, a distinguishing feature from goods or properties. Article 4, §2 of the original proposition reads as follows: 'animals must be accorded the dignity of treatment reserved for sentient beings'.[44]

One of the main goals of the bill was creating a legal regime for animals, which would have the right to be represented before courts despite not having legal personality. In addition, a change in Article 32 of Law 9.605 to determine that animals no longer be considered things under the 2002 Brazilian Civil Code was proposed.

Notwithstanding, for some animal advocates, if approved, the legal proposal would actually represent a dismantling of the fundamental rights granted to animals by the Brazilian Constitution. According to an open letter created by the bill's opponents, animals are already not considered things by the Brazilian legal order, as demonstrated by Article 225 of the Constitution, as well as by the many pro-animal rulings issued by the Brazilian Supreme Court. For them, animal sentience is already tacitly acknowledged by the Constitution and by other statutes,

[43] Animals Are Not Things, Bill No 6.054/2019, 'Adds a single paragraph to art. 82 of the Civil Code to provide for the legal nature of domestic and wild animals', available at www.camara.leg.br/propostas-legislativas/601739.

[44] ibid Art 4, §2.

such as Law 9.605 (Environmental Crimes Act); therefore, there would be no need to explicitly state that. Beyond that, the indetermination of the proposed *suis generis* legal nature would, they argued, leave room for interpretations and new laws that could diminish the protection of animals.[45]

During the proceedings, the Senate proposed an amendment to the bill to exclude from the *suis generis* legal nature – and thus from its rights and protections – the following: farmed animals; animals used in scientific research; and animals used in cultural manifestations.[46] Following the understanding that Brazilian Constitution (Article 225, §1, VII) recognises all animals as equally sentient and deserving of protection, without any distinction of species, the approval of the bill with this amendment could indeed diminish the rights of those animals encompassed by the exception.

That, however, is not the opinion of many animal law scholars, including Daniel Braga Lourenço and Vicente de Paula Ataíde Júnior. They argue that there is no consensus in the Brazilian legal community that animals are subjects of rights under Article 225. In that sense, according to them, the approval of the bill would consolidate animal law in Brazil, significantly expanding the legal protection of animals in the country.[47]

The amendment included by the Senate needs to be approved by the House of Representatives before resuming ordinary proceedings. Since March 2023, the suggested amendment is awaiting schedule to be voted by the House of Representative's Commission of Agriculture, Livestock, and Rural Development (CAPADR).

B. Live Animal Exports (PL 3316/2021)

This bill aims to add just one sentence to the national law on agricultural policy: 'The export of live animals for slaughter or reproduction is prohibited.'[48] Even though the inclusion would be made in the format of a new section to an Article on health surveillance, it seems clear that sentience is the real framework to support this proposal. The bill is currently awaiting analysis by the House of Representative's Commission for the Environment and Sustainable Development (CMADS).

[45] Vanice Cestari, 'Animal Political Letter' Saber Animal (12 August 2019), available at saberanimal.org/carta-aberta.

[46] Bill Amendment proposal No 3, Author: Senator Davi Alcolumbre (Brasília, 18 November 2019), available at www.camara.leg.br/proposicoesWeb/prop_mostrarintegra?codteor=1835164&filename=EMS+6054/2019.

[47] Vicente de Paula Ataíde Júnior and Daniel Braga Lourenço, 'Considerations on the Bill Animals Are Not Things' Conjur (1 September 2020), available at www.conjur.com.br/2020-set-01/ataide-junior-lourenco-pl-animais-nao-sao-coisas.

[48] Ban on Live Animal Exports, Bill No 3.316/2021, 'Amends art. 28-A of Law no. 8171 to prohibit the export of live animals', available at www.camara.leg.br/proposicoesWeb/prop_mostrarintegra?codteor=2079805.

C. *Foie Gras* (PL 7125/2014)

The extreme cruelty in the making of *foie gras*, which involves purposefully inducing hepatic steatosis by force-feeding ducks or geese with huge amounts of food,[49] has been exposed by major animal protection organisations. Intensive advocacy work has resulted in increasing public outcry and support for a ban on its production and consumption globally.

Following the footsteps of other nations such as the Czech Republic, Denmark, Finland, Germany, Italy, Luxembourg, Norway, Poland and Israel,[50] Brazil has a bill to prohibit the selling of any product made from duck or goose liver obtained through forced feeding.[51] The bill is still being debated at the National Congress, and the only protection birds have against such horrendous practice are those provided by the municipal laws that have banned it locally.[52]

D. Slaughter of Pregnant Animals (PDL 387/2021)

While standard industrial animal agriculture practices are far from a compassionate ideal, they are especially harmful when performed on pregnant animals. Similarly to non-ambulatory animals, gestating animals are also in a delicate condition both physically and psychologically due to the alterations in their bodies. Being pregnant automatically puts females in a more vulnerable condition in comparison with non-pregnant peers. Because of that, it is not an exaggeration to say that there is an inextricable aggravated cruelty in farm industry practices performed on gestating animals.

Brazil, the world's largest beef exporter,[53] has adopted measures to protect pregnant animals. Slaughtering animals during the gestational period is considered mistreatment by the Animal Welfare and Defense Code of the State of Paraíba.[54] The State of Rio Grande do Sul does not allow the transport of animals

[49] Animal Equality, 'What is Foie Gras?' (10 May 2023), available at animalequality.org/blog/2022/02/08/what-is-foie-gras/#:~:text=Foie gras is one of,ten times its normal size.

[50] Vanessa Gischkow Garbini, 'A constitucionalidade da proibição do foie gras no brasil: um estudo à luz do re no 1030732 e da discussão sobre a competência legislativa municipal em matéria de meio ambiente e de proteção dos animais não-humanos' (2020) *Anais do VII Congresso Mundial de Bioética e Direito Animal* 378.

[51] Ban on Foie Gras, Bill No 7.125/2014, 'Prohibits the marketing of any food product made from duck or goose liver (foie gras), obtained through forced feeding of animals', available at www.camara.leg.br/propostas-legislativas/606202.

[52] Garbini (n 50) 393.

[53] Mustafa Zia, James Hansen, Kim Hjort and Constanza Valdes, 'Brazil Once Again Becomes the World's Largest Beef Exporter' USDA (1 July 2019), available at www.ers.usda.gov/amber-waves/2019/july/brazil-once-again-becomes-the-world-s-largest-beef-exporter.

[54] State law No 11.140/PB, Establishes the Code of Law and Animal Welfare of the State of Paraíba, 8 June 2018, Art 7, § 2, VII.

in an advanced state of gestation,[55] and a Decree from the same state mandates the disposal of the carcasses soon after slaughter (Article 121, III).[56]

However, all those advances are currently under threat. In 2021, a Federal Ordinance was created to regulate the handling of pregnant females and other practices performed on foetuses after the mother's slaughtering. Its Article 7 prohibits the slaughter or transport of pregnant females during the last 10 per cent of the gestational period, and has been harshly criticised by animal advocates.[57] It is considered a backlash in comparison to the total ban on transport and slaughter of gestating animals towards which the country had been previously leaning.

A coalition of animal protection organisations, supported by the Association of Agricultural Inspectors of the State of Rio Grande do Sul and the National Confederation of Workers in the Food and Related Industries, elaborated an open letter repudiating Article 7 of the Ordinance. At the same time, Bill 387 was proposed with the sole goal of suspending the same Article.[58] The bill's description of the matter supports that creating rules that protect animals is within the constitutional prohibition of animal cruelty commandment.[59]

The same coalition also filled a class action calling for a ban on transport and slaughter of females in advanced stages of pregnancy.[60] It all started after an undercover investigation revealed the outrageous situation of pregnant cows in the Brazilian agricultural system. Footages showed pregnant cows enduring a long journey to the slaughterhouse in a crowded truck, with no room to sit or lie down even for a second. The situation does not improve once they arrive at the slaughterhouse. When the mother is slaughtered, the calf often struggles too, dying from asphyxia.[61] Thus, when it comes to slaughtering gestating animals, the suffering of more than one sentient being might be at stake.

E. Multi-species Family (PL 179/2023)

This bill acknowledges the existence of multi-species families as communities composed by human beings and their companion animals (Article 1, §1).[62]

[55] State Law No 15.434/RS, Institutes the State Environmental Code of the State of Rio Grande do Sul, 9 January 2020, Art 13, III.

[56] State Decree No 53848, Regulates Law No 15,027 of August 21 2017, which provides for the inspection and supervision of products of animal origin in the State of Rio Grande do Sul, 21 December 2017, Art 13, III.

[57] ibid.

[58] Legislative Bill No 387, 'Suspends the application of art. 7 of Ordinance no. 365 of 16 July 2021 of the Agricultural Defense Secretariat of the Ministry of Agriculture, Livestock and Supply', available at www.camara.leg.br/propostas-legislativas/2294678.

[59] ibid.

[60] Animal Equality Brasil, 'Precisamos Impedir O Abate De Vacas Grávidas!', available at animalequality.org.br/participe/abate-vacas-prenhes.

[61] ibid.

[62] Multi-species family, Bill No 179/2023, 'Recognizes the multispecies family as a family entity', available at: www.camara.leg.br/proposicoesWeb/prop_mostrarintegra?codteor=2232359&filename=PL 179/2023.

Besides presenting a list of fundamental rights to pets (Article 2), the bill aims to regulate a wide range of situations a multi-species family may endure, such as divorce, requests for custody, and even their coexistence in condos.

Animals are considered totally incapable of performing any civil act by the bill, and must be legally represented. In fact, access to justice to seek existential, moral or material damages is one of the fundamental rights enjoyed by companion animals according to this bill.

F. Specialised Animal Protection Police Stations (PL 211/2023)

The increasing number of complaints about animal abuse and mistreatment prompted the proposal of this bill. It aims to create specialised police stations that will only deal with animal-related criminal cases involving wild or domestic species (Article 3).[63]

V. Conclusion

Sentience has been the guiding concept of Brazilian animal law from the outset. It is implicit in the constitutional prohibition of animal cruelty rule and the fundamentals of animal dignity, from which all fundamental rights stem. As seen in chapter one, animals' capacity of suffering was acknowledged even before the 1988 Constitution and the formal beginning of animals legal protection through a cutting-edge 1934 Decree that still serves as a interpretative legal resource today.

Following the constitutional command, animal protection spread within Brazilian legal order. It became either the main subject (eg states' animal protection statutes) or part of the content of laws (eg Article 32 of the Environmental Crimes Act) in the most different areas of law. Even where no formal change was made (eg Brazilian Civil Code), animal protection has been progressively accommodated the more animal law and the notion of animal dignity develops in the country.

Thus, the study of Brazil's animal welfare legal framework so far demonstrates that sentience is part of the past of the country's animal law (ie its origins). Yet, it did not stop there. The judiciary has been playing an essential role by reaffirming it, either directly (through an explicit reference to animal sentience) or indirectly (by acknowledging and applying Article 225, §1, VII of the Constitution as an animal law rule, created to grant individual rights to animals).

[63] Specialized Animal Protection Police Station, Bill No 211/2023, 'Provides for the creation and functioning of Specialized Animal Protection Police Stations', available at www.camara.leg.br/proposicoesWeb/prop_mostrarintegra?codteor=2232420&filename=PL 211/2023.

Brazilian animal jurisprudence, especially that of the Supreme Court, is proof that sentience is also part of the present of the country's legal culture. The rulings scrutinised in chapter two demonstrate that judges have been going above and beyond by resorting to comparative and international law, as well as animal ethics and rights scholarship to ground their pro-animals decisions.

Due to written or codified laws' important role in civil law tradition, the bills under debate by the legislative power is an excellent indicator of the direction the country is taking and the main values it intends to consecrate. Section IV provided an overview of some animal-related topics that are currently being debated by Brazilian political representatives, whose job is safeguarding society's claims through law in a democratic way.

Despite the divided opinions and political hindrances, Brazil's animal protection bills are quite promising. Covering a variety of topics, they range from specific subjects (eg a *foie gras* ban) to broader issues (eg a Statute for Animals) and, in general, propose progressive measures – some of which may even need further thought before being put into practice, or else they might backfire. All things considered, Brazilian animal-related bills point towards a better future for animals, when their sentience will hopefully not even be subject of debate.

Recognising animal sentience means overthrowing the fallacy of the cartesian separation between humans and animals. In order to erase this abstract human-created dividing line, Law, another abstract human-created science, might be a great tool. At least in the Brazilian legal system, it is possible to affirm that all roads – past, present and future – lead to the recognition of animal sentience.

8

The Judicial Recognition of Animal Sentience: Developments in Pakistan and India

HIRA JALEEL

I. Introduction

India and Pakistan have a lot in common. Both countries are former British colonies that gained independence in the year 1947, inheriting similar colonial laws and justice systems. Both countries, while internally very diverse, have somewhat similar cultures, languages and customs. Both countries also have similar political systems: both are democratic republics with a federalist structure and a tripartite system of government. In Pakistan, legislative and executive power is divided between the Federal Government and the four provincial governments, while in India, legislative and executive mandate is shared between the Central Government and 28 state governments. Another common factor between the two states has been the judiciary's active role in interpreting laws and constitutional provisions alike. The term 'judicial activism' in Pakistan and India is used to describe this unique phenomenon whereby elected judges sometimes step into the shoes of the legislature, or issue instructions to the legislature (despite the ostensibly strict separation of powers), especially when it comes to matters pertaining to the 'public interest'.[1]

The focus of this chapter is on the judiciary's role in recognising animal sentience and advancing animal protection in Pakistan and India. While the two countries are on different trajectories vis-à-vis legislative advancements in the field of animal protection, enforcement of animal protection laws has historically been inadequate and the legislature has been slow to act. Additionally, religious and cultural customs, some of which can be seen as being cruel to animals, have further

[1] Syed Jazib Shamim, 'A Review on Judicial Activism in Pakistan' [2018] Social Science Research Network, available at ssrn.com/abstract=3126641; and Jamie Cassels, 'Judicial Activism and Public Interest Litigation in India: Attempting the Impossible?' (1989) 37 *The American Journal of Comparative Law* 495, available at doi.org/10.2307/840090.

hindered political action on animal issues. In the absence of adequate legislative action, courts in both countries have stepped up to acknowledge animal sentience and to advance nonhuman animal interests. This has generally been accomplished by creatively interpreting existing constitutional provisions to conclude that nonhuman animals are rights-bearing beings and, in the case of India, to declare that animals are legal persons.

The goal of this chapter is to provide an overview of the steps taken in India and Pakistan, especially by the judiciary, to recognise animal sentience and advance animal protection through the law. The chapter will examine and analyse various approaches and justifications that have been employed by the judiciary in both countries to extend constitutional protections to nonhuman animals, and will examine the implications of granting personhood status to the entire animal kingdom, as has been done in India.[2]

Section II examines key animal protection legislation in India and Pakistan, and will attempt to explain some of the reasons behind why the animal protection legislation in the two countries has taken differing trajectories, despite both inheriting similar colonial-era anti-cruelty laws. Section III will examine certain landmark animal protection legislation in India and Pakistan, and explain why the legislative branch of government has historically refused to formally acknowledge animal sentience, requiring the courts to step in. Section IV will then discuss religious justifications employed by the judiciary in animal protection decisions to bolster the argument that animals are sentient beings deserving of legal protections, and will comment on why courts in these two countries feel the need to employ religio-legal arguments to boost the credibility of their decisions and to support the argument that animals are sentient beings. Finally, section V will analyse implications of judicial decisions that have recognised animal sentience (or in the case of India, declared all animals to be legal persons), and will argue that such declarations, while being the ultimate formal recognition of animal sentience, hold little meaning when it comes to enforcing the law to protect and serve the interests of animals.

In examining what it means to recognise 'sentience', this chapter defines the term as used by philosopher and author Martha Nussbaum in her book, *Justice for Animals*. This includes both an ability to apprehend the good and the bad, which in more rudimentary terms is the way sentience is usually understood: an aversion to pain and a movement towards pleasure or good. It also refers to a subjective awareness of the world coupled with a sense of salience, including making decisions based on what is significant for the animal, based on emotions that transcend simple pain or pleasure and include things such as fear, joy, grief, anger or compassion.[3]

[2] Through cases such as *Karnail Singh & ors v State of Haryana* (2019) SCC OnLine P&H 704 (India); and *Naryana Dutt Bhatt v Union of India & Ors* 2018 SCC OnLine Utt 645 (India).

[3] Martha Nussbaum, *Justice for Animals: Our Collective Responsibility* (Simon & Schuster, 2023) 126–31.

II. Animal Protection Laws in Pakistan and India

While animal sentience has not expressly been recognised either by India or Pakistan in their constitutional provisions or legislation, we see these laws, especially in India, acknowledge sentience in implicit ways. Despite this implicit recognition, no legislative measures have been taken in either Pakistan or India to transition the legal status of animals away from property, with animals' legal status very much remaining entrenched (though courts in India have declared animals to be legal persons, as will be discussed below).

A. The Indian Constitution

The cultural and religious makeup of India and Pakistan affects the animal protection laws (or lack thereof) in each country. While India is officially a secular state, almost 80 per cent of its population subscribes to Hinduism,[4] with Muslims being the largest religious minority at 14 per cent followed by Christians and other religious groups. Within Hinduism and in India in particular, the female cow has been considered sacred and has served as a long-standing symbol of resistance.[5] Cow protection, namely resistance to the slaughter of cows and beef consumption has been a part of Hindu nationalism and political resistance since at least the 1800s.[6] Even apart from the cow, many different animals have religious significance in Hindu culture, and have historically been revered or treated as sacred.[7] It is perhaps for this reason that animal protection is featured heavily in the Indian Constitution, with at least three constitutional provisions addressing animal protection in some shape or form.

Firstly, Article 48 of the Constitution of India, which forms part of the Directive Principles of State Policy, states that the state shall endeavour to organise agriculture and animal husbandry on modern and scientific lines and shall, in particular, take steps for preserving and improving the breeds and prohibiting the slaughter, of cows and calves and other milch and draught cattle. While on the one hand, the constitutional provision appears to be focused on improving animal production (premised on the continued exploitation of farmed animals), it also places emphasis on prohibiting the slaughter of cows and calves in particular (which, some scholars argue, is a nod to Hindu religious beliefs).[8]

[4] Stephanie Kramer, 'Population Growth and Religious Composition' (Pew Research Center's Religion & Public Life Project, 21 September 2021), available at www.pewresearch.org/religion/2021/09/21/population-growth-and-religious-composition.

[5] Sambaiah Gundimeda and VS Ashwin, 'Cow Protection in India: From Secularising to Legitimating Debates' (2018) 38 *South Asia Research* 156, available at doi.org/10.1177/0262728018768961.

[6] ibid.

[7] Lisa Kemmerer, 'Hindu ethics and Nonhuman Animals' (May 2014), available at www.la.utexas.edu/users/bump/Hindu%20Ethics%20and%20Nonhuman%20Animals.pdf.

[8] Ian Copland, 'Cows, Congress and the Constitution: Jawaharlal Nehru and the Making of Article 48' (2017) 40 *South Asia: Journal of South Asian Studies* 723.

In 1976, the 42nd Amendment to the Indian Constitution introduced two further provisions that directly or indirectly addressed animal protection. Article 48A encourages the state to protect and improve the environment and to safeguard the forests and wildlife of the country. Furthermore, Article 51(A)(g) imposes a fundamental duty on all Indian citizens to 'protect and improve the natural environment including forests, lakes, rivers and wildlife, and to have compassion for all living beings'. While the Indian Constitution does not explicitly acknowledge animal sentience, an implicit recognition is present insofar as the duty for all citizens to show compassion for all living beings. Firstly, the usage of the term 'living beings' instead of 'humans' or 'persons' indicates the legislature's intention to expand the circle of compassion to include the nonhuman world. Furthermore, Article 51(A)(g) has repeatedly been interpreted by Indian courts to include animals, which implies that animals are deserving of compassion. The use of the term 'compassion' here is also interesting since in ordinary English, it denotes consciousness or awareness of the distress of another and a desire to alleviate it.[9] It could be argued that by using the term 'compassion' and implying that animals feel distress, (which human beings have a fundamental duty to try and alleviate), the Indian Constitution gives a nod to animal sentience.

B. Indian Legislation and Federal Executive Actions

The primary anti-cruelty/animal welfare legislation in India, enacted at the Central Government level, is the Prevention of Cruelty to Animals Act 1960 (hereinafter referred to as 'the 1960 Act'). The law does not explicitly acknowledge animal sentience, but does so implicitly by recognising nonhuman animals' ability to feel pain and suffering, and also appreciating that animals suffer not only physically, but also mentally and emotionally. The term 'animal' is broadly defined to include 'any living creature other than a human being',[10] and the preamble of the law acknowledges that the law is intended to address the prevention of unnecessary pain and suffering on animals, thereby recognising that animals suffer. Additionally, section 9(e) of the 1960 Act, which deals with the functions of the Animal Welfare Board of India,[11] acknowledges that animals experience not only physical pain, but also mental pain and suffering in connection with slaughter, especially during the pre-slaughter stage.

The law also creates positive as well as negative duties vis-à-vis human beings and animals, which can be interpreted as an affirmation that not only do animals

[9] 'Compassion Definition & Meaning' (Merriam-Webster), available at www.merriam-webster.com/dictionary/compassion.

[10] Prevention of Cruelty to Animals Act, 1960 (the '1960 Act'), s 2(a).

[11] The Animal Welfare Board of India is a federal body established under s 4 of the 1960 Act, for the promotion of animal welfare generally and for the purpose of protecting animals from being subjected to unnecessary pain and suffering.

have the capacity to suffer, but also to flourish. For example, section 3 of the Act states that it is the duty of every person having the care or charge of an animal to take all reasonable measures to ensure its well-being, and to prevent the infliction of unnecessary pain and suffering on the animal. The twin goals of preventing suffering and promoting animal welfare are also found in other parts of the law.[12]

While the 1960 Act is one of the many pieces of animal protection legislation in India, after the Constitution, it is the most notable in terms of its implicit recognition of animal sentience.

In May 2013, the Central Government's Ministry of Forests and Environment issued a notification under the Wildlife (Protection) Act, 1972, prohibiting the establishment of any dolphinariums in the country. The notification further advised the state governments to reject proposals to establish dolphinariums that involve import or capture of cetacean species for commercial entertainment, exhibition or interaction.[13] The reasoning behind the decision explicitly acknowledged dolphin sentience and intelligence, with the Ministry stating that:

> Whereas cetaceans in general are highly intelligent and sensitive, and various scientists who have researched dolphin behaviour have suggested that their unusually high intelligence, as compared to other animals, means that dolphin should be seen as 'non-human persons' and as such should have their own specific rights and [that it] is morally unacceptable to keep them captive for entertainment purpose.
>
> Whereas cetacean in general do not survive well in captivity, [and] confinement in captivity can seriously compromise the welfare and survival of all types of ceteaceans by altering their behaviour and causing extreme distress.[14]

An analysis of the notification illustrates several points. Firstly, the notification contains a recognition that cetaceans in general are highly intelligent and sensitive, moving beyond a mere recognition of sentience but also acknowledging other traits besides an ability to feel pain and pleasure. Secondly, the Ministry notes that even among cetaceans, dolphins are unusually intelligent. On the one hand, this observation can be seen as problematic insofar that it apparently establishes a hierarchy among cetaceans based on intelligence, with dolphins at the higher rungs of this hierarchy and thus exempt from the pain and suffering inflicted on captive animals used for entertainment and exhibition. On the other hand, while the notification is an executive order and not legislation, it seems to confer personhood on dolphins and acknowledge that they should have rights, one of which would entitle them bodily liberty insofar as being free from captivity for the purposes of entertainment is concerned. Lastly, the Ministry is affirming that dolphins suffer tremendously under conditions of captivity and recognising that at least some of

[12] Such as s 4(1) and s 9(k) and (l) of the 1960 Act.

[13] Circular No F No 20-1/2010-CZA(M) dated 17 May 2013 issued by the Ministry of Environment, Forest and Climate Change India, available at awbi.gov.in/uploads/regulations/168257671136may_june2013_compressed.pdf.

[14] ibid.

this distress is mental/psychological in nature, as evidenced by the acknowledgement that captivity alters dolphin behaviour. Insofar as the recognition of sentience is concerned, the notification contains several encouraging observations regarding dolphin sentience in particular.

C. Constitution of Pakistan

In stark contrast to India, animal protection and recognition of animal sentience is completely missing from Pakistan's constitutional scheme. The Constitution of the Islamic Republic of Pakistan 1973 (the 'Pakistan Constitution') makes no mention of animals either in the chapter devoted to fundamental rights, or the principles of public policy. Although superior courts in Pakistan have interpreted certain constitutional provisions (such as Article 9, which deals with safeguarding a person's life or liberty) to include environmental protection and, more recently, animal protection, there is nothing in the text of the Pakistan Constitution that lends itself well to such interpretations.

D. Legislation – Pakistan

Similar to India, Pakistan's main anti-cruelty legislation is titled the Prevention of Cruelty to Animals Act 1890 ('the 1890 Act'). The 1890 Act has not been meaningfully updated since 1937, before Partition and when India (of which Pakistan was still a part) was still under colonial rule. Therefore, it is not inaccurate to say that the State of Pakistan has never legislated to formally or even implicitly recognise animal sentience in its main anti-cruelty legislation.[15] The 1890 Act prohibits inflicting unnecessary pain and suffering on nonhuman animals,[16] which are circularly defined as 'domestic' or 'captured' animals with neither of those terms being further defined.[17] Furthermore, unlike the Indian legislation, the 1890 Act does not place any emphasis on animal welfare or well-being, and instead focuses only on the prevention of cruelty to animals. In contrast to the Indian law, the 1890 Act also does not recognise animals' ability to experience mental or emotional pain. The 1890 Act can only be said to implicitly acknowledge animal sentience by virtue of its prohibition on infliction of unnecessary pain and suffering on animals, thereby conversely implying that animals have the capacity to experience pain and suffering. However, this recognition of sentience is limited to 'domestic' and 'captured' animals, and is not as expansive as that found in Indian legislation. At

[15] Under s 18 of the Indian Independence Act 1947, all Acts of Parliament, Orders of Council, orders, rules or regulations made before independence as part of the law of British India continued in force as laws of India and Pakistan, until repealed or replaced by the legislatures of the respective countries. Therefore, Pakistan and India inherited the exact same laws upon partition.

[16] s 3 of the Prevention of Cruelty to Animals Act, 1890 (the '1890 Act').

[17] s 2(a) of the 1890 Act.

the time of writing this chapter, almost all express recognition of animal sentience in Pakistan has been through the judiciary, making the judicial arm a key player in recognising and protecting animal interests in the country.

III. Judicial Efforts to Recognise Animal Sentience

As section II above outlined, animal sentience is not expressly acknowledged in either Indian or Pakistani constitutional provisions or legislation, but is implicitly acknowledged to varying extents in both (with India having stronger recognition than Pakistan). This section will examine certain landmark animal protection decisions from both jurisdictions and examine the animal sentience-based justifications used by the court to link and expand human beings' constitutional right to life to include the right to life for nonhuman animals.[18]

A. India

The most notable case from India that set the tone for recognition of animal sentience and protection of animal rights was the landmark decision issued by a Division Bench[19] of the Supreme Court of India's in *Animal Welfare Board of India v Nagaraja*.[20] The *Nagaraja* decision laid the groundwork for other important animal protection jurisprudence emerging from India, but its impact was recently tempered by another decision of the Supreme Court in *Animal Welfare Board of India v Union of India*,[21] as will be discussed below.

The case related to various challenges to the cultural and traditional practices of bull-cart racing and *Jallikattu* (a sport whereby people attach themselves to the horns of bulls in an attempt to tame them) in the Indian States of Tamil Nadu and Maharashtra. The judgment starts by laying down the facts of the case and recording the arguments of counsel. Immediately afterwards, the Supreme Court notes that since the cases being adjudicated arose out of the 1960 Act, the standard the court will apply is one of 'species-best interest'. The justification for this is that the court is dealing with a welfare legislation of 'a sentient being, over which human beings have domination'.[22] Right off the bat then, the judgment acknowledges that the animals in question (bulls) are sentient and that the 1960 Act is a legislation

[18] In cases such as *Islamabad Wildlife Management Board v. Metropolitan Corporation Islamabad* 2021 CLC 262 (Pakistan); and *Animal Welfare Board of India v Nagaraja and Ors* 2014 (7) SCC 547 (India).

[19] A Division bench consists of two to three judges. In this case, it was a two-judge bench.

[20] *Animal Welfare Board of India v Nagaraja and Ors* 2014 (7) SCC 547 (India).

[21] Decision dated 18 May 2023 in Writ Petition No 23 of 106 and ors, available at main.sci.gov.in/supremecourt/2016/1216/1216_2016_3_1501_44624_Judgement_18-May-2023.pdf.

[22] *Nagaraja* (n 20) para 12.

enacted for their welfare. The court then proceeds to quote from a report filed by the board, which describes natural behaviours of bulls at great length, including their eating patterns and social behaviours, noting that bulls' natural tendency, when faced with threats, is to flee and not fight.[23] The report also observes that when separated from their herd, bulls experience mental anguish and anxiety, in another nod to the emotional suffering of the animals.[24] Additionally, the report notes how, when forced to engage in the practice of *Jallikattu*, bulls cannot escape and suffer mental as well as physical harm when, as the court puts it, they are 'pushed, hit, prodded [and] abused'.[25]

In describing the harms inflicted on bulls before, during and after *Jallikattu*, the report uses a mix of scientific information and legal provisions to draw out some other features of the animals that affirm their sentience. For example, when describing how the ears of bulls are frequently cut by their owners (in a misplaced attempt to improve the animal's hearing), the report acknowledges that bulls whose ears have been 'mutilated' resist being touched around the head because of 'painful past experiences'.[26] This observation affirms that the animals have a subjective view of the world and can remember past harms inflicted on them. In further describing how bulls are mistreated, the report (and the Supreme Court's judgment) refers to 'mental trauma', the bulls being 'terrified', and frequent defecation and urination being 'indicators of fear and pain' to confirm that the animals are not merely objects, but sentient beings who are severely harmed, both emotionally and physically, as a result of these practices.

The court notes that section 3 the 1960 Act places certain duties on human beings, and correspondingly, confers rights on the animals.[27] It observes that the festival/practice of *Jallikattu* does not safeguard the well-being of the animal, but instead deprives bulls of their rights under the 1960 Act and also uses the animals as instruments, ignoring their intrinsic worth. Through this observation, the Supreme Court acknowledges that animals have inherent value and worth, and should not merely be treated as a means to an end[28] (an argument similar to one contemporary Kantian philosophers like Christine Korsgaard have made in arguing for expanding our moral circle of concern to animals).[29]

The manner in which the judgment acknowledges sentience clearly goes beyond the simple understanding that animals avoid pain and seek pleasure. The Supreme Court of India is obviously attempting to acknowledge that animals have a subjective view of the world and therefore, their experiences involve an awareness of their environment. Furthermore, there is a recognition that the suffering

[23] ibid para 13.
[24] ibid para 17.
[25] ibid para 15.
[26] ibid para 17.
[27] ibid para 27.
[28] ibid para 27.
[29] Christine M Korsgaard, *Fellow Creatures: Our Obligations to the Other Animals* (Oxford University Press, 2018).

of animals has an emotional as well as physical component when subjected to prolonged pain and suffering:

> Suffering has the same function [as pain], but instead of informing the animal about stimuli to avoid, which informs it about a situation to avoid. An animal might be regarded as suffering, if is in pain, distress, or acute or unduly prolonged discomfort. Consequently, to experience the suffering, the animal needs an awareness of its environment, the ability to develop moods that coordinate a behavioural response, and the capacity to change adverse situation or avoid them.[30]

The Supreme Court also acknowledges that animals have inherent dignity and a right to have their well-being protected, which again, goes beyond the simple concept of seeking pleasure.[31] In talking about the anthropocentric bias that humans often have towards animals, the court not only recognises the inherent worth of the animals, but also their dignity, honour and the right to privacy.[32] When discussing the human right to life, guaranteed under Article 21 of India's Constitution, the Court states that as far as animals are concerned, the term 'life' means something more than mere survival or existence or instrumental value for human beings, but to lead a life with some intrinsic worth, honour and dignity.[33]

It is however, important to note that despite the Court's acknowledgment that animals are sentient beings protected as such under law, the judgment also holds that under the 'doctrine of necessity', rights afforded to nonhuman animals by the 1960 Act are limited by human beings' need to use animals for various purposes.[34] The Court therefore holds that the exceptions under the 1960 Act, which dealt with destruction of stray dogs, experimentation on animals and killing animals for food are carved out because of necessity (although the Court does observe that these are also forms of speciesism within society).[35] Hence, the Court does not hold animal rights to be absolute but instead holds them to be subject to the restrictions imposed by the law (which are all a result of the human need to use animals). At the same time, however, the Court holds that activities like *Jallikattu* or bull-cart racing, which cause serious pain and suffering for the animals for recreation, entertainment or human pleasure, are non-essential activities and thus the animals' rights to be treated in a dignified manner are violated by these activities.[36]

When discussing whether bulls are inherently performing animals, the Supreme Court notes that the bodies of bulls, their gait and their historic usage (as draught animals) disfavours the idea that bulls are performing animals.[37] The

[30] *Nagarja* (n 20) para 30.
[31] ibid para 32.
[32] ibid para 51.
[33] ibid para 62.
[34] ibid para 71.
[35] ibid para 31.
[36] ibid para 61.
[37] ibid para 33.

Court notes that bulls are not anatomically designed to run fast and cannot be used for racing, comparing them to horses, whose anatomy, according to the court, makes them faster and thus able to be used for racing.[38] This part of the judgment attempts to inject some sort of equity into the process of determining whether an animal can be used as a performing animal, but falls prey to the same speciesist and anthropocentric reasoning that the Court critiques throughout the judgment. A 'performing animal' is an inherently anthropocentric and arbitrary term, with both the types of performances and animals chosen to participate determined by human beings. Of course, no animal is inherently meant to perform for humans, and who qualifies as a performing animal in any society could widely vary by historical, cultural and social influences. By noting that bulls are biologically unfit to race, and horses inherently better at participating in racing, the Court fails to acknowledge that regardless of whether horses or bulls are used, the activity is one solely meant to benefit human beings and not the animals themselves (and that the animals have not consented to participate in these races).

Eventually, the court held that *Jallikattu*, bull-cart racing and other such events violate the 1960 Act and declared that bulls cannot be used as performing animals either for *Jallikattu* or bull-cart races in the States of Tamil Nadu, Maharashtra or anywhere else in the country.[39] The Court declared that the legal rights guaranteed to bulls under the 1960 Act could not be taken away or restricted except as the law itself allows. It also declared that it expects Parliament to elevate the rights of animals to the status of constitutional rights so as to protect their honor and dignity.[40]

The *Nagaraja* judgment has proven to be the building block for other cases that have relied on the decision to take a step further and delve into questions of animal rights and animal legal personhood. For example, the Uttarkhand High Court in the case of *Narayan Dutt Bhatt v Union of India and ors*[41] went as far as to declare the entire animal kingdom, including avian and aquatic species, as being legal entities with a distinct persona, having corresponding duties, rights and liabilities of a living person. Similarly, the Punjab-Haryana High Court in *Karnail Singh & ors v State of Haryana* also declared the entire animal kingdom to be legal entities, and declared all citizens throughout the State of Haryana to be persons in *loco parentis* as the human face for the welfare/protection of animals.[42] Both these cases relied on *Nagaraja* to arrive at their conclusions, taking an express acknowledgement of animal sentience one step further into fully fledged animal personhood.

[38] ibid.
[39] ibid para 77.
[40] ibid.
[41] *Naryana Dutt Bhatt v Union of India & Ors* 2018 SCC OnLine Utt 645 (India).
[42] *Karnail Singh & ors v State of Haryana* (2019) SCC OnLine P&H 704 (India).

B. Pakistan

In May 2020, Pakistan's Islamabad High Court rendered an unprecedented decision in *Islamabad Wildlife Management Board v Metropolitan Corporation Islamabad*.[43] Authored by the court's Chief Justice, J Athar Minallah, the decision resulted in the shutting down of the Marghazar Zoo in Pakistan's capital city, Islamabad.[44] All the zoo's animals, among them an Asian elephant named Kaavan, were ordered to be relocated to appropriate sanctuaries either within Pakistan or abroad.[45] The Court's judgment, hereinafter referred to as the '*Kaavan* decision', was groundbreaking in several important ways. Firstly, it recognised that nonhuman animals have certain natural and legal rights, which are implied and protected by the relevant anti-cruelty legislation in Pakistan.[46] Secondly, the decision linked the rights of animals with the right to life and liberty of human beings as enshrined in Article 9 of Pakistan's Constitution, by concluding that animal maltreatment violates the fundamental right to life and that state authorities have a duty to prevent cruelty against animals.[47]

Gifted to Pakistan by the Sri Lankan Government in 1985,[48] Kaavan had resided in the zoo for the better part of four decades at the time of the Court's decision. After his sole elephant partner at the zoo, Saheli, died due to infection in 2012, Kaavan quickly became depressed and aggressive, resulting in him being kept chained.[49] Kaavan also exhibited clear signs of psychological distress, including swaying and pressing his head into a wall. His plight resulted in him being referred to as the 'world's loneliest elephant'.[50]

In 2019, a petition was filed before the Islamabad High Court, challenging the conditions in which animals were kept at the zoo and seeking that Kaavan be relocated to a sanctuary.[51] Deciding this petition along with two others, the Court posed two fundamental questions: Do nonhuman animals have legally enforceable rights? And does the Constitution impose duties on the state to safeguard the welfare of nonhuman animals?[52] The Court answered both these questions in the affirmative. In reaching its conclusions, it examined international and domestic animal law jurisprudence, including, notably, efforts made by the Nonhuman Rights Project and PETA in the US.[53]

[43] *Islamabad Wildlife Management Board v Metropolitan Corporation of Islamabad* (2021) PLD (Islamabad) 6 (Pak).
[44] ibid.
[45] ibid.
[46] ibid.
[47] ibid.
[48] ibid.
[49] Rachel Nuwer, 'How Cher Helped Rescue the World's Loneliest Elephant' *Smithsonian Magazine* (21 April 2021), available at www.smithsonianmag.com/science-nature/how-cher-helped-rescue-worlds-loneliest-elephant-180977562.
[50] ibid.
[51] *Islamabad Wildlife Management Board* (n 43).
[52] ibid.
[53] ibid.

In noting the conditions in which the animals were being kept in the zoo, the Court noted that the animals are suffering 'pain, distress and agony'. With respect to Kaavan specifically, who was exhibiting tell-tale signs of zoochosis, ie swaying and bobbing his head as well as pressing his head against the wall of his enclosure, the Court observed that Kaavan was expressing loneliness, distress and suffering. The court observed that Asian elephants are intelligent, social beings, with emotions similar to those of human beings and that Happy the elephant (residing in the Bronx Zoo in New York) has also passed the mirror test. The Court noted that:

> They [elephants] feel pain, disress, happiness as well as sadness. The birth of a baby elephant is celebrated while they cry and mourn the death of a member of the herd … Kaavan is indeed suffering and is being treated in a manner that has subjected him to unnecessary pain and suffering. He is lonely and the extent of his suffering is unimaginable.

With respect to the question of whether animals have legal rights, J Minallah concluded that nonhuman animals are the subject of a life and sentient beings, who have emotions and can feel pain or joy. Therefore, they possess certain natural rights, such as the right to live in an environment that meets their social, behavioural and physiological needs and the right to not be subjected to unnecessary pain and suffering.[54] The Court found these natural rights have been codified within the anti-cruelty law in Pakistan, specifically the 1890 Act, which prohibits, among other things, subjecting animals to unnecessary pain and suffering.[55] Hence, according to the Court, since animals have certain natural rights recognised by law, they possess legal rights, which the Court defined, relying on *Black's Law Dictionary*, as 'a right related to or recognised by law'.[56] This holding by the Court is also interesting because it draws from a nineteenth-century statute to establish the relatively recent concept of 'animal rights' in Pakistan's legal context, even though it is highly unlikely that the drafters of the 1890 Act had any conception of animal rights in mind.

Because the zoo authorities were not fulfilling their obligations to its inhabitants and were subjecting the animals to unnecessary pain and suffering, the Court ordered the zoo be shut down and the animals relocated to sanctuaries.[57] By the end of 2020, all the animals from the zoo, including Kaavan, had been relocated to various sanctuaries.[58]

The *Kaavan* decision has also been groundbreaking in terms of starting a wave of successful animal law litigation in Pakistan, with other High Courts and

[54] ibid.
[55] ibid.
[56] ibid.
[57] ibid.
[58] Rvel Zahid, 'Lonely Elephant Kaavan Moves to Cambodia from Controversial Islamabad Zoo' Zenger News (6 December 2020), available at www.zenger.news/2020/12/06/lonely-elephant-kaavan-moves-to-cambodia-from-controversial-islamabad-zoo.

regulatory bodies relying on the principles enshrined in *Kaavan* to affirm animal sentience and rights. One such example is the case of *Zawar Hussain v Province of Punjab*, decided by the Lahore High Court in 2022.[59]

The case arose out of a notification issued by the Punjab Wildlife and Parks Department banning the use of electronic decoys, mojos and pre-charged pneumatic airguns in hunting. The governing law, the Punjab Wildlife (Protection, Preservation, Conservation and Management) Act 1974, already prohibited the use of live decoys in hunting.[60] However, hunters had increasingly been using electronic decoys to hunt waterfowl since the law did not expressly address their use, leading to a decline in the waterfowl population in the province of Punjab.[61] The ban was challenged by the petitioner, a hunter, on the grounds that the department had exceeded its jurisdiction by imposing a ban the law did not expressly envision.[62]

In ultimately upholding the ban, the Lahore High Court partially relied on the *Kaavan* decision to affirm that since animals are sentient beings, they have legal rights, including the right to life, and that it is the duty of the state to ensure these rights are not infringed upon.[63] Since one of the core purposes of the Punjab Wildlife Act 1974 is to protect wildlife, the Court held that the Wildlife Department has discretion to adopt measures to protect the lives of wild animals and birds.[64]

Therefore, even though the Lahore High Court was not bound by the *Kaavan* decision, it adopted *Kaavan*'s principles and declared that animals have legal rights, further linking those rights to Article 9 of the Pakistan Constitution. The adoption of the holding in *Kaavan* by the Lahore High Court, which is the High Court for Pakistan's most populous province, indicates further entrenchment of animal rights within Pakistan's jurisprudence.

As the decisions discussed above illustrate, while legislation in Pakistan and India recognise animal sentience to varying extents, it is in fact the courts in both countries that have gone beyond the implicit recognition of sentience present in legislation to explicitly acknowledging animal sentience, by conceding that animals are complex, social creatures with a subjective view of the world. Judicial recognition of animal sentience in both countries has accomplished what legislation has not, and has elevated the status of animals under the law by stating that anti-cruelty legislation affords animals legal rights, and places corresponding duties on human beings to have regard for animal sentience and nonhuman animals' unique needs.

[59] *Zawar Hussain v. Province of Punjab* (2022) PLD (Lahore) 445 (Pak).
[60] The Punjab Wildlife (Protection, Preservation, Conservation and Management) Act 1974, s 9.
[61] *Zawar Hussain* (n 59).
[62] ibid.
[63] ibid.
[64] ibid.

IV. Religious Recognition of Animal Sentience in Jurisprudence

This section will discuss religious justifications employed by the judiciary in animal protection decisions to bolster the argument that animals are sentient beings deserving of legal protection.[65] Given the deeply religious contexts of both countries, such justifications are helpful, if not necessary, to lend credence to the argument that the interests of animals should be considered on a somewhat equal footing to those of human beings.

A. India

Although India is a secular country with a secular constitution, religion plays an important role in the country and, as highlighted in the introduction, has historically done so even in the context of constitutional animal protection. Therefore, it might be unsurprising that the judiciary in India often relies on religious justifications to bolster animal sentience arguments in animal-related cases. Such arguments highlight the recognition of animal sentience in the underlying religious laws, and therefore add strength to the judgments. For example, the *Nagaraja* case, when discussing whether practices like bull-cart racing and *Jallikattu* are an inherent part of Tamil tradition and culture, relies on ancient Hindu texts of the Isha-Upanishads, from which it reproduces the following quote: 'The universe along with its creatures belongs to the land. No creature is superior to any other. Human beings should not be above nature. Let no one species encroach over the rights and privileges of other species.'[66] While this excerpt does not expressly acknowledge sentience, it puts animals and the natural world on an equal ground to human beings. This portion of the judgment, along with other parts, were later relied on in *Narayan Dutt Bhatt* to draw a clearer connection to sentience. In *Narayan Dutt Bhatt*, the Uttarkhand High Court notes that cruelty to animals is a cause for psychological pain to them and that: 'In Hindu Mythology, every animal is associated with [a] God. Animals breathe like us and have emotions. The animals require food, water, shelter, normal behavior, medical care, self-determination.'[67] The Uttarkhand High Court uses this argument (with its clearly religiously grounded justification) to conclude that every species has an inherent right to live and to be protected by the law, and that such protection does not just extend to a protection from pain but also extends to animals' right to be healthy, comfortable, well-nourished, safe and able to express innate behaviour without pain, fear and stress.[68] Hence, the High Court relies, at least in part, on religious

[65] ibid.
[66] *Nagaraja* (n 20) para 44.
[67] *Narayan* (n 41) para 83.
[68] ibid para 98.

justifications, both in its own decision and from *Nagaraja* to conclude that animals are sentient beings and deserve the status of legal entity/legal person.

However, in other cases, especially those having to do with animal sacrifice on religious grounds, some courts in India have also given priority to animal sentience over religious justifications for continued exploitation. For example, in *Ramesh Sharma v State of Himanchal Pradesh & Ors*,[69] a case challenging the practice of animal sacrifice in Hindu temples in the State of Himachal Pradesh, the Himanchal Pradesh High Court held that animal sacrifice is not an inherent part of Hindu religion[70] (or even if it was, modern sensibilities dictate that society move away from the practice). Additionally, the Court held that constitutional values take precedence over personal religious values and because animals have emotions and feelings (are sentient), religion cannot be allowed to become a tool to inflict unchecked pain and misery on animals.[71] The Court therefore banned the practice of animal/bird sacrifice in temples and public places throughout the State of Himanchal Pradesh.

We therefore see courts in India draw on religious justifications to lend credence to the argument for recognising animal sentience, but at the same time in certain cases, when the recognition of sentience directly conflicts with religious freedom, certain courts have given priority to acknowledging sentience and upholding legal rights for nonhuman animals.

B. Pakistan

Unlike India, Pakistan's constitutional scheme is not secular. Pakistan is an Islamic Republic, and therefore, all laws made by the legislature must not only conform to broader constitutional principles, but also the injunctions of Islam. It is for this reason that the judiciary has a greater incentive to not only rely on constitutional and legal provisions, but also Islamic principles in its decisions.

For example, in the *Kaavan* decision, the Islamabad High Court similarly relies extensively on sources of Islamic law to bolster the argument for legal rights for nonhuman animals. The judgment notes that 'there is consensus amongst all religions of the world that animals are 'sentient beings i.e. able to perceive and feel'. However, since Pakistan is a primarily Muslim country and officially an Islamic Republic, the Court chooses to focus on sources of Islamic law for the purposes of the decision. Some of the quotes from the *Quran* and *Ahadith* reproduced in the judgment clearly emphasise the sentience of nonhuman animals, for example:

> Although there is no animal that walks on earth and no bird that flies on its two wings which is not God's creature like yourself.
>
> *Surrah Al-Anam 6:38*

[69] *Ramesh Sharma v State of Himanchal Pradesh & Ors.* 2014 SCC Online HP 4679.
[70] ibid para 82.
[71] ibid para 83.

> Seest thou not that it is Allah Whose praise all beings in the heavens and on earth do celebrate, and the birds (of the air) with wings outspread? Each one knows its own (mode of) prayer and praise, and Allah knows well all that they do.
>
> *Surrah An-Noor 24:41*

The quotations exhibit a clear bent towards acknowledging that humans and animals are on an equal footing and that, for the higher power, while animals might not act or behave exactly the same way human beings do, does not mean they do not share similar qualities or intentions.

Reliance on religious justifications for supporting animal sentience in Pakistan could be a double-edged sword. While religious arguments are perhaps easier to make when discussing captive wild animals, Islamic sources can also be relied upon for example to support the continued consumption of farmed animals or to justify causing harm to stray dogs. In India, the secular nature of the courts give judges more leeway when invoking religious justifications for animal protection. However, the fact remains that the primary motivation for some of India's constitutional animal protection provisions, as well as at least some animal protection legislation, is primarily religion and religious beliefs around protecting certain sacred animals, such as cows.[72] On the other hand, in Pakistan, an animal-friendly law can potentially be struck down on the basis of religion alone. Going forward, it would be interesting to note how the judiciary continues to employ religious arguments either in favour of or against animal protection in the region.

V. Animal Personhood and the Path Forward

On the face of it, judicial recognition of animal sentience appears to be a promising step towards meaningful protection of animal interests through the law. This is and is not the case. This chapter will draw out some of the arguments why animal advocates tracking judicial developments on animal sentience in this region of the world ought to be cautious when celebrating the progress made for animals through the courts.

Firstly, even though courts have acknowledged animal sentience, even beyond the rudimentary concept of sentience as the ability to feel pain and pleasure (to acknowledging that animals have subjective experiences and require more from their surroundings than a simple ability to avoid pain and seek out pleasure), the recognition of sentience remains subservient to human needs and desires. In the *Nagaraja* case, the Supreme Court of India lays down a limiting test in the form of 'doctrine of necessity', which allows animal exploitation in the form of animal testing and consuming animals for food, even though the Court expressly states

[72] A list of India's various cow protection laws (as of December 2018) can be found www.hrw.org/sites/default/files/report_pdf/india0219_appendix_1.pdf.

that this is a form of speciesism. Similarly, the practices that formed the underlying premise of the case, ie festivals and cultural traditions that exploit animals for entertainment, were not absolutely prohibited. While on the one hand, the Court attempts to alleviate suffering of bulls by recognising that anatomically, psychologically and physically, bulls are not meant to be performing animals, it also throws other performing animals like horses under the bus by implying that those animals are somehow better suited to use in races and performances. Therefore, on closer reading, *Nagaraja* reads like a censure of specific practices using a certain animal (the bull), not a general critique of using animals for performances or entertainment (whether commercially or as part of a cultural festival).

In the case of Pakistan, similarly, even though the *Kaavan* case ostensibly acknowledges sentience for all animals, not just Asian elephants, the case does not comment on the myriad of ways animals are exploited for human use outside of the zoo context, and what implications the decision may have for those animals (since the Court does declare all animals, not just elephants, to possess legal rights and draws linkages between those rights and constitutional rights).

Secondly, it is difficult to establish what the judicial recognition of animal sentience changes for nonhuman animals in practice, outside the limited immediate effect of the judgments themselves. For example, the Indian case law discussed in the preceding sections culminates in at least two High Courts in India declaring the entire animal kingdom to be 'legal persons'. However, the judgments refuse to delve into the complicated and messy question of what that changes in the day-to-day lives of nonhuman animals in the respective states. Are animals now able to bring legal challenges on their own behalf? Can human beings not exploit animals because they are legal persons and thus have inalienable rights? It doesn't appear that the decisions foresee grand changes beyond the immediate evil they're looking to address, despite pronouncements of animal legal personhood and legal rights for animals. Iin the *Kaavan* decision, even though animals are held to have legal rights, it is unclear whether the decision has had any real impact beyond the release of animals from the Marghzar zoo to sanctuaries at home and abroad (and this section argues, in fact, that it did not).

Arguably, one positive impact of these decisions has been to embolden other courts into passing similar pro-animal judgments. For example, the *Nagaraja* case is relied upon in both *Narayan Dutt Bhatt* and *Karnail Singh*, which dive into questions of animal legal personhood. Similarly, *Kaavan* has been relied upon in decisions by for eg the Lahore High Court, upholding governmental actions aiming to protect wild animals.[73]

However, besides their precedential value, it is not immediately obvious what the impact of these decisions are. In fact, some recent developments in both India and Pakistan seem to indicate a retrogression from the pro-animal stance taken by

[73] *Zawar Hussain* (n 59).

the decisions discussed above. For example, after the *Nagaraja* decision, the States of Tamil Nadu,[74] Maharashtra[75] and Karnataka[76] passed laws circumventing the decision in *Nagaraja* and allowing for practices such as *Jallikattu* and bull-cart racing to continue in those states. The new laws legitimised the practices while at the same time regulating the way the festivals are carried out, inserting provisions to account for aspects of animal welfare (such as stipulating the length of the race, time for rest periods, prohibition on physically abusing the animals, etc). The laws were challenged before the Supreme Court of India on the grounds that the state legislatures, by enacting these laws, are seeking to circumvent the Court's decision in *Nagaraja.* In its second decision on this issue in *Animal Welfare Board of India v Union of India*,[77] the Supreme Court of India adopted a much more restrained position than it originally had in *Nagaraja.* For starters, while the Court reaffirmed animal sentience, it refused to acknowledge that animals hold any constitutionally guaranteed fundamental rights[78] and also denied that animals are considered legal persons under India's constitutional scheme, capable of bringing suits or petitions by themselves, leaving that question to be decided by the legislature.[79]

On the question of whether the new state laws circumvent the Court's holding in *Nagaraja*, the Supreme Court of India held that they do not, on the grounds that new laws attempt to regulate the manner in which the practices are carried out and attempt to cater more to the welfare of the animals than was previously the case[80] (while acknowledging that even despite the amendment in the laws, there cannot be any guarantees that bulls will experience no pain and suffering when used during these events.)

Interestingly enough, in the *Animal Welfare Board* decision, the Supreme Court addresses the incongruity in *Nagaraja*, whereby the Court had held that the practices in question are particularly cruel to bulls because bulls are not designed to be performing animals, while horses are. In ruling on whether the new laws were arbitrary and unreasonable, the Court considers that the 1960 Act allows for infliction of pain and suffering on sentient animals out of human necessity, and that there is no logical need to single bulls out for this purpose. In fact, the Court also cites the sentience of horses and animals that are slaughtered for food to make the point that infliction of pain and suffering is necessary if animals are to be used by human beings, but what the Court can consider is whether the degree of pain and suffering is unnecessary. It therefore concludes that it is up to the legislature to decide whether a particular form of animal use is unnecessary, and refrains from commenting on whether it is appropriate to use bulls for entertainment (as the

[74] Through the Prevention of Cruelty to Animals (Tamil Nadu Amendment) Act, 2017.
[75] Through the Prevention of Cruelty to Animals (Maharashtra Amendment) Act, 2017.
[76] Through the Prevention of Cruelty to Animals (Karnataka Second Amendment) Act, 2017.
[77] *Union of India* (n 21).
[78] ibid para 24.
[79] ibid.
[80] ibid para 28.

Court in *Nagaraja* had done).[81] While this position is more intellectually consistent than that of the Court in *Nagaraja*, the result strips bulls of the protection they had been afforded by the *Nagaraja* Court (against being used as performing animals).

Overall, while the *Animal Welfare Board* decision continued to reaffirm the sentience of animals, it also stripped bulls of many of the protections allowed under *Nagaraja*, and essentially allowed the practices that had been challenged under the original decision to continue. Furthermore, the Court also expressly refused to acknowledge the legal personhood of nonhuman animals, or that they have constitutionally guaranteed fundamental rights under Article 21 of the Indian Constitution. This decision challenges the premise that judicial recognition of animal sentience has much meaning to begin with, or whether the judiciary is even the appropriate forum for such recognition, considering that the legislature can step in to undo the effects of such judicial pronouncements (as was clearly attempted in this case).

Similarly, in Pakistan, after the progressive decision in the *Kaavan* case, one might have anticipated the conditions for animals in Pakistan's zoos, especially elephants, to improve. While the *Kaavan* decision was not binding on all zoos in Pakistan, the lack of impact it had on any zoo outside the Marghzar Zoo is significant. In April 2023, a 17-year-old African elephant named Noor Jehan, housed in the Karachi Zoo – a government-run facility in Pakistan Sindh's province, collapsed after falling in a pond. Noor Jehan had been suffering from an undiagnosed ailment that left her back legs severely weakened, and became the subject of national and international attention after public outcry over the lack of appropriate care and attention she and three other African elephants had been receiving at the zoo.[82] After Noor Jehan's death, despite immense public pressure to relocate the remaining three elephants to suitable elephant sanctuaries abroad, no governmental or judicial action has been taken to do so, with the three remaining elephants likely to live out the rest of their lives in captivity and under conditions of neglect in the zoo.

Lastly, it is pertinent to frame any legislative or judicial advancements in recognising animal sentience within this region in the appropriate cultural, religious and political context. As was seen in the case of the Indian Supreme Court's attempt to ban the long-standing cultural festival of *Jallikattu*, cultural and social sentiments can often lead to immense public pressure which limits the changes the judiciary can or is willing to make to the lives of animals, even if sentience is expressly recognised. In India specifically, questions of animal protection can be fraught with tensions with other social justice movements, and have, in the past, been

[81] ibid para 31.

[82] Alex Hardie, Sugam Pokharel and Ivana Kottasová, 'Critically Ill Elephant Noor Jehan Dies at Pakistan Zoo' (CNN, 22 April 2023), available at www.cnn.com/2023/04/22/asia/pakistan-karachi-zoo-elephant-death-intl/index.html.

linked to attempts by the Government to oppress religious minorities.[83] Similarly, in Pakistan, since all laws are tested on religious grounds, courts and legislatures must find religious support for all animal decisions, which can be a difficult line to tread.

VI. Conclusion

The rich cultural, political and religious landscapes of Pakistan and India make the two countries interesting case studies from an animal law perspective. Despite inheriting the exact same colonial laws at independence, Pakistan and India have taken very different trajectories when it comes to animal protection through legislation. When it comes to judicial decisions that recognise animal sentience or attempt to cement animal rights within the existing legal framework, the two nations' judiciaries have followed somewhat parallel paths, though jurisprudence from India is still ahead in terms of the number of favourable animal protection decisions and how far those decisions go. Despite the developments in recognising animal sentience through the judiciary, it is not immediately clear how much impact notable animal law decisions have had on the lives of nonhuman animals in India and Pakistan, outside the immediate cases they concern. Nevertheless, despite the limitations and practical difficulties with implementing changes as a result of recognising animal sentience, the developments in Pakistan and India on this front, especially through the judiciary, have been some of the most progressive anywhere in the world, and have undoubtedly contributed to the advancement of animal law jurisprudence (and hopefully firmer embodiment of animal sentience within the law). The South Asian region is one to keenly watch in the future for further developments in this space.

[83] 'Deaths Raise Fresh Fears over Cow Vigilantism in India' (BBC News, 8 May 2023), available at www.bbc.com/news/world-asia-india-65229522.

9

Legal Recognition of Sentience in New Zealand

MB RODRIGUEZ FERRERE

I. Introduction

New Zealand explicitly recognised in legislation the sentience of non-human animals in 2015. The Animal Welfare Amendment Act (No 2) 2015 amended the long title – a type of preamble – of the Animal Welfare Act 1999, such that it now reads: 'An Act … to reform the law relating to the welfare of animals and the prevention of their ill-treatment; and, in particular … to recognise that animals are sentient'. At the time of this enactment, Government and regulatory agencies predicted that the amendment would have no significant legal effect, so long as the recognition remained in the preambular section of the Act. Other commentators expected the amendment to represent a sea change in the way animals were treated and viewed in New Zealand law.[1]

This chapter will review the history behind – and the impact of – this amendment. It proceeds in two sections. First, it briefly reviews New Zealand's animal welfare legislative history and the steps leading to the 2015 amendment. Second, it assesses the impact of that amendment both within the courts and beyond. The chapter will conclude that the recognition of animal sentience in the Animal Welfare Act has not had any significant direct legal effect. However, the introduction of the concept into the law has had a far more meaningful indirect effect by socialising the term, both within the judiciary and the wider community. That socialisation provides the necessary vocabulary to advocate for the interests of animals, which has the potential to lead to a conceptual shift far beyond what the legislative drafters intended.

[1] See, eg, Ian Robertson and Daniel Goldsworthy, 'To feel or not to feel; that is the legal question' [2017] *New Zealand Law Journal* 10.

II. Recognition of Sentience and its History

A. New Zealand's Historical Approach to Animal Welfare Regulation

New Zealand's animal welfare regulatory system is underpinned by the Animal Welfare Act 1999 (AWA) and it is in this legislation that we find both explicit and implicit recognition that animals are sentient.[2] New Zealand remains one of a handful of jurisdictions to have such legislative recognition, which aligns with the country's reputation of making significant – but symbolic – advances in animal welfare. To understand that reputation and its limitations, it is important to briefly outline the legislative history of New Zealand's approach to animal welfare regulation.

Upon becoming a colony, New Zealand was first bound by English legislative instruments, before converting much of the content of that law into indigenous counterparts.[3] The regulation of animal welfare was no exception to this rule. Animal cruelty legislation began in the United Kingdom with Martin's Act of 1822,[4] and a 'furious' period of piecemeal legislative activity in the United Kingdom followed, culminating in the Cruelty to Animals Prevention Act 1849.[5] This Act applied in New Zealand for nearly 30 years, creating offences for those that 'cruelly beat, ill-treat, over-drive, abuse, or torture'[6] domestic animals as well as requiring those who 'confine or impound' domestic animals to provide them with adequate food and water.[7]

The first indigenous animal cruelty legislation in New Zealand took the form of the Cruelty to Animals Act 1878. This Act adopted the United Kingdom's 1849 provisions relating to cruelty almost verbatim, but was innovative in two important respects.[8] The first was its remarkably expansive definition of 'animal' which included all animals of any species, regardless of whether they were domesticated or wild, native or exotic.[9] The second was that it expanded its scope to the treatment of animals in slaughterhouses and on farms, meaning those who treated such animals in a manner which caused 'unnecessary pain or suffering' would face liability.[10] The Act only lasted two years before being succeeded by a new version,

[2] Animal Welfare Act 1999 (NZ), long title, ss 80 and 100.

[3] English Laws Act 1858 (NZ), s 1: the laws of England were deemed in force (where applicable in the circumstances) in New Zealand since 14 January 1840.

[4] Named after its sponsor, Richard Martin MP. Officially titled the Cruel Treatment of Cattle Act 1822 (3 Geo IV c 71).

[5] Thomas G Kelch, 'A Short History of (Mostly) Western Animal Law: Part II' (2013) 19 *Animal Law* 347, 350–51.

[6] Cruelty to Animals Prevention Act 1849 (12 & 13 Vict Cap 92), s 2.

[7] ibid, s 5.

[8] Neil Wells and Marcelo B Rodriguez Ferrere, *Wells on Animal Law in New Zealand* (Brookers, 2018) 48.

[9] Cruelty to Animals Act 1878, s 4.

[10] ibid, s 5.

which itself was repealed and subsumed into the Police Offences Act 1884.[11] Once again, New Zealand excepted itself as an innovator in animal cruelty legislation, with this Act providing for the appointment of Royal Society for the Prevention of Cruelty to Animals (SPCA) inspectors as 'special constables', which gave them wide powers to inspect and even arrest, an approach which was at that time unique in the British Empire.[12]

After this point, however, animal cruelty legislation in New Zealand went into a period of stasis for nearly 80 years. Minor amendments and consolidations occurred, entrenching the concept of 'unnecessary suffering' as a touchstone for animal cruelty offences, which remained part of the Police Offences Act in its various iterations rather than standalone legislation.[13] However, until the passage of the Animals Protection Act in 1960 (the APA), little changed in the legislative landscape. The sponsor of the APA noted Parliamentary debate that that this new legislation was described in the media as 'some of the most enlightened legislation in the world' and described it herself as an 'animals' Bill of Rights'.[14]

Such descriptions were the result of two important changes ushered in by the APA. First, its coverage was significantly more comprehensive. The offences of cruelty in section 3 of the APA listed 26 different offences, ranging from the general cruel ill-treatment offence to the very specific 'burying of poison' offence.[15] More significantly, however, there was a subtle shift in the principles underlying the legislation. Whereas previous legislation had focused on acts of cruelty attracting liability on the basis that they were harmful to an owner's interest in animals as chattels, some offences included in the APA imposed liability on the basis that certain acts of cruelty were harmful to animals *ipso facto*.[16] For example, the APA created offences of failing to provide sufficient food, shelter and water or otherwise wantonly neglecting an animal.[17] This animal-centric approach was a major step forward.

B. The Animal Welfare Act 1999

In other respects, however, the APA stood for, bizarrely, a step backwards. Its predecessors' definition of 'animal' for example – simple and inclusive – was replaced with one that limited the application of the Act to horses, cattle, sheep, pigs, goats, dogs, cats, mules, asses, birds and marine mammals.[18] Similarly, significant

[11] Wells and Rodriguez Ferrere (n 8) 48–49.
[12] ibid, 163.
[13] ibid, 163–64.
[14] (1960) NZPD 2036–2037 per Hon Mabel Howard, MP.
[15] Animals Protection Act 1960 (NZ), ss 3(a) and (s).
[16] Peter Sankoff, 'Five Years of the New Animal Welfare Regime: Lessons Learned from New Zealand's Decision to Modernize Its Animal Welfare Legislation' (2005) 11 *Animal Law* 7, 12.
[17] Animals Protection Act 1960 (NZ), ss 3(a) and (b).
[18] ibid, s 2.

exemptions to the application of the APA – including wholesale exemptions for hunting and scientific research – further reduced its coverage.[19] Finally, perhaps most oddly, the ground-breaking extensions of inspectorate and enforcement powers given to the SPCA under the old legislation were removed, and it required significant lobbying by that organisation to be later appointed as 'honorary' inspectors.[20]

As Pete Hodgson MP noted during the third reading of the legislation that would repeal and replace the APA:

> This legislation replaces legislation that is now nearly 40 years old. The legislation that it replaces is a crock of old garbage. It is no good for animal welfare. It is no good for animal ethics. It is no good for a nation that trades in animal products to the extent that we trade in them. It is legislation that is terribly out of date.[21]

Yet as the sponsor of the new legislation – the AWA – made clear, it adopted an animal welfare rather than an animal rights philosophy, and that while 'some in the community feel that Parliament perhaps should have considered the animal rights issue, [he did] not believe that it should be with this Bill'.[22] That Bill became law on 14 October 1999, and while the AWA did not usher any revolution in the fundamental principles underlying animal welfare regulation, it was undoubtedly 'very, very significant'.[23] The Act completely transformed the legislative scheme alongside introducing major, albeit symbolic, advances in the way the New Zealand views animals.

It is those symbolic advances that made headlines throughout the world. The doyen of the animal liberation movement, Peter Singer, thought that the legislation was a 'major breakthrough'[24] and its progress in Parliament was noted in both major United Kingdom[25] and United States[26] newspapers. The attention was arguably solely due to section 85, which put significant restrictions (but not a complete prohibition) on research, testing and teaching on non-human hominids: chimpanzees, orang-utans and bonobos.[27] Such a restriction was the first of its kind in the world.[28] Although it fell short of giving anything more than a quasi-right to these species and fell significantly short of the aims of those who lobbied Parliament on the issue, it was an important first step.[29] However, the symbolism of the change was laid bare by the fact that of the 34 non-human hominids

[19] ibid, s 19.
[20] Wells and Rodriguez Ferrere (n 8) 50.
[21] (1999) NZPD 19747.
[22] (1999) NZPD 19745.
[23] (1999) NZPD 19746.
[24] Sankoff (n 16) 8.
[25] Nigel Hawkes, 'Declaration on Human Rights – for Chimps' *The Times* (11 February 1999) 1.
[26] Allan Coukell, 'New Zealanders Press Plan for Apes' Rights' *New York Times, Late Edition (East Coast)* (16 March 1999) 3.
[27] As defined by s 2 of the Animal Welfare Act 1999.
[28] Rowan Taylor, 'A Step at a Time: New Zealand's Progress toward Hominid Rights' (2001) 7 *Animal Law* 35, 38.
[29] ibid, 35–36.

that were in New Zealand at the time of the AWA's passage, not one was kept for the purposes of scientific research, and thus section 85 had no practical effect on these animals.[30] This meant that, despite the special treatment that non-human hominids received (and the press coverage that was generated) by s 85, they were for all practical purposes, treated exactly the same as any animal under the AWA. Symbolism is not without value, but it was important to keep the impact of this change in perspective.[31]

A far more important – but barely noticed – change was the AWA's implicit recognition of sentience. This recognition was simply the corollary of the bigger step of recognising and implementing the '3Rs' in scientific research involving animals. The 3Rs – replacement, reduction and refinement – were first articulated by Russell and Burch in 1959,[32] and New Zealand was one of the first jurisdictions to recognise them in legislation. It is the Act's articulation of the principle of 'replacement' that we see the implicit recognition of animal sentience: one of the AWA stated purposes in regulating scientific research involving animals is to promote efforts 'to replace animals as subjects for research and testing by substituting, where appropriate, non-sentient or non-living alternatives'.[33] That reference to 'sentience' was the first time the word had appeared in New Zealand legislation, and by stating that the principle seeks to replace animals with non-sentient alternatives, the Act implies that animals *are* sentient.

This was, of course, hardly revolutionary, given the scientific community had long recognised the sentience of animals for decades by this point, and this implicit recognition in the purpose section of the legislation has little direct impact. Still, as will become a theme, it represented an important step in socialising the term; the recognition indicated that it was a legitimate descriptor in legislation that deals with regulating the welfare of animals. Thus, the most significant impact of the AWA implicitly recognising sentience might have been that it helped usher in the later explicit recognition of sentience.

C. The Animal Welfare Amendment Act 2015

Fifteen years after the introduction of the AWA, its deficiencies were beginning to show. Gaps in its coverage, and inconsistencies in its application, prompted a comprehensive set of amendments to the Act. That took the form of the Animal Welfare Amendment Act (No 2) 2015, and one of the amendments in that legislation was the explicit recognition of sentience.

[30] Paula Brosnahan, 'New Zealand's Animal Welfare Act: What Is Its Value Regarding Non-Human Hominids' (2000) 6 *Animal Law* 185, 186.

[31] ibid, 192.

[32] William Russell and Rex Burch, *The Principles of Humane Experimental Technique* (Meuthen, 1959) 64.

[33] Animal Welfare Act 1999 (NZ), s 80(2)(b)(iii).

This recognition was not, however, part of the original amendment bill. New Zealand legislation usually passes through three stages. A bill is introduced into the House of Representatives, and if it passes its first reading, it is then referred to a select committee of representatives which hears public submissions on the bill. Changes are recommended by the committee, and the bill is returned to the House for its second and third readings, before it receives Royal Assent and is then enacted into law. It was at the select committee stage of the Animal Welfare Amendment Bill that sentience was raised as an issue, then a recommended by the committee as an amendment.[34]

While many submissions to the committee raised the issue of sentience, it was the submission of the World Society for the Protection of Animals (WSPA), now known as World Animal Protection, that was the most comprehensive. Noting that the Ministry for Primary Industries (the government department in charge of administering the AWA) had already recognised animal sentience in its 2013 Animal Welfare Strategy, WSPA argued that it would 'seem logical that the recognition of sentience be included in the legislation, which underpins this strategy and WSPA considers that not to do so would be a significant missed opportunity'.[35] Crucially, it noted that 'New Zealand has always prided itself on being a global leader in animal welfare. The inclusion of sentience language in the Animal Welfare Act would ensure New Zealand remains at the forefront of animal protection policy and legislation globally.'[36] WSPA encouraged two amendments. First, to the long title of the AWA – essentially a preamble, where the Act's intent and purpose is outlined – to include: 'to recognise that all sentient beings are capable of feeling positive and negative emotions and are therefore deserving of protection wherever possible'.[37] Secondly, WSPA argued that the definition of 'animal' in the AWA should refer to sentience.[38]

The committee asked for advice from the Ministry of Primary Industries about the implications of including such a reference.[39] In its advice, the Ministry posited three scenarios: the status quo (ie, the implicit recognition of sentience), an amendment to the long title, or a more substantive amendment to the body of the AWA, such as the change of the definition of 'animal'. Of the second scenario, the Ministry noted that 'it would be an important symbolic gesture that could help to influence the future operation of the Act [which] in practical terms … is unlikely to lead to any immediate change to the way in which Courts would interpret the Act.'[40]

[34] Animal Welfare Amendment Bill (107-2), cl 3A.

[35] Bridget Vercoe, World Society for the Protection of Animals, Submission on Animal Welfare Amendment Bill to Primary Production Committee, 25 September 2013.

[36] ibid.

[37] ibid, Appendix A, 87.

[38] ibid.

[39] Ministry of Primary Industries, 'Animal Welfare Amendment Bill: Report of the Ministry of Primary Industries' (2014).

[40] ibid, 69.

Ultimately, it recommended such an amendment, perhaps swayed by WSPA's appeal to New Zealand's reputation:

> Including sentience within the preamble to the Act would not impact the detail of any of the rights, duties and obligations set out within the Act, but it would shape the overall spirit and intent of the Act. This change would also bring New Zealand legislation into line with international animal welfare legislation and with our stated international position.[41]

The committee accepted the recommendation, but curiously, rejected the wording WSPA proposed. Instead, the committee recommended the following, far more minimal, wording: 'to recognise that animals are sentient'. The committee did not explain why changed the wording, and specifically, why it removed reference to the definition of sentience. In its report, it simply noted that: 'Although the concept of animal sentience is commonly accepted in New Zealand, we recommend inserting new clause 3A to make it clear that animals are sentient beings.'[42] Even so, however, the sponsor of the legislation (who was also the Minister of Primary Industries) seemed to happily acknowledge the definition of sentience. In the Minister's comments to the House of Representatives after receiving the committee's report, he notes that:

> The committee has recommended that the bill expressly recognise the sentience of animals – that is, that animals can have feelings, perceptions, and experiences that matter to them. Animal sentience has been proven in science for some time, and a number of overseas jurisdictions already recognise that animals are sentient. It is, therefore, appropriate that New Zealand's primary piece of animal welfare law also recognise animal sentience.[43]

Thus, given the common understanding of what sentience means in general terms, it is unclear why the committee was reticent to make clear what sentience meant. My supposition is that the lack of a definition in the new wording would help ensure the Ministry's predicted outcome that it would have little practical impact.

The 2015 amendment legislation also included another reference to sentience, making the extent to which a researcher has assessed the suitability of replacing animals as subjects with non-sentient or non-living alternatives as a key criterion for the acceptance of any research project.[44] But it was the amendment to the long title and explicit recognition of sentience that generated headlines.[45] Alongside other symbolic amendments (for example, a ban on testing of cosmetics

[41] ibid, 69–70.
[42] Animal Welfare Amendment Bill 2013 107-2 (NZ), Commentary, 2.
[43] (2014) 702 NZPD 898.
[44] Animal Welfare Act 1999 (NZ), s 100.
[45] Sophie McIntyre, 'Animals are now legally recognised as 'sentient' beings in New Zealand' *The Independent* (online) (19 May 2015), available at www.independent.co.uk/news/world/australasia/animals-are-now-legally-recognised-as-sentient-beings-in-new-zealand-10256006.html; Jonathan Carson, 'New Zealand legally recognises animals as 'sentient' beings' *Stuff* (online) (9 May 2015), available at www.stuff.co.nz/nelson-mail/68363264/new-zealand-legally-recognises-animals-as-sentient-beings.

on animals,[46] despite New Zealand never having engaged in such testing), the amendment legislation continued a trend that began in 1878. Largely driven by optics – the desire to be seen a world leader in the field – each iteration of animal welfare legislation is heralded as major advancement in progressive action to protect and enhance the lives of animals. Each time, however, it is clear that those advances are largely symbolic, in that they lead to little systemic change. Indeed, some fundamentals have largely remained unchanged in the 145-year history of indigenous animal welfare legislation in New Zealand.

For example, in the Cruelty to Animals Act 1878, 'ill-treat' was defined as: 'Any person slaughtering, branding, conveying, or carrying, or causing or procuring to be slaughtered, branded, conveyed, or carried, any animal in such a manner or position as to subject such animal to unnecessary pain or suffering.' In 2023, 'ill-treat' is defined as: 'causing the animal to suffer, by any act or omission, pain or distress that in its kind or degree, or in its object, or in the circumstances in which it is inflicted, is unreasonable or unnecessary'. These are essentially the same definition of 'ill-treat': causing an animal to suffer unnecessary pain or suffering. If fundamental substantive aspects of New Zealand's animal welfare legislation have not changed, it makes it very unlikely that any symbolic change to the long title of that legislation could have an impact beyond making headlines and securing New Zealand's reputation.

III. Recognition of Sentience and its Impact

A. Judicial interpretation of the AWA

Notwithstanding that symbolism, many viewed New Zealand's recognition of animal sentience by the AWA as momentous. For instance, soon after the enactment of the amendment legislation, Robertson and Goldsworthy argued the AWA's recognition of sentience could have dramatic legal implications.[47] They argued that the recognition of sentience would necessarily expand existing negatively framed responsibilities of those in charge of animals, viz ensuring that they do not have experiences of unreasonable pain or distress.[48] Eventually, they reasoned, since sentience encompasses both negative *and* positive emotive experiences, those in charge of animals will not only have to prevent negative experiences, but also appropriately provide for positive experiences.[49] Courts could 'require an assessment, based on best practice and scientific knowledge, of whether [an] animal is experiencing (and demonstrating) positive states of consciousness'.[50]

[46] Animal Welfare Act 1999 (NZ), s 84A.
[47] Robertson and Goldsworthy (n 1).
[48] ibid, 12.
[49] ibid, 13.
[50] ibid, 14.

For a number of reasons, my view has been that this expected effect – although very desirable – is an unlikely one.[51] First, as the Ministry of Primary Industries argued, the AWA:

> [A]lready implicitly recognises sentience, by requiring owners and persons in charge to meet the physical, health and behavioural needs of their animals. These needs are further described in codes of welfare, and include behaviours that could be described as indicating a positive or negative emotional state. Arguably there is no tangible benefit to be gained by including sentience in the Act, and not doing so would avoid any unintentional change to the status quo.[52]

If the AWA implicitly recognised animal sentience before the amendment – and that had long reflected the consensus of the scientific community – why had it not led to courts interpreting the AWA as requiring those in charge of animals to ensure positive experiences?

Simple statutory interpretation principles provide the answer: a court cannot imply additional obligations in a criminal statute unless such implication is clear and obvious,[53] and thus the implicit recognition of sentience was insufficient to expand existing offences. However, that same problem of uncertainty remains in the AWA's explicit recognition of sentience because it is unaccompanied by a legislative definition. While the common law can (and has) supplement that absence by providing a definition,[54] that still might not suffice to provide the necessary degree of legislative certainty. As Blattner has noted, 'despite the widespread avowal to sentience, the function and operability of the legal recognition of animal sentience are ebulous and lack scholarly conceptualisation'.[55] Without external consensus about the specific breadth and depth of animal sentience, a court cannot know the legislative intent behind the recognition of animal sentience, and thus is not in a position to authoritatively define the impact of such recognition on the scope of obligations for those in charge of animals.[56]

Moreover, given the breadth of application of the AWA,[57] while it is possible to see how those in charge of companion animals have the capacity to provide for positive experiences, it is near impossible to see how those in charge of animals used in industrialised agriculture could do the same.[58] Fishes are covered by the AWA, for instance, but it is difficult to see a court imposing obligations on commercial fishers to provide for positive experiences of those animals, given

[51] Marcelo B Rodriguez Ferrere, 'The (Symbolic) Legislative Recognition of Animal Sentience' (2022) 28 *Animal Law* 117, 123–24.

[52] Ministry of Primary Industries (n 39) 69.

[53] Francis Bennion, *Bennion on Statutory Interpretation*, 5th edn (LexisNexis, 2008) 495.

[54] *Haenga v Porirua City Council* [2021] NZHC 1549, [35]; see discussion below.

[55] Charlotte E Blattner, 'The Recognition of Animal Sentience by the Law' (2019) 9 *Journal of Animal Ethics* 121, 122.

[56] Rodriguez Ferrere (n 51) 124.

[57] Animal Welfare Act 1999 (NZ), s 2. Essentially, all animals except insects, and those in a larval, pre-natal or pre-hatched stage, are included in the definition of 'animal'.

[58] Rodriguez Ferrere (n 51) 124.

that industry presently measures its catch by the tonne rather than individual animals.[59] Desirable as it might be, the courts simply do not have the interpretative mandate to bring about such a significant expansion to the obligations of those in charge of animals.

Unfortunately, this prediction has so far proved true, and the AWA's explicit recognition of sentience has not yet had a significant substantive impact. Only six cases in New Zealand's senior courts have mentioned the AWA's recognition of sentience since its 2015 amendment, and three of those were only quoting or describing the overall scheme of the Act.[60] The three remaining cases, however, are worth examining, for while they do not show the imposition of positive obligations as forecast by Robertson and Goldsworthy, they do seem to show that the explicit recognition has 'shape[d] the overall spirit and intent of the Act', as predicted by the Ministry of Primary Industries.[61]

The first case to substantively consider the explicit recognition of sentience was *Wallace v Royal Society for the Prevention of Cruelty to Animals Auckland*.[62] In this case, the Court was considering whether it could grant an order for the sale or destruction of seized animals at the same time as the trial for their ill-treatment was occurring. The Court held this was not the same situation as the prejudice to a fair trial that could arise from an application for forfeiture of criminal proceeds, in part because of the 'negative impacts for the animals if disposal proceedings had to wait for the criminal prosecution to conclude'.[63] While it relied on many factors to arrive at this conclusion, it explicitly noted that this approach reflected the purpose of the Act to recognise the sentience of animals.[64]

Similarly, in *Kondratyeva v Royal New Zealand Society for the Prevention of Cruelty to Animals*,[65] the recognition of sentience assisted the Court in coming to an interpretative conclusion. This case involved against an appeal against a forfeiture order (requiring the owner to relinquish their animals) and a disqualification order (preventing her from owning animals in the future) after she was convicted of failing to provide for the physical, health and behavioural needs of 50 cats in her care.[66] Justice Duffy rejected the appellant's submission that the court below had acted improperly by imposing a forfeiture order. She first notes that:

> [A]nimals are clearly treated differently than inanimate property under the law … The purpose of the Act is to 'recognise that animals are sentient'. The Act is not concerned

[59] Seafood New Zealand, 'New Zealand Seafood Exports: Summary Report May 2023', available at www.seafood.co.nz/fileadmin/Export_Statistics/2023-05-Summary-Prov.pdf.

[60] *Erickson v Ministry for Primary Industries* [2017] NZCA 271, [2017] NZAR 1015; *McCartney v Canterbury Society for the Prevention of Cruelty to Animals* [2018] NZHC 2624; *New Zealand Animal Law Association v Attorney-General* [2020] NZHC 3009.

[61] See n 39.

[62] *Wallace v Royal Society for the Prevention of Cruelty to Animals Auckland (SPCA Auckland)* [2019] NZHC 1599, [2019] NZAR 1393.

[63] ibid, [23].

[64] ibid.

[65] *Kondratyeva v Royal New Zealand Society for the Prevention of Cruelty to Animals (SPCA)* [2022] NZHC 449.

[66] ibid, [1]–[4].

> with a property rights regime for animals, rather ensuring that animals are treated properly both by the people to whom they belong and to others who may temporarily be in charge of them.[67]

In coming to her conclusion on the appropriateness of the order, she reiterated that the 'Act recognises animals as sentient beings. They should not be left in the ownership of someone the Court has found to be unsatisfactory because it might be helpful to her psychological wellbeing.'[68] Once again, while the explicit recognition of sentience may not have been determinative in the outcome in this case, it buttressed those commonsense conclusions, giving the court an interpretative hook.

Despite the positive impact of the explicit recognition of sentience in these two cases, they also show that the impact has been muted, merely providing the court with purposive guidance when engaging in interpretation. This is welcome additional tool, but it certainly does not represent a sea change in the status or nature of the AWA itself.

B. Within the Common Law Generally

It is thus rather ironic that the most significant impact that the explicit recognition of sentience in the AWA has had was in a case that had nothing to do with the AWA. Instead, *Haenga v Porirua City Council* involved an appeal against a conviction and sentence for a dog attack causing serious injury under s 58 of the Dog Control Act 1996.[69] That section stipulates that 'the court shall, on convicting the owner, make an order for the destruction of the dog unless satisfied that the circumstances of the attack were exceptional and do not justify destruction'. There is thus a presumption that where a dog has attacked and caused injury that the court will order its 'destruction'. It was the use of this term that piqued Isac J's interest, and it is worth quoting his analysis in full:

> [35] I note the Act refers to the 'destruction' of the dog. Such wording reflects the fact that animals have historically been classed as personal property that can be 'destroyed'. Of course, most New Zealanders would not classify their dog as an inanimate object that can be 'destroyed'. But neither does the Animal Welfare Act, which recognises animals are sentient. Although sentience is not defined in the Animal Welfare Act, it refers to the capacity to have feelings and requires a certain level of consciousness and intellectual capacity.
>
> [36] The Dog Control Act's reference to 'destruction' is therefore surprising. Sentient beings are generally not 'destroyed'; they are put to death or killed. Of course, the Dog Control Act serves a different purpose to the Animal Welfare Act. The Dog Control Act is very much focussed on public safety and control of dogs, whereas the Animal

[67] ibid, [53].
[68] ibid, [72].
[69] Above n 54.

> Welfare Act serves to impose obligations on people in charge of animals. Given the Animal Welfare Act's recognition of the sentience of animals, the continuing reference to destruction in the Dog Control Act remains curious, as does its classification of a destruction order as a criminal sentence. One might think that the question of public safety and what is to be done with a dangerous dog ought to be unshackled from the criminal responsibility of its owner.

This is a remarkable passage for several reasons. Most significantly, it represents the first (and to date, only) judicial definition of sentience, relying upon the work of Jane Kotzmann.[70] The common law now has a recognised and accepted definition of sentience; something that is, as noted above, lacking in the AWA. While that acceptance of a definition is only at the High Court level, if it is adopted by the senior appellate courts, it would go some way to quelling my doubts about the potential impact of the legislative recognition of sentience: it would have a common and understood meaning, thereby reducing the uncertainty of its impact. At the very least, the provision of a common law definition to supplement the legislative recognition of sentience certainly gives the concept both texture and substance, and is a welcome advance.

Second, Isac J has highlighted the deficiencies of legislation that sits in parallel to the AWA: the language of destruction is only appropriate for inanimate property, not a sentient being, and given that sentience, it makes little sense to punish the animal for the faults of its owner. Justice Isac may have simply used the words 'surprising' and 'curious' but that sentiment belies the utterly antiquated and inappropriate scheme of the Dog Control Act. Finally, an important aspect of this case is the power that the AWA's explicit recognition of sentience has had beyond the four corners of that legislation itself. Although the appellant did not succeed, and the dog (Chop) was killed – not destroyed – as a result, that result might not be in vain should it represent the start of judicial questioning of legislative regimes that seek to deny the sentience of animals.

By referring to another piece of legislation, and only as an aside in his analysis, Isac J's comments were obiter dictum. Nevertheless, his decision in *Haenga* represents an important step in the continuing judicial socialisation of the concept of 'sentience' in cases involving the Dog Control Act, which itself makes no explicit reference to sentience whatsoever. The judicial recognition of sentience with regards to dogs has occurred in parallel to the AWA's recognition of sentience, as evidenced by the first senior court decision to ever refer to animal sentience, *Turner v South Taranaki District Council*,[71] which occurred two years before the AWA's recognition of sentience. In this case, the Court was interpreting what amounted to an 'attack' by a dog, and held that 'Physical contact between dog and victim will suffice so long as it results from deliberate aggressive action. The legislation thus recognises that dogs are sentient creatures, and that from a dog's

[70] Jane Kotzmann 'Recognising the Sentience of Animals in Law: A Justification and Framework for Australian States and Territories' (2020) 42 *Sydney Law Review* 281, 282.

[71] *Turner v South Taranaki District Council* [2013] NZHC 1603, [2013] NZAR 1046.

perspective contact need not always signify hostility.'[72] In coming to this conclusion, the judge was able to use a commonsense understanding and implication of animal sentience – that dogs will have different emotional states – to provide a gloss on the idea of an attack: physical contact is not sufficient, and there needs to be some sort of quasi-aggressive intent on the part of the dog. *Turner* was accepted and applied in later High Court cases,[73] indicating the recognition of sentience has had a lasting impact on the way courts interpret the Dog Control Act's reference to 'attack'.

Similarly, the High Court in *Risdom v Auckland Council* recognised the sentience of dogs without the need for any explicit legislative reference.[74] This case was an appeal against the order for the destruction of a dog after he committed an attack. The appeal was filed after the relevant deadline, but 'taking into account the merits of the proposed appeal as bearing on the life of a sentient being',[75] the Court extended the time for filing. While this may seem merely administrative, it is a recognition that the dog-owner's failure might have life-threatening consequences for the dog, and is therefore an example of judicial consideration for the dog's emotional well-being.

Neither *Turner* (and the cases relying upon it) nor *Risdom* make explicit reference to the AWA's recognition of sentience. Still, as *Haenga* shows, that recognition has allowed the concept to cross-pollinate into other areas, and this dovetails into the existing judicial recognition of sentience in Dog Control Act cases. This provides some small hope for the future development of sentience as a concept at the common law, showing that it has the potential to go beyond merely an interpretative tool by also providing a basis for challenging existing legislative systems.

C. Beyond the Courts

It is important not to overstate these developments. While there is indeed future potential for the development of sentience, the six cases that have referred to the concept since 2015 are a small proportion of the 206 involving the AWA in that period.[76] Nevertheless, that limited penetration of the concept in the courts is not reflective of the penetration of sentience in the animal regulatory framework generally.

One of the arguments advanced by WSPA in its submission in support of explicitly recognising sentience was that the Ministry of Primary Industries had already done so.[77] In its 2013 New Zealand Animal Welfare Strategy, the Ministry

[72] ibid, [21].
[73] *Snodgrass v Kapiti Coast District Council* [2014] NZHC 1333, [2014] NZAR 834 [29]; and *Newlands v Nelson City Council* [2021] NZHC 652.
[74] *Risdom v Auckland Council* [2020] NZHC 905.
[75] ibid, [8].
[76] Westlaw New Zealand search (18 May 2023).
[77] See n 39.

of Primary Industries places sentience at the forefront for the rationale behind the strategy, noting that:

> Animals are sentient – they can feel pain and distress – and as a humane society we have responsibilities to ensure our animals' needs are met. Animals play an important role in many aspects of New Zealand life, and New Zealanders have high expectations of our animal welfare system.[78]

Other rationales for the strategy included the fact that New Zealand's economy relies upon animals and that 'Cases of poor animal welfare can have a negative impact on our reputation and result in a loss of export markets',[79] perhaps indicating that sentience was not the driving reason behind such a strategy. Certainly, the undercooked definition of sentience within the strategy – 'Animals are sentient, which means they can feel pain and distress and have other experiences' – indicates that the inclusion was an afterthought.[80] Still, it was an important first step, and since the explicit recognition of sentience by the AWA in 2015, the concept has become firmly embedded within the animal welfare regulatory infrastructure. The National Animal Welfare Advisory Committee (NAWAC), for instance:

> [A]cknowledges the explicit recognition of animal sentience within the Animal Welfare Act in 2015. Sentience is the ability to perceive or feel things. The understanding that animals are sentient has always been integral to NAWAC's development of the codes of welfare and the minimum standards contained within them. With sentience now explicitly recognised within the Act, NAWAC will continue to integrate the concept of animal sentience into future codes and standards as they are developed and reviewed.[81]

This sounds like a very important development. Codes of welfare – another major change to the regulatory framework ushered in by the AWA in 1999 – are intended to provide specificity and minimum standards for different species of animals or specific industries, and are designed to complement and enhance the AWA itself. For much of their existence, however, they have been an abysmal failure, routinely *undermining* the AWA.[82] NAWAC is charged with overseeing the development of the codes, and so it is important that it now acknowledges it must consider, and indeed integrate, the concept of sentience within its codes of welfare. Whether it does so remains to be seen: presently, sentience is not mentioned anywhere within its 19 codes currently in force, even if it is a concept consistently raised by submissions in the consultation processes that lead to their creation.[83]

[78] Ministry for Primary Industries, 'New Zealand Animal Welfare Strategy' (2013) 3.

[79] ibid.

[80] ibid, 4.

[81] Ministry of Primary Industries, 'All animal welfare codes', available at www.mpi.govt.nz/animals/animal-welfare/codes/all-animal-welfare-codes.

[82] Danielle Duffield and Marcelo B Rodriguez Ferrere, '*New Zealand Animal Law Association v Attorney General:* New Zealand's most significant animal law case in a generation' (2021) 29 NZULR 593; Sankoff (n 16).

[83] National Animal Welfare Advisory Committee, 'Report To Accompany An Amendment To The Code Of Welfare For Dairy Cattle' (31 October 2019), available at www.mpi.govt.nz/dmsdocument/

Nevertheless, despite that lack of substantive action, NAWAC continues to engage work on the meaning and parameters of the concept. In November 2017, NAWAC held a workshop attended by '150 participants representing a diverse sectors, industries and organisations'[84] on the impact of the AWA's recognition of sentience. In 2021, it produced an explainer website,[85] and in its work programme for 2023–24, it intends to publish guidance about sentience, hopefully leading to the more substantive consideration of sentience within its work on code development.[86] Although the impact to date is minimal, the Ministry of Primary Industries' view that the explicit recognition of sentience would have little practical impact does seem to underestimate the power of that recognition.

Most tellingly, sectors within industrialised agriculture seem to be both alive to (and concerned by) the recognition of sentience. For instance, the Egg Producers Federation of New Zealand has criticised NAWAC for suggesting an implication of sentience is that animals can feel human-like emotions:

> The discrepancy in NAWAC's position arises when it applies human emotions to animals, stating: 'situation-related experiences can be negative or positive for animals, for example, feeling secure and safe, frustration, boredom, helplessness, loneliness, anxiety or fear.' The word 'sentience', along with others such as emotions and feelings, imply a greater ability to measure subjective states in animals scientifically, than is currently possible.[87]

This concern seems to mirror the anticipated impact of the explicit recognition by Robertson and Goldsworthy. If sentience does encompass the capacity to feel subjective emotions, then industrialised agriculture – which almost by definition causes the negative emotions described above and hinders positive emotions – then any legal obligation to recognise and respect that sentience could have dramatic implications. Accordingly, it is clear that industry will push back on any expansive definition and/or attempt to limit the legal implications.

Likewise, just as industry has accepted that the recognition of sentience has a potential impact, so too are those non-governmental organisations seeking greater levels of regulation. All major animal interest organisations have position statements on sentience. For instance, the SPCA notes that 'recognising sentience means that SPCA acknowledges animals as individuals who have meaningful and

41782-Report-to-accompany-an-amendment-to-the-code-of-welfare-for-dairy-cattle-2019. This report, for instance, summarises six submissions that mention that cattle are sentient but neither NAWAC's report nor the code mentions the term.

[84] National Animal Welfare Advisory Committee, 'Animal Sentience Workshop Report' (15 November 2017), available at www.nawac.org.nz/assets/NAWAC-documents/Report-on-the-Animal-Sentience-Workshop-Wellington-2017.pdf.

[85] National Animal Welfare Advisory Committee, 'Animal Sentience', available at www.nawac.org.nz/animal-sentience.

[86] National Animal Welfare Advisory Committee, 'Work Programme 2023–2024' (3 May 2023), available at www.nawac.org.nz/assets/Uploads/NAWAC-Work-Programme-2023-2024.pdf.

[87] Michael Brooks, 'Sentience' in *Welfare Pulse*, Issue 32 (Wellington, Ministry for Primary Industries, 2021) 7.

unique emotions and experiences'.[88] The recognition of sentience has allowed many of these organisations to use the term as a shorthand for the meaningfulness of the emotive experiences of animals, and has also allowed the community to better understand and critique New Zealand's animal welfare regulatory regime.[89] It is clear the recognition of sentience has allowed the term to become socialised within the community in a way that longstanding scientific recognition had not yet achieved. This is powerful, providing a vocabulary to those who care about the interests and experiences of animals allows them to better advocate for those interests, perhaps another reason why industry groups remain wary.

Finally, it is worth noting that New Zealand's explicit recognition of sentience may have had a minor part to play in sentience being recognised in the New Zealand–United Kingdom Free Trade Agreement, signed on 28 February 2022. As stated in Article 6.2 in the Animal Welfare chapter of the Agreement, 'The Parties recognise that animals are sentient beings. They also recognise the connection between improved welfare of animals and benefits to food production systems.'[90] The AWA's recognition of sentience was almost certainly not the core reason this Article was included, since Australia, which has very limited legislative recognition of sentience, also agreed to the same terminology in its own free trade agreement with the United Kingdom.[91] Like Australia, this is the first time any free trade agreement signed by New Zealand has contained such a term or a specific chapter on animal welfare. As Kotzmann notes with regards to the Australian agreement:

> [I]t is unclear what, if any, impact this provision might have in Australia … The most likely impact will be in political terms, in that the federal government may come under pressure from the UK government to improve its animal welfare standards.[92]

Certainly, it does not help that the Agreement's reference to sentience is footnoted with the following: 'As defined in each Party's respective animal welfare laws and regulations.'[93] As stated above, New Zealand has not defined sentience, and despite the passage of the Animal Welfare (Sentience) Act 2022, nor has the United Kingdom.[94] However, the terms of reference for the Animal Sentience Committee that the Act created does give it the power to determine and apply a definition.[95]

[88] SPCA New Zealand, 'Animal Sentience', available at www.spca.nz/advice-and-welfare/article/animal-sentience.

[89] Lynley Tulloch, 'Animal Sentience and how the Law is truly an ass' Scoop (18 May 2021), available at www.scoop.co.nz/stories/HL2105/S00048/animal-sentience-and-how-the-law-is-truly-an-ass.htm.

[90] Free Trade Agreement Between New Zealand and the United Kingdom of Great Britain and Northern Ireland, 28 February 2022, Art 6.2.

[91] Jane Kotzmann, 'A Typology of Australian Animal Sentience Recognition Provisions – Enacted and Proposed' (2023) *Federal Law Review* 1, 12–13.

[92] ibid, 21.

[93] n 90.

[94] Animal Welfare (Sentience) Act 2022 (UK).

[95] Department for Environment, Food and Rural Affairs 'Animal Sentience Committee Terms of Reference' (17 November 2021) 22, available at data.parliament.uk/DepositedPapers/Files/DEP20220007/Animal_Sentience_Committee_Draft_Terms_of_Reference.pdf.

Both the creation of a committee and the creation of a definition might assist in encouraging New Zealand to do the same. At the very least, New Zealand is now committed to using 'its best endeavours not to weaken or reduce the protection afforded to the welfare of farmed animals in its animal welfare laws and regulations, in a manner materially affecting trade or investment between the Parties'.[96] Vague as that commitment might sound, it is another reason why the explicit recognition of sentience by the AWA is here to stay: politically or diplomatically, the New Zealand cannot risk its reputation by removing that recognition.

IV. Conclusion

New Zealand has a history of enacting progressive advances in animal welfare regulation and being very proud of those advances. That history, however, shows that many of those advancements are symbolic, and have not led to systemic change. Legislation touted as an 'animals' Bill of Rights' upon its enactment becomes 'a crock of old garbage' upon the eve of its repeal.

The recognition of animal sentience may well fall into this category of a symbolic legislative advance. Certainly, its implicit recognition in 1999 by the AWA had no impact. However, there are signs that amendments in 2015 to explicitly recognise sentience in the long title of the Act might still have broader consequences.

Its inclusion in the long title of the AWA and the lack of any accompanying definition means that it is unlikely that this recognition will single-handedly lead to the imposition of broader and positive duties of care for those in charge of animals. However, this legislative recognition of sentience has helped buttress the socialisation of the term that was already occurring within the common law. We now have several cases which have used to the recognition of sentience as an interpretative tool, and one case that both defined sentience and used it to critique other discordant legislation. Beyond the court, the term is now widely used by regulatory agencies, NGOs and appears in New Zealand's trade agreements.

This is a limited impact, but an impact all the same, and it is one that can only expand rather than contract. The government's assertion that the legislative recognition of sentience in New Zealand will have little practical impact might well come to pass, but presently, that prediction seems both premature, and fortunately for animals, an understatement.

[96] n 90, Art 6.3.

10

A Field Trip into Québec Law: Exploring the Theoretical Ramifications of Sentience Recognition

MICHAËL LESSARD*

I. Introduction

Québec offers a fascinating playground for exploring the theoretical intricacies of animal law. This Canadian province, characterised by a civil law tradition with a common law court system, whose laws are enacted both in English and in French, exemplifies the movement towards recognising animal sentience within a bilingual and bijural North American context.

Since 2015, the Civil Code of Québec (CCQ) has not only recognised that animals are sentient beings endowed with biological needs, but it has also dereified them by explicitly declaring that they are not things.[1] In addition to this general provision, the Animal Welfare and Safety Act (AWSA) has aimed to operationalise this new recognition.[2] Section II of this chapter offers an overview of these legislative changes to provide an international readership with a better understanding of Québec's animal law.

These legislative changes have transformed Québec into a fertile ground for theoretical reflections on animal law that are relevant to other jurisdictions. In section III of this chapter, I set out the seeds of these reflections. First, I examine how the dereification of animals – the assertion that they are no longer things – can impact their categorisation in civil law. Second, I examine theoretical factors that can influence the impact of the statutory recognition of sentience and biological

* I would like to thank Marcelo Rodriguez Ferrere, Dena Kia, Hira Jaleel and Paulien Christiaenssen for their comments on previous drafts. Some of this chapter's passages are adapted from Michaël Lessard, 'Beyond Sentience: Legally Recognizing Animals' Sociability and Agency' (2024) *Journal of Animal Ethics* (forthcoming) and Michaël Lessard, 'Pour quelques harfangs des neiges. Le Québec au coeur d'un dialogue transsystémique sur les droits des animaux' in Aloïse Quesne (ed), *Quel(s) droit(s) pour les animaux?* (Mare et Martin, 2023).

[1] Civil Code of Québec (CCQ), CQLR c CCQ-1991, Art 898.1.

[2] Animal Welfare and Safety Act (AWSA), CQLR c B-31, preamble.

needs in both civil law and common law. These factors include the prescriptive force attributed to the statutory recognition, the location and invocability of the statutory recognition, and the interpretation of the concepts of sentience and biological needs. Thirdly, I explore this last point in more depth, highlighting that the notions of sentience and biological needs can be interpreted by legal officials in many different ways.

As a result, this chapter will be of interest not only to individuals interested in comparative law seeking a better understanding of Québec law, but also to anyone interested in legal theory considerations regarding the recognition of animal sentience and biological needs.

II. The Animal Law Reform of 2015

In 2015, the Parliament of Québec reformed the legal status of non-human animals.[3] On one hand, it added a provision to the CCQ stating that animals are not things but rather sentient beings with biological needs (section A below).[4] This declaration serves as the foundation for the development of animal law in Québec. On the other hand, the Parliament also enacted AWSA to give teeth to this new legislative declaration (section B).[5] The AWSA outlines a significant part of the obligations that humans have towards animals. Let us take a closer look at these two sides of the animal law reform in Québec.

To fully appreciate the legal context in which this reform took place, one needs to understand the division of legislative powers in Canada and the structure of animal law in Québec. In Canada, legislative powers are shared between the federal and provincial parliaments. The 2015 animal law reform was enacted by the Parliament of Québec, which was acting within its legislative jurisdiction, particularly in the area of property and civil rights. However, the provincial animal law reform could impact the application of federal law in Québec. Indeed, any federal law incorporating concepts or terms from provincial property and civil rights law must be interpreted in accordance with the provincial law.[6] Therefore, in my opinion, the specific understanding of animals conveyed by this reform could influence federal law relating to animals.

Regarding the structure of animal law, one must understand that animals are essentially divided into two categories by the Parliament of Québec: domesticated and wild. Domesticated animals include species, sub-species or breeds that have been selected by humans to meet their needs. This includes animals 'such as cats, dogs, rabbits, cattle, horses, pigs, sheep, goats and chickens, and their hybrids'.[7]

[3] An Act to improve the legal situation of animals, SQ 2015, c 35.
[4] ibid, s 1.
[5] ibid, s 7.
[6] Interpretation Act, RSC 1985, c I-21, s 8.1–8.2.
[7] AWSA (n 2) s 1.

Until the implementation of AWSA, domesticated animals had limited legal protection. With the exception of a brief period from 2012 to 2015, during which rules similar to those now found in AWSA were put in place, only dogs and cats were protected as members of the domesticated animal category.[8] On the other hand, the Act respecting the conservation and development of wildlife provides protections for so-called wild animals. These are animals whose genus, species or sub-species naturally reproduce in the wild and do not descend from a lineage selected by humans, or are difficult to distinguish from such animals, even if they were born or kept in captivity.[9] However, these so-called wild animals receive the majority of their legal protection when they are kept in captivity.[10] This domesticated/wild diptych is overlooked by the Civil Code, enacted by the Parliament of Québec, which, since 2015, acknowledges animals as sentient beings, regardless of their categorisation as domesticated or wild. It is also overlooked by criminal law, established by the Parliament of Canada, which provides protections primarily against animal cruelty, regardless of how animals are categorised.[11] Finally, in addition to these legal regimes, there are specific protections scattered throughout federal and provincial statutory law, often aimed at regulating particular industries. For example, since 1959, federal law has required the slaughter of the majority of animals intended for human consumption to be conducted using methods that ensure rapid or immediate loss of consciousness.[12] Within this legal structure, there was previously no protection regime for domesticated animals comparable to that provided by AWSA.

A. Article 898.1 of the Civil Code of Québec

From a legal standpoint, the relationship between human and non-human animals is now structured by the recognition that animals are sentient beings with biological needs. This results from the implementation of Article 898.1 CCQ, which is listed as the only 'General provision / *Disposition générale*' of the book 'Property / *Des Biens*' of the Civil Code of Québec. This Article establishes that animals are not things but rather sentient beings with biological needs to which property law applies:[13]

> **898.1.** Animals are not things. They are sentient beings and have biological needs.
>
> In addition to the provisions of special Acts which protect animals, the provisions of this Code and of any other Act concerning property nonetheless apply to animals.

[8] Michaël Lessard and Marie-Andrée Plante, 'Where the Wild Things Are (and Have Been): An Archeology of Legal Discourses on Animals in Québec' (2024) 61 *Alberta Law Review* (forthcoming).

[9] Act respecting the conservation and development of wildlife, CQLR c C-61.1, s 1. This legal regime has provided protections for the welfare of so-called wild animals since 1962, see ibid.

[10] Regulation respecting animals in captivity, CQLR c C-611, r 51.

[11] Criminal Code, RSC 1985, c C-46, s 445.1-447.1; Lessard and Plante (n 8).

[12] Lessard and Plante (n 8).

[13] CCQ (n 1) Art 898.1.

> ***898.1.*** *Les animaux ne sont pas des biens. Ils sont des êtres doués de sensibilité et ils ont des impératifs biologiques.*
>
> *Outre les dispositions des lois particulières qui les protègent, les dispositions du présent code et de toute autre loi relative[s]*[14] *aux biens leur sont néanmoins applicables.*

Article 898.1 CCQ modifies the *jus commune* by recognising the sentience and biological needs of animals.[15] This legislative change directly impacts the foundation of all other laws.[16] Any legal area reliant on the Civil Code must align with the recognition of animals as sentient beings.[17]

In 2019, the Court of Appeal of Québec, the province's highest court, explicitly recognised the normative force of Article 898.1 CCQ in *Road to Home Rescue Support c Ville de Montréal*. Here, the Court of Appeal heard a case where a borough in Montréal sought to put to death a dangerous dog while a shelter in the United States sought to provide refuge for the animal. The Court of Appeal clarified the scope of Article 898.1 CCQ, emphasising that it does not prohibit the killing of animals, but rather establishes a behavioural standard that dictates how human beings must interact with animals:[18]

> [56] … The fact that animals (including, of course, dogs of all kinds) are sentient beings does not preclude them from occasionally being a nuisance or danger and being subject to measures aimed at counteracting or remedying one or the other, either temporarily or permanently. These measures include euthanasia, which, according to the regulations in question, may be ordered when the dog is declared dangerous.
>
> [57] There is nothing in this [municipal by-law] that contravenes Article 898.1 C.C.Q. By affirming that animals are sentient beings with biological needs, the legislator is also dictating the conduct *of all those who interact with such beings. This provision, which is therefore a behavioural standard*, certainly applies to the manner in which cities implement their by-laws adopted under the *Municipal Powers Act* to manage animal nuisances or stray or dangerous animals. Thus, when a by-law (as in this case) provides for the euthanasia of an animal, it must be done in a manner that is consistent with Art. 898.1 *C.C.Q.*, that is, respectful of the animal sentience recognized by the legislator. It is not impossible either that Art. 898.1 *C.C.Q.* has a direct effect on the content of such a by-law, which could not, among a range of possibilities, prescribe the use of the cruelest or most painful means to euthanize an animal (in this case, the by-laws do not prescribe anything of this sort).

[14] There seems to be a mistake in the French version of Article 898.1 CCQ; see *Michaël Lessard, 'Le droit de vie et de mort sur l'animal : quelle évolution depuis la reconnaissance des animaux comme êtres sensibles?' (2021) 55 Revue juridique Thémis de l'Université de Montréal* 137, 144.

[15] Until then, the *jus commune* considered animals as things although it recognised some of their unique characteristics. Therefore, the reform of animal law can be more accurately described as an evolution in continuity with the views of jurists up to that time, see Lessard and Plante (n 8).

[16] CCQ (n 1), preliminary provision.

[17] Michaël Lessard, 'Can Sentience Recognition Protect Animals? Lessons From Québec's Animal Law Reform' (2021) 27 *Animal Law Review* 57; Alain Roy, 'Commentaire sous l'article 898.1' in Benoît Moore (ed,) *Code civil du Québec : Annotations – Commentaires 2022–2023* (Yvon Blais, 2022) 1013–17.

[18] *Road to Home Rescue Support c Ville de Montréal*, 2019 QCCA 2187 at 56–58 [*RHRS c Montréal*] (my translation).

> [58] That being said, Art. 898.1 *C.C.Q.* does not, in itself, prohibit the slaughter or euthanasia of an animal that constitutes a nuisance or poses an undue danger.
>
> [Emphasis added, references omitted.]

Therefore, the Court of Appeal suggests that Article 898.1 CCQ has implications for municipal by-laws. For instance, a by-law could not prescribe a cruel method of animal killing since this would contradict the standard of respecting animal sentience established by the provision.

With the advent of Article 898.1 CCQ, the concepts of sentience and biological needs acquire significant normative force in law as an increasing number of judges and scholars understand the legal recognition of sentience as imposing legal obligations on humans towards animals, thereby reshaping the legal relationship between humans and animals.[19] Since Article 898.1 CCQ applies to all animals, relations with every animal must now respect their sentience and biological needs. However, it is important to explore the legal definitions of sentience and biological needs, as these concepts are influenced by academic research, evolving social understandings, and the laws of other jurisdictions. Before addressing these dynamics in section III, it is worth considering how the concepts of sentience and biological needs are operationalised in the AWSA, which purports to crystallise these concepts into clear rules.

B. The Animal Welfare and Safety Act

The AWSA aims to provide a range of protections for domesticated animals and certain wild animals in Québec.[20] This statute holds the promise of transforming the new legal recognition of animals' sentience and biological needs into concrete rules.[21] Its preamble also emphasises that 'the human species has an individual and collective responsibility to ensure animal welfare and safety'.[22]

The AWSA provides protections to ensure the welfare and safety of animals covered by the Act, but it does not prevent their exploitation or killing. Section 5 AWSA provides that the owner or custodian of an animal must ensure that its 'welfare / *bien-être*' and 'safety / sécurité' are not compromised.[23] The welfare or

[19] In addition to the Court of Appeal decision, see Alexandra Popovici, 'Chercher la petite bête : les animaux dans le Code civil du Québec' in Nathalie Vézina, Pascal Fréchette and Louise Bernier (eds), *Mélanges Robert P Kouri : l'humain au coeur du droit* (Yvon Blais, 2021) 135; Alain Roy, 'La garde de l'animal de compagnie lors de la rupture conjugale' (2022) 51 *Revue de droit de l'Université de Sherbrooke* 249; Michaël Lessard and Marie-Andrée Plante, 'L'animal de la famille: un sujet sensible' (2023) 52:3 *Revue de droit de l'Université de Sherbrooke* 729.

[20] AWSA applies to domesticated animals, red foxes and American mink kept in captivity for breeding purposes with the intention of trading in fur, as well as any other animals designated by regulation, AWSA (n 2) s 1.

[21] AWSA (n 2) preamble.

[22] ibid, preamble.

[23] ibid, s 5.

safety of an animal is presumed to be compromised when the animal does not receive care that is consistent with their biological needs.[24] Section 5 AWSA offers a non-exhaustive list of such care, which includes having access to sufficient food and water of suitable quality; being kept in a sanitary, clean, suitable, spacious and well-lit place; having the opportunity for adequate exercise; being protected from excessive heat, cold and bad weather; being transported in a suitable manner in an appropriate vehicle; receiving necessary care in case of injury, illness or suffering; and not being subjected to any abuse or mistreatment that may affect the animal's health.[25]

If an animal does not receive any of the care listed in section 5 AWSA, or any other care consistent with its biological needs, its welfare or safety is presumed to be compromised. In such cases, the owner or custodian must prove that neither the welfare nor the safety of the animal has been compromised, or at least demonstrate that they have taken steps to ensure the welfare and safety of the animal was not compromised. Failure to rebut the presumption would indicate a failure in the owner or custodian's duty and they would be subject to a fine or imprisonment.[26]

The Act also imposes an obligation that extends beyond owners and guardians. According to section 6 AWSA, no person may, by their act or omission, cause an animal to be in distress.[27] Distress is defined as being subjected to conditions that could result in death or serious harm, acute pain or extreme anxiety for the animal.[28] Failure to comply with this obligation could result in a fine or imprisonment.[29]

However, both the obligations outlined in section 5 (concerning welfare and safety) and section 6 (concerning distress) have significant exceptions. Indeed, section 7 AWSA states that sections 5 and 6 do not apply to activities related to agriculture, veterinary medicine, teaching, or scientific research that are carried out in accordance with generally recognised rules. In so doing, section 7 relieves those engaged in most animal exploitation of any obligation to ensure animal welfare and safety and to alleviate the animal's distress. It should be noted, however, that since those activities must still be carried out in accordance with generally recognised rules, a breach of the generally recognised rules would trigger the application of sections 5 and 6. Therefore, these generally recognised rules, often set out in industry codes of practice, may take on a de facto legal force insofar as a breach of an industry code rule means that sections 5 and 6 are once again enforceable, even though the activity relates to agriculture, veterinary medicine, teaching or scientific research. Violating a rule of practice that also contravenes an obligation under sections 5 and 6 would result in the same consequences as if the

[24] ibid.
[25] ibid.
[26] ibid, ss 68, 70.
[27] ibid, s 6.
[28] ibid; for an analysis of the notion of distress for the purpose of this Act, see Lessard (n 14).
[29] AWSA (n 2) ss 68, 70.

violation had been committed outside the context of agriculture, veterinary medicine, teaching or scientific research.[30] However, it should be noted that industry codes of practice authorise a number of infringements on animals' welfare and safety in their general rules.

The AWSA also imposes specific obligations that are not subject to explicit exceptions. Owners and custodians of cats, dogs, equines or any other animal designated by regulation must provide them with stimulation, socialisation and environmental enrichment consistent with their biological needs.[31] No one may train an animal to fight another animal.[32] No one may transport an animal in a vehicle if the animal would suffer unduly during transport due, among other reasons, to infirmity, illness, injury or fatigue, unless the transport is necessary for providing required care and suffering is minimised during transport and boarding.[33] Finally, the Act stipulates that the killing of an animal must be done in a manner that is not cruel and must minimise the animal's pain and anxiety.[34] The method must result in rapid loss of sensibility, followed by a quick death.[35]

Hence, throughout a series of provisions, the AWSA mobilises the notion of biological needs to outline obligations towards animals.[36] Based on section 5 AWSA, a failure to provide care that aligns with an animal's biological needs triggers a presumption that the welfare or safety of the animal has been compromised. Moreover, the requirement of stimulation, socialisation and environmental enrichment for certain animals, as stated in section 8 AWSA, is conceived in terms of their biological needs. It is important to recognise that these obligations could evolve alongside our understanding of the notion of biological needs. This permeability will be further discussed in section III.

III. Theoretical Considerations

This section provides an overview of the various theoretical reflections that may emerge from the Québec experience and their relevance to the broader animal law community. Québec law allows us to reflect on the impact of the dereification of animals, especially in a civil law context (section A below). It also allows us to interrogate the parameters of statutorily recognising sentience and biological

[30] Michaël Lessard and Marie-Andrée Plante, 'Les codes de pratique de l'industrie animale sont-ils obligatoires ? Analyse des articles 5, 6 et 7 de la Loi sur le bien-être et la sécurité de l'animal' (2023) *Repères* 3577.

[31] AWSA (n 2) s 8.

[32] ibid, s 9.

[33] ibid, s 10.

[34] ibid, s 12.

[35] ibid.

[36] See also how the notion of biological needs is used in Regulation respecting the safety and welfare of cats and dogs, CQLR c P-42, r 101 at 2; Regulation respecting the welfare and safety of domestic companion animals and equines, CQLR c B-31, r 01; Regulation respecting animals in captivity (n 10).

needs (section B), as well as the possible interpretations of sentience and biological needs (section C). However, it is important to note that this section only provides a preliminary exploration of these topics and further in-depth discussions are needed to delve into these issues.

A. The Legal Status of Animals after Dereification

Civil law generally divides the world into two categories: persons and things.[37] The category of persons is considered the dominant one, while the category of things is viewed as residual. Therefore, only those individuals identified by the law as persons are recognised as such, while all others are classified as things. The mere fact of not falling into the category of persons is enough to qualify as a thing.

Québec law challenges this classic *summa divisio* by removing animals from the category of things – dereifiying them – without placing them in the category of persons. Indeed, Article 898.1 CCQ explicitly states that 'Animals are not things' but rather sentient beings with biological needs.[38] In so doing, Québec civil law seems to create a new category that, to my knowledge, is not found in other civil law systems.[39] For example, in France, although the Civil Code recognises animals as sentient beings,[40] they still remain in the legal category of things.[41]

Thus, Québec law could be understood in one of two ways. Firstly, Québec law may create a third category parallel to persons and things, that of sentient beings. Alternatively, Québec law could modify the *summa divisio* from persons/things to beings/things. In this chapter, I do not need to decide the issue or defend either position. Instead, I would like to simply point out that animals can no longer be understood as belonging to the category of things. Animals now occupy a distinct legal space that, while not equivalent to that of persons, also sets them apart from things.

I believe that this departure from the realm of things must have legal consequences. It goes against the logic of law that the categorisation of an element – especially when it concerns a *re*categorisation explicitly brought about by democratic legislative action – could be conceived as merely cosmetic, devoid of normative

[37] Regarding the statements in this paragraph, see Gaële Gidrol-Mistral and Anne Saris, 'La construction par la doctrine dans les manuels de droit civil français et québécois du statut juridique de l'embryon humain. Volet 1 : la maxime « infans conceptus »' (2013) 43 *Revue de droit de l'Université de Sherbrooke* 209, 222.

[38] CCQ (n 1) Art 898.1.

[39] In the Czech Republic, the Civil Code seems to state that animals are not things, but the provisions applicable to things apply to them as long as the provisions do not contradict their nature. I think this implies that animals are still classified within the legal category of things, even though they are not things in the colloquial sense. See Czech Republic, Občanský Zákoník, Art 494. The Spanish Civil Code seems to adopt a similar approach by stating that the regime of things applies to animals as long as it is compatible with their nature. See Spain, Código Civil, Art 333bis.

[40] France, Code civil, Art 515-14.

[41] Cour d'appel de Poitiers, 1re chambre civile, 24 avril 2018, n 16/00881.

impact. Moreover, the statement in Article 898.1 CCQ that property law still applies to animals does not negate the assertion that animals are no longer legally considered as things, but rather beings.[42] For these reasons, this new categorisation of animals can be understood, in the words of Professor Alexandra Popovici, as a 'revolution … in our legal relationship with animals'.[43]

Further clarifications from judges and scholars seem necessary to fully understand the implications of this new categorisation of animals. In my view, this new category of sentient beings implies, at the very least, that its members should be treated with respect for their sentience and biological needs, in the same spirit as expressed by the Court of Appeal in *Road to Home c Montréal* when explaining the legal consequences of recognising these animal characteristics. With this in mind, let us now explore the theoretical considerations surrounding the legal recognition of the concepts of sentience and biological needs.

B. The Normative Ramifications of Recognising Animal Sentience and Biological Needs

The primary consideration in determining the normative ramifications of recognising animal characteristics in law is whether a descriptive statutory statement – ie, for Québec, the declaration in the Civil Code that animals are sentient beings – will be interpreted by legal officials as having prescriptive force. In my view, statutory statements recognising animals' sentience or biological needs should have some normative force, at least in terms of interpretative value. This viewpoint stems from a general principle of statutory interpretation mandating that every provision, paragraph, and even word of a statute must be given some effect.[44] No part should be understood as inoperative, void or superfluous, to the extent possible, given other principles of statutory interpretation.

In Québec law, this presumption of effect is evident, as the Court of Appeal concluded that the recognition of animals' sentience and biological needs has prescriptive force. As we have seen, the Parliament declared in the Civil Code of Québec that 'Animals are not things. They are sentient beings and have biological needs.'[45] At first glance, this provision might seem like a descriptive statement that does not invite normative consequences. It could also be perceived as merely having interpretative value, meaning its use is limited to providing guidance in interpreting other provisions impacting animals. However, the Court of Appeal

[42] This suggests that animals are beings that can be appropriated by a person or appropriated for a purpose. See Lessard (n 14) 144–45.
[43] Popovici (n 19) 134 (my translation).
[44] Pierre-André Côté, Stéphane Beaulac and Mathieu Devinat, *Interprétation des lois* (Thémis, 2009) 1048–50.
[45] CCQ (n 1) Art 898.1.

concluded that this provision directly imposes a new legal obligation to respect animals' sentience. The Court stated that:

> By affirming that animals are sentient beings with biological needs, the legislator dictates at the same time the conduct that must be followed by all those who interact with such beings. This provision … therefore has the value of a behavioural standard.[46]

The legal recognition of sentience has thus been understood as establishing a legal obligation to act in a manner that respects animals' sentience.[47]

Besides the issue of whether a descriptive statement recognising an animal characteristic would have a prescriptive consequence, the normative impact of the legal recognition of animal sentience and biological needs may be limited by three other factors: (1) location; (2) invocability; and (3) interpretation.

First, a recognition of animal sentience and biological needs could have an overarching impact only if it is located in an overarching source of law. For example, if sentience recognition is merely mentioned in a parliamentary motion, its impact may be quite limited or even non-existent. Similarly, if sentience recognition is solely present in a statute's title (such as the legislation in New Zealand[48] or in the United Kingdom[49]), or not contained in a statute applying to most (if not all) human–animal interactions (such as New Zealand and the United Kingdom, as well as the European Union treaty[50]), its impact may be doubtful, although this will ultimately depend on the legal particulars of each jurisdiction. For a recognition of an animal characteristic to have a significant impact on the law, it must be contained in an appropriate legal instrument, that is, a source of law that is understood to have a general impact on the law. This source of law could be a constitution or a statute of general application. In the context of civil law, it could be a civil code. Indeed, civil codes, such as Québec's civil code, are understood as laying the *jus commune* of a given jurisdiction and serving as the foundation of all other laws in matters related to private law.[51] Therefore, the recognition of animal characteristics in a civil code has the potential to significantly impact the law in general.[52] It thus makes sense to see civil law jurisdictions adopt a recognition of animal sentience in their civil codes (such as Belgium, Columbia, the Czech Republic, France, Québec and Spain).[53] The location of a sentience recognition provision may thus affect the scope of its impact on the law.

[46] *RHRS c Montréal* (n 18) at para 57 (my translation).

[47] Lessard (n 17).

[48] Animal Welfare Act 1999, 1999 No 142, title.

[49] Animal Welfare (Sentience) Act 2022, UKPGA 2022 c 22, title. Note that the British statute also provides for the creation of an advisory Animal Sentience Committee.

[50] European Union, Treaty on the Functioning of the European Union, Art 13.

[51] See, for example, CCQ (n 1) preamble.

[52] See ch 5 of this volume.

[53] Belgium, Code civil, Art 3.39; Columbia, Codigo Civil, Art 655; Czech Republic, Občanský Zákoník, Art 494; France, Code civil, Art 515-14; Québec, Civil Code of Québec (n 1), Art 898.1.; Spain, Código Civil, Art 333bis.

Second, the question of who can invoke a recognition provision may further affect its impact. In Québec, although we know that the recognition of sentience and biological needs in Article 898.1 CCQ imposes legal obligations, it is still unclear who has the legal standing to enforce those obligations. The Court of Appeal has stated that an animal's owner has legal standing to ensure the animal's protection.[54] However, more court cases are needed to determine whether other humans may also have legal standing and in what context. For example, could an animal's custodian have similar legal standing? What about interested parties, especially when the person violating an animal's sentience or biological needs is the owner? Can animal rights groups have public standing in some circumstances? These questions remain unanswered, but could have important implications for how the legal obligations deriving from sentience recognition are enforced.[55] Ultimately, these questions can all be reduced to a simple one: to whom are the legal obligations deriving from sentience recognition owed?

Third, the interpretation of sentience and biological needs by legal officials may also impact the extent of obligations resulting from their legal recognition. Three factors concerning the interpretation of these concepts may influence their normative impact: their isolation from scientific knowledge; their departure from the raison d'être of using these concepts; and the content of their interpretation.

An animal characteristic that is recognised in law runs the risk of being transformed into a legal concept, that is, a concept that is shaped by court decisions, legislative actions and scholarly writings. Once seized by the law, such a concept can take on a life of its own, potentially deviating from its original meaning and latest understandings in other fields. In the case of sentience and biological needs, these concepts seem intuitively connected with the current state of scientific knowledge about animals.[56] However, divergence is possible, as seen in the case of sentience where most jurists in Québec seem to interpret it narrowly as referring to the capacity to feel pain, while many scientists have broader conceptions of sentience, understanding it as the capacity to have subjective experiences. In my view, this discrepancy raises concerns insofar as the legal concepts may not keep pace with advancements in scientific knowledge. If legislators decide to use the concepts of sentience and biological needs to describe and integrate the reality of animals in law, as is the case in Québec,[57] the gap between the legal understanding

[54] *RHRS c Montréal* (n 18) at para 22.

[55] During the writing of this chapter, the Superior Court of Québec concluded that rights groups cannot have standing, but this decision is currently under appeal. See *Communauté Droit Animalier Québec – DAQ c Festival Western de St-Tite inc*, 410-17-002039-225, 21 April 2023, Justice Marc Paradis.

[56] For a discussion on the relationship between law and other fields regarding the concepts of sentience and biological needs, see Lessard (n 1).

[57] See, for example, National Assembly of Québec, Committee on Agriculture, Fisheries, Energy and Natural Resources, 'Clause-by-clause consideration of Bill 54, An Act to improve the legal situation of animals', *Hansard*, vol 44, nº 52, 41st legislature, 1st session, 20 October 2015, p 1 ('Il n'y a plus de doute en 2015 pour nous et nos concitoyens que les animaux ne sont pas des biens meubles. C'est pourquoi la première partie de ce projet de loi modifie le Code civil du Québec afin que les animaux soient considérés légalement non plus comme des biens meubles, mais plutôt comme des êtres doués de sensibilité et

of these concepts and scientific knowledge regarding animals' reality would drive the law away from the legislative intent. Incorporating knowledge and consensuses from other scientific fields into the law after those notions become legal concepts can be a slow process, subject to the uncertainties of court decisions and legislative action.

Moreover, by becoming legal concepts, sentience and biological needs also run the risk of becoming *liminal legal concepts*, ie, concepts whose shapes are negotiated by jurists in a space perceived as proto-legal before being formally integrated into the law, an integration that often robs concepts of their raison d'être.[58] The raison d'être of sentience and biological needs in animal law discourses is, above all, to achieve greater respect for animals and their interests. This purpose is reflected in the parliamentary debates surrounding the recognition of these animal characteristics in Québec,[59] as I believe it is in other jurisdictions that have recognised animal sentience. However, when these concepts are appropriated by the law, they can be used to justify various forms of exploitation and suffering as being supposedly respectful.[60] This mechanism can be observed in several countries that have legally recognised animal sentience. Despite such recognition, the exploitation and slaughter of animals continues, with some arguing that these practices still respect animal sentience or are justified by it, even in the absence of concrete changes. This suggests a gap between the law and the reasons for recognising animal sentience in law.

In addition, the interpretation of sentience and biological needs significantly affects their normative impact. These concepts are subject to multiple possible interpretations, with some interpretations being broader and others narrower. For example, in Québec, legal officials have interpreted sentience narrowly, mostly as referring to the capacity to experience pain. A discussion of these possible interpretations requires a separate exploration, which we shall undertake in the next section.

C. The Interpretation of Key Concepts

This section explores how the concepts of sentience and biological needs can be subject to different interpretations – some broader and some narrower. To

ayant des impératifs biologiques. … Le Québec peut et doit faire mieux en matière de bien-être animal.', Pierre Paradis, Minister of Agriculture, Fisheries and Food), 5 ('L'animal n'est pas un bien meuble, l'animal est un être doué de sensibilité, voilà des choses qui sont acquises maintenant, je pense, dans la société québécoise et qui méritent d'être inscrites dans une loi … le ministre a dit aussi que le bien-être de l'animal est une priorité. Moi, je pense, c'est là-dessus qu'on va travailler.', Agnès Maltais, official opposition). See also Martine Lachance, 'Le nouveau statut juridique de l'animal au Québec' (2018) 120 *Revue du notariat* 333, 342. I would like to thank Daphnée B Ménard for those sources.

[58] Jonas-Sébastien Beaudry, 'Welcoming Monsters: Disability as a Liminal Legal Concept' (2017) 29 *Yale Journal of Law & Humanities* 291, 292–93.

[59] National Assembly of Québec (n 57).

[60] ibid.

highlight these differences, I will use Martha Nussbaum's capabilities approach to illustrate the possible content of both broad interpretations. It is interesting to note that the capabilities theory reveals that broad interpretations of sentience and biological needs may yield similar outcomes. A broad interpretation of sentience could require respect for the aspirations of animals, listed by Nussbaum as capabilities. Similarly, a broad interpretation of biological needs requires placing animals in conditions where they can exercise all the possibilities of their bodies, which can be understood as being their capabilities. That said, it is important to clarify that this section does not aim to defend the capabilities approach as the desirable interpretation of sentience and biological needs. Rather, it uses the capabilities approach to illustrate the potential that lies within each of these concepts.

i. The Concept of Sentience

The concept of sentience may be interpreted in several ways, some broader and others narrower. The choice of interpretation adopted by legal officials necessarily has an impact on the legal consequences of recognising animal sentience.

Until now, it seems that legal officials have interpreted the animal sentience recognised in the Civil Code of Québec as referring only to the capacity to feel pain.[61] This restricted interpretation of the notion of sentience may partly explain why the recognition of animal sentience has not led to any significant change in the treatment of animals. Indeed, this pain-focused interpretation is co-extensive with the state of Québec law prior to the 2015 animal law reform, where several provisions already aimed to reduce and minimise animal suffering, notably through criminal law. As a result, the legal obligations arising from the pain-focused interpretation of sentience were already addressed through existing anti-cruelty and welfare regulations.

However, other interpretations of sentience exist in scholarly literature. Many scholars understand sentience as the ability to feel subjective experiences, including but not limited to the ability to feel pain and pleasure.[62] A number of

[61] Lessard (n 17).

[62] See, for example, Martha C Nussbaum, *Justice for Animals: Our Collective Responsibility* (Simon & Schuster, 2023) ('capable of having a subjective point of view on the world and feeling pain and pleasure' at xxiv; 'those who have a point of view on the world, for whom things matter' at 8; 'conscious awareness' at 51; 'the ability to feel, to have a subjective perspective on the world' at 97; 'capable of perception and desire, and of moving in response to that combination. By perception I mean … the capacity to focus on objects in the world, in a way that's not just a causal collision, that has real directedness or what philosophers call intentionality. The world *looks like something* to these creatures. They have some sort of subjective experience. With desire, it is similar: the creatures we are looking for don't just mechanically jump away from harm or move toward food; they have a felt orientation toward what is seen as good and a felt aversion to what is seen as bad. That is what makes their striving significant.' at 119; 'Sometimes sentience is reduced to the ability to feel pain; but it is really a much broader notion, the notion of having a subjective point of view on the world' at 119; 126–31); Sue Donaldson and Will Kymlicka, *Zoopolis: A Political Theory of Animal Rights* (Oxford University Press, 2011) 25. (tying the concepts of sentience and self: 'Beings who experience their lives from the inside, and for whom life can go better or worse are selves, not things, whom we recognize as experiencing vulnerability–to pleasure

philosophers have developed theories and proposals that enable us to implement normative consequences to such a broader interpretation.

For instance, let us consider Martha Nussbaum's capabilities approach, according to which sentient animals can be understood as forming subjective experiences of striving for something, a movement to which moral value must be ascribed. So, one way to conceptualise, and ultimately implement, a broader interpretation of sentience is to start by ascribing moral value to beings' aspirations. The potential for the capabilities approach becomes clearer when we examine its rationale, which I suggest reconstructing based on Nussbaum's extension of the theory to animals in her recent book, *Justice for Animals: Our Collective Responsibility*:

1. Animals value the ends they strive for (empirical statement).[63]
2. One must not interfere with another being's active strive towards a valued end (moral intuition).[64]
3. Humans interfere with animals' strives in various ways (empirical statement).
4. Humans must not interfere with animals' strives (application of statement 2 to 3).
5. Humans stepping back is not an adequate course of action:
   a. Humans control and influence the entire planet to such an extent that completely stepping back to allow animals to strive without any human interference is impossible (empirical statement).[65]
   b. Stepping back might not improve the striving potential of animals, especially in the case of domesticated animals, since other animals would gravely interfere with their aspirations (empirical statement).[66]
6. Enabling animal striving in a context of human control implies that humans must adapt their behaviour to allow animals to strive towards some ends (application of statements 4 to 5).[67]
7. Striving for an end implies being able to choose that end (empirical statement).[68]
8. Enabling animals to strive requires providing them with a reasonable range of opportunities to choose from (a combination of statements 6 and 7).[69] Those

and pain, to frustration and satisfaction, to joy and suffering, or to fear and death'); Gary Steiner, *Animals and the Moral Community: Mental Life, Moral Status, and Kinship* (Columbia University Press, 2008) xi–xii ('sentience is a capacity shared by all beings for whom the struggle for life and flourishing *matters*, whether or not the being in question has a reflective sense of which things matter or how they matter'); Gary L Francione, *Introduction to Animal Rights: Your Child or the Dog?* (Temple University Press, 2000) 6 ('To be sentient means to be the sort of being who is conscious of pain and pleasure; there is an 'I' who has subjective experiences').

[63] Nussbaum (n 62) 67, 69–71, 119, 131.

[64] ibid, xxiv, 2, 67, 71, 119, 137–38, 180. Therefore, animals who do not strive for ends are not proper subjects of her theory of justice, see ibid at 138–48.

[65] Nussbaum (n 62) 193–254.

[66] ibid.

[67] ibid, 8, 112.

[68] ibid, 67, 87, 90.

[69] ibid, 80–81, 102.

options are called capabilities[70] and each individual animal can choose which options she would like to pursue.

The broad interpretation of sentience, viewed through the lens of the capabilities approach, enables us to ascribe moral value to animal capabilities. Thus, an obligation to respect animal sentience would require respecting animals' capabilities. Of course, further clarification is needed to determine upon whom this duty is imposed. That said, the purpose of this chapter is not to explain how to operationalise the capabilities approach or to defend it as the preferred interpretation of sentience. Rather, my intention is simply to show the existence and scope of broader interpretations of sentience. The capabilities approach serves as just one example. Let us now consider how the concept of biological needs can also be subject to various interpretations.

ii. The Concept of Biological Needs

The concept of biological needs can also be interpreted in different ways. However, in comparison to sentience, this concept seems less debatable because the term itself refers to the notions of 'needs' and 'biological'. Furthermore, the concept of biological needs is also more clearly defined in Québec law. Let us first examine how the law defines the concept of biological needs, before addressing areas that are potentially open to interpretation.

Indeed, unlike sentience, biological needs are defined in Québec law. The AWSA defines biological needs as follows:[71]

> 'biological needs' means the basic physical, physiological and behavioural needs related to such factors as the animal's species, subspecies, race, age, stage of growth, size, level of physical or physiological activity, sociability with humans and other animals, cognitive abilities and state of health and those related to the animal's capacity to adapt to the cold or heat or to bad weather;
>
> *«impératifs biologiques»: les besoins essentiels d'ordre physique, physiologique et comportemental liés, notamment, à l'espèce, la sous-espèce ou la race de l'animal, à son âge, à son stade de croissance, à sa taille, à son niveau d'activité physique ou physiologique, à sa sociabilité avec les humains et autres animaux, à ses capacités cognitives, à son état de santé, ainsi que ceux liés à son degré d'adaptation au froid, à la chaleur ou aux intempéries;*

Accordingly, biological needs include not only needs of a purely physical nature, but also those related to the sociability and cognitive capacities of animals. More broadly, any 'behavioural/*comportemental*' need constitutes a biological need. Therefore, the definition crystallised in law is broader than one might have initially imagined for such a term. Once this definition is established, the specific requirements of the obligation to satisfy animals' biological needs may depend on the state of scientific knowledge about their physical, physiological, and behavioural needs.

[70] ibid, 8, 86–89.
[71] AWSA (n 2) s 1.

However, according to Québec law, the life of an animal itself does not constitute a biological need.[72] While biological needs are generally understood as the animal's needs to stay alive, they do not seem to include the need to stay alive itself. This debatable conception of biological needs may evolve over time.[73] Staying alive is necessary to fulfill the biological needs that have already been recognised. Moreover, insofar as scientific knowledge establishes, for example, that some animals have a need to sustain meaningful long-term relationships – either with other animals or with humans – and to carry out long-term projects – such as raising their children – such needs may give rise to a corollary need to live long enough to fulfil these relationships and projects.

As a result, the norm of satisfying animals' biological needs may evolve based on advancements in scientific knowledge regarding animals' physical, physiological, and behavioural needs, but also according to philosophical and political perspectives on what falls into these categories of needs. In this sense, fostering a dialogue between the various disciplines would be fruitful in clarifying the meaning and content of the legal notion of biological needs.

The capabilities approach, discussed in the previous section, offers an example of a possible interpretation of biological needs. Under this approach, animals' capabilities, which are defined as striving options particular to their bodies, are given a moral value. Indeed, capabilities are species-specific elements that depend on bodily characteristics. This approach calls for animals to be placed in conditions where they can choose to exercise all the possibilities of their bodies, ie their capabilities. Having the opportunity to exercise the possibilities of one's body – a form of freedom – can be understood as a biological need. Moreover, a certain element of freedom is already understood as a biological need in Québec law. For example, according to the AWSA, animals must be allowed to socialise or move if they desire.[74] This recognition of animals' need for elements of freedom within the current conception of biological needs indicates that the need for freedom per se as a biological need is possible in the future.

This chapter has sought to demonstrate that Québec animal law may offer many insights for comparative law scholars and legal theorists. I outlined the animal law regime adopted in 2015, with recognition of the sentience and biological needs of animals in the Civil Code of Québec and the adoption of a new AWSA. Perhaps more interestingly for an international readership, I have also highlighted some theoretical avenues for reflection arising from the Québec experience. We examined how the dereification of animals into the new category of sentient beings, and how the sentience statutory recognition's location, invocability and interpretation can impact the law. I invite readers to explore these avenues for further theoretical reflection on the recognition of animals' sentience and biological needs.

[72] *RHRS c Montréal* (n 18) para 58.
[73] For a more detailed argument, see Lessard (n 17) 77–81.
[74] AWSA (n 2) ss 5, 8.

11

Perspectives on the Recognition of Animal Sentience in Spain

CARLOS ANDRÉS CONTRERAS LÓPEZ[1]

I. Introduction

The Spanish Civil Code (hereinafter CC), enacted in 1889, referred to animals as things in order to regulate the way of acquiring them and to establish that their owners are liable for any damages the animals cause. 132 years had to pass before the CC would be amended by Law 17/2021 of 15 December[2] which introduced the consideration of all animals as 'living beings endowed with sensitivity' and as 'sentient beings' (to distinguish them from things or goods).

The amendment to the CC was not merely theoretical as it established legal consequences based on the new classification of animals, linking animal sentience with the obligation to ensure animals' welfare and interests. However, the recent legislative changes are certainly insufficient to effectively halt the exploitation and suffering of the vast majority of animals in Spain, in part because almost all the consequences of the declaration of animal sentience are focused on companion animals. The general public already recognises that companion animals are sentient, and they therefore include them into their moral circles, while rejecting farm animals (which are also sentient).[3] This could turn animal law into 'companion animal' law exclusively, which is not desirable.

Now that animals are legally considered sentient beings, people are bound by more responsibilities. Although people can still exercise the right to ownership over animals, this right is increasingly limited, not only due to anti-cruelty laws, but also by laws that are starting to treat companion animals, at the very least, as

[1] Carlos Andrés Contreras López is a Visiting Fellow at the Brooks McCormick Jr Animal Law & Policy Program at Harvard Law School. He is the current President of the Barcelona Bar Association's Commission for the Protection of Animal Rights.

[2] Available at www.boe.es/diario_boe/txt.php?id=BOE-A-2021-20727.

[3] See Hank Rothgerber, 'Meat-Related Cognitive Dissonance: A Conceptual Framework for Understanding How Meat Eaters Reduce Negative Arousal from Eating Animals' (2020) 146 *Appetite* 104511.

family members. It is merely a question of time before Spanish judges and courts include animal sentience and the new legal precepts as part of their decisions in the arguments supporting animals. Legislative changes are a response to the need to tailor Spanish legislation to current societal values.

Two years after the amendment to the CC and the enactment of this 'Sentience Law', and thanks to the creation by the Spanish Government of the General Directorate for Animal Rights, two highly important changes happened in Spanish animal law in 2023: 1) the enactment of the Law on the protection of animal rights and welfare applicable nationwide (hereinafter LPDBA after the Spanish initials); and 2) the amendment of crimes against animals in the Spanish Criminal Code (hereinafter CP after the Spanish initials).

The consideration of animals as sentient beings in the CC confirms that animals are no longer property in the Spanish legal system. In the section II, I examine the background and concept of ownership, as well as the importance of animal sentience in legislation. I then analyse the amendment to the CC and the most important consequences of the new status of animals as sentient beings. I also discuss LPDBA, which mostly focuses on companion animals. The chapter ends with some comments on the recent modification to the Spanish criminal code.

II. Animals are not Property

A. Background and Concept of Ownership

Article 333 of the CC expressly set forth that for a thing to be a considered a 'good', it must be possible to take ownership of it.[4] Animals are understood to be included within the classification of chattel as they can be owned by people. This provision from 1889 kept the tradition of the European Civil Codes that derives directly from the consideration of animals as things and from the regulation of their ownership in Roman Law.[5]

By studying the Institutes of Gaius[6] we realise that for this Roman jurist, a *res* (thing) necessarily has an economic value. Gaius's intention was to classify all the elements of assets as 'things'.[7] This way, we can state that a *res* (thing) is anything

[4] Código civil español; redactado por el gobierno en cumplimiento de la Ley de 11 de mayo de 1888, y publicado á virtud de autorización concedida al mismo por real decreto de 6 de octubre del mismo año (1888), available at nrs.harvard.edu/urn-3:HUL.FIG:004693224.

[5] See Carlos Andrés Contreras López, *Régimen jurídico de los animales en Chile, Colombia y Argentina: (antecedentes, codificación y desarrollo legislativo)* (Tirant lo Blanch, 2016).

[6] T Radford Potts, *Summary of the Institutes of Gaius (Books I, I, 1–97, and III, 88–225) with Historical Introduction and Notes* (H Giles; Simpkin, Marshall, Hamilton, Kent & Co, 1907), available at nrs.harvard.edu/urn-3:hul.ebookbatch.MOML_batch:GALEMOML6001745.

[7] Sandro Schipani, *La codificazione del diritto romano comune* (Rist accresciuta, G Giappichelli, 1999).

that can be legally included in trade. Property is considered as such, not only when it is useful for man, but also when it can be owned. Thus, for example the sea and the sun are essential things for life on land; however, they are not property because they cannot be owned for the benefit of a private individual, a citizen or a nation.[8] The legal concept of ownership has been linked to the economic development of every nation and has been defined by the needs of each civilisation. Animals were classified as property in Roman law because they were fundamental to the agricultural economy of the era.

If we transfer this to our time and think about animals of species whose trade is prohibited by international treaties such as CITES,[9] domestic-bred companion animals, animals protected by the rights of nature,[10] or wild animals that live freely in cities, clearly these animals would not enter into the classical concept of property as they cannot be owned (as their trade is prohibited) or because they lack relevant economic value. Until now, when a decision has been made to protect or to grant rights to animals, they have been animals belonging to species with the closest biological traits to human (such as the great apes), with a close connection to humans (such as dogs and cats), or whose survival is in danger (wild animals). What animals from these species have in common is that their meat is not normally eaten by humans. That is why I believe that banning their trade or ownership would not face widespread rejection by society, due to the mere fact that few humans would be affected in their daily life. What about farm animals? Unfortunately, they are still important to the agricultural economy of many countries, and they can still be owned. This means they would enter into the classical concept of property.

But economic value is not the only important matter for the law today. There are humans who are an economic 'asset' for a corporation, yet they are not deemed 'property'. For example, the soccer player Erling Haaland has a market value of €170,000,000 and is 'owned' by Manchester City.[11] The Colombian Constitutional Court analysed the constitutionality of the law that spoke of the transfer of athletes which said that sports clubs were owners of the players and that they could buy or loan them. The Court understood that the term 'transfer' was unconstitutional because it disregards the dignity of athletes, as it turns them into things and clubs into the owners of individuals.[12] Thus, the protection of human rights is not based solely on sentience, or on whether they are an 'asset' for a company. Intrinsic value, and human dignity is morally relevant, and this is why I believe that in addition to sentience, intrinsic value and animal dignity is a relevant issue.

[8] See Marcel Planiol, *Tratado elemental de derecho civil*, 12th edn (JM Cajica, 1945).

[9] Over 38,000 species, subspecies and populations are protected under CITES; see cites.org/eng/app/index.php.

[10] See Kristen Stilt, 'Rights of Nature, Rights of Animals' (2021) 134 *Harvard Law Review* 276.

[11] 'Erling Haaland – Evolución Del Valor de Mercado | Transfermarkt', available at www.transfermarkt.es/erling-haaland/marktwertverlauf/spieler/418560.

[12] CCOC, *Sentencia C-320/1997*, available at www.ddc.com.co/data/SENTENCIAS/C-320-97.htm.

B. Animal Sentience and Legislation

We find sentience as an aspect to be considered in law in the work by Jeremy Bentham, *An Introduction to the Principles of Morals and Legislation II*, specifically in his famous phrase 'The question is not Can they reason? nor, Can they talk? but Can they suffer?'.[13] According to Rowan and others, Bentham's phrase, contained in a footnote, almost at the end of Volume II of his work, has become a foundational concept in considerations of animal welfare.[14] Thus, the first step in our ladder of moral values is to avoid unnecessary pain. When we see another being in pain, we empathise instantly without experiencing their pain.[15]

The word sentience is derived from the Latin verb *sentire*, meaning *to feel*, but it has many elements and has been understood to mean very different things by different writers.[16] While the term is correct to describe the capacity to suffer, sentience goes beyond that. For many, it implies a holistic approach to the needs of animals on the understanding that they are able to experience emotions associated with pleasurable states such as joy, and aversive states such as pain and fear.[17] Along those lines, Robertson and Goldsworthy argue that the acceptance of animal sentience in law should be based not just on how to avoid negative experiences for animals but also on how to provide them with opportunities for positive affective states.[18]

Vertebrates are not the only sentient beings. Studies have shown that motivational trade-offs in hermit crabs[19] and conditioned place preference in octopuses[20] are responses to injury that go beyond simple reflexes. When conveyed to policymakers, this kind of scientific evidence leads to more sensible judgments and better policy. Crump and others developed their criteria for a UK government report, which recommended regarding all cephalopod molluscs and decapod crustaceans as legally sentient.[21] The Government responded by including both

[13] Jeremy Bentham, 'An Introduction to the Principles of Morals and Legislation (Chapters I–V)' in *Utilitarianism and on Liberty* (Blackwell Publishing Ltd, 2003).

[14] Andrew Rowan et al, 'Animal Sentience: History, Science, and Politics' (2021) 6 *Animal Sentience*, available at www.wellbeingintlstudiesrepository.org/animsent/vol6/iss31/1.

[15] See Arthur Reber, Frantisek Baluska and William Miller, 'All Living Organisms Are Sentient' (2022) 6 *Animal Sentience*, available at www.wellbeingintlstudiesrepository.org/animsent/vol6/iss31/3.

[16] Barry Hughes, 'Defining and Assessing Sentience' (2022) 6 *Animal Sentience*, available at www.wellbeingintlstudiesrepository.org/animsent/vol6/iss31/13.

[17] Katy Sowery, 'Sentient Beings and Tradable Products: The Curious Constitutional Status of Animals under Union Law' (2018) 55 *Common Market Law Review* 55.

[18] Ian Robertson and Daniel Goldsworthy, 'Recognising and Defining Animal Sentience in Legislation: A Framework for Importing Positive Animal Welfare through the Five Domains Model' (2022) 48 *Monash University Law Review* 244.

[19] Mirjam Appel and Robert W Elwood, 'Motivational Trade-Offs and Potential Pain Experience in Hermit Crabs' (2009) 119 *Applied Animal Behaviour Science* 120.

[20] Robyn J Crook and Edgar T Walters, 'Neuroethology: Self-Recognition Helps Octopuses Avoid Entanglement' (2014) 24 *Current Biology* R520.

[21] Andrew Crump et al, 'Invertebrate Sentience and Sustainable Seafood' (2022) 3 *Nature Food* 884.

taxa in the Animal Welfare (Sentience) Act 2022.[22] Declaring octopuses and other similar species as sentient beings can be the first step to banning cruel practices such as boiling them alive.

A part of the animal rights movement believes that declaring animals as sentient beings in the law has not had major practical consequences. As Rowan correctly notes, 'if one examines the consumption of animals for food and research and the decline in wild animal populations, then it is just as clear that the condition of many animals has worsened considerably since Bentham penned his famous phrase'.[23] Sowery highlights this interesting paradox: the increased use of animals for human purposes, on the one hand, and the increased moral concern for the welfare of animals, on the other hand.[24] Bekoff goes further, stating that 'declaring nonhumans to be sentient beings is more of a "feel good" move, just another instance of humane-washing'.[25] In fact, despite the scientific consensus on animal sentience and increasing numbers of countries incorporating this into law, most terrestrial sentient beings on this planet live in cages.[26]

It is true that Bentham penned his famous phrase in 1789. Yet we must consider that animal law and public policies concerning animal welfare have a very recent origin. Countries in Western Europe experienced severe scarcities during and after World War II,[27] so once the war was over, meat production was increased steadily to meet the demand for food and feed the population. Based on these changes, concern for animals' quality of life increased.[28]

The Treaty of Amsterdam (1997) recognised animals as 'sentient beings', a mere 26 years prior to the publication of this chapter. Modifications to Civil Codes are also very recent: Austria (1988), Germany (1990), Switzerland (2002), Catalonia (2006) and the Czech Republic (2012) have established a negative definition of animals as 'not things' in their respective legal frameworks. Belgium (2009), France (2015), Portugal (2017) and Spain (2021) have recognised that animals are sentient beings in their legal frameworks.[29]

[22] Andrew Crump, 'Animal Sentience Science and Policy' (2022) 6 *Animal Sentience* 2, available at www.wellbeingintlstudiesrepository.org/animsent/vol6/iss31/15.

[23] Rowan et al (n 14).

[24] Sowery (n 17) 57.

[25] Marc Bekoff, 'Time to Stop Pretending We Don't Know Other Animals Are Sentient Beings' (2022) 6 *Animal sentience* 2.

[26] 'Animal Cruelty in Factory Farm Statistics – Dreadful Numbers' (27 January 2023), available at worldanimalfoundation.org/advocate/factory-farming-statistics.

[27] EM Collingham, *The Taste of War: World War II and the Battle for Food*, 1st American edn (Penguin Press, 2012).

[28] David Fraser, 'Farm Animal Production: Changing Agriculture in a Changing Culture' (2001) 4 *Journal of Applied Animal Welfare Science* 175.

[29] See Enrique Alonso García and Ana Recarte Vicente-Arche, 'La Diversidad de Fundamentos de Las Distintas Normas Que Constituyen El "Derecho Animal": La Ciencia Aplicada Del Bienestar Animal y Las Restantes Ciencias Cognitivas, Los Paradigmas Filosóficos y Éticos y Los Movimientos Sociales En Los Que Se Basa Dicho Derecho (I). Paradigmas Culturales, Científicos, Filosófico-Éticos y Movimientos Sociales En Los Que Se Basó La Primera Oleada de Normas de Bienestar Animal En El Siglo XIX y Primera Mitad Del Siglo XX' [2017] *Journal of Animal Law & Interdisciplinary Animal Welfare Studies / Revista General de Derecho Animal y Estudios Interdisciplinares de Bienestar Animal –* JAL&IAWS 81.

In the EU, the development of the science of animal welfare applied to legislation has exploded in the last 25 years. During this short time, the EU has improved welfare standards for farm animals based on the recognition of sentience.[30] In 2020 the EU outlined a new path to promote plant-based diets within the Union in its 'from farm to fork' strategy.[31] The strategy provides importance to the positive impact that it would have on people's health to follow a plant-based diet.[32] According to Bender and Brauer, the most effective behavioural change an individual can adopt to benefit the planet is to shift to a plant-based diet.[33] However, the only way to make the plant-based food system a reality is if government institutions assume a leading and interventionalist role. The declaration of sentience was a necessary first step for the development of the science of animal welfare applied to legislation in Europe.

The public still does not know enough about animals. Some prefer not to believe that animals are sentient, while others live in denial. Some people avoid the conflict between enjoying meat and concern for animal sentience by still perceiving animals as unfeeling. For example, in research conducted in 2010, subjects randomly assigned to eat beef afterwards reported that cows are less capable of suffering, and they showed less moral concern than subjects randomly assigned to eat nuts.[34] It is very important to continue working both at the academic level and at the institutional level to educate society about the sentience of animals and the corresponding moral consequences. Animal welfare scientists (and animal rights advocates) have

> a responsibility not only to do research and publish papers to be read by other scientists, but also to communicate new knowledge and understanding in a manner that it is most appropriate to the full spectrum of individuals in society.[35]

Sentience is a concept with a scientific basis which is in turn irrefutable and easily understandable by judges, legislators and the general public. But we need to raise awareness of this better. Defining animals as sentient beings will be an important step to giving them rights. Kotzmann[36] proposes using the concepts of sentience and intrinsic worth as a pluralist foundation for prospective animal rights.[37]

[30] John Anthony Webster, 'Sentience and Sentient Minds' (2022) 6 *Animal Sentience*, available at www.wellbeingintlstudiesrepository.org/animsent/vol6/iss31/6.

[31] Carlos Andrés Contreras López and Macarena Montes Franceschini, 'De La Granja A La Mesa: La Estrategia De La Unión Europea Contra Las Pandemias' (2020) 15 *Revista Brasileira de Direito Animal*.

[32] ibid.

[33] Yana Bender and Juliane Bräuer, 'The Dissonance between Knowing Animals Are Sentient Beings yet Eating Them' (2022) 6 *Animal sentience*.

[34] See Steve Loughnan, Nick Haslam and Brock Bastian, 'The Role of Meat Consumption in the Denial of Moral Status and Mind to Meat Animals' (2010) 55 *Appetite* 156.

[35] See Webster (n 30).

[36] Jane Kotzmann, 'Sentience and Intrinsic Worth as a Pluralist Foundation for Fundamental Animal Rights' [2023] *Oxford Journal of Legal Studies* gqad003.

[37] According to Kotzmann, sentience and intrinsic worth as a conceptual underpinning for animal rights hold clear benefits in that (i) the concepts are already embedded in many legal systems, (ii) sentience would enable the development of animal rights to be built on the established interest theory

In Singapore, research was carried out to determine whether intrinsic/relational values of sentient beings/non-sentient beings/ecosystems better explain people's sense of moral duty towards global nature conservation for the future. Participants from a representative sample of the population of Singapore (n = 1,508) were randomly allocated to two 'last human' scenarios. Scientists found that the best predictor of such a sense of moral duty for future nature conservation is the recognition of the intrinsic values of sentient beings. The study suggests that the concern for animal welfare may enhance rather than compete with the sense of moral duty towards nature conservation.[38]

The declaration of animals as sentient beings can in fact affect and has positively affected the lives of many animals. Sentience and even the science of animal welfare do not tell us that we should eat animals. It is up to us as a society to decide what to do with this scientific information. The application of animal sentience could lead to a highly significant improvement for animal rights, in constitutional, civil, administrative, and criminal law.

III. Animals as Sentient Beings in the CC

A. Sentient Beings and Living Beings Endowed with Sensitivity

Thanks to the Sentience Law, since 2021, animals are no longer things in the CC and have a different system, name and consideration: namely that they are sentient beings. The consequences of the consideration of animals as sentient beings in the CC has focused on companion animals. We can find the definition of companion animal that judges must use in the new (2023) Spanish Law on the protection of animal rights and welfare (LPDBA) and that will be studied in the section IV below. The LPDBA established that a companion animal is any *domestic-bred or wild* animal in captivity, kept by human beings, provided that its welfare can be maintained and that its possession is not intended for consumption or the exploitation of its products or any industrial, commercial or lucrative use and that, in the case of wild animals, its species is included in a list of companion animals to be published by the government in the near future.[39]

The CC divides animals into three categories: wild; domesticated; and domestic-bred. I consider it a mistake for this provision to remain. The central point of

of rights, and (iii) sentience directly links to the justification of rights as being primarily concerned with the prevention of pain and suffering.

[38] Tianxiang Lan, Neil Sinhababu and Luis Roman Carrasco, 'Recognition of Intrinsic Values of Sentient Beings Explains the Sense of Moral Duty towards Global Nature Conservation' (2022) 17 *PloS one* e0276614.

[39] 'BOE-A-2023-7936 Ley 7/2023, de 28 de Marzo, de Protección de Los Derechos y El Bienestar de Los Animales', available at www.boe.es/buscar/act.php?id=BOE-A-2023-7936.

the classification is the animal's dependence on man, but not its nature or genetics. Traditionally, the CC stablished that a domesticated animal will become wild once it loses the habit of returning to humans for protection or dependence. But, it is well known that the domestic-bred nature of an animal or a plant is due to morphological, physiological and genetic factors of its own species, which are transmitted from generation to generation. This distinction made sense when the CC was enacted, in 1889, because animals where considered property, but, now that animals are considered sentient beings in the CC, It should not be possible to own wild animals or those that live in freedom, simply because it is against their interests. In Spain, the few wild animals that remain are either protected or in danger of extinction.

Article 333bis.1 expressly states that animals are 'living beings endowed with sensitivity'. The legal technique used to amend the CC was similar to the one used to amend the French Code Civil.[40] However, Article 333bis.2 of the CC states that animals are also 'sentient beings'. It is a bit confusing, because being endowed with sensitivity is not the same than being sentient. What the Spanish congress was looking for was to finally adjust the CC to what Article 13 of the Treaty on the Functioning of the European Union (2009) had established: that animals are sentient beings.[41]

The 'Sentience Law' sought the definitive separation in private law between the legal status of things and the status of animals.[42] However, the new Article 333 of the CC clarifies that animals 'can also be subject to ownership'.[43] Thus, at present, animals, despite not being things, retain an economic value within a person's belongings.

B. Animals and Property

For its part, the new Article 333bis.2 of the CC represents a limitation to the right of ownership over animals. It confirms that the right of ownership is not absolute and that the capacities that traditionally comprise it (use, disposal, enjoyment) do not apply to animals if they are intended to be exercised against the animal's welfare, or against the applicable laws of animal protection.

[40] On the contrary, the legal technique to modify the Colombian Civil Code was not as precise or coherent because it considered animals as semi-chattel which are at the same time sentient beings. See: Carlos Andrés Contreras López, 'Sentient Beings Protected by Law. Analysis of Recent Changes in Colombian Animal Welfare Legislation' (2016) 2 *Global Journal of Animal Law*, fn 2, 3.

[41] See: Enrique Alonso García, *El bienestar de los animales como seres sensibles-sentientes: su valor como principio general, de rango constitucional, en el Derecho español* in Juan Alfonso Santamaría Pastor, *Los Principios Jurídicos Del Derecho Administrativo*, 1st edn (Wolters Kluwer, 2011).

[42] María José Vaquero Pinto, 'Ley 17/2021, de 15 de diciembre, de modificación del Código Civil, la Ley Hipotecaria y la Ley de Enjuiciamiento Civil, sobre el régimen jurídico de los animales [BOE-A-2021-20727]' (2022) 10 *Ars Iuris Salmanticensis* 347.

[43] Ley 17/2021, de 15 de diciembre, de modificación del Código Civil, la Ley Hipotecaria y la Ley de Enjuiciamiento Civil, sobre el régimen jurídico de los animales. [17/2021].

In that same context, Article 333bis.4 expressly enshrines that animal owners and those that live with animals have the right to request compensation for damages for emotional distress due to the loss or severe injury of their companion animal caused by a third party. Expressly recognising compensation for moral damage due to the loss of an animal in the Civil Code is undoubtedly highly relevant. This moves animals even further from the category of thing. Traditionally, in the countries with a continental law tradition, there is no compensation for moral damage due to the loss of a thing.[44]

Furthermore, for the first time the Code regulates cases in which a person finds a lost animal in the Article 611. First, the animal should be restored to its owner or its caretaker if their identity is known. If there are 'well-founded' indications that the animal found is a victim of abuse, the person who found it is not obliged to return the animal but is obliged to report it. The text also sets forth the possibility of demanding payment for all the costs the person who found the animal has incurred for the animal's care.

Regarding the sale and purchase, the reform establishes that the seller of an animal is liable to the buyer for the breach of their duties in terms of the veterinary assistance and care necessary to guarantee the animal's health and welfare if the animal suffers an injury, illness or significant alteration of behaviour that originates prior to the sale. It also establishes that in no case can the right of collateral be established over companion animals. Banning animals as collateral yet permitting ownership is a paradox. In other words, it is possible to sell a companion animal, but it cannot be given as a guarantee to pay off a debt. The reform declared that companion animals could not be subject to seizure. However, the inability to be subject to seizure limits the right of ownership and alienation by means of executing a seizure. This could be seen as recognition of an animal's right not to be separated from its human, as this would imply emotional suffering for the animal. However, it can also be seen as a human right. It is important for companion animals to be exempt from seizure.

C. Marital Crises in which Animals are Treated in a Similar Fashion as Underage Children

Article 92 of the Spanish Civil Code regulates the guardianship and custody of underage children and the parents' obligations after divorce. Additionally, it establishes when it will be possible to agree on shared custody between the parents. However, the Article set forth that starting now, prior to awarding joint custody, the judge must verify the existence of animal mistreatment, or the threat thereof,

[44] See Macarena Montes Franceschini, 'La indemnización del daño moral por la pérdida o lesión de un animal de compañía. BIDA. AOL-18-G7-8' (intercids.org, 16 November 2018), available at intercids.org/la-indemnizacion-del-dano-moral-por-la-perdida-o-lesion-de-un-animal-de-compania-bida-aol-18-g7-8/.

as a means of controlling or victimising the other spouse or cohabiting children. For the first time in the CC, animal abuse is considered a form of psychological aggression against the victim, recognising the connection between animal abuse and domestic or gender violence. In effect, some provincial courts in Spain already recognised the link between animal abuse and domestic/gender violence.[45]

In Spain, a substantial percentage of women who have been victims of violence have suffered abuse towards their companion animals by their partners. These acts and threats to harm or kill their animals are also committed to intimidate the women, make them suffer, silence and coerce them.[46] Aggressors typically use minors or animals to indirectly hurt women.[47] According to the judge of the Court of Violence against Women number 1 in Bilbao, in Spain it is common for male aggressors to threaten their victims that they will harm what the victims love most: their children or their animals.[48] In the United States of America, 35 states, Washington DC and Puerto Rico have enacted legislation that include provisions for pets in domestic violence protection orders.[49] Studies have shown that women residing at domestic violence shelters were nearly 11 times more likely to report that their partner had hurt or killed pets than a comparison group of women who said they had not experienced intimate violence. Hence, pet abuse is a significant predictor of physical violence.[50]

Under the new law, unless there is an agreement between the two spouses, in cases of separation and divorce judges will decide whether companion animals are entrusted to one or both spouses, exclusively considering the animal's welfare rather than ownership, the limitation of which resides in the animal's own interests (in terms of health and welfare). Judges will decide, when appropriate, the way in which the spouse who has not been entrusted with the care of the animal can visit it, as well as how the economic burdens associated with the animal's care will be distributed. This means that, for example, if one of the spouses can confirm during the proceedings that they have forged an emotional bond with the animal, they will

[45] Macarena Montes Franceschini 'Reconocimiento del vínculo entre la violencia interpersonal y el maltrato animal en las sentencias españolas. BIDA. AOL-19-G3' (intercids.org, 16 October 2019), available at intercids.org/reconocimiento-vinculo-violencia-genero-y-maltrato-animal-jurisprudencia-espanola.

[46] CoPPa, 'España: "Violencia de género: cuando se agrede a la víctima a través de sus animales", resumen y conclusiones | CoPPA' (7 May 2021), available at coppaprevencion.org/violencia-genero-agrede-victima-a-traves-animales-resumen-conclusiones.

[47] Soraya F Sánchez, Cristina Mateos Casado and Isabel Tajahuerce Ángel, 'Maltrato Animal, Violencia Vicaria y Violencia de Género: La Integración de Recursos Animalistas En La Intervención Integral En Violencia de Género En El Ámbito de La Pareja o Expareja' (2022) 9 *Visual Review. International Visual Culture Review / Revista Internacional de Cultura Visual* 1.

[48] See 'Derecho y Animales', available at intercids.org/episodio-62-maltrato-animal-violencia-genero-con-leticia-badiola.

[49] 'Domestic Violence and Pets: List of States That Include Pets in Protection Orders | Animal Legal & Historical Center', available at www.animallaw.info/article/domestic-violence-and-pets-list-states-include-pets-protection-orders.

[50] Frank R Ascione et al, 'Battered Pets and Domestic Violence: Animal Abuse Reported by Women Experiencing Intimate Violence and by Nonabused Women' (2007) 13 *Violence Against Women* 354.

have the right to be entrusted with the pet's care, despite not being the owner. In 2019, before the reform of the CC was approved, a judge in Valladolid had awarded shared custody of a dog named Cachas to a couple who were in court disputing the ownership of the dog. The judge considered that the *can* is not a thing, but rather a sentient being, and approved that Cachas would spend six months with each partner bearing in mind the animal's welfare.[51] Additionally, prior to the approval of the reform of the CC, a court in Madrid awarded shared custody of a dog named Panda to both members of a separated couple. This 'ruling marked a step toward the recognition of companion animals as sentient beings under the law'.[52] Both members of the unmarried couple were presented as 'jointly responsible' and 'joint caretakers' of Panda, not 'joint owners', which avoided treating Panda as a 'thing' or 'shared good'.[53]

D. Wills and Testaments

On the fate of companion animals in last wills and testaments, the reform established certain important principles. In Spain companion animals often survive their human caretaker. The bond between a pet owner and a companion animal is strong: recent studies show that this bond can be deeper in older owners.[54] In the absence of an express will of the successor in title, special attention must be paid to the animal's care and resources must be dedicated to the inheritance to ensure the animal's welfare. First, the animal will be given to the heirs or legatees, though the legal authority must guarantee the animal's care. It is interesting to analyse whether these provisions, which arise as a response to the consideration of animals as sentient beings, actually grant rights. This case involves the right for a part of an inheritance to be dedicated to caring for the animal's health and welfare. Here the CC lost the opportunity to establish what in US law is known as a pet trust. A pet trust allows an individual to name a pet guardian 'and if they wish, to leave funds providing for the continued maintenance of animals, in the event that the Pet Owner is unable to'.[55]

[51] 'C.G.P.J – Noticias Judiciales', available at www.poderjudicial.es/cgpj/es/Poder-Judicial/Noticias-Judiciales/Un-juez-de-Valladolid-otorga-la--custodia-compartida--de-un-perro-a-una-pareja-que-pleiteaba-por-la-propiedad-del-animal.

[52] Maite Fernández Simon, 'Couple in Spain Granted Joint Custody of Their Pet Dog, Panda, in Rare Ruling' *Washington Post* (27 October 2021), available at www.washingtonpost.com/world/2021/10/27/spain-dog-joint-custody-panda.

[53] See 'Sentencia pionera sobre custodia compartida de un perro: reconoce la "corresponsabilidad"' (Derecho & Animales, 9 November 2021), available at www.derecho-animales.com/sentencia-pionera-custodia-compartida-perro-reconoce-corresponsabilida.

[54] See 'Study Shows Relationship between Older Owners, Dogs Deepens over Time | CTV News', available at atlantic.ctvnews.ca/study-shows-relationship-between-older-owners-dogs-deepens-over-time-1.3884939.

[55] Rachel Hirschfeld, 'The Perfect Pet Trust: Saving Your Dog from the Unexpected' (2016) 9 *Albany Government Law Review* 107, 110.

IV. Law on the Protection of Animal Rights and Welfare (LPDBA)

On 16 March 2023, the Bill for the Protection of Animal Rights and Welfare – an administrative law – was passed into law in Spain. The preamble of the law recognises that there is increasing evidence in Spain of growing concern among citizens about the need to safeguard the protection of animals in general considering that they are sentient beings whose rights must be protected. Furthermore, it references the intrinsic value of animals, highlighting that the main goal of the law is not so much about guaranteeing the welfare of animals by assessing the conditions offered them, but rather about regulating society's recognition and protection of the dignity of animals.[56] The law recognises the need to provide coherence to the legal system for the protection of animals in Spain, establishing a shared minimum level of rights of and duties towards animals regardless of the region. This means that each autonomous community in Spain can implement legislation that provides greater protection to animals.

Interestingly, while the Spanish legislature is not afraid of speaking about the 'rights of animals' or 'animal dignity' when it creates animal protection laws in the administrative field, they are much more reserved when seeking to amend the CC or the Constitution. The new administrative law establishes the ban on sacrificing companion animals and the conditions of ownership of companion animals, as well as regulating access to means of transportation and establishments open to the public. Concerning dog owners, the law sets forth that prospective owners must attend a training course, thereby seeking to facilitate responsible animal ownership. Furthermore, the Article 29 seeks to guarantee the access of people with their companion animals, to transport, as well as to public buildings, hotels, etc.

LPDBA regulates the sale and adoption of companion animals, establishing that this can only be done by professional breeders, authorised specialised stores and animal protection centres. Although it is an important step, I believe it is insufficient as oversight of animal breeding will be extremely complicated. Moreover, LPDBA is incoherent because its field of application excludes animals used in bullfights, production animals, animals used in experimentation, wild animals, animals used in sports or work activity, and hunting dogs. The Spanish animal rights movement protested these exclusions, in particularly the exclusion of hunting dogs.[57]

It is possible that people are motivated to disengage from resonating with animal suffering when it comes into conflict with human needs and desires.[58]

[56] Ley 7/2023, de 28 de marzo, de protección de los derechos y el bienestar de los animales 2023 45618 Preamble.

[57] See 'Abogados animalistas califican de "varapalo" la nueva ley animal' (*La Vanguardia*, 10 February 2023), available at www.lavanguardia.com/vida/20230210/8747623/abogados-animalistas-califican-varapalo-nueva-ley-animal.html.

[58] See David Fraser, 'Toward a Global Perspective on Farm Animal Welfare' (2008) 113 *Applied Animal Behaviour Science* 330.

I believe that gaining a better understanding of animal sentience and of the cognitive and affective experiences of a pig, a chicken, or a cow, might be effective for people to reduce their meat consumption.

The third transitory provision of the Law on the Protection and Defense of Animals (LPDBA) banned circuses and public shows that use wild animals in captivity. I believe this is a success of the new law, and one of the provisions that does not focus solely on companion animals. However, many of the regulations that have recently been adopted in Spain because of the declaration of animals as sentient beings create a type of legislation that guarantees the right of human beings to 'have a pet'.[59] This is a mistake, because instead of incentivising the purchase of companion animals, the goal of animal law should be to reduce the rate of dog and cat ownership. I do not believe that humans have the right to have a pet due to the mere fact of being humans. Not all the species can live in captivity with humans in proper conditions to ensure their welfare, and having a pet has also an environmental impact.[60] In the US, there are more than 163 million dogs and cats that consume, as a significant portion of their diet, animal products and therefore potentially constitute a considerable dietary footprint.[61] This does not mean that we should not worry and take care of the companion animals that exist on this planet, but the overpopulation and abandonment of dogs and cats is a real global issue, so the breeding and trade of companion animals should be strictly regulated.

Stilt points out that in general, in legal systems 'animal interest are protected to the extent that humans want them to be and benefit from those protections and limitations'.[62] What Stilt describes is what is happening with animal law regarding companion animals in Spain. The reason for protecting companion animals, is so that we can have them in our apartments; travel with them; go to restaurants with them, etc.

This new law continues to allow people to own wild animals provided that the species is included in a list of companion animals to be published by the Government in the future. Although I do not support people possessing wild animals as companion animals, the law allows it. Thus, the procedure to include a wild species on the list must be very strict and based on scientific reports guaranteeing that all the species included can live in captivity with humans in proper conditions to ensure their welfare. In other words, all species included in the list must have a life worth living.

[59] See: Ley 2/2023, de 13 de marzo, de Protección, Bienestar y Tenencia de animales de compañía y otras medidas de bienestar animal 2023 42739.

[60] Leslie Albrecht, 'U.S. Pets Are Responsible for 30% of the Environmental Impact of Meat Eating' (MarketWatch), available at www.marketwatch.com/story/americas-163-million-cats-and-dogs-are-responsible-for-30-of-the-environmental-impact-of-meat-consumption-2017-08-03.

[61] Gregory S Okin, 'Environmental Impacts of Food Consumption by Dogs and Cats' (2017) 12 *PloS one* e0181301.

[62] Stilt (n 10) 278.

Although humans can create bonds with wild animals, this does not justify allowing humans to own them. Including wild animals in the list will encourage the illegal international trafficking and the sale and possession of these species. Regardless of high welfare standards, wild animals will always suffer in captivity because humans cannot offer what their habitats and natural communities can offer. Particularly, primates must not be included in the list of companion animals because they suffer greatly in captivity, especially when they are kept as pets, and because the same law established in the fourth additional provision that the government has three months to present a bill to protect great apes. Hence, the law should ban any primate from being kept in private homes as companion animals or pets.

Only native local species that are not in danger of extinction, and that do not represent a danger to the physical integrity of the owners or neighbours should be included in the list. An educational training course and a revision of the animal's housing conditions should be required for those who intend to acquire wild animals included in the list of companion animals.

As previously mentioned, the LPDBA bans euthanising companion animals in animal protection centres and veterinary clinics throughout the Spanish territory for economic reasons, overcrowding, lack of space, not finding an adopter within a certain period, age, illness or injury with the possibility of treatment either palliative or curative, due to behavioural problems that can be redirected, etc.

Chapter VI of the LPDBA regulates everything related to the 'Feline Colonies' that live in the streets, to control their population in an ethical manner, in accordance with their condition as sentient beings. The above means that the population control of stray cats must be done solely through the method of capture, sterilisation and return (Trap-Neuter-Return).

Perhaps the most interesting aspect of this new law is that in the fourth additional provision, the Spanish Government was given a three-month period to present a bill for great apes. It is a fact that the lack of legal protection for great apes is leading to an increasingly imminent risk of extinction.[63]

V. Amendment to the Criminal Code (CP)

The Spanish Congress, in its session on 16 March 2023, passed the most recent amendment to the Criminal Code (CP). The preamble of this law explains that the reason for amending the CP is to adapt the offence to the new legal status of animals as living beings endowed with sensitivity recognised by the 'Sentience Law' (2021), considering the legal good to be protected in crimes against animals, which is none other than their life, health and integrity, in both physical and

[63] Paula Casal and Peter Singer, 'The Threat of Great Ape Extinction From COVID-19' (2021) 11 *Journal of Animal Ethics* 6.

psychological terms. The reform includes the expression 'vertebrate animal' in the CP, which expands the list of animals protected by the previous CP. This way, not only domestic-bred animals, or those that live with human beings, will see their physical and emotional integrity safeguarded by criminal legislation, but also vertebrated wild animals will be added. This change, which comes as a direct consequence of the protection of animals as 'sentient beings', rectifies one of the most obvious shortcomings of the previous CP.

The CP reform introduced criminal liability for legal persons. Although natural persons can continue to be held materially liable for animal abuse, if appropriate 'we will be able to punish' legal persons, with penalties ranging from the ineligibility to receive public subsidies to the temporary closure of facilities. One recent highly publicised case was a criminal case against Vivotecnia,[64] a contract testing facility conducting tests for chemical, tobacco, pharmaceutical and agrochemical companies. A whistleblower uncovered incidents of physical abuse, verbal abuse and neglect. There was systemic, improper handling of the animals, where for example rabbits would fall and severely injure their backs. With CP in force at that time, it was nor possible to report the laboratory as a legal person for the offence of animal abuse, as only administrative regulations could be applied. From now on, a company can be reported for the offence of animal abuse.

While this all sounds great, animal law attorneys were dissatisfied with the CP reform in Spain.[65] One of the concerns is that by recognising that animals are not things, but rather sentient beings, they stop being covered by crimes 'over things' that could be beneficial for them when there are no similar crimes applicable only to animals. For example, the reform did not include the 'theft or robbery of companion animals'. Thus, if a person steals another person's companion animal, with or without violence, this would not be a crime, as it is not possible to apply the crime of theft or robbery to animals since they are no longer considered things. The judge Pilar de Lara claimed that some animals were better protected when they were considered 'things' than now that civil legislation considers them 'sentient beings'.[66] Her reasoning was that animal abuse that does not cause injuries or does not require veterinary treatment can be punished with a maximum sentence of two months, but if animals were considered a thing, the offenders could be punished for the misdemeanour of property damage, with a maximum sentence of three months.

[64] Natalie Grover and Ashifa Kassam, 'Undercover Footage Shows "Gratuitous Cruelty" at Spanish Animal Testing Facility' *The Guardian* (8 April 2021), available at www.theguardian.com/environment/2021/apr/08/undercover-footage-shows-gratuitous-cruelty-at-spanish-animal-testing-facility-madrid-vivotecnia.

[65] See 'Reforma del Código Penal en materia de maltrato animal: Tratamiento de la explotación sexual y actos sexuales con animales' (intercids.org, 20 February 2023), available at intercids.org/reforma-codigo-penal-maltrato-animal-explotacion-sexual-actos-sexuales.

[66] See Concha López, 'La jueza Pilar de Lara, sobre el nuevo Código Penal en materia de maltrato animal: "Había una línea roja, y se ha cruzado"' (*elDiario.es*, 4 March 2023), available at www.eldiario.es/caballodenietzsche/jueza-pilar-lara-nuevo-codigo-penal-materia-maltrato-animal-habia-linea-roja-cruzado_132_10002866.html.

Another issue that aroused indignation among the animal rights movement in Spain concerns sexual acts with animals as the legislature decided not to intervene to punish bestiality that does not result in injuries, deeming abstaining from criminal punishment as morally superior. In 2015 sexual exploitation of animals was included in Spain as an offence in the CP. Currently the approval of the new law implies the decriminalisation of the sexual exploitation of animals.[67] Using sentience as the only basis to protect animals can lead, for example, to sexual acts with animals being considered an offence only if it is possible to prove that the act has caused an injury. Animal law associations proposed that the offence of abuse include 'all acts of a sexual nature with an animal'[68] applying the same sentence (a maximum of 18 months in prison). But, what would acts of a sexual nature entail? Does it include acts such as: caressing, kissing, masturbating, cunnilingus? Or 'does it refer only to penetration of the mouth, anus or vagina?'

Several questions may arise regarding this topic. Is bestiality not in any case a form of violence against animals? If all sexual acts with animals are considered an offence without the need to prove physical or psychological injury, what would the Criminal Code be protecting? Would it protect human morality? Or animal dignity? Or the animal's sexual freedom and integrity? Yet if we sterilise our pets, are we not also infringing on their sexual freedom?

What is clear is that even if an act is not violent or does not cause injuries, it is not necessarily acceptable. Thus, although sentience is the current basis to protect animals, this should not be the only criterion to consider. We must also consider the vulnerability and dignity of animals. Furthermore, I believe that if bestiality will be penalised in Spain, it should be specified with the most explicit and concrete terms.

Although these are highly controversial topics, what animal law experts in Spain criticise most about this new law is the introduction of fines as an alternative to prison sentences in cases in which the abuse does not lead to an animal's death. The judge Pilar de Lara is certain that prison has a dissuasive effect, while fines, on the contrary, do not.[69]

I personally think that animal abusers should take educational courses focused on explaining why animals have rights and why they should not be mistreated. The animal protection movement's enthusiasm for criminal punishment is a phenomenon not exclusive to Spain. I have significant doubts about whether increasing prison sentences for animal abuse (without working on education) effectively helps animals. As Marceau notes, these criminal policies can become 'oppressive, discriminatory on racial and class lines, unproven as tools of crime reduction, and strikingly lacking in empathy'.[70]

[67] The term 'sexual exploitation' entailed problems of applicability and interpretation, as it was not clear what it covered. In fact, to my knowledge there has not been any complaint filed, nor has a single proceeding taken place between 2015 and 2023 in Spain for the sexual exploitation of animals.

[68] See González Lacabex (n 65).

[69] See López (n 66).

[70] See Justin Marceau, *Beyond Cages: Animal Law and Criminal Punishment* (Cambridge University Press, 2019).

VI. Conclusions

(1) Animal law and public animal welfare policies have a very recent origin and incorporating language regarding animal sentience into legislation can be good for the interests of animals, depending on what sentience is for the law and the level of protection. The recognition of sentience has played an important role in improving animal welfare in Europe and in important advances like the banning of battery cages, although the recognition of sentience has not been enough to decrease the impact on the climate. Reducing meat consumption and moving towards plant-based diets is fundamental. We urgently need more action and more education.

(2) The evolution of the application of sentience in legislation must:
- define what sentience is for the law and clearly establish the level of protection;
- ban the breeding, trade and ownership over animals or species of animals that it seeks to protect;
- recognise the environmental impact of mass animal breeding worldwide;
- start considering animals (or some species of animals) as subjects of rights or persons;[71]
- include policies to improve education on animal issues;
- effectively protect animals with special procedural actions which need urgent attention to safeguard their most fundamental rights. Nothing will change unless we move forward from statements of principles to actions.

(3) Only a legal system that is drafted with a correct technique, without contradictions and with rules that are easy to apply can advance in the protection of animal rights. One of the challenges for future legislative reforms will be to include all animals excluded from current animal protection laws, recognising the existence of their own interests.

(4) Thanks to the creation of the General Directorate for Animal Rights by the Spanish Government, important changes are happening in Spain. It is a fact that the recognition of animal sentience has been crucial in the evolution of animal rights protection in Spain.

[71] Some scholars like Montes argue that nonhuman animals can be considered persons according to the traditional legal concepts of person See: Macarena Montes Franceschini, 'Traditional Conceptions of the Legal Person and Nonhuman Animals' (2022) 12 *Animals (Basel)* 2590.

12

The Animal Sentience Committee: Evolution or Revolution in the Recognition of Animal Sentience in the UK?

RACHEL DUNN AND JOSHUA JOWITT

I. Introduction

As one of the first countries in the world to ban fur farming,[1] the use of great apes in scientific research and the testing of cosmetics on animals,[2] the UK is often viewed as a world leader with regards to animal welfare protections.[3] In passing the Animal Welfare (Sentience) Act 2022 (the 'Sentience Act'), the UK Government again appears to be at the forefront of legal innovation through the creation of an Animal Sentience Committee (the ASC) whose purpose is to scrutinise all government policy at the pre-legislative stage for the extent to which drafters have paid due regard to any adverse effect their proposals might have on the interests of sentient animals.

Yet the legislation is not without its critics, as it offers wide discretion without clear definitions and appears to diverge in its definition of 'animal' from other key legislation such as the Animal Welfare Act 2006 (the AWA) – meaning that even though the law now recognises certain invertebrates are capable of experiencing pain and suffering, it also holds that they do not benefit from the same protection as companion animals such as cats and dogs.[4] Although the extent to which

[1] Rachel Dunn, 'For Fur's Sake: Can the UK Ban Imports of Fur from other Countries?' (2019) 3*UK Journal of Animal Law* 42.

[2] Paula Sparks and Simon Brooman, 'Brexit: A New Dawn for Animal Used in Research, or a Threat to the 'Most Stringent Regulatory System in the World?' (2017) 2 *UK Journal of Animal Law* 1.

[3] Defra, 'Action Plan for Animal Welfare', available at assets.publishing.service.gov.uk/government/uploads/system/uploads/attachment_data/file/985332/Action_Plan_for_Animal_Welfare.pdf.

[4] Universities Federation for Animal Welfare, 'The UK has recognised Animal Sentience in Law, Now the Hard Work Begins' (*UFAW News*, 11 April 2022), available at www.ufaw.org.uk/ufaw-news/news/post/254-the-uk-has-recognised-animal-sentience-in-law-now-the-hard-work-beginsa.

the Sentience Act will succeed in increasing protection for animal interests is unknown, a key fact remains: for the first time in the domestic law of the UK, there has been a clear legislative choice to ensure that the interests of specified sentient animals are considered as part of the policy-making process. A new benchmark for advancing animal welfare and interests has been set that firmly locates animal welfare concerns at the heart of the legislative agenda, rather than pursuing the more complex rights-based arguments that appear to motivate attempts to protect animal interests through litigation in various jurisdictions.[5] This chapter will attempt to ascertain whether this choice can be vindicated, by firstly outlining the extent to which sentience has been explicitly or implicitly recognised by UK law prior to the Sentience Act's passing. It will then introduce the substantive provisions of this new legislation, addressing both the extent to which it might redress issues faced by previous animal welfare legislation and the potential effect of new problems that might arise from the discretion that the Sentience Act gives to various actors. The chapter will close by considering various means by which the problems we identify might be resolved.

We would like to caveat this chapter with the observation that the full membership of the ASC was only announced on 25 May 2023, just six weeks before this chapter was submitted to the editors of this collection. It is possible that there will have been further developments in our understanding of the ASC and its operation that may have emerged between the submission of this chapter and its publication.

II. A History and Evaluation of Animal Sentience and Legal Protection in the UK

It is important to fully contextualise the Sentience Act, which will be fully scrutinised in section III. First, it must provide an account of how legal recognition of animal sentience has been implicit in the law of the UK for several hundred years, even though explicit recognition is a much more recent phenomenon. Secondly, it must consider what problems have arisen in this framework, so that we can understand the extent to which the Sentience Act might serve to remedy them.

A. The Concept of Sentience in UK Legislation: A Historical Overview

The claim that the UK is a world leader with regards to animal welfare legislation is often grounded in the fact that the earliest national legislation that gave significant

[5] Examples include inter alia the rights-based approach taken by the Nonhuman Rights Project in New York, most recently on behalf of Happy the Elephant in *Matter of Nonhuman Rights Project, Inc v Breheny* 2022 NY Slip Op 03859.

protection to animal interests was created there.[6] Presented to the Westminster Parliament by Richard Martin in 1822 (and subsequently known as 'Martin's Act'), it made it an offence to 'cruelly beat, abuse, or ill-treat' specified farmed animals, including horses, cows and sheep. Though this was the first legislation to explicitly claim to be for the protection for animal welfare in the UK, older examples of legislative attempts to protect animal interests exist – for example, an Act Against Cruelty to Horses-Sheep (Ireland) 1635[7] was introduced to end the:

> [b]arbarous custom of ploughing, harrowing, drawing and working with horses … by the tail, whereby (besides the cruelty used to the beasts) … the like barbarous custom of pulling off the wool yearly from living sheep instead of clipping or shearing them.

In accepting that behaviour toward 'the beasts' can be cruel, this provision presupposed their sentience – even though this was neither explicit nor a clear motivational factor in its creation.[8] In a later, ultimately failed attempt to introduce legislation, Lord Erskine challenged the House of Lords 'in the name of that God who gave to man his dominion over the lower world, to acknowledge and recognise that dominion to be a moral trust'.[9] Erskine was clear in his belief that we possess a moral duty to protect animals from harm, later alluding to sentience as the reason behind this obligation by noting that: 'Almost every sense bestowed on Man is equally bestowed upon them seeing – hearing – feeling – thinking – the sense of pain and pleasure'.[10] We can therefore see that, whether implicitly or explicitly, sentience was a consideration for UK lawmakers seeking to protect animal interests even before Martin's Act came into force.

What we would now recognise as the concept of sentience began to appear more explicitly in Parliamentary debates related to animal welfare towards the end of the nineteenth century, even if it was not explicitly referred to by that name. For example, during the creation of The Cruelty to Animals Act 1876 it was argued that experimentation on cats, dogs, horses, mules and asses should be prohibited as they 'were the most intelligent, and consequently most sensitive to pain'.[11] On the other side of this coin, in the same debate it was argued that 'A salmon caught with a fly pulls in a way which would be impossible to a creature of sensitive organization. In fact, if we had not some assurance of this, many of our common practices would be intolerably cruel.'[12] Both arguments evidence lawmakers' belief

[6] It is important to note that Reddy's chapter in this book outlines how Massachusetts introduced legislation in 1641, which outlawed cruelty to some working/farmed animals. The UK had the first legislation that applied nationally, which is why it is often cited to be the first to introduce animal welfare laws.

[7] An Act against Plowing by the Tayle, and pulling the Wooll off living Sheep (1635) 10&11 Chas 1 c 15.

[8] Piers Beirne, *Confronting Animal Abuse: Law, Criminology, and Human-Animal Relationships* (Rowman & Littlefield Publishers, 2009).

[9] *Hansard* HL Deb Vol 14, cols 554–571 (15 May 1809) (Lord Erskine).

[10] Ibid.

[11] Cruelty to Animals Bill (Friday 11 August 1876) col 1151.

[12] *Hansard* HC Deb Vol 231, cols 927–28 (9 August 1876) (Lyon Playfair MP). Recent research into fish sentience shows this view to be misplaced; see Lynne U Sneddon and Matthew C Leach,

that a species' sentient capacities provide a reason to protect them. Sentience again found implicit recognition when the Protection of Animals Act 1911 introduced the concept of 'unnecessary suffering'. In acknowledging that animals can suffer and feel pain, this concept, which still exists in law today, not only presupposes their sentience but establishes the principle that causing unnecessary suffering ought to be criminalised. Sentience is therefore a necessary precondition of this offence, showing that it can implicitly underpin criminal sanctions even if not explicitly acknowledged by the legislation.[13]

The main statute governing the welfare and protection of animals in England and Wales today is AWA,[14] which both consolidated older legislation and introduced new offences based on the concept of animal welfare.[15] Again, though the term is not expressly used, we find implicit recognition of sentience in AWA; for example in section 62(1), which brings both physical *and* mental suffering within the scope of the Act. The term was, however, used explicitly during the passing of the legislation – such as in Baroness Miller's comment that 'the opinion of the scientists who have worked on the Bill … is that vertebrate animals, including goldfish, are demonstrably sentient'.[16] It should be noted at this point that the scope of protection offered to sentient beings by the AWA is limited; it applies only to nonhuman vertebrates,[17] and excludes wild animals and those used in experiments from its protection.[18]

Sentience was first explicitly incorporated into UK law not from a domestic source, but through Article 13 of the Treaty on the Functioning of the EU (TFEU).[19] This Article reads as follows:

> In formulating and implementing the Union's agriculture, fisheries, transport, internal market, research and technological development and space policies, the Union and the Member States shall, since animals are sentient beings, pay full regard to the welfare requirements of animals, while respecting the legislative or administrative provisions and customs of the Member States relating in particular to religious rites, cultural traditions and regional heritage.

This provision explicitly identifies an animals' sentience as a sufficient reason to consider them worthy of additional legal protection. It does this through imposing

'Anthropomorphic denial of fish pain' (2016) 3 *Animal Sentience*; Joao L Saraiva et al, 'Farming Fish' in Andrew Knight, Clive Phillips and Paula Sparks (eds), *Routledge Handbook of Animal Welfare* (Routledge, 2022).

[13] Charlotte E Blattner, 'The Recognition of Animal Sentience by the Law' (2019) 9 *Journal of Animal Ethics* 121, 121–122.

[14] Animal welfare is presently mostly a devolved competence in the UK.

[15] This includes the s 9 Welfare Offence, which places a positive duty on owners of animals to provide for their welfare. This is based on the Five Freedoms, which came out of the Brambell Report when reviewing intensive farming practices. The UK has moved on slightly from this, focusing more on ensuring animals have a life worth living, but the Five Freedoms are still prevalent in legislation, both domestically and internationally.

[16] Animal Welfare Bill, Hansard, HL Vol 685, col 1015 (23 October 2006).

[17] AWA, s 1.

[18] ibid s 58.

[19] Treaty on the Functioning of the European Union, Art 13.

a duty on all EU institutions and Member States to 'pay full regard' to the welfare requirements of animals because they are sentient beings. It is, however, fairly limited in its scope; it only applies to the policy areas explicitly listed and is subject to the limitations provided for. As will be addressed below with regards to farmed animals, this led to a situation where certain classes of animal did not benefit from any increase in welfare standards that might have been expected from an explicit legal acknowledgment that their sentience makes them worthy of additional legal protections. When the UK left the EU, however, the Government did not retain this provision, meaning that until the coming into force of the Sentience Act in 2022, the UK was again without explicit legal recognition of the importance of sentience to animal welfare.

B. Problems with this Framework and the Introduction of the Sentience Act

Having presented a historical overview of the extent to which sentience was recognised by UK law, we can move to a brief assessment of what problems arose from this framework. Firstly, despite sentience being implicitly recognised as important for animal welfare, it is far from certain that this was a primary motivational factor in introducing early legislation. Contemporary scholars are of the belief that more likely explanations for the introduction of early legislation are economic[20] or connected to the civilising mission of protecting the working classes from themselves through prohibiting popular pastimes such as bull-baiting.[21]

Secondly, it must be observed that the social use of specific animals is still a key determining factor with regards to the legal protection they are entitled to; though the EU recognised sentience in law, its limited scope and express limitations noted above meant that animal welfare standards on UK farms remained poor in comparison to those experienced by companion animals.[22] The Animal Protection Index acknowledges that the recognition of animals as sentient has 'become a matter of symbolic importance' and the UK has no history of relying on Article 13.[23] For example, it has long been known that the conditions for broiler chickens is not conducive to their welfare, as they are genetically bred to grow significantly faster than is natural, causing significant health issues such as leg

[20] Thomas Kelch, 'A short history of (mostly) western animal law: Part I' (2012) 19 *Animal Law* 23.

[21] Deborah Legge and Simon Brooman, *The Law Relating to Animals* (Routledge-Cavendish, 1997), 41. It is noted in this text that early attempts at animal welfare legislation were perceived to be 'anti-working class'.

[22] UK Centre for Animal Law, 'Brexit, Article 13, and the Debate on Recognising 'Animal Sentience' in Law' (A-LAW Briefing Note, November 2017).

[23] Animal Protection Index, 'United Kingdom' (2020), available at api.worldanimalprotection.org/country/united-kingdom.

disorders and cardiovascular diseases.[24] The UK Government has not committed to legislating for better conditions for farmed animals that would reduce intensive farming practices, even when Article 13 was applicable. Though it required the UK to pay full regard to animals as sentient beings it has not prevented the UK from continuing to ignore a certain level of harm and suffering due to the societal need of the animal, and the legal recognition of sentience has had little impact on that.[25] Blattner suggests this difference in how legal systems treat different animals is due to 'cognitive biases in society', which explains why the law allows the continued mistreatment of some animals despite acknowledging their sentience.[26] She also highlights the risk of scientific biases that may favour assessments of sentience that permit the continued use of animals, and the anthropocentric bias of ascribing sentience to animals with more human-like physiological traits.[27] Any benefit to legally recognising an animal as sentient under Article 13 TFEU is thus contingent on a limiting factor: that public bodies merely need to show they have paid 'full regard' to the impact of their policies on animal welfare. This provides a means by which the biases identified by Blattner could influence the ability of this legislation to properly protect all sentient animals from pain and suffering.[28]

The extent to which animal interests are fully protected is also contingent on the existence of proper investigation and enforcement of legislation, and too often the potential benefits of animal welfare legislation are limited by an 'enforcement gap' between the written law and its enforcement.[29] For example, though the AWA is centrally overseen by the Department of Environment, Food and Rural Affairs (Defra), its implementation and enforcement is mainly delegated to resource-poor local authorities which are often unable to fulfil their obligations under the legislation due to an absence of central government support. Even in jurisdictions where government agencies are responsible for animal law enforcement, few, if any, details on enforcement activities are made publicly available.[30] It often falls to NGOs to fill this gap, despite them having little to no statutory authority to do so.[31] In England and Wales, this is mainly the RSPCA[32] – which, it is claimed, is

[24] KM Hartcher and HK Lum, 'Genetic selection of broilers and welfare consequences: a review' (2020) 76 *World's Poultry Science Journal* 154.

[25] Angus Nurse, 'A Question of Sentience: Brexit, Animal Welfare and Animal Protection Law' (2019) 10 *Journal of Animal & Environmental Law* 32.

[26] Charlotte E Blattner, 'The Recognition of Animal Sentience by the Law' (2019) 9 *Journal of Animal Ethics* 121.

[27] Ibid.

[28] Debbie Legge, 'Key Animal Law Across Europe' in Andrew Knight, Clive Phillips and Paula Sparks (eds), *Routledge Handbook of Animal Welfare* (Routledge, 2022).

[29] Rochelle Morton, Michelle L Hebart and Alexandra L Whittaker, 'Explaining the Gap Between the Ambitious Goals and Practical Reality of Animal Welfare Law Enforcement: A Review of the Enforcement Gap in Australia' (2020) 10 *Animals* 482, available at dx.doi.org/10.3390/ani10030482.

[30] Ibid.

[31] Ibid.

[32] This has been the case since the Society's formation in response to Martin's Act. See Jerry L Anderson, 'he Origins and Efficacy of Private Enforcement of Animal Cruelty Law in Britain' (2012) 17 *Drake Journal of Agricultural Law* 263.

responsible for around 90 per cent of prosecutions under the AWA[33] with a success rate of 98 per cent.[34] Seen next to the Crown Prosecution Service's success rate of 50 per cent in the 10 per cent of prosecutions it is responsible for,[35] the near invisibility of the Government with regards to enforcing its own legislation is stark. It is therefore clear that government has done little to ensure proper enforcement of legislation, instead choosing to rely on NGOs and animal welfare groups to investigate and prosecute breaches. This could be interpreted as a lack of due regard to the sentience of animals and a dereliction of proper governmental support and dedication, and is an issue which has become highly politicised in the UK. In response to the Wooler Review, which was highly critical of the RSPCA's prosecutorial powers, the charity has transferred its private prosecutorial role to the CPS and recalibrated its workings to focus on its role as an investigator. Though it ultimately hopes this may lead to firmer statutory powers under any revisions to the AWA,[36] the practical impact that this pivot will have on the enforcement and prosecution of animal welfare offences in the UK remains to be seen.

Against this pessimistic background, it might not come as a surprise that the UK dropped from an A to a B rating in the six years between the most recent reports from the Animal Protection Index.[37] This decline can in part be attributed to specific legal issues, such as the UK's comparatively slow reform with regards to sentences available for animal cruelty offences when compared with other jurisdictions[38] and its failure to retain the legal recognition given to sentience in EU law following Brexit.[39] But it could equally be argued that such a marked decline

[33] Environment, Food and Rural Affairs Committee, 'Animal Welfare in England: Domestic Pets: Third Report of Session 2016–17' (HC 117 2016–17) 27.

[34] *Hansard*, HC Deb Col 557, col 201WH (29 January 2013).

[35] ibid.

[36] RSPCA, 'We're reviewing or prosecutor role to focus on frontline cruelty' (28 January 2021), available at www.rspca.org.uk/-/news-reviewing-prosecutor-role-to-focus-on-frontline-cruelty; Advocates for Animals, 'RSPCA Reviews Prosecutorial Role: Implications for Animal Protection' (23 September 2021),availableatwww.advocates-for-animals.com/post/rspca-reviews-prosecutorial-role-implications-for-animal-protection.

[37] Animal Protection Index, 'United Kingdom' (2020), available at api.worldanimalprotection.org/country/united-kingdom. It is worth noting that no country was awarded an A in the latest report, but our point remains: a country that sees itself as 'world-leading' ought not to be regressing in these rankings.

[38] Alice Collinson and Robert Sardo, 'Increased Maximum Sentences for Deliberate Animal Abuse: Part of the Armoury of the Criminal Justice System in Tackling Violent Crimes Towards People and Animals' (2017) 1 *UK Journal of Animal Law* 29; The Animal Welfare (Sentencing) Act 2021 introduced penal sentences from six months to five years, which was passed after the last API ratings were released.

[39] Article 13 of the Treaty on the Functioning of the European Union was the EU law which stipulated that animals are sentient beings and when to take animal welfare into account when enacting new policies. The Animal Protection Index awarded the UK a C for not formally recognising animal sentience in legislation and recommended that the UK Government introduce animal sentience legislation as soon as possible: Animal Protection Index, 'United Kingdom' (2020), available at api.worldanimalprotection.org/country/united-kingdom; See also, Steven McCulloch, 'Animal sentience bill is necessary for the UK to be a true world leader in animal welfare' (The Conversation, 5 August 2021), available at theconversation.com/animal-sentience-bill-is-necessary-for-the-uk-to-be-a-true-world-leader-in-animal-welfare-165576; Simon Brooman, 'Animal sentience in UK law: does the new clause need claws?' (2018) 2 *The UK Journal of Animal Law* 21.

requires more radical reconsideration of how UK law treats sentient animals currently excluded from legal protections – such as those on farms, in the wild and in laboratories. The Government's 2021 Action Plan for Animal Welfare responded by 'laying out our aims and ambitions for animal welfare domestically and internationally' and claimed that the UK's 'departure from the EU have provided us with an opportunity to do things better'.[40] This plan noted that legally recognising the importance of sentience 'will be at the very heart of central government decision making going forward',[41] and this appears to have been a driving motivation behind the Sentience Act. The following section will introduce this legislation before asking whether it might be successful in addressing the concerns we have raised here.

III. The Animal Sentience Committee: Advancing the Legal Recognition of Sentience

The Sentience Act is a short piece of legislation of only six sections whose main purpose (contained in section 1) is the creation of the ASC. The ASC's role is to scrutinise and report on the extent to which the formulation or implementation of any government policy has paid 'due regard to the ways in which the policy might have an adverse effect on the welfare of animals as sentient beings'.[42] It is notable that the Sentience Act brings all policy decisions within the remit of the ASC; this is a huge and significant expansion from the limited list of policy areas within which EU institutions and Member States are obliged to consider the welfare of sentient animals per Article 13.[43] Yet with this breadth comes considerable discretion, with the legislation purposefully granting the ASC the power to choose which policies it wishes to scrutinise. At the time of writing the membership of the committee has only just been announced, meaning how they will choose to exercise this discretion remains to be seen; as such, it is impossible at this stage to fully ascertain whether the ASC has been successful in improving the legal protection afforded to the interests of animals who fall within its remit.[44] This section will instead present

[40] Department for Environment Food & Rural Affairs, 'Action Plan for Animal Welfare' (12 May 2021), available at www.gov.uk/government/publications/action-plan-for-animal-welfare/action-plan-for-animal-welfare.

[41] ibid.

[42] Animal Welfare (Sentience) Act 2022, ss 2(1)–(2).

[43] See p **210** for these policy areas. The breadth of the UK's legislation compared to its EU counterpart was criticised during the Bill's passing through the House of Commons; see *Hansard* HC Deb Vol 707, col 248 (18 January 2022) (Sir Geoffrey Clifton Brown MP).

[44] Animal Sentience Committee Home Page, available at www.gov.uk/government/groups/animal-sentience-committee. This announcement came over a year after the legislation received Royal Assent, and a full eight months after the announcement of the committee's chairperson, Michael Seals CBE. See DEFRA 'Michael Seals confirmed as first chair of the new ASC (2 September 2022), available at www.gov.uk/government/news/michael-seals-confirmed-as-first-chair-of-the-new-animal-sentience-committee.

the discretion possessed by the ASC in order to demonstrate how the legislature may have intended this discretion to be exercised, before moving to an assessment of whether the ASC might succeed in increasing the level of protection offered to the interests of sentient animals.

A. Definitional Difficulties

Before we can fully engage in this task, two definitional issues must first be brought to the fore – one that the legislature has addressed head-on, and another which appears to have been left to the discretion of the committee. The first of these is what is meant by the term 'animal'. The layman may be surprised to hear that, rather than apply to all animals – or even all sentient animals – the legislation only applies to a limited list of beings:[45] 'any vertebrate other than *homo sapiens*; any cephalopod mollusc;[46] and any decapod crustacean'.[47] Three things must be noted with regards to this list. Firstly, the definition is heavily weighted towards vertebrates, with comparatively little representation for invertebrate species. Good pragmatic reasons may exist for this limitation; should insects or all marine invertebrates be included within its remit, the ASC may find itself overwhelmed and less able to spend time scrutinising policy that affects animals who are considered of greater moral – or even economic – significance.[48] But invertebrates are the most common form of life on earth, and their complete exclusion from early drafts of the Bill was questioned[49] and ultimately partially addressed during the legislative process.[50] Secondly, and connected to the inclusion of some invertebrates, comes the fact that although this list is fixed, section 5(2) allows for amendments for the inclusion of additional invertebrates through secondary legislation. This was requested during the legislative process[51] and it is welcome that the provision exists; however, the power to expand the list appears to be at the exclusive discretion of the Secretary of State[52] rather than at the suggestion of the ASC or in

[45] Animal Welfare (Sentience) Act 2022, s 5(1).

[46] Octopus, squid or cuttlefish are common examples of cephalopod molluscs found in UK waters.

[47] Such as lobsters, crab, shrimp, prawns and crayfish.

[48] For a recent overview of the moral issues raised by insect sentience in particular, see Jeff Sebo, 'The Rebugnant Conclusion: Utilitarianism, Insects, Microbes, and AI Systems' (2023) *Ethics, Policy and Environment*, available at doi.org/10.1080/21550085.2023.2200724.

[49] *Hansard* HL Deb Vol 812, col 1903 (16 June 2021) (Baroness Fookes).

[50] Only after reviewing evidence presented by the Foundations of Animal Sentience Project headed by Professor Jonathan Birch at the LSE that convinced Parliament to include cephalopod molluscs and decapod crustaceans within the scope of the ASC. See Jonathan Birch, Charlotte Burn, Alexandra Schnell, Heather Browning and Andrew Crump, 'Review of the evidence of sentience in cephalopod molluscs and decapod crustaceans' (LSE Consulting 2021) 17, available at www.lse.ac.uk/news/news-assets/pdfs/2021/sentience-in-cephalopod-molluscs-and-decapod-crustaceans-final-report-november-2021.pdf23.

[51] *Hansard* HL Deb Vol 812, cols 1917–18 (16 June 2021) (Lord Dodds of Duncairn).

[52] In the UK, a Secretary of State is a political appointee. The title is typically given to a cabinet minister in charge of governmental department, and indicates that the holder is a senior minister of the

response to emerging scientific consensus. Any expansion of this list is thus highly vulnerable to prevailing political currents that may serve to ossify the scope of the Sentience Act. And thirdly, although cephalopods and decapods are recognised as sentient under this Act, they do not receive any further protection in law as a result of being included. Most importantly, the definition of 'animal' under the AWA has not been extended to include them, meaning they remain excluded from its protections. In practical terms, this means that, despite their sentience being recognised in law, practices such as boiling lobsters alive remain legal in the UK. This lack of harmonisation has the potential to create future problems, and ought to be corrected to ensure legal consistency.

The second term that might raise definitional difficulties is 'sentience'. This may not raise practical difficulties for the ASC given that their remit is narrowly defined by section 5(1), but it seems unusual that an attempt to reintroduce legal recognition of the importance of sentience should not attempt to define it. That this lack of definitional focus might raise future problems was raised in the House of Commons,[53] where it was also suggested that an appropriate definition might be that offered by the Global Animal Law Project and later adopted by the British Veterinary Association: 'sentience shall be understood to mean the capacity to have feelings, including pain and pleasure, and implies a level of conscious awareness'.[54] It might be that a definition was excluded due to fears that scientific advances might render it out of date, but there is no reason why the Sentience Act could not have provided for secondary legislation in which sentience could have been defined and more easily amended should this become desirable.[55] We may perhaps see a hint at the Government's reasoning for keeping definitions relating to 'sentience' out of both the Sentience Act and any secondary legislation in remarks made by Lord Benyon in the House of Lords[56] – 'The Government are trying to sail a path between creating something that is meaningful and effective and keeping Parliament as the deciding force on this, not the courts'.[57] Instead of including any definition that could be judicially challenged, the Terms of Reference for the ASC instead allow the Committee wide discretion, stating sentience 'may be defined by the Committee for its own purposes'.[58] Though this may be desirable from the

Crown. The current Secretary of State for the Department for the Environment, Food and Rural Affairs, who has oversight of this particular process, is The Rt Hon Thérèse Coffey MP of the Conservative Party. However, as different animal laws are overseen by different governmental departments, multiple Secretaries of State are responsible for making decisions connected to their welfare.

[53] *Hansard* HC Deb Vol 707, col 258 (18 January 2022) (Richard Drax MP).

[54] *Hansard* HC Deb Vol 710, col 704 (14 March 2022) (Dr Neil Hudson MP).

[55] ibid.

[56] The Right Honourable Lord Benyon is currently a member of the House of Lords, which forms part of the legislative process in the UK. The House of Lords is an unelected body and does not represent individual constituencies.

[57] *Hansard* HL Deb Vol 812, col 1944 (16 June 2021) (Lord Benyon).

[58] Defra, 'Animal Sentience Committee: Terms of Reference' (17 November 2021) 22, available at data.parliament.uk/DepositedPapers/Files/DEP2022-0007/Animal_Sentience_Committee_Draft_Terms_of_Reference.pdf.

perspective of responsiveness to changing scientific consensus, it also makes the term vulnerable to being narrowly defined should the membership of the ASC wish to pursue this route.

It therefore seems difficult to avoid the conclusion that a potential consequence of these definitional difficulties is a severe limiting of the breadth of animals that could benefit from the protection of the ASC, and that this might have been intentional on the part of the drafters.

B. Parliamentary Oversight of the Remit of the ASC

Having discussed these initial definition difficulties, we can turn to the substantive powers of the ASC. Lord Benyon was very clear that Dicey's orthodox conception of Parliamentary Sovereignty was never far from the drafters' minds[59] when determining the role of the ASC within the legislative process when he stated:

> It is important to understand what the Bill is and what it is not. It is intended to embed consideration of animal welfare into the policy decision-making process. It does not change existing laws, nor does it dictate to ministers which decisions they should ultimately make. It is for ministers to make those calls, taking all relevant considerations into account, and for Parliament to hold them to account. The Bill is designed to support Parliament in doing so.[60]

This, however, raises two interesting disconnects. The first is that, despite this stated desire to maintain Parliament's role at the heart of the legislative process, section 2(1) of the Sentience Act does not require the ASC to scrutinise *all* government policy – rather, it bestows a general power to scrutinise. This wide discretion was criticised during the legislative process, with some expressing concern that it may create the impression that the ASC is politically biased or otherwise hostile to what might be perceived to be exclusively rural interests.[61] Others suggested that this power may overwhelm the ASC,[62] and that organising principles similar to those used by the New Zealand National Animal Welfare Advisory Council[63] ought to be put in place to provide the ASC with a framework to ensure transparency in how policies were selected for review.[64] These recommendations were not acted upon, meaning that an immense amount of power – functionally equivalent to absolute discretion – rests with the ASC to determine which policies it wishes to scrutinise, with no possibility of parliamentary oversight of how these choices

[59] AV Dicey, *Introduction to the Study of the Law of the Constitution* (Liberty Fund, 1982) 3–4.

[60] *Hansard* HL Deb Vol 812, col 1900 (16 June 2021) (Lord Benyon).

[61] *Hansard* HC Deb Vol 710, col 697 (14 March 2022) (Greg Smith MP).

[62] *Hansard* HL Deb Vol 813, col 276-277 GC (6 July 2021) (Baroness Bakewell).

[63] New Zealand National Animal Welfare Advisory Council Guideline 12: Prioritisation Framework (March 2016), available at www.nawac.org.nz/assets/NAWAC-documents/Guideline-12-Prioritisation-framework.pdf.

[64] *Hansard* HL Deb Vol 813, col 284GC (6 July 2021) (Baroness Hayman).

are made. The ASC appears to have similarly wide-ranging powers when it comes to interpreting what is meant by 'due regard', which needs to have been paid to the interests of sentient animals in the implementation or development of the policy under their consideration.[65] Baroness Meyer asked 'how can one prove to have had all due regard',[66] presumably in the hope that some guidance on how to interpret this term may have been included in the legislation. Lord Benyon again gave us a clue in the House of Lords, when he appears to suggest that 'due regard' indicates the need for a balancing act between human and animal interests:

> This Bill … provides a statutory basis for the welfare needs of sentient animals to be properly reflected in all government policy-making, in a reasonable and proportionate way – I emphasise 'reasonable' and 'proportionate' – and it is vital that, throughout the process of this Bill, we recognise that.[67]

But no such guidance made its way into the legislation itself, again suggesting that the ASC themselves may have a significant role in determining the meaning of the term – and, by extension, the extent to which the Government ought to consider the interests of sentient animals in the formulation and implementation of policy. They could follow Lord Benyon's lead and ask whether these interests were acknowledged, even if ultimately disregarded as being outweighed by human interests.[68] Yet an alternative reading of the legislation is also possible; a functional reading of the requirement that they consider the adverse impact policy may have on nonhuman animal interests may lead the ASC to ask whether the policy is one that has the least detrimental impact possible on these interests. Much, it seems, depends on the composition of the ASC itself. But for now, it will suffice to say that when it comes to the setting of the ASC's agenda, Parliament may not have as much control as Lord Benyon suggested the Government desired.

The second disconnect between Lord Benyon's claim and the extent to which power actually rests with Parliament can be seen when we consider how the legislation provides for input from the ASC into the legislative process. Should the ASC feel due regard has not been paid to the interests of animals as sentient beings, it is entitled to issue a report that contains recommendations on how it can be paid in future formulation and implementation of the policy.[69] Reports are to be published in a manner the ASC sees fit,[70] and cannot address issues relating to devolved competencies.[71] The Secretary of State is then required to lay a response before

[65] Note that this is a different (and seemingly lesser) standard to that of 'full regard' required by Art 13 TFEU.

[66] *Hansard* HL Deb Vol 813, col 274GC (6 July 2021),.

[67] *Hansard* HL Deb Vol 812, cols 1947–48 (16 June 2021).

[68] Universities Federation for Animal Welfare, 'The UK has recognised Animal Sentience in Law, Now the Hard Work Begins' (11 April 2022), available at www.ufaw.org.uk/ufaw-news/news/post/254-the-uk-has-recognised-animal-sentience-in-law-now-the-hard-work-beginsa.

[69] Animal Welfare (Sentience) Act 2022, s 2(3)–(4).

[70] ibid s 2(6).

[71] ibid s 2(7)–(8). This is particularly frustrating, as many animal welfare matters in the UK are devolved.

Parliament no later than three months after the report is issued. There is, however, no need for ministers to accept any recommendations the ASC may choose to make; nor is there a requirement that Parliamentary time must be set aside for the consideration of ASC reports and recommendations and the Government's response to them. Both omissions were criticised during the legislative process, with members of both Houses suggesting that a failure to require Parliamentary scrutiny of ASC reports and the Government's response to them risks making the ASC merely symbolic, and may hinder the possibility of meaningful scrutiny.[72] It is hard to disagree that this sidelining of Parliament could have this effect.

C. Broad Discretion and Membership of the ASC

Perhaps this wide discretion to set its own remit is why Sir Geoffrey Clifton Brown stated in the House of Commons that the appointments process must be extremely transparent so as to ensure that those who are at the table are 'there for the right reasons'.[73] Yet appointments to the committee are at the sole discretion of the Secretary of State,[74] which – deliberately or otherwise – means they are the de facto gatekeeper not just to initial appointments, but to the viewpoints that will shape the remit of the ASC for years to come. This discretion on the part of the Secretary of State was criticised during legislative debates as excessively broad[75] and having potential to bake biases against certain pursuits into the ASC without sufficient parliamentary oversight,[76] but no specific guidance was included in the final Act.

As noted above, it remains too early to draw any conclusions as to what direction the ASC will take as, at the time of writing, its membership has only been publicly known for six weeks. However, it seems notable that the membership appears dominated by those whose approach to animal welfare is informed by a scientific, veterinary or economic background, with no appointees from law, philosophy and ethics or other disciplines within the humanities and social sciences.[77] As such, there is a non-negligible chance that the choices they make when exercising their discretion may be vulnerable to the group-think that could emerge from a narrow range of expertise.[78] Although admittedly speculative, an example of this could be found in how the ASC choose to interpret the term 'adverse' as per section

[72] *Hansard* HL Deb Vol 812, col 1902 (16 June 2021) (Baroness Young of Old Scone); HC Deb Vol 710, col 691 (14 March 2022) (Jim McMahon MP).

[73] *Hansard* HC Deb Vol 707, col 247 (18 January 2022) (Sir Geoffrey Clifton Brown).

[74] Animal Welfare (Sentience) Act 2022, s 1(2)–(3).

[75] *Hansard* HL Deb Vol 812, col 1903 (16 June 2021) (Baroness Fookes).

[76] ibid, col 1920 (Lord Hannan of Kingsclere).

[77] Animal Sentience Committee Home Page, available at www.gov.uk/government/groups/animal-sentience-committee.

[78] For an overview of how ethics and science must interact in order to avoid groupthink and unhelpful narrowing of welfare outcomes, see Sarah Wolfensohn, 'Too cute to kill? The need for objective measurements of quality of life' (2020) 10 *Animals* 1054, available at doi.org/10.3390/ani10061054.

2(2) of the Sentience Act. The inclusion of this limiting factor was not without controversy during the legislative process, with some questioning why it needs to be present at all[79] and others suggesting that freeing the ASC to consider positive developments would help the UK become a 'beacon of standards'.[80] But given it has been included, the composition of the ASC may serve to interpret this claim narrowly according to their own expertise – rather than a broader, more holistic view of 'adverse' that might be preferred by the academic lawyer who may be better placed to locate the rules under scrutiny within the broader landscape of legislation relating to animal welfare.[81]

Another example of potential self-limitation resulting from a narrow expertise could be that the ASC may be unwilling to challenge the hierarchy of animals that was briefly outlined in section II.B above. This hierarchy can be identified in existing legislation; for example, section 4(3) of the AWA notes the context in which an animal is kept – including common practices and other connected legislative considerations – are relevant considerations for determining whether suffering is 'unnecessary'; and section 9(3) of the AWA holds that the purpose for which the animal is kept is a relevant consideration when determining whether a cruelty offence has been committed. This can result in justification of companion animals receiving better welfare protection than others used for a specific purpose, such as farmed animals, due to the purpose and context for which they are kept.

The hierarchy is also present in the political process itself; a good example of this is the comparatively high proportion of legislative time spent increasing protections for companion animals – such as the new offence of 'dognapping' proposed by the Government's Pet Taskforce[82] – compared to the comparatively minimal time spent addressing the needs of farmed animals. This hierarchy is, however, not acknowledged at all in the Sentience Act. There is therefore no prima facie reason why it ought to feature in reports of the ASC. Whether its newly appointed membership defer to the legal status quo and accept this hierarchy as inevitable or instead act in a way that questions why the law treats farmed animals differently to companion animals is therefore something that may also be informed by their own backgrounds, including their familiarity with the legislative landscape and/or how they view the species under consideration.

To conclude this section, although it remains too early to predict how the ASC will operate in practice, it does seem clear that the Sentience Act – rather than ensure that ultimate power over this area remains with Parliament – has instead concentrated power with the executive. This chapter will now move on to briefly consider how the Sentience Act could be strengthened to better strengthen legal protection of animal interests.

[79] *Hansard* HC Deb Vol 707, col 244 (18 January 2022) (Caroline Lucas MP).
[80] *Hansard* HC Deb Vol 710, col 704 (14 March 2022) (Dr Neil Hudson MP).
[81] *Hansard* HC Deb Vol 707, col 255 (18 January 2022) (Luke Pollard MP).
[82] Defra, UK Government Pet Taskforce, New 'Pet Abduction' Offence' Report (2021) 9, available at www.gov.uk/government/publications/pet-theft-taskforce-report.

IV. Future Directions of Animal Sentience and Protection in the UK

This chapter has so far outlined the historical presence of sentience in legislation designed to protect animal interests in the UK, before addressing how the new Sentience Act has embedded the concept of sentience within the UK's legislative process. This final section will now offer some suggestions as to how the UK law could be improved so as to better protect the interests of animals as sentient beings. It will firstly look at the discretion of the ASC before going on to suggest stronger obligations of Parliament.

A. The Discretion of the ASC

The absolute discretion of the ASC to choose which policies to investigate *and* whether to issue a report could be problematic. Contrary to a proposal made in the House of Lords, the ASC is not obliged to scrutinise all policies that might have an adverse effect on the interests of animals as sentient beings,[83] nor does the Government – or Parliament – have the explicit power to direct the ASC to consider a policy are that they think would benefit from their attention.[84] There is also an absence of a broader 'sentience strategy' framework through which the Government or Parliament could indirectly guide the ASC towards which policies may benefit from scrutiny, even if they consider direct referrals to be inappropriate.[85] This should be seen in contrast to the Scottish Animal Welfare Committee (SAWC), which can be asked to issue a report on specific issues by Scottish ministers or their dedicated representatives.[86] The strong discretion given the ASC to issue reports is also in stark contrast to the requirement to issue annual reports imposed by similar committees in other jurisdictions; annual reports into its activities must be issued by the National Animal Welfare Advisory Council in New Zealand,[87] and academics have argued that the requirement that the SAWC issue annual reports into its operations mean that it has become a true 'guardian of sentience'.[88] Baroness Young suggested that such a requirement, together with a right to an oral response from the Government in Parliamentary time, would be beneficial for the ASC[89] – but this was rejected on the basis that this would reduce the ability of the ASC to determine its own remit and, by extension, damage its

[83] *Hansard* HL Deb Vol 812, col 1902 (16 June 2021) (Baroness Young of Old Scone).
[84] ibid.
[85] ibid.
[86] Scottish Animal Welfare Regulations 2020, s 5(2)(a)–(b).
[87] Animal Welfare Act 1999 (New Zealand), s 60.
[88] Libby Anderson and Iyan Offor, 'Animal welfare measures in Scotland: penalties, protections, powers and a Commission' (2020) 4 *The UK Journal of Animal Law* 29.
[89] *Hansard* HL Deb Vol 812, col 1902 (16 June 2021) (Baroness Young of Old Scone).

independence.[90] This may be true, but it also has the effect of completely removing any set role for Parliament in the process of scrutinising the reports of the ASC; such scrutiny would therefore be contingent on an issue being taken up by either an individual MP or Select Committee, which may make their reports vulnerable to the political winds at Westminster and the extent to which such scrutiny may be politically valuable at a given moment in time. We are of the opinion that the Sentience Act would be strengthened had these proposals been adopted.

B. Declarations of (In)compatibility

A more radical way of strengthening the Sentience Act might be to take inspiration from the Human Rights Act 1998 (the HRA), which made the European Convention on Human Rights domestically enforceable by courts in the UK. Section 3 of this Act provides that legislation must be read in a way which is compatible with Convention rights and, if legislation cannot be read in this way, the courts may issue a Declaration of Incompatibility under section 4. This sends a message to Parliament that the legislation needs to be reconsidered to meet our obligations under the Convention. Allowing the courts to make similar declarations should the Government fail to act on reports of the ASC would send a similarly strong message to Parliament that the law in its current form would benefit from reform. By way of example, The Humane League UK had recently been granted a full hearing to judicially review the use of fast-growing chickens in intensive farming, under the Welfare of Farmed Animals (England) Regulations 2007, challenging the Secretary of State for permitting farmers to continue to keep fast-growing chickens in contrary to the Regulations.[91] The judicial review was unsuccessful, with the court deciding that the Secretary of State had not acted contrary to her legal duties and the onus in on the farmers to decide whether the chickens can be kept in conditions without an obvious impact on their health and welfare.[92] It may have been that as fast-growing chickens make a significant proportion of those who enter our market,[93] the courts were reluctant to pass a decision which greatly impacts on the common intensive farming methods and the economy in which they operate. If the Sentience Act had emulated the HRA and allowed the courts to make declarations of incompatibility, a mechanism could have been provided whereby they could signal their belief that 'due regard' had not been paid to the interests of animals as sentient beings in a way that left the ultimate decision to Parliament, and thus kept them out of any political controversy.

[90] *Hansard* HL Deb Vol 814, col 16GC (20 July 2021) (Lord Benyon).

[91] Cordelia Britton, *Our Judicial Review Challenging the use of Frankenchickens has been* Granted (The Humane League UK, 23 September 2022), available at thehumaneleague.org.uk/article/judicial-review-challenging-the-use-of-frankenchickens-granted?mc_cid=7076ba2e0c&mc_eid=c3e6c91816.

[92] *Humane League UK v Secretary of State for Environment, Food and Rural Affairs and others* [2023] EWHC 1243 (Admin).

[93] They make up approximately 90% of over one billion chickens slaughtered for meat each year. Britton (n 92).

Such a mechanism may also allow the courts a means to acknowledge deficiencies in the implementation of government policies which, at the time of their formulation, were not scrutinised by the ASC as there may not have been an appreciable impact on the interests of sentient animals. An example might be the UK Government's Freeport Policy contained in the Finance Act 2021; following the implementation of this policy, significant dredging of the River Tees was undertaken – an event that coincided with several mass-mortality events affecting decapod crustaceans in the North Sea in the areas where dredged material was dumped. Scientists believe the two could be connected as dead crabs that they examined tested positive for the highly toxic chemical pyridine; this chemical was formerly produced by the well-established petrochemicals industry in Teesside, and sediment containing high levels of the toxin may have been disturbed in the dredging process.[94] It is unlikely that crabs off the Yorkshire coast would have been high on the list of policy-makers when formulating this policy, and it may be equally unlikely that the ASC would have scrutinised the proposals for their effect on the interests of crabs as sentient beings. Empowering the courts to highlight this problem in the policy implementation stage would be a means of flagging these blind spots to both Parliament and the ASC, and may help prevent similar situations from arising in future.

Lessons from the HRA could also be applied to the legislative process. Section 19 of the HRA requires a minister responsible for a Bill to inform Parliament whether it is compatible with the ECHR. Including a similar requirement in the Sentience Act, whereby a minister must assure Parliament that a Bill has taken 'due regard' of the interests of sentient animals may help avoid the creation of legislation which the ASC has found to be problematic. We are of the belief that both measures would increase the potential for meaningful parliamentary scrutiny of government policy, in line with the purposes of the Sentience Act.

V. Conclusion

We believe that legally recognising sentience is symbolically important. We also believe that, in creating a place in the legislative process for an independent assessment of how all government policies might have an adverse effect on the interests of sentient animals, the UK has taken a novel and potentially highly effective step in the right direction with regards to ensuring animals' interests are appropriately protected. But we cannot rest on our laurels in this regard, as both Article 13 TFEU and domestic legislation throughout history show us that protections that are enshrined into law are not always reflected in practice on the ground. Perhaps one of the failures of Article 13 is the lack of an official committee or body to

[94] Gary Caldwell et al, 'Determining the toxicity and potential for environmental transport of pyridene using the brown crab *Cancer pagarus* (L) (2022) bioRxiv, available at doi.org/10.1101/2022.11.17.516169.

oversee the implementation and progress of it and report back to the European Commission, which could arguably strengthen the impact of it. We at least now have that with the ASC in the UK.

What we can learn from this is that it is all well and good that the ASC can recognise animals as sentient and consider their interests during the creation and implementation of government policy, but this does not mean the policy will go in the favour of sentient animals. Its initial discretion to determine when and how its reports should be issued, and how certain terms such as 'adverse' ought to be interpreted is wide; as such, it could be heavily influenced by a membership whose expertise seems narrow. It remains to be seen whether this will be the case, but we are hopeful that the ASC will not succumb to the executive dominance we have warned of above – and will instead provide a new and invaluable means through which the interests of sentient animals can be protected at the pre-legislative stage. This proactivity, even if limited, can only be a good thing – and we hope that this indicates a clear direction of travel in our jurisdiction.

13

Affirmative Acts of Recognition: How Codifications of Animal Sentience Are Ushering Animals into the Focus of US Law

RAJESH K REDDY

I. Introduction

The evolution of US animal protection laws enjoys a rich, if complex, history, one whose origins predate the founding of the nation itself. Indeed, more than a century before the American Revolution, the Massachusetts Bay Colony took the historic step of enshrining protections for certain categories of animals by outlawing acts of cruelty toward them and advancing considerations for cattle welfare.[1] Codified in 1641, these provisions constituted the first formal animal protection laws in America,[2] with the US inheriting this legacy upon its founding in 1776.[3] Soon after, individual states began to give rise to a diverse tapestry of animal protection laws, with every state then part of the country featuring an animal protection law on its books by 1907.[4] In the federal context, the US codified its first nation-wide animal protection law in 1873 by providing for the welfare of farmed animals in interstate transport.[5] Notably, what animated these and other early frameworks were complementary yet competing impulses to cultivate a more compassionate society and safeguard living property, with animals themselves marginalised by the very laws that ostensibly provided for their visibility.

[1] Massachusetts Bay Colony Body of Liberties § 92, 93 (1641).

[2] Janet M Davis, 'The History of Animal Protection in the United States' (The American Historian), available at www.oah.org/tah/issues/2015/november/the-history-of-animal-protection-in-the-united-states.

[3] 'The Declaration of Independence: A History' (National Archives), available at www.archives.gov/founding-docs/declaration-history.

[4] Alyssa S Robinson, 'Animal Cruelty Legislation, Part I' (NC State University Libraries, 26 February 2019), available at www.lib.ncsu.edu/news/special-collections/animal-cruelty-legislation-part-i.

[5] Animal Welfare Institute, 'Legal Protections For Farm Animals During Transport' (Animal Welfare Institute), available at awionline.org/sites/default/files/uploads/legacy-uploads/documents/FA-LegalProtectionsDuringTransport-081910-1282577406-document-23621.pdf.

In the 100 years since, the US has seen advocates at the state and federal level strive to bring animals into greater focus with the hope of offering them relief. With that said, the overarching goal of many modern-day advocates has been to not only pass more and strengthen existing animal protection laws but also transform perspectives of animals from objects into subjects, with the latter viewed as having intrinsic interests that the law should secure both procedurally and in substance.[6] Against the backdrop of this decades-long effort to increase the visibility of animals by 'subjectivising' them in the law's eyes, this chapter frames attempts to codify animal sentience as not merely another step towards but rather an inflection point in the effort to elevate the profile of animals, with greater visibility and more robust protections, as well as the prospective affirmation of their personhood, flowing from this recognition. In light of these implications, this chapter frames the codification of animal sentience as a promising, if pragmatic, approach for advocates to advance the status of animals. In doing so, it observes how paradigmatic shifts entailed by such recognitions have destabilised the historically informed anthropocentric foundation of US animal protection laws and interrogates if and how such advancements might usher forth the recognition of animals as legal persons.

Developing this argument, section II interrogates the historical premises of America's early animal protection frameworks, which contemplated animals as their partial and at times even unintended beneficiaries, a view that entrenched their status as legal objects among other forms of property over which legal subjects could otherwise exert dominion. In parallel with this examination, the chapter observes the extra-legal distinction between subjects, who possess sentience, and objects, which do not, as a means to convey how animals have seen their intrinsic interests marginalised vis-à-vis the entrenchment of their legal objectification in animal protection frameworks. Against this backdrop, section III frames recent attempts to formally recognise the sentience of animals as a means to centre their interests, long relegated to the periphery of such frameworks. Scrutinising the impact of this development across three noteworthy cases in Oregon, the only US jurisdiction to have celebrated the passage of an animal sentience bill into law, the chapter attests to how the state's centring of animals in its animal protection laws has increased their visibility and enhanced their protections while disrupting their historical objectification as mere property. Characterising the jurisprudence arising out of these cases as progressive stepping stones, section IV touches upon the monumental *Justice v Vercher* case,[7] which concerned a civil suit brought on behalf of a horse, Justice, against his former owner for the suffering he endured as a result of her neglect.[8] Examining the context of this 'case for Justice', the chapter interrogates the promise that subjectivising animals holds for their prospective

[6] Gary Francione, 'Animal Rights Theory and Utilitarianism: Relative Normative Guidance' (1997) 3 *Animal Law* 75, 83–84.

[7] Just. by and through *Mosiman v Vercher*, 321 Or App 439, 446, 518 P.3d 131 (2022) (*Justice v Vercher*).

[8] ibid, 441–43.

recognition as legal subjects – that is, as legal persons, or rights-bearers, under the law. Observing the concerns raised by the state judiciary, the chapter reassesses Oregon's codification of animal sentience, with a view toward gleaning lessons it offers advocates hoping to shift the status of animals not only from the objects to the subjects of animal protection laws but also, and more broadly, from legal property to legal persons.

II. The Anthropocentric Foundations of US Animal Protection Laws

A. Individual Colony and State-Level Protections

More than 100 years before the founding of the US, the Massachusetts Bay Colony had already assumed a vanguard role in providing for the protection of animals under human control. The pair of provisions it enacted in 1641 featured prohibitive and permissive aspects. The first outlawed cruelty toward 'bruite creatures … usuallie kept for man's use',[9] whereas the second entitled herders of cattle to rest and refresh them on another's land under certain conditions.[10] Codified in the *Liberties of the Massachusets Collonie in New England*, the laws are noteworthy, not only representing the first of their kind within the Colonies but also predating England's Dick Martin's Act, which similarly prohibited the cruel treatment of working animals and has been hailed in some circles as the first animal protection law in the West.[11]

Although animals necessarily represented the *subject matter* of these early protections, their incorporation into the body of the law, or *corpus juris*, entrenched their status as objects as opposed to subjects, with the latter enjoying, among other benefits, being seen as the law's intended beneficiaries. While the distinction between legal object and legal subject defies rigid binaries, the estimation of animals as mere objects by the Massachusetts Bay Colony's leadership was encoded into the provisions enacted to protect them. Indeed, their codification as 'bruite' creatures betrays the diminution of their status, with the term's root stemming from the Latin *brutus*, meaning 'dull',[12] or slow to understand or lacking distinct perceptions, if not sensitivity altogether.[13] With its characterisation of animals as having a diminished sensitivity if not lacking sensitivity outright, the law undermines the notion of animals being able to subjectively experience and thus even enjoy their protections.

[9] Massachusetts Bay Colony Body of Liberties § 92 (1641).

[10] ibid, § 93.

[11] Jess Terry, 'Celebrating 200 Years of Animal Welfare Legislation' (World Animal Protection, 29 June 2022), available at www.worldanimalprotection.org.uk/blogs/animal-welfare-legislation-200-years.

[12] 'brute (adj)' (Online Etymology Dictionary), available at www.etymonline.com/word/brute.

[13] 'dull' (Collins), available at www.collinsdictionary.com/us/dictionary/english/dull.

But if not those of animals, then whose interests did the anti-cruelty law have in mind? The answer demands an appreciation of the anxieties of the Puritans,[14] who considered their 'cruel dominion' over animal life to be a consequence of mankind's fall from Eden.[15] In the case of the Massachusetts Bay Colony, its leadership expressed a desire to foster, if not recreate, that Edenic paradise, which did not feature such cruelty.[16] This consideration concerned the depravity of the human heart rather than a concern with the subjective experience of animals, whom the law viewed as having been created for the sake of man and over whom mankind had been granted dominion.[17] With this anti-cruelty protection predicated upon animals being 'kept for man's use', the law served to entrench their status as living commodities. Taking into account even the permissive allowance for cattle to be fed and refreshed, the law's principal concern was the preservation of cattle, who held an instrumental value – not only for the owners of cattle but also for the community as a whole.[18] Together, these and other anthropocentric impulses would give rise to similar provisions after the fight for independence from England and the founding of the US.

Despite this separation, it would be the animal protection movement in England that informed animal protection efforts in numerous states across the US. Similar to the anthropocentric concerns that gave rise to the Massachusetts Bay Colony's anti-cruelty law a century earlier, this historic achievement came off the heels of animal welfare societies calling attention to the link between human and animal violence, as exemplified by William Hogarth's *Four Stages of Cruelty*, a set of printed engravings from 1751 that illustrated how acts of cruelty inflicted upon animals hardened the hearts of society, which would 'graduate', so to speak, from committing acts of cruelty to animals to committing them against fellow humans.[19] To be sure, the view that animals should merit protections regarded the security of humans as its focal point, with animals relegated to being the indirect beneficiaries of mounting calls for the law to safeguard them. After numerous failed attempts, England passed its first animal protection law, Dick Martin's Act, in 1822.[20] Drawing inspiration from the landmark legislation in England,[21]

[14] Massachusetts Bay Colony Body of Liberties § 93 (1641), (after these animal-related protections were provisions that would put people to death if they worshipped another god).

[15] Davis (n 2).

[16] ibid.

[17] ibid. The law likewise prescribed the death penalty for bestiality, a severe punishment that served to protect animals from sexual violence on the one hand yet also demanded that the animal in question be 'slain, buried, and not eaten' on the other. Massachusetts Bay Colony Body of Liberties § 94.7 (1641). Again, viewed holistically, the Massachusetts Bay Colony's animal-related laws predominantly reflect a concern with the debasing of a people rather than an interest in the protection of animals for their own sake.

[18] Charles R Lee, 'Public Poor Relief and the Massachusetts Community, 1620–1715 (1982) 55 *New England Quarterly* 564, 568–69.

[19] 'The Four Stages of Cruelty' (The History Of Art), available at www.thehistoryofart.org/william-hogarth/four-stages-of-cruelty.

[20] Terry (n 11).

[21] Davis (n 2).

New York codified the first state-based animal protection law in the US six years later, in 1828.[22] Seven years after that, in 1835, Massachusetts became the second.[23] Other states followed suit, and by 1907, every state then part of the nation featured an anti-cruelty law on its books.[24]

Despite this rich tapestry of animal protection laws, animals found their interests marginalised by courts, who saw it as their duty to simply effectuate the intent of the legislature when the laws were passed. Nearly half a century after New York enacted its first animal protection law, for example, its courts were still neglecting to locate the interests of animals as the law's primary concern. As one judge opined in a decision concerning an act of cruelty against a stage coach horse,

> It is not correct to assert that the policy of this kind of legislation, especially that which has for its purpose the prevention of cruelty to *brutes*, is a regulation of the dominion of the private citizen over his own private property merely. It truly has its origin in the intent to save a just standard of humane feeling from being debased by pernicious effects of bad example – the human heart from being hardened by public and frequent exhibitions of cruelty to dumb creatures, committed to the care and which were created for the beneficial use of man.[25]

Notably, the court's pronouncement expressly affirms that the underlying policy the legislature intended to advance goes beyond the state's interest in regulating the private ownership of animals, whose existence for human use and over whom humans may exert dominion is presumed, if not reinforced. Despite the term failing to appear in the text of the law itself,[26] the court nevertheless renders animals as 'brutes' when addressing the law's underlying purpose. With animals and their interests diminished by virtue of the lack of sensitivity implied by the term, the court hews to an anthropocentric reading of the law's intent as being the prevention of human morals from being debased, or 'hardened'. Again, the dispositive question was not the subjective state or experience of animals themselves but where along the spectrum between humane and inhumane their treatment situated the individual who harmed them. While the suffering inflicted upon animals necessarily constituted part of this assessment, absent a recognition of and concern over their subjective experience, animals served as little more than objective measures of a human-focused assessment.

B. Federal Protections

The rationale driving early animal protection laws at the national level likewise concerned the impact of their poor treatment on society: vis-à-vis both the owners

[22] Robinson (n 4).
[23] ibid.
[24] ibid.
[25] *Christie v Bergh*, 15 Abb Pr (ns) 51 (NY 1873) (emphasis added).
[26] NY Rev Stat Tit. 6, 26 (1829).

of the animals in question and the public generally. The first such law, the Act to Prevent Cruelty to Animals while in Transit by Railroad or Other Means of Transportation within the United States,[27] focused squarely on the treatment of farmed animals being transported by rail across state lines.[28] At the time, animals farmed in western states were transported hundreds and even thousands of miles to slaughterhouses in eastern states.[29] Given that the railroads operated as de facto monopolies, they had little incentive to ensure the welfare of the animals consigned to their care.[30] As a result, many animals lost significant weight, suffered physical injuries, grew sick, or died.[31] While these harms necessarily affected the animals, the principal concern focused on the lost profit of farmers, as well as the cost paid by the consuming public.[32] In response to their complaints, Congress required, among other considerations, that cattle, pigs, and sheep be given at least five consecutive hours of food, water and rest for every 28 hours of live transport.[33] As with state-level developments, the first anti-cruelty measure in the federal landscape saw protections afforded to animals for their owners' economic benefit. As a further testament to the anthropocentric concerns at the heart of the law, subsequent amendments provided for the animals' owner to authorise carriers to extend the time transported animals could be confined without such care by an additional eight hours.[34] Notably, as rail no longer represents the predominant form of transport for farmed animals being sent to slaughter, the agricultural industry today coordinates the trucking of its own animals and proves the primary opponent of the protections provided by the Twenty-Eight Hour Law, as it is commonly known today.[35]

Even more modern laws passed to promote the welfare of animals fail to truly centre their interests. For example, the Animal Welfare Act, which represents the predominant federal animal protection law in the US and addresses the treatment of animals in the context of exhibitors, dealers and research facilities,[36] marginalises the suffering of animals in function. Indeed, in order for an advocate to bring suit to enforce the law, courts require them to demonstrate both that they are suffering the type of harm the law was intended to prevent and that they have actually suffered that harm.[37] To this end, courts have determined that seeing an animal suffering in violation of the Animal Welfare Act constitutes an 'aesthetic

[27] AWI (n 5) (observing that the law is today known as the 'Twenty-Eight Hour Law').
[28] Transportation of Animals, 49 USC § 80502 (a)(1) (Twenty-Eight Hour Law).
[29] S Rep No 41-1, at 1612–14 (1879).
[30] ibid 1614–15.
[31] ibid 1612–13.
[32] ibid 1612–1615.
[33] Twenty-Eight Hour Law (n 28) (a)(1)–(b).
[34] ibid (a)(2)(B).
[35] 'A Review: The Twenty-Eight Hour Law and Its Enforcement' (Animal Welfare Institute) 2–3, available at awionline.org/sites/default/files/uploads/documents/20TwentyEightHourLawReport.pdf.
[36] Animal Welfare Act, 7 USC § 2131 et seq, § 2131(b)(1) (AWA).
[37] *Animal Legal Def Fund, Inc v Glickman*, 154 F.3d 426, 432 (DC Cir 1998).

injury' for the advocate bringing the case.[38] Yet while the suffering of the actual animal matters, it is the impact of that suffering on the person seeking to prevent the harm that determines whether the case can be heard in court.[39] While this may prove an easy threshold to clear in certain circumstances, such as with a captive animal exhibited by zoos, because research facilities are not intended to be open to the public, courts have held that even if an advocate is harmed by witnessing the suffering of a research animal, their injury may not constitute a legal one.[40] Akin to its counterpart in the state context, what this jurisprudence betrays is that absent an impact on humans – and under specified conditions, no less – the subjective experience and suffering of animals matters little to the law.

III. Bringing Animals into Focus: The Impact of Animal Sentience

A. Legislating to Codify Animal Sentience

Whereas the EU and numerous countries have formally enshrined the sentient status of animals into law,[41] the US lacks a similar provision in the federal sphere, and it is in this absence that a small handful of states have attempted to codify this recognition within their respective jurisdictions.[42] To date, however, only Oregon has witnessed the passage of a sentience bill into law, with SB 6 clearing the legislative process in 2013 to subjectivise animals and pave the state's path to becoming one of the most progressive jurisdictions for animal protections globally.[43]

Of course, which animals are recognised as having sentience, how the term itself is defined, and any accompanying policy statements as to its effect offer key insight into a bill's potential impact on a jurisdiction's animal protection landscape. While Oregon's animal sentience law is not explicitly limited to specific species or categories of animal use,[44] its anti-cruelty code defines an 'animal' as 'any nonhuman mammal, bird, reptile, amphibian or fish',[45] thereby excluding

[38] ibid, 445.

[39] ibid.

[40] ibid (observing how in the case of research facilities oversight committees are established with private citizens whose aesthetic injury is considered as part of their representation of the interests of the community). Note, however, that such private citizens serving on oversight committees face incredible difficulty demonstrating that they have actually suffered an aesthetic injury. *Animal Legal Def Fund, Inc v Espy*, 23 F.3d 496, 501 (DC Cir 1994).

[41] Rajesh K Reddy, 'Enshrining Animal Sentience into Law: Global Developments and Implications' (2019) Fall, *American Bar Association Tort, Trial, and Insurance Practice Section Newsletter* 23.

[42] Ross Kelly, 'Recognition of animal sentience on the rise' (VIN News, 14 May, 2020), available at news.vin.com/default.aspx?pid=210&catId=633&id=9639465.

[43] ibid; SB 6, 77th Leg. Assemb, Reg Sess (Or 2013) (enrolled).

[44] OR REV STAT § 167.305 (2023).

[45] OR REV STAT § 167.310 (2023).

from its purview numerous species and taxonomic classes, such as cephalopods, decapod crustaceans and insects, which studies have found to possess markers of sentience.[46] Codified in ORS 167.305, Oregon law declares animals to be 'sentient beings capable of experiencing pain, stress and fear', with the principal policy implication being that animals 'should be cared for in ways that minimise pain, stress, fear and suffering'.[47] Notably, this recognition of animal sentience and its attendant policy impact operate as an inflection point. Indeed, whereas courts in other states may unilaterally cite scientific studies or even common sense to establish that that animals are sentient beings and that it is their interests that animal protection laws principally concern, the Oregon legislature affords its courts a *statutory* foundation to ground such determinations.

While Oregon's sentience statute does not explicitly define 'sentience', a notoriously plastic term whose meaning is contested even within the scientific community,[48] it is noteworthy that the context and accompanying policy impact statement contemplates not just physical but also mental suffering, with this provision attesting to the subjective experiences of animals. That said, both the declaration and policy statement limit its application to the prevention of negative affective states.[49] Despite Oregon's minimum care standards speaking to the need to preserve animal 'well-being',[50] a term considered by some to contemplate positive affective states,[51] this narrow definition of the subjective experiences implicated by sentience arguably limits the ability of courts to advance the interests of animals beyond the prevention of their pain and suffering. Furthermore, it is important to note that Oregon's definition of animal sentience also excludes cognitive capacities, such as self-awareness, self-reflection, and the ability to appreciate the mental states of others. To be sure, this narrowed scope likewise serves to limit what advances might be gained for animals, as discussed below.

[46] Meghan Barrett, 'Short Research Summary: Can insects feel pain? A review of the neural and behavioural evidence by Gibbons et al. 2022,' (Effective Altruism, 22 November 2022), available at forum.effectivealtruism.org/posts/yPDXXxdeK9cgCfLwj/short-research-summary-can-insects-feel-pain-a-review-of-the.

[47] OR REV STAT (1)–(2). Other pronouncements under ORS 167.305 include findings that: the state has a pecuniary interest in reducing the cost to care for impounded animals; the suffering of impounded animals can be alleviated by expediting their disposition while their owners await trial; and requiring unlicensed rescue organisations to follow regulations can likewise reduce animal suffering; among other determinations. ORS 167.305(3)–(6).

[48] Amelia Cornish et al, 'Demographics Regarding Belief in Non-Human Animal Sentience and Emotional Empathy with Animals: A Pilot Study among Attendees of an Animal Welfare Symposium' (2018) 8 *Animals* 174.

[49] This limitation to negative affective states is informed by where the recognition is codified. Located under Oregon's statutory framework regarding 'Offenses Against General Welfare and Animals', its scope is arguably confined to the negative experiential states of animals.

[50] OR REV STAT 167.310(9) (2023).

[51] David Fraser, 'Assessing Animal Well-Being: Common Sense, Uncommon Science' (1993) *Wellbeing International*, 37, 37–38.

B. The Impact of Animal Sentience in Criminal Law Cases

Despite its inherent limitations, Oregon's codification of animal sentience has empowered its judiciary – as exemplified by three high-profile rulings handed down by the highest court in the state – to shape Oregon into a model for other states to draw inspiration from. Taken together, what these three cases affirm is that Oregon takes animals, as opposed to society at large or the owners of animals, as the principal beneficiaries of its animal protection laws. Considering that the centring of human interests in the sphere of animal protections implicates the marginalisation of animals' interests, the decisions handed down by the Oregon Supreme Court privileging the interests of animals has entailed the curtailing of certain human rights and interests – even going so far as to abridge some of society's most fundamental constitutional guarantees.

The first of three high-profile cases to address who – the public or animals – represent the primary beneficiaries of Oregon's animal protection laws reached the Oregon Supreme Court just one year after the legislature formally enshrined the recognition of animal sentience into law.[52] The case in question, *State v Nix*, concerned 20 counts of second-degree animal neglect by the defendant, Nix, who was found guilty of the underlying crimes at the trial level, which saw the 20 misdemeanor offences merged into a single offence.[53] Appealing the trial court's decision to merge the 20 offences into one, the State cited Oregon's anti-merger statute,[54] which provides that where a defendant may have violated a single statute, there are nevertheless 'as many separately punishable offenses as there are *victims*'.[55] With the appellate court reversing the lower court's determination, the lone question before the Supreme Court of Oregon concerned whether, for sentencing purposes, Nix had committed 20 individual offences or just one.[56] Notably, because the underlying events arose in 2009 – four years before Oregon's codification of animal sentience – the Court observed the changes to the State's animal protection framework in 2013 and made clear that it would refer only to the pre-amendment statutes, as codified in 2009.[57] With this context laid bare, the Court stated that it 'express[es] no opinion *about the effect of the 2013 amendments* on the issue presented in this case'.[58] Critically, this refusal to state whether the legislature's subsequent finding and policy declaration that animals, as sentient beings, are capable of feeling pain and thus should be cared for in ways that minimise that pain and suffering affected its decision is telling if only by virtue of what is implied by omission. Indeed, while the Court neglected to state that the amendments to the law constituted a *shift* in Oregon's view that animal protection laws

[52] *State v Nix* 334 P.3d 437, 438 (Or 2014).
[53] ibid.
[54] ibid.
[55] OR REV STAT § 161.067 (2023) (emphasis added).
[56] *Nix* (n 52) 438.
[57] ibid, 438 fn 1.
[58] ibid (emphasis added).

principally concern the interests of animals, the statement potentially serves to clarify that this may have been the state legislature's position all along. As such, while the case technically does not address the impact of Oregon's codification of animal sentience, it would be naïve to dismiss its impact on the court's decision.

As to the substantive matter at issue in *Nix*, whether the offences should be merged into a single offence or remain 20 separate offences under the state's anti-merger statute turned on the question of whether animals are 'victims' under Oregon's animal protection laws. That said, the inquiry itself implicated more fundamental questions. Indeed, as animals have historically been considered mere commodities and thus the objects of animal law crimes as opposed to their subjects, the prospect of recognising their victimisation would entail an acknowledgement that the purpose of the law was to prevent the harm animals subjectively experience. Such a view would render animals the subjects of animal protection laws and thus more than mere objects. To be sure, Nix's defence rested on the historical indelibility of such lines, arguing that the scope of the term 'victim' encompassed only humans and legal 'persons', which he distinguished from animals, whom the law classified as personal property.[59] Turning to the legislative intent of the law to guide its determination,[60] the Court rejected the view that only legal persons could be victims.[61] And while it affirmed that Oregon law classified animals as legal property, it rejected the view that animals could not likewise be victims under the general meaning of the term and as contemplated by the legislature, as well as by prior rulings.[62]

Here, the Court distinguished the foundation of Oregon's current animal protection laws from those of other states. Pointing specifically to statutes modeled after New York's, it observed how, 'In the nineteenth through the twentieth centuries, some states began to pass anti-cruelty laws that were intended to deter immoral conduct; the emphasis still was not on protecting the animals themselves.'[63] While the Court acknowledged that Oregon had also followed New York's lead, passing its first animal protection law in 1885, it observed how its courts had long determined animals to be the focus of its laws,[64] with public moral concern simply reflecting an 'additional' consideration.[65] The focus of its laws was the care of the animals suffering the underlying harm of neglect or abuse. Although it did not cite Oregon's codification of animal sentience the year before to arrive at this holding, the Court affirmed that the state's animal protection laws took the suffering of individual animals, an implicit recognition of their sentience, as their primary concern.[66] As

[59] ibid, 438–39.
[60] ibid, 439.
[61] ibid, 442.
[62] ibid, 444.
[63] ibid, 445.
[64] ibid, 446–47 ('Oregon's animal cruelty laws have been rooted – for nearly a century – in a different legislative tradition of protecting individual animals themselves from suffering.').
[65] ibid, 447.
[66] ibid, 443–44.

such, its decision to uphold the intermediate court's determination that animals represent the focal point of animal protection laws ushered them from the margins of the law to its centre as a means of offering them individual relief. While it should be noted that the Court had to vacate its decision due to a procedural deficiency, it has nevertheless affirmed this holding through subsequent decisions,[67] two of which would limit owners' dominion over the animals in their care and in doing so curtail fundamental constitutional liberties.

One of these cases considered whether the state has an interest in conducting a blood test on a legally seized animal thought to be abused, and, if so, whether that state interest implicated and overcame the owner's constitutional rights to be secure in their property against warrantless searches. The case, *State v Newcomb*, concerned a dog named Juno, who was reported to have been beaten and underfed.[68] Arriving at the residence of the defendant, Newcomb, an animal welfare officer observed Juno's near-emaciated state and suspected him to be the victim of criminal neglect.[69] Determining Juno to be in need of medical care, the officer seized him without a warrant.[70] As part of the medical testing performed to understand Juno's condition and provide any necessary medical care, the State procured a blood test, which helped determine that he was malnourished, a key piece of evidence used to convict Newcomb of criminal neglect.[71]

With the case arriving at the Oregon Supreme Court, Newcomb, who had refused to sign a medical release form for the authorities to conduct an examination of Juno, argued that the blood drawn from Juno amounted to a warrantless search of her property and thus constituted a violation her right to be secure in her effects under both the US Constitution, as well as its counterpart in Oregon's law.[72] To buttress her argument, she asserted that because Oregon classified animals as personal property, they were 'no different [from] a folder or a stereo or a vehicle or a boot', alongside other forms of personal property.[73] Seeking to uphold Newcomb's conviction, the State asserted that Newcomb's right to be free from warrantless searches had not been implicated because a 'search' had not been conducted; in particular, they observed how an animal was 'one thing [in] itself', with a dog not containing anything other than 'more dog'.[74] But even if a search had been conducted, the State said, warrantless searches were prohibited only if unreasonable, and the State's statutory protections calling for animals to be cared for, they argued, trumped an owner's privacy interest in their property.[75]

[67] 'Update: Each Animal Counts!' (Animal Legal Defense Fund, 20 August 2015), available at aldf.org/article/update-each-animal-counts.

[68] *State v Newcomb* Or 375 P.3d 434, 437 (Or 2016).

[69] ibid, 436–37.

[70] ibid, 437.

[71] ibid.

[72] ibid.

[73] ibid, 437–38.

[74] ibid, 438.

[75] ibid.

Informing its determination, the Court began with the observation that not everything that can be owned and possessed as property merits the same constitutional protections in the same circumstances.[76] With regard to animals, and domestic pets in particular, it said, Oregon recognised that 'some animals, such as pets, occupy a unique position in people's hearts and in the law', a position not well-reflected in the 'cold characterization of a dog as *mere* property'.[77] As to whether owners have a privacy interest that is invaded by the withdrawal and testing of their animal's blood, the answer, the Court said, turns on the nature of the property in question.[78] Citing the state's recognition of animals as sentient beings, the Court stressed that the law affords them additional considerations in that they are the actual subjects of animal protection laws.[79] The question, therefore, was not whether the law allows humans to treat animals in ways they are prohibited from fellow humans; rather, it was whether the law prohibits humans from treating animals in ways that they are free to treat other forms of personal property.[80] While preserving the fundamental property status of animals, the Court maintained that those having custody over animals have an obligation to secure their welfare needs – a duty with no analogue in the realm of inanimate property.[81] As such, when animals are *lawfully seized*, as was the case with Juno, the State's examination of them to in order provide medical treatment does not constitute a 'search' of the owner's property. The dividing line carved out by the Court in this case, then, was informed by the sentient nature of the property in question. Owners may hold property rights over animals; however, due to the state's recognition of the sentient status of animals, who, again, are the subjects of animal protection laws, those property interests are qualified in the context of warrantless *searches*.

The concern over animal well-being moved Oregon's Supreme Court to chip away at an owner's dominion over the animals in their care in the context of warrantless seizures as well. The underlying case, *State v Fessenden*, concerned reports of an emaciated horse on the property of the defendant, Fessenden.[82] Observing the horse's condition, with the time needed to obtain a warrant threatening to see the horse collapse, the animal welfare officer entered Fessenden's property and seized the animal without a warrant.[83] Here, the defendant sought to suppress the evidence, arguing that it was obtained in violation of both Oregon and US constitutional protections against warrantless seizures.[84] Acknowledging that exceptions to the warrant requirement exist in cases of exigent circumstances,[85]

[76] ibid, 440.
[77] ibid (emphasis added).
[78] ibid.
[79] ibid.
[80] ibid, 441.
[81] ibid.
[82] *State v Fessenden* 333 P.3d 278, 280 (Or 2014).
[83] ibid.
[84] ibid, 280–81.
[85] ibid, 281.

such as to prevent danger to life, Fessenden argued that its scope should be limited to human life – not property, even living property at that.[86] Even if the Court considered animals to be 'sentient life' and not 'property', Fessenden continued, the constitutional right to be secure in one's effects nevertheless trumped society's interest in protecting animals.[87] Supporting this view, Fessenden characterised society's interest in animal protection as 'deriving not from a recognition that animal life is *inherently* worthy of protection, but from various benefits that humans receive by protecting animals'.[88] Rather, Fessenden argued, the protection of animals flowed only from their property value to their owners and the impact of animal cruelty on society at large.[89]

In its review, the Court scrutinised whether, under Oregon law, the exigent circumstances exception to the warrant requirement – which required the State to establish that swift action was necessary to prevent the danger to life – overcame Fessenden's constitutional guarantees.[90] Arguing that whose life mattered should be informed by modern developments, the State observed that the exception should include interventions to protect animal life.[91] Siding with the State, the Court found that an officer acts in concert with the legislative intent of the animal protection laws when they determine that a 'specific animal *deserves* and is *in need of* aid or protection'.[92] Holding that the exception to prevent danger to life was not limited to human life, the Court found that the officer had acted with probable cause to prevent further 'imminent harm to the *victim* of the crime', with animals qualifying as 'victims' under its previous ruling in *Nix*.[93]

Taken together, the legislature's codification of animal sentience and the progressive jurisprudence coming out of Oregon's highest court attest to the impact of this recognition for animals, a series of developments that merit revisiting to establish the new paradigm they have engendered. Notably, it is unclear whether the codification of animal sentience represented a clarification of or shift in the legislature's position as to the purpose of animal protection laws. That said, its determination that animals are sentient beings with the capacity to 'feel pain, stress and fear' and the view that they should thus be cared for in ways to prevent such suffering has affirmed the standing of animals as the primary beneficiaries of Oregon's animal protection laws. As exemplified by the decisions handed down by the Supreme Court of Oregon, the implications of this determination have proved far-reaching. Beyond this centring of animals as the primary beneficiaries of the state's animal protection laws, what the Oregon trilogy – *Nix*, *Newcomb* and *Fessenden* – dismantle is the historical view of animals as mere objects within

[86] ibid, 281, 286–87.
[87] ibid, 282–83.
[88] ibid, 283 (emphasis added).
[89] ibid, 282–83.
[90] ibid, 285.
[91] ibid, 285.
[92] ibid, 287 (emphasis added).
[93] ibid, 286 (emphasis added).

the law. Indeed, despite being property, animals are the 'victims' of the crimes committed against them, and compelling interest in preventing their suffering has abridged some of society's most fundamental liberties, even those grounded in constitutional property guarantees. To follow the arc of these cases, then, the codification of animal sentience has enabled animal protection laws to make 'justice' for animals possible.

That said, while the jurisprudence coming out of the Oregon trilogy has cemented the view that animals are not *mere* property, it did not provide that animals represent something *more or other than* property. As discussed in the next section, the case to test whether these holdings might serve as jurisprudential stepping-stones to find that animals can be legal persons would arrive in 2018.[94]

IV. The Case for Justice

In light of the progressive decisions handed down by Oregon's highest court, advocates sought to argue that animals should be able to sue their abusers for damages under a negligence per se claim, a cause of action arising under Oregon common law.[95] Broadly, to succeed under a negligence per se claim, the plaintiff must demonstrate four prima facie elements: first, the defendant must have violated a criminal statute defining the duty of care; second, the plaintiff must have suffered serious and permanent injuries; third, the plaintiff must be a member of the class of 'persons intended to be protected by the statute in question'; and, finally, the injuries suffered must have been of the type the statute was enacted to prevent.[96] Notably, the question of who constitutes a 'person' under relies on the state's definition of a 'victim', or a 'person … against whom the defendant committed the criminal offense, if … the person … has suffered … as a result of the offense'.[97] Given the Supreme Court of Oregon's determination in *Nix* that 'In any reasonable sense of the word, the "victim" of [animal cruelty] offenses is the individual animal that suffers the neglect',[98] animals necessarily qualify as 'persons' for these purposes because they are the ones whom animal protection laws are intended to protect. With this prospect of animal neglect victims being legal persons in a negligence per se action under the precedent established by Oregon's highest court, it was simply a matter of finding a compelling victim of animal neglect.

This prospective 'person' would come in the form of Justice,[99] a horse who suffered life-threatening injuries, including frostbite, malnourishment and other

[94] 'Justice the Horse Sues Abuser' (Animal Legal Defense Fund, 7 March 2023), available at aldf.org/case/justice-the-horse-sues-abuser.
[95] Brief of Petitioner-Appellant at 2, Just by and through *Mosiman v Vercher*, 321 Or App 439, 446, 518 P.3d 131, 135 (2022) (Appellant Brief).
[96] ibid, 10.
[97] OR REV STAT § 137.103(4)(a).
[98] *Nix* (n 52) 444.
[99] *Justice v Vercher* (n 7) 441.

harms at the hands of his former owner, Gwendolyn Vercher, who pled guilty to criminal neglect in 2017.[100] On its face, Justice met the state's statutory definition of a 'victim' given that he 'suffered' as a result of Vercher's violation of Oregon's animal neglect laws – an argument bolstered by the Oregon Supreme Court's own determination that animals constitute the victims of such offences because they are the ones suffering from the neglect. With precedent weighing in Justice's favour as to this third element, the primary question was whether Oregon courts would uphold the presumed right of an animal who otherwise met the other prima facie elements to sue their abuser in court, just as a human crime victim could.[101]

Despite this precedent established by the state's highest court, it was arguably unlikely that either the trial or intermediate court would embrace prospect of legal personhood for animals due to its novelty. In 2019, the trial court held that Justice could not bring the cause of action simply because animals are not legal persons.[102] Notably, its decision simply stated that because animals could not bear duties, they were ineligible to enjoy rights.[103] Engaging with the case more critically, the intermediate court cited the state's recognition of animal sentience and its implications in cases such as *Nix* and *Newcomb*.[104] In doing so, it reiterated that the law considered animals to be 'a special form of property', which entailed additional considerations as to their treatment compared to inanimate forms of property.[105] With respect to the prospect of their legal personage, however, it distinguished between animals on the one hand and human beings and legislatively created entities, such as corporations, on the other.[106] What distinguished the two groups, the intermediate court said, was that the former possessed the 'capacity' to sue whereas the latter lacked it.[107] According to the court, the incapacity of animals 'exists in perpetuity such that it would be difficult to say that a court – or any human being – may actually discern the animal's own interests in pursuing a legal action'.[108] Contrasting this perceived incapacity of animals to the incapacity of a minor or a human with a severe cognitive disability, the court argued that the former's lack of 'self-determination' was 'inherent' and 'distinctive'.[109] As such, it concluded that animals were not legal persons for the purposes of the law.[110] Although the ruling

[100] ibid, 442.

[101] The first element is satisfied, as Vercher pled guilty to the offence of animal neglect, which established the duty of care. The second element is also satisfied given the serious and permanent injuries Justice suffered as a result of Vercher's violation. As noted, the third element is satisfied by virtue of Justice belonging to the class of persons that intended to be protected by the state's animal neglect laws, which extend to mammals. Finally, the injuries Justice sustained, including frostbite and malnourishment, were of the nature the statute was intended to prevent. Appellant Brief (n 95) 10.

[102] Washington County Circuit Court, Case No 18CV17601, A169933 (2018).

[103] ibid.

[104] *Justice v Vercher* (n 7) 454.

[105] ibid, 451–52.

[106] ibid, 458.

[107] ibid.

[108] ibid, 446.

[109] ibid.

[110] ibid.

was appealed, the Supreme Court of Oregon declined to take up the case, with its order denying review neglecting to offer a reason why.[111] In doing so, it left the intermediate court's holding in place as current law, yet not itself cementing it as such.

V. Conclusion

To be sure, the unfolding of the *Justice* saga in the US's most progressive state raises the question of whether justice for animals, as exemplified by the affirmation of their legal personage, has been delayed, denied or both. As it concerns the codification of animal sentience that helped pave the path to the *Justice* case, what the intermediate court's decision attests to are the ramifications of the codification of 'animal sentience' being limited to pain and suffering. Although the intermediate court did not explicitly state what cognitive capacities animals would need to possess in order to be received as legal persons, a broader definition of what sentience entails as it concerns animals could one day incline courts to determine that they do. Indeed, broadly conceived, sentience implicates aspects of metacognition, such as the ability to self-reflect and empathise with and appreciate the perspectives and viewpoints of others,[112] elements that, if formally recognised by a legislature, might provide a pathway to 'capacitate' animals like Justice into legal persons.

As of June 2023, only a small minority of states have considered legislation to codify the sentience of animals in law. The first state to enact statutory protections for animals over 100 years ago, New York has witnessed the introduction of a bill in its 2022–23 legislative session to declare animals sentient beings capable of 'experiencing pain, stress, and fear' and who should therefore be 'treated humanely', as well as be 'considered the victims of animal cruelty crimes' by courts.[113] To be sure, the bill's definition of sentience echoes Oregon's sentience legislation and aspires to codify what Oregon's courts have expressly affirmed: that animals are the victims and thus intended beneficiaries of the state's animal protection laws. Yet, as with Oregon's sentience law, the New York bill's narrow definition contemplates only negative affective states and arguably limits its impact where the prospect of animals as legal persons is concerned. Conversely, Oklahoma's proposed sentience bill, likewise introduced in 2023, offers a more expansive definition of sentience yet ostensibly narrows the category of animals to whom it would apply.[114] Referred to as the 'Dog and Cat Bill of Rights Act', the Oklahoma bill states that 'Dogs and

[111] Animal Legal Defense Fund, 'Oregon Supreme Court Denies Petition to Review Case Involving Lawsuit on Behalf of Abused Horse' (Animal Legal Defense Fund, 7 March 2023), available at aldf.org/article/oregon-supreme-court-denies-petition-to-review-case-involving-lawsuit-on-behalf-of-abused-horse.
[112] Lori Marino, 'Introduction and Definitions' (2010) *Encyclopedia of Animal Behavior* 132, 132–38.
[113] AB 0041 2022–2023 Leg Assemb, Reg Sess (NY 2023).
[114] Dog and Cat Bill of Rights Act, HB 1992, 59th Reg Sess (OK 2023).

cats have the right to be respected as sentient beings that experience complex feelings that are common among living animals while being unique to each individual animal.'[115] In speaking to the 'complex feelings' that dogs and cats possess, the bill offers a more expansive conception of what sentience entails, contemplating both negative and positive affective states while also not disclosing the prospect of cognitive capacities. Notably, while the Oklahoma bill appears to afford this consideration to cats and dogs alone, by observing the commonality of these capacities among living animals, it extends this consideration to other species. Although Oklahoma's animal sentience bill has yet to be enacted, it offers insight into how jurisdictions, even those considered less progressive, may shift historical views as to whom animal protection laws are intended to benefit, as well as expand the implications of that recognition. Ultimately, while codifications of animal sentience may not transform the legal classification of animals in the near future, what is clear is that they are ushering animals into the focus of animal protection frameworks. In doing so, they are redressing the flawed foundations of those frameworks so that new gains for animals might be scaffolded from them.

[115] ibid.

PART THREE

Applications and Limitations

14

Sentiency, Exceptionalism and Farm Animal Protection

STEVEN WHITE

I. Introduction

Farm animals are clearly sentient – no less so than other domesticated animals or wild animals.[1] The sentiency of farm animals has long been established as a scientific fact.[2] Importantly, as long ago as 1965 this scientific fact was recognised as being significant in a policy sense, with the influential Brambell Report in the United Kingdom explicitly recognising the principles of sentience and animal welfare.[3] The Brambell Report, prompted by concerns about the intensive farming of animals, led to development of the Five Freedoms as principles to guide good animal welfare, in turn underpinning development of standards for the protection of farm animals in a range of jurisdictions. Explicit recognition of the sentiency of animals has, until relatively recently, been largely absent from domestic legislation. There is, though, an increasing willingness on the part of some jurisdictions to legislatively do so.[4] This chapter examines how legal recognition of sentiency might affect the level of protection extended to the largest class of domesticated animals: commercial farm animals. The focus is on Australian law, with some relevant international developments also considered. As a federation, and with responsibility for farm animal protection largely assumed by the six states and two self-governing territories, the potential exists to compare farm animal outcomes for jurisdictions recognising sentiency with those yet to do so. While this remains something of a speculative exercise at this point, with just one jurisdiction so far

[1] For a detailed account by a leading animal welfare science researcher of the sentience and cognitive abilities of a range of animals, including farm animals see Donald M Broom, *Sentience and Animal Welfare* (CABI, 2014).

[2] ibid.

[3] Francis W Brambell, 'Report of the Technical Committee to Enquire into the Welfare of Animals kept under the Intensive Livestock Husbandry Systems' (HMSO, 1956).

[4] For a summary of recent developments see J Kotzmann, 'Legal Recognition of Animal Sentience: The Case for Cautious Optimism' (2022) 6 *Animal Sentience* 7.

explicitly legislating recognition of sentiency, international developments suggest Australian jurisdictions will be under increasing pressure to take this step.

The early indications are that explicit recognition of sentience in animal protection law may not by itself materially change the status of farm animals under law. This chapter analyses why this might be the case. A central reason is the longstanding differential legal protection accorded to farm animals, often excluded from many of the basic protections extended to some other categories of animal. This chapter shows how legislation in Australia effaces the application of basic standards of protection – a duty of care and prohibition of cruelty – to farm animals. Although the precise legislative mechanism varies across the states and territories, all adopt the same broad approach of creating an exception to the application of protection offences where there is compliance with a relevant code of practice or regulation for farm animals.[5] The codes of practice and regulations largely reflect the agenda of farm animal industries and compromised agricultural departments, so that a range of practices harmful to farm animals are legally sanctioned.

One consequence of this legislative approach is a perceived gap between what the law would seem to promise farm animals and what is achieved in practice. Another consequence is that dissatisfaction with the development of government-sanctioned codes of practice has prompted the emergence of voluntary, private standard-setting schemes for farm animals, such as the RSPCA Approved Farming Scheme. Understanding the nature of these schemes and the extent to which they formally recognise sentience is important, given they sit outside the requirements of the law. It is argued that to the extent that farm animals are understood to be sentient, this is largely implicit, not just in the formal law, but also in the regulatory processes in place to develop farm animal standards, whether state-sponsored or private.

Scope exists, therefore, to ensure not just that legislation formally acknowledges the sentience of all animals, including farm animals, but also that this recognition is an explicit feature of standards development, whether government or private. Shifting expectations about the protection that should be afforded to farm animals is grounded in an understanding that farm animals are sentient and, importantly, as sentient beings farm animals possess certain capabilities and should have their interests protected. In particular, there is a gap between 'what people are expecting of the regulator and the perceived regulatory reality'.[6] This chapter, then, explores this gap and whether explicit recognition that farm animals are sentient may contribute to closing that gap.

[5] Codes of practice may be adopted in stand-alone form or translated into regulations under primary legislation. Newer standards and guidelines are superseding codes of practice, but they perform the same functional role: see section II.B below.

[6] Futureye, 'Commodity or Sentient Being? Australia's Shifting Mindset on Farm Animal Welfare' (Research Report, 2018) 6.

II. Protection of Farm Animals – The Status Quo

Regulation of the protection of farm animals in Australia is complex, given the distinct legal regimes in each state and territory, the lack of national oversight[7] and the significant standard-setting role played by some non-state institutional actors. This section will provide a brief overview of some of the key features of farm animal protection in Australia,[8] before considering the legal recognition of sentiency and its implications for farm animals in subsequent sections.

A. Qualified Legislative Protection of Farm Animals

Australia does not have national animal protection legislation, even if the national Commonwealth Government has at different times played a role in coordinating policy development, particularly for farm animal protection.[9] Each state and territory has animal protection legislation which nominally applies to 'animals', including farm animals. This means that protections such as a prohibition of cruelty and obligations to meet the welfare needs of animals – such as food, shelter, the opportunity to express normal patterns of behaviour, access to veterinary care and proper handling – prima facie apply to farm animals. The obligation to meet the welfare needs of an animal in some jurisdictions is styled as a distinct 'duty of care', with Queensland specifically defining this duty of care by reference to the Five Freedoms.[10] In a novel development, Queensland has recently extended this approach by introducing what is, in effect, an aggravated duty of care breach.[11] Most jurisdictions incorporate aggravated cruelty offences in their animal protection legislation, while New South Wales and Queensland have an offence of 'serious animal cruelty' in omnibus criminal legislation.[12]

In practice, the application of these protective provisions to farm animals is highly circumscribed. The first limitation is found in the qualifying language of the offences, a familiar feature of legislation in many jurisdictions internationally.

[7] The national Government, elected in 2022, committed to establishing a national independent office of animal welfare. This looks likely to go no further than extending the existing Inspector General of Live Animal Exports to an Inspector General of Animal Welfare and Live Animal Exports, with a limited role in policy setting: see Department of Agriculture, Fisheries and Forestry, 'Inspector General of Animal Welfare and Live Animal Exports', available at www.agriculture.gov.au/biosecurity-trade/export/controlled-goods/live-animals/animal-welfare/igaw.

[8] For a detailed jurisdiction-by-jurisdiction account of the law in this area, see Deborah Cao, *Animal Law in Australia*, 3rd edn (Thomson Reuters, 2023) ch 7; see also Elizabeth Ellis, *Australian Animal Law: Context and Critique* (Sydney University Press, 2022) ch 4.

[9] For an overview see Steven White, 'Farm Animal Protection Policymaking and the Law: The Impetus for Change' (2018) 43 *Alternative Law Journal* 244.

[10] Animal Care and Protection Act 2001 (Qld), s 17. A similar approach is taken in the UK: see Animal Welfare Act 2006, s 9.

[11] Animal Care and Protection Act 2001 (Qld), s 17(2)(a).

[12] See Crimes Act 1900 (NSW), s 530; Criminal Code 1899 (Qld), s 242.

Terms such as 'appropriate', 'reasonable' and 'no unnecessary, unjustified or unreasonable pain or suffering' are commonplace. There is no significant higher court consideration of the scope of these qualifications in an Australian context, for several reasons. For one thing, the availability of defences or exemptions, including for compliance with a relevant code of practice, forecloses consideration of the offence provision (addressed in section B below). And, even where a defence of that type may not be available, animal welfare offences are generally summary offences, with prosecutions occurring at the lowest level of the court hierarchy. Finally, as Wolfson and Sullivan argue, by reference to comparably worded United States legislation:

> By including in the definition of *cruelty* the otherwise undefined requirement that the conduct must be unjustifiable or unnecessary, the law may invite the conclusion that a practice, though capable of causing great suffering, is not legally cruel if it is related, in any way, to food production.[13]

B. Exemptions, Defences and Codes of Practice

Two key types of exemptions or defences may mean that conduct which might otherwise draw the potential application of the cruelty prohibition or failure to meet the welfare needs of an animal does not give rise to liability in a commercial farm animal context. The law is structured to nominally protect all animals but then, as an exception, remove that protection for farm animals. This form of exceptionalism also occurs for some other categories of animal, most notably animals used for research purposes[14] and some wild animals, but the sheer number of farm animals raised and killed each year means that it is perhaps most significant for this category of animal. As Lovvorn has argued, this type of structural approach creates a 'gap' between the promise of anti-cruelty legislation and its realisation, especially for farm animals.[15]

The first and less common means, at least in Australia, to exclude farm animals from protection is to excuse conduct which is consistent with an 'accepted animal husbandry practice'. For example, the serious animal cruelty offence in New South Wales does not apply where the relevant conduct 'occurred in the course of or for the purposes of routine agricultural or animal husbandry activities'.[16] Similarly, in Western Australia, the cruelty prohibition does not apply where the relevant act was done 'in accordance with a generally accepted

[13] David J Wolfson and Mariann Sullivan, 'Foxes in the Hen House – Animals, Agribusiness and the Law: A Modern American Fable' in Cass R Sunstein and Martha C Nussbaum (eds), *Animal Rights: Current Debates and New Directions* (Oxford University Press, 2004) 205, 211 (emphasis in original).

[14] See Jane Kotzmann and Hope Ferdowsian's contribution to this volume.

[15] JR Lovvorn, 'Animal Law in Action: The Law, Public Perception, and the Limits of Animal Rights Theory as a Basis for Legal Reform' (2006) 12 *Animal Law* 133, 139.

[16] Crimes Act 1900 (NSW), s 530(2)(b).

animal husbandry practice … that is used in … farming or grazing activities'.[17] This form of exemption is concerning from an interpretative perspective since, as Sharman points out, it 'suggests that those who profit from animal use have made themselves the arbitrators of the meaning of cruelty, instead of enabling the definition to be determined chiefly by the Courts or those with a more objective approach to the interests of farmed animals'.[18]

More common, and a feature of nearly every jurisdiction, is an exemption or defence for compliance with a relevant code of practice or regulation.[19] For example, the South Australian animal protection statute provides that 'Nothing in this Act renders unlawful anything done in accordance with a prescribed code of practice relating to animals'.[20] The consequence of this type of exemption is that the standards of protection for almost all farm animals are not set by the Act. Rather, the relevant standards are to be found in a relevant code of practice or regulation. Model Codes of Practice for farm animals were first developed in Australia in the 1980s. Over the past decade and a half, there has been a process of reinvigorating Model Codes of Practice as Australian Animal Welfare Standards and Guidelines,[21] with the goal that these new standards and guidelines are adopted as delegated legislation in the form of a regulation by the states and territories.[22] While some degree of consistency has been achieved, there remain significant gaps and differences across the jurisdictions. The process has been hindered by the waxing and waning of the Commonwealth Government's commitment to coordinating the process. Most notably, periods of government by the Liberal-National Parties have undermined any improvement in animal welfare regulatory processes at the national level.[23]

Crucially, even where codes of practice are adopted by state and territory jurisdictions as delegated legislation, the codes still permit a range of ostensibly cruel practices to be committed against farm animals. For example, the codes allow practices such as the use of battery cages for laying hens,[24] mulesing of

[17] Animal Welfare Act 2002 (WA), s 23(a).

[18] Cao (n 8) 286.

[19] In NSW compliance or non-compliance with a relevant regulation is admissible in court proceedings: Prevention of Cruelty to Animals Act 1979 (NSW), s 34A(3).

[20] Animal Welfare Act 1985 (SA), s 43.

[21] For detail of this process until 2020 see Australian Animal Welfare Standards and Guidelines, available at www.animalwelfarestandards.net.au.

[22] See White (n 9).

[23] The National Party of Australia is the party of agricultural Australia, effectively a sectional interest group, with party representatives often having a rural background. Their small numbers are disproportionately amplified by 'opportunities to shape the policy approach of the Liberal Party, thanks to formal coalition agreements and a tendency by the Liberal Party to defer to its junior partner on issues affecting rural Australia': Peter Chen, *Animal Welfare in Australia: Politics and Policy* (Sydney University Press, 2016) 292.

[24] Commonwealth Department of Agriculture, Fisheries and Forestry, 'Australian Animal Welfare Standards and Guidelines for Poultry', available at www.agriculture.gov.au/agriculture-land/animal/welfare/standards-guidelines/poultry. The use of battery cages for hens is to be phased out, but not until 2036.

sheep,[25] and tail docking, castration and sterilisation of sheep, including without pain relief for animals less than six months of age.[26] This approach reflects the key role played by farming industry interests and agricultural departments in the agenda-setting and writing process. Consultation has been improved but remains impervious to widespread public concerns about some practices (eg the practice of mulesing of sheep and the use of battery cages for hens). The process of review has been drawn-out, marked by compromised use of animal welfare science research, a failure to engage with international developments and a focus on the machinery of standard-setting while avoiding change in the content of standards.[27] The overall result is that it is difficult to argue that there has been any significant, meaningful improvement in government-sanctioned animal welfare standards since 2005.[28] The extent of failure in this area has led to proposals for the creation of an independent statutory body to assume responsibility for coordinating the development of farm animal welfare standards, including from a source as unlikely as the Productivity Commission, a national agency sitting in the Treasury portfolio, historically focused on economic issues, but with a mandate to provide 'quality, independent advice and information to governments', with a focus on 'key policy or regulatory issues bearing on Australia's economic performance and community wellbeing'.[29] The Productivity Commission identified three key problem areas to be addressed in standard-setting for farm animal welfare:

- The objective of the national standards and guidelines needs to be clearer.
- Standards and guidelines should be evidence-based, drawing on independent and credible evidence on animal welfare science and research on community values for animal welfare …

[25] Mulesing 'is the removal of skin from the breech and/or tail of a sheep using mulesing shears' and is employed 'to reduce urine and faecal soiling or dag formation in the breech and tail wool and thus minimise susceptibility to breech and tail flystrike': Sheep Standards and Guidelines Writing Group, 'Sheep Standards and Guidelines – Mulesing Discussion Paper' (January 2013) 1, available at www.animalwelfarestandards.net.au/sheep/consultative-process. People for the Ethical Treatment of Animals (PETA), a US-based animal advocacy organisation with branches all over the world, has targeted the Australian wool industry over a range of cruel animal husbandry practices, including mulesing of sheep. The mulesing campaign involved PETA targeting large US and European wholesale wool buyers and informing them of the mulesing of Australian sheep, with the goal of discouraging purchase of Australian 'mulesed' wool. Australian Wool Innovation (AWI), a representative wool industry organisation, sued PETA on the basis that PETA was in breach of secondary boycott laws under the Trade Practices Act 1974 (Cth) (since repealed). The litigation did not proceed to trial, with settlement in 2007 including AWI paying its own significant costs and agreeing to pursue the phasing out of mulesing by 2010. The latter has still not occurred.

[26] Australian Animal Welfare Standards and Guidelines, 'Sheep', available at www.animalwelfarestandards.net.au/sheep. For a more detailed account of the range of harms permitted under codes of practice see Ellis (n 8) 123–42.

[27] Ellis (n 8); White (n 9); Jed Goodfellow, 'Regulatory Capture and the Welfare of Farm Animals in Australia' in Deborah Cao and Steven White (eds), *Animal Law and Welfare – International Perspectives* (Springer International Publishing, 2016) 195.

[28] Ellis (n 8); White (n 9).

[29] Productivity Commission, 'How we contribute' (Australian Government), available at www.pc.gov.au/about/contribute; Productivity Commission, 'Regulation of Australian Agriculture' (Australian

- There needs to be more independence in the standards development process so that outcomes are not overly influenced by the views of any one group, either industry or animal welfare groups. Judgments made to balance conflicting considerations should be transparent and apply rigorous scientific principles. Surveys of community values for animal welfare should be statistically robust and transparent.[30]

The Productivity Commission focused on government-led development processes for farm animal protection standards, only briefly considering co-regulatory or private standards. Before considering the significance for farm animals of explicit recognition of sentience, it is necessary to address the increasingly important role played by non-state standard setting processes in farm animal protection.

C. Non-state Standard-setting and the Protection of Farm Animals

Private standard-setting schemes addressing animal welfare have been pursued for a range of reasons, including the haphazard and meandering state-sanctioned process, addressed in the previous sub-section; the commercial need of the farming industry for seamless compliance processes; and to meet demands from consumers for higher standards than those provided through state-sanctioned codes of practice. Two key mechanisms in this context in Australia are quality assurance (QA) systems (essentially industry-driven) and the RSPCA Approved Farming Scheme.[31] Industry-driven QA schemes add little to no value to state-sanctioned standards of protection for farm animals. For example, APIQ, a QA scheme administered by the pig industry representative group Pork Australia, covers 90 per cent of production in Australia but, in the area of animal welfare, certifies only that producers comply with regulated codes of practice.[32]

By contrast, the RSPCA Approved Farming Scheme extends existing state-sanctioned regulation, with incrementally higher protection standards, and includes a commitment to regular review, regular compliance monitoring and a focus on animal welfare science. The assurance scheme, administered by RSPCA Australia, focuses on six of the most intensively farmed animals in Australia:

> The RSPCA has developed animal welfare standards for layer hens, pigs, meat chickens, turkeys, farmed Atlantic salmon and dairy calves. These standards go well beyond legal

Government, Report No 79, 15 November 2016) ch 5. The left-of-centre national Government elected in 2022 had committed to an independent, nationally coordinated standards approach, although it is not clear whether this will be achieved in practice: see Department of Agriculture, Fisheries and Forestry (n 7).

[30] Productivity Commission, 'Regulation of Australian Agriculture' (Australian Government, Report No 79, 15 November 2016) 228.

[31] Comparable schemes operate in other jurisdictions: see, eg, RSPCA Assured in the United Kingdom (www.rspcaassured.org.uk) and SPCA Certified in New Zealand (www.spcacertified.nz).

[32] Australian Pork, 'What is APIQ', available at australianpork.com.au.

> requirements and are based on the best available animal welfare science, RSPCA policy, leading farming practices in Australia and overseas and take account of the commercial realities associated with farming. They are detailed and specific to each species, publicly available, and are reviewed every five years. By regularly reviewing the standards, continual improvements can be made to the welfare of millions of farm animals. The RSPCA's standards prohibit many unnecessary or inhumane farming systems such as the use of battery cages for layer hens or sow stalls and farrowing crates for pigs.[33]

RSPCA Australia states that 'More than 2.5 billion hens, pigs, chickens, turkeys and farmed Atlantic salmon have benefitted from higher welfare conditions since the Scheme began in 1996'.[34]

RSPCA Australia's standards have gained traction in recent years, not least because the two largest supermarket retailers in Australia, Coles and Woolworths, have required some of their animal product suppliers to comply with them. In doing so, those retailers are seeking to respond to consumer demand. Underlying this instrumental purpose are a range of factors, including the desire to achieve a competitive advantage, managing the risk of misleading claims about the welfare status of animal products, addressing gaps in existing state-sponsored standards, concerns about a lack of enforcement of state-sponsored standards, and a concern that state-sponsored development of standards takes too long. This expanding role in standard-setting for RSPCA Australia is consistent with the trend in other areas of protective regulation where NGOs are playing increasingly significant roles in standard-setting.[35] The requirement that suppliers of the large retailers comply with the RSPCA Australia standards is, for RSPCA Australia, a pragmatic means of effecting faster change in the protection of farm animals than would otherwise be the case.[36]

The RSPCA Approved Farming Scheme now applies to most of the total market in meat chickens in Australia, and to a lesser extent of farmed salmon, but otherwise farm animal market coverage is low.[37] This point highlights one of the potential limitations of private standards approaches. Participation is purely voluntary and often instrumental, with large supermarket retailers, for example, not concerned about animal welfare per se. If the scheme standards are regarded as being too high to be achievable, if consumer perceptions about the significance

[33] RSPCA Australia, 'What is the RSPCA Approved Farming Scheme' (RSPCA Knowledge Base, updated 23 June 2023), available at kb.rspca.org.au/knowledge-base/what-is-the-rspca-approved-farming-scheme.

[34] ibid.

[35] Colin Scott, 'Standard-Setting in Regulatory Regimes' in Robert Baldwin, Martin Cave and Martin Lodge (eds), *The Oxford Handbook of Regulation* (Oxford University Press, 2010) 104, 112.

[36] RSPCA Australia is clear about the scope of what might be possible in standard-setting, stating that 'the RSPCA Standards are … created with the aim of meeting the needs of animals while also being commercially achievable. This means the Scheme can work with large scale producers and improve the lives of a greater number of animals': RSPCA Australia, 'RSPCA Approved Farming – Impact Report 2020' (2021) 17.

[37] ibid, 8.

of animal protection issues were to change (including adversely, for example due to increased cost) or farming industry groups were to object, retailers may not engage.[38] The consumer base of the large retailers is diverse. Given RSPCA Approved Farming Scheme standards are not applied across the board by large retailers to their animal products, this might suggest a limited, selective implementation of more robust animal protection standards.[39] Finally, the existence and adoption of private standard-setting schemes contributes to a fragmentation of the farm animal protection regulatory regime,[40] leaving continuing gaps and uncertainty in the standard of animal protection. There is the risk that private regulatory schemes, as incomplete as they are, might provide justification for state retreat from the field of standard-setting and enforcement:

> An optimistic view suggests that private regulatory activity might have a capacity building effect, raising local awareness, higher standards, and inspiring states to develop more rigorous regulatory institutions. At least, it might help states overcome inhibitions to greater regulation. A more pessimistic prediction would see the existence of private actors move the state to withdraw to the sidelines, and existing institutions to become atrophied.[41]

The presence of private standards schemes complicates the question of what it means to recognise sentience on the part of farm animals, beyond legislative declaration, and what the effects of such action might be.

[38] One of the large supermarket retailers, Woolworths, has reportedly disavowed its commitment to reach the highest level (Tier 1) ranking in the Business Benchmark of Farm Animal Welfare, an international assurance scheme operated by Compassion in World Farming and Four Paws International (www.bbfaw.com). Farming industry groups had expressed their concern to Woolworths about assessment criteria giving weight to efforts to source non-animal based protein: see 'Woolworths ends alignment with controversial animal welfare benchmark' Beef Central (23 May 2023), available at www.beefcentral.com/news/woolworths-ends-alignment-with-controversial-animal-welfare-benchmark. Notably, a Woolworths spokesperson is quoted as suggesting that 'the international benchmark fails to recognise the unique context of Australian farming, and the ways our farmers care for animals in a different climate and geography': ibid. Parochial claims of this nature have historically been made in the state-sanctioned development of codes of practice to resist improved standards, with a lack of engagement with international developments one of the criticisms of the process made as long ago as 2005: Geoff Neumann and Associates, *Review of the Australian Model Codes of Practice for the Welfare of Animals* (Final Report, 9 February 2005).

[39] McInerney argues that 'the obvious place where ethical standards relating to animal treatment could influence the food supply chain is in the purchasing decisions of the supermarkets – and they have singularly failed to adopt a principled stance on this issue. Those that do claim to do so have been selective in their efforts, focussing just on specific products, carrying "high end" brands for one segment of the market while offering across the range down to budget brands of ill-described and minimal quality characteristics. This, of course, is an entirely rational commercial strategy in a competitive market; supermarkets, too, realise they need to have principles but can't afford them to be universal': John McInerney, 'Principles, Preference and Profit: Animal Ethics in a Market Economy' in Christopher M Wathes et al (eds), *Veterinary & Animal Ethics* (John Wiley-Blackwell, 2013) 271, 278.

[40] See, generally, Julia Black, 'Constructing and Contesting Legitimacy and Accountability in Polycentric Regulatory Regimes' (2008) 2 *Regulation & Governance* 137.

[41] Peter Grabosky, 'Beyond Responsive Regulation: The Expanding Role of Non-State Actors in the Regulatory Process' (2013) *Regulation & Governance* 114, 121.

III. Law, Sentiency and Farm Animal Protection

To what extent is sentience recognised in the context of farm animal protection? The answer to this question, at least in Australia, is very little, at least explicitly. The Australian Capital Territory (ACT) is the only jurisdiction to date to amend animal protection legislation to formally recognise sentience. Section 4A(1) of the Animal Welfare Act 1992 (ACT) provides that:

> The main objects of this Act are to recognise that –
>
> (a) animals are sentient beings that are able to subjectively feel and perceive the world around them; and
>
> (b) animals have intrinsic value and deserve to be treated with compassion and have a quality of life that reflects their intrinsic value; and
>
> (c) people have a duty to care for the physical and mental welfare of animals.

Two further jurisdictions are likely to explicitly recognise sentience in their respective animal protection statutes.[42] As part of a broader reform process, the Victorian Government has stated an intention to incorporate explicit reference to sentience in revised animal protection legislation, either in an objects section, as a legislative principle and/or in the definition of 'animal'. The Western Australian Government has endorsed the recommendation of an independent panel to include recognition of sentience in the objects section of the Animal Welfare Act 2002 (WA), even if this will be achieved by describing sentience without using the term.[43]

Other jurisdictions have ruled out recognition, including the Northern Territory, Queensland and New South Wales. The rationale offered by each jurisdiction for declining to do so is, essentially, that sentience is implicit in legislation, whether through the existence of protective provisions and/or in the definition of 'animal'.[44] In Queensland, reliance on the argument that sentience is implicit in legislation occurred in the face of rhetoric that reform of Queensland law was designed to examine 'all aspects of the Act to ensure that our laws continue to meet changing community expectations and modern animal welfare practices'.[45]

[42] For a detailed account of these proposals see Jane Kotzmann, 'A Typology of Australian Animal Sentience Recognition Provisions' (2023) 51 *Federal Law Review* 157.

[43] See Department of Regional Industries and Regional Development, 'Government Response to the Report of the Independent Review of the Animal Welfare Act 2002', available at www.agric.wa.gov.au/animalwelfare/review-animal-welfare-act-2002-government-response.

[44] Kotzmann (n 42). The Queensland Government response relied on both, with the responsible department stating that the 'Act implicitly recognises sentience in animals through the section 11 definition of animal. Only sentient animals are prescribed as an animal under section 11 of the Act. In addition, the inclusion of sections 17 (duty of care) and 18 (cruelty) in the Act recognise that animals can experience different feelings such as suffering or pleasure. These provisions also recognise that animals can suffer negative feelings or emotions including pain, fear, boredom and frustration': Queensland Government, 'Departmental Final Response to Public Submissions – Inquiry into the Animal Care and Protection Amendment Bill 2022' (Prepared by the Department of Agriculture and Fisheries for the State Development and Regional Industries Committee, 16 June 2022) 29.

[45] Minister for Agricultural Industry Development and Fisheries and Minister for Rural Communities, 'Thousands of Queenslanders help to update animal welfare laws' (Ministerial Media Statement, 13 December 2021).

The agenda for change put forward by the State Government was limited to a few narrow issues, excluding recognition of sentience as a specific proposal. Despite this 'Respondents in almost half … of the written submissions called for animal sentience to be explicitly recognised in the [Act]'.[46] Tasmania has also rejected statutory recognition of sentience, but in commentary on a 2022 amendment bill has 'proposed that any statements regarding sentience be considered for inclusion (on a case-by-case basis) in future animal welfare guidelines, not as part of the amendment Bill'.[47]

Overall, then, there is a mixed approach in Australia to explicit legislative recognition of sentience. Some jurisdictions have legislated this, or intend to do so, while others have not considered it or have rejected it. The different approaches create the possibility of a comparative consideration of the effect of such recognition on animal protection standards, even if more time is needed for a fuller consideration as more jurisdictions give effect to their intention to act.

Has recognition of sentience in the ACT proved to be significant, in a way which places it apart from other jurisdictions for protection of farm animals? Like most animal protection legislation in Australia, the reference to 'animal' in the Animal Welfare Act 1992 (ACT) is a reference to animals generally, with no distinction drawn between categories of animal, so that section 4A(1) encompasses farm animals. Also consistent with most other state and territory legislation, the ACT legislation has a provision which provides an exemption from application of cruelty and welfare obligation offences where there is compliance with an approved or mandatory code of practice.[48] Section 21 contemplates codes of practice addressing 'animal welfare in intensive farming', 'transport of livestock' and 'livestock and poultry slaughtering establishments', and a range of codes affecting farm animals have been adopted. In form, then, notwithstanding section 4A(1), the ACT entrenches a familiar legislative structure of nominal protection of farm animals, undercut by substantive exclusions.

Notably, though, the ACT prohibits battery cage farming,[49] close confinement of pigs[50] and beak removal or trimming in chickens (unless conducted by a vet for therapeutic purposes),[51] standards of protection which place it ahead of other Australian states and territories. These provisions, though, were in place prior to the introduction of explicit recognition of sentience in section 4A(1). This might suggest that the jurisdictions most likely to take the step of recognising sentience

[46] Queensland Government, 'Review of the Animal Care and Protection Act 2001 – Consultation Outcomes' Report (2021) 36.

[47] Department of Natural Resources and Environment Tasmania, 'Animal Welfare Amendment Bill – Summary of Online Consultation', available at nre.tas.gov.au/biosecurity-tasmania/animal-biosecurity/animal-welfare/legislation-standards-guidelines/animal-welfare-act/animal-welfare-act-amendment-bill.

[48] Animal Welfare Act 2022 (ACT), s 20.

[49] Ibid, s 9A.

[50] ibid, s 9B.

[51] ibid, s 9C.

are also those already willing to consider or extend at least some protections beyond the baseline requirements of farm animal codes of practice, so that a pattern of correlation rather than causation exists.

This analysis is broadly consistent with Kotzmann's conclusion, after comparing the effects of explicit legislative recognition of sentience in international settings including New Zealand, Quebec and the European Union, that:

> While there are differences between the jurisdictions considered here, the relevant provisions bear striking resemblance to each other. In each jurisdiction, concern for animal welfare and a perceived need to improve legal protections for animals provided the context for legal recognition of animal sentience. In this respect, the sentience provisions were the product of domestic pressures, but also pressures that transcend individual jurisdictions. At the same time, it is not clear that explicit recognition of sentience in any of the jurisdictions has yet had any significant consequence for animals.[52]

Beyond legislation, in Australia contemporary codes of practice, which as shown in the previous section, are the farm animal welfare standards adopted as regulations under primary statutes, do not have statements explicitly recognising the sentience of farm animals or the significance of sentience. Notably, some earlier sets of standards were not afraid to invoke a responsibility towards farm animals grounded in at least implicit recognition of their sentience, and perhaps even extending beyond the narrow requirements of the law. For example, the Model Code of Practice for Cattle included the statement:

> Whatever the form of husbandry, owners and managers have a legal and moral responsibility to care for the welfare of the animals under their control … The basic needs of cattle must be met, irrespective of the nature of the husbandry or farming system.[53]

Similarly, standards produced as part of private standard-setting schemes, including the RSPCA Approved Farming Scheme, do not refer to sentiency. This is despite RSPCA Australia separately endorsing explicit legislative recognition as a policy objective.[54]

Finally, Australia and the United Kingdom recently entered into a free trade agreement in which paragraph 1 of the animal welfare chapter states that the

[52] Jane Kotzmann, 'Recognising the Sentience of Animals in Law: A Justification and Framework for Australian States and Territories' (2020) 42 *Sydney Law Review* 281, 296. A similar conclusion is expressed by Rodriguez Ferrere after a survey of statutes in Oregon, Quebec and New Zealand, with such an outcome 'entirely expected': Marcelo Rodriguez Ferrere, 'The (Symbolic) Legislative Recognition of Sentience' (2022) 28 *Animal Law* 117, 135.

[53] Primary Industries Standing Committee, 'Model Code of Practice for the Welfare of Animals – Cattle', 2nd edn (CSIRO Publishing, 2004) 3.

[54] The organisation states that 'Fundamentally, animal welfare is important because animals are sentient. The sentience of animals is the core reason for why their interests count and why it is wrong to treat animals cruelly. Such recognition reflects developments in community attitudes in moving beyond simply valuing animals for their instrumental worth. Accordingly, the objects of animal welfare legislation should be to … recognise that animals are sentient beings with intrinsic value': RSPCA Australia, 'Animal Welfare Legislation' (Position Paper GP2, adopted 6 June 2021) 3.

parties 'recognise that animals are sentient'.[55] This does not have any immediate implications for farm animal protection standard-setting in Australia. However, it does put the issue back on the policy agenda of the Commonwealth Government, a point taken up in the next section as part of a broader consideration of whether explicit recognition of sentiency on the part of farm animals is worth seeking.

IV. Sentience, Farm Animals and Improved Protection

If explicit recognition of sentience in law has so far been limited and, where it has occurred, not yet improved the protection accorded to animals, is it worth pursuing? This question has recently been addressed in thorough and nuanced ways with differing views, including in this volume,[56] and so this section will focus more narrowly on three issues particularly relevant for the interests of farm animals.

First, it might be argued that explicit recognition of sentience of farm animals can play an important role in undermining the property status accorded to farm animals. There is an incongruity between the idea of sentience and continuing to legally classify farm animals as property, valued as fungible commodities or livestock. It is notable that in the farm animal sector, the deep disagreements between stakeholder groups, the fragmented and contested nature of standards development, and often compromised animal welfare science arguably reflect two competing justifications for regulatory intervention. On the one hand, there is a justification which assumes farm animals to be commodities, but which recognises that market failures may necessitate limited intervention, including where distress felt by consumers concerned about animal harm is not adequately reflected in the price of animal products. Such a justification is consistent with an approach which structures animal protection legislation in a way which systematically limits basic statutory protections against cruelty and fulfilment of welfare needs for farm animals.[57] On

[55] Australia–United Kingdom Free Trade Agreement, Australia–United Kingdom, signed 17 December 2021, Art 25.1. Kotzmann points out that this is the first trade agreement involving Australia which has a chapter addressing animal welfare: n 42 above, 169. The inclusion of an animal welfare chapter was at the insistence of the UK. Australia and the EU have been negotiating a free trade agreement since 2018. While it is not clear when or if an agreement will be finalised, the EU has requested the inclusion of provisions addressing animal welfare: see Department of Foreign Affairs and Trade, 'Australia–EU FTA – Report on Negotiating Round Nine, 30 November – 11 December 2020', available at www.dfat.gov.au/trade/agreements/negotiations/aeufta/news/australia-eu-fta-report-negotiating-round-nine-30-november-11-december-2020.

[56] See, for example, Kotzmann (n 52), who is of the view that recognition is, on balance, positive. Rodriguez Ferrere (n 52) has argued that, on balance, recognition is symbolic only and ultimately counter-productive in the quest to achieve meaningful reform for the protection of animals. In ch 17 of this volume, Rodriguez Ferrere suggests that whether recognition leads to better outcomes for animals is yet to be seen but is by itself no panacea. See also Max Carpendale, 'Does Sentience Legislation Help Animals?' (Animal Ask, 9 December 2022), available at www.animalask.org/post/does-sentience-legislation-help-animals.

[57] In this context, private interest theories of regulation can provide useful insights into regulatory outcomes. As Morgan and Yeung describe it, in 'political versions of private interest theory, political

the other hand, there is a non-instrumentalist, public interest justification which assumes farm animals have an intrinsic moral worth requiring protection consistent with that extended to other, similar animals, such as companion animals. Recognition of sentiency would be consistent with this non-instrumentalist, public interest justification and reinforce a shared understanding of why it is that the state intervenes at all to protect farm animals, even if this does not by itself change the property status of farm animals.[58]

Second, there is a gap between the promise of the law for farm animals and what it achieves in practice. Kotzmann has summarised a growing level of concern about the treatment of animals across developed countries, including in Australia, much of this underpinned by the work of animal activists in exposing routine treatment of animals in a range of settings.[59] Notably, concerns about the treatment of farm animals have perhaps been most significant of all. A large sample social survey commissioned by the Commonwealth Department of Agriculture suggests that this concern is underpinning dissatisfaction with the regulation of farm animal protection on the part of the general public in Australia. Significantly, an understanding of animals as sentient is at the heart of this dissatisfaction:

> [F]indings clearly show that the Australian public's view on how farm animals should be treated has advanced to the point where they expect to see more effective regulation. In Australia today, 95% of people view farm animal welfare to be a concern and 91% want at least some reform to address this. This perceived gap between expectations and regulation spells increasing risk for the Australian federal government … The major driver of this shift is an increased focus on animals' level of sentience and related capabilities. Research indicates a fundamental community belief that animals are entitled to the protection of relevant rights and freedoms, closely aligning with activist sentiment. The public has a clear expectation for effective regulation to uphold these freedoms and expect highly transparent practices, regulation and enforcement.[60]

This suggests that explicit recognition of sentience is likely giving effect to a widely held assumption on the part of the general public about the nature of animals, including farm animals. However, consistent with the public interest justification

outcomes, and the regulatory rules in which they are embedded, are the aggregate result of different groups pursuing their own versions of the public interest … inequality of resources will inevitably give some groups advantages over others': Bronwen Morgan and Karen Yeung, *An Introduction to Law and Regulation: Text and Materials* (Cambridge University Press, 2007) 44. The farming industry, represented through powerful and narrowly focussed industry representative groups, has dominated standard-setting, and this influence is embedded in farm animal welfare standards.

[58] The failure of declarations of sentiency to address the fundamental issue of the property status of animals is emphasised by Ferrere Rodriguez (n 52) 126.

[59] Kotzmann (n 42) 163–65, citing among others Amelia Cornish, David Raubenheimer and Paul McGreevy, 'What We Know about the Public's Level of Concern for Farm Animal Welfare in Food Production in Developed Countries' (2016) 6 *Animals* 74.

[60] Futureye (n 6) 4. Some caution is needed around the language of 'rights and freedoms' used in the report, which appears to refer essentially to the Five Freedoms (even if they have been argued to constitute a set of 'rights': see Clare McCausland, 'The Five Freedoms of Animal Welfare are Rights' (2014) 27 *Journal of Agricultural and Environmental Ethics* 649).

for state intervention to protect animals, identified above, this recognition is tied to an expectation that farm animal protection is reformed in ways that make it more effective, including ensuring application of at least basic welfare principles such as those embodied in the Five Freedoms, transparency in regulatory processes and effective enforcement – all of which are currently not a feature of Australian farm animal protection law.

Third, explicit recognition of sentiency in animal protection statutes by itself may not reach far enough into the arena of farm animal welfare regulation, where the standards for protection are determined outside the formal legislative process. This suggests that if legislation is to explicitly recognise the sentiency of animals, then similar acknowledgement also needs to be made in codes of practice for farm animals, including as they are adopted as delegated legislation. The Tasmanian Government has stated a willingness to consider such an approach, as noted in section III. Given the increasingly significant role played by private standards schemes, this recognition should also be a feature of standards established in those schemes. Finally, if there is to be a reshaping of the way in which farm animal protection standard-setting occurs, including a greater role for the Commonwealth Government and, especially, the creation of an independent commission, as urged by the Productivity Commission, as well as a range of NGOs and left-of-centre political parties in Australia, then explicit acknowledgment of sentience should be a foundation principle for such an institution, including in the legislation establishing the agency.

V. Conclusion

The protection of farm animals is arguably the arena in which the legal recognition and meaningful application of a principle of sentience might be most significant, given the sheer number of animals farmed for food, fibre and a multitude of other uses. In Australia alone, more than 700 million farm animals are raised and killed annually,[61] with limited protection for them under animal protection statutes, instead subject to government-sanctioned standards developed through compromised standard-setting processes or, for some, incremental improvements in protection under market-based private standard-setting schemes. There is mounting evidence that the general public expects the law to do much more for farm animals, and this expectation is tied to the idea of sentience. The question is what meaningful application of a legislative declaration of sentience might entail. The potential for such declarations to usher in improved protection for animals is still to be determined. However, if statements of recognition are institutionalised,

[61] For example, in 2022/23 713 million chickens were slaughtered for chicken meat: Australian Chicken Meat Federation, 'Australian Industry Facts and Figures', available at www.chicken.org.au/facts-and-figures.

cascading through standard-setting processes and outcomes, finding expression not just in statutes, but in regulations and non-statutory standards, this might help to develop or reinforce a shared understanding of farm animals as comparable to other animals, such as companion animals, with intrinsic interests worthy of protection. It would make more transparent standards which compromise that understanding. This may create the space to shift the 'burden of justification from those who would protect animals to those who would harm animals'.[62]

[62] Taimie L Bryant, 'Similarity or Difference as a Basis for Justice: Must Animals be like Humans to be Legally Protected from Humans?' (2007) 70 *Law and Contemporary Problems* 207, 251.

15

Err on the Side of Sentience: The European Precautionary Principle, Article 13 of the Treaty on the Functioning of the European Union, and Invertebrates*

PAULIEN CHRISTIAENSSEN

I. Introduction

This chapter looks at the implications of the legal precautionary principle for the protection of animals, and particularly invertebrates, as sentient beings in European law. In primary EU law, Article 13 of the Treaty on the Functioning of the European Union[1] (TFEU) requires the Union and Member States to pay full regard to animal welfare, *since* animals are sentient beings.

At the same time, invertebrates are largely excluded from secondary European animal welfare legislation (directives and regulations).[2] Invertebrate animals do not have a central spine; their nervous system is structured fundamentally differently than that of vertebrates. It was therefore long assumed that they could not

* This is the English and shortened version of the contribution 'In dubio pro animale – Levend koken van kreeften in het licht van het juridisch voorzorgsbeginsel' in Bernard Tilleman, Maarten Herbosch, Bram Devolder and Frederik Van den Abeele (eds), *Gastronomie & Recht*, forthcoming.

[1] Consolidated Version of the Treaty on the Functioning of the European Union [2012] OJ C326/47; this Treaty is part of 'primary' EU law, since it is a binding agreement between all EU Member States laying down the foundational rules of the EU, eg the EU objectives and the relation between the EU and its Member States.

[2] Secondary EU law is made by the EU institutions and based on primary EU law. A regulation has general application. It is binding in its entirety and directly applicable in all European Member States. A directive is binding to Member States as to the result to be achieved, upon each Member State to which it is addressed, but it leaves it up to the national authorities to choice the form and methods to achieve the results. See Art 288 TFEU. The ordinary European legislative procedure consists in the joint adoption by the European Parliament and the Council of a regulation, directive or decision on a proposal from the Commission. See Art 289 TFEU.

sense pain (or other feelings) and were not sentient.[3] Yet recent scientific studies show strong indications to the contrary for some invertebrate species.[4] Research on invertebrate sentience is of course not yet as advanced as it is for vertebrates, and given sentience is a subjective experience, it is impossible to measure it directly and with certainty. Notwithstanding the remaining elements of scientific doubt on invertebrate sentience, scientists have argued that the welfare of particular species of invertebrates should be protected, based on the *scientific* precautionary principle: when in doubt about whether an action harms the physical or psychological integrity of an animal, we should avoid the action (*in dubio pro animale*). In other words, once we know, beyond reasonable doubt, that an animal species can feel/suffer, we should act accordingly. The precautionary principle also has a *legal* variant in national, European and international laws. Legally, the precautionary principle has so far been predominantly applied in environmental and public health matters.

This chapter will start by explaining the meaning of the European legal precautionary principle. It then argues that the broad European definition of principle, in combination with Article 13 of the TFEU, allows for its application to animal welfare. Section III highlights the particular relevance of precautionary reasoning in determining the scope of animal welfare legislation. Section IV outlines the consequences of the precautionary principle for the protection of invertebrates in European law, and argues in particular for a proportionate broadening of the scope of secondary EU legislation to certain (orders of) invertebrates and a clear ban on the killing method of live cooking.

II. European Precautionary Principle and its Applicability to Animal Welfare

A. European Precautionary Principle

How can legislators still act carefully when faced with scientific uncertainty about a socially relevant issue? Given the increase in evidence-based policy, this question is becoming ever more important.[5] Legislators found an answer in the

[3] For the definition of sentience, this contribution looks to animal welfare science. There, the term is defined as 'the capacity to have feelings'. Feelings include for instance pain, hunger, joy, etc. See eg Jonathan Birch, Charlotte Burn, Alexandra Schnell, Heather Browning and Andrew Crump, 'Review of the evidence of sentience in cephalopod molluscs and decapod crustaceans' (London School of Economics and Political Science, November 2021) 12, available at www.lse.ac.uk/news/news-Assets/PDFs/2021.

[4] See ibid, 14.

[5] Science Communication Unit, 'Science for Environment Policy. The Precautionary Principle: decision making under uncertainty' (Future Brief 18, Produced for the European Commission DG Environment, University of the West of England, Bristol, 2017) 5, available at www.ec.europa.eu/science-environment-policy.

ethical-scientific precautionary principle, and transformed it into a legal norm, which first appeared in German environmental law of the 1970s.[6] Underlying the German 'Vorsorgeprinzip' was scientific uncertainty about the adverse environmental effects of certain toxic substances.[7]

The United Nations subsequently defined the principle for environmental matters, in the 1992 Rio Declaration:[8]

> [I]n order to protect the environment, the precautionary approach shall be widely applied by States according to their capabilities. Where there are threats of serious or irreversible damage, lack of full scientific certainty shall not be used as a reason for postponing cost-effective measures to prevent environmental degradation.

Nowadays, the precautionary principle is part of a number of international treaties, declarations, resolutions and directives, and has even, according to some, already acquired the status of customary international law.[9]

Many different definitions and applications of the legal precautionary principle have arisen over time. In its weak version, the precautionary principle does not necessarily mandate government action in the face of a scientifically uncertain risk, but neither does it automatically accept that uncertainty as an excuse for inaction by policy-makers.[10] Determination of risk in the weak form does not imply an obligation to ban, but an obligation to take an appropriate measure (restrictions, conditions, etc), in light of the principle of proportionality.[11]

On the other end, the strongest version of precaution obliges the government to take action ('when in doubt, opt-out'[12]) unless proponents of the practice can prove that it is not harmful.[13]

Within the moderate application of the precautionary principle too, uncertainty leads to action, but only when an opponent of the practice can demonstrate a sufficiently serious threat.[14]

[6] Stephen M Gardiner, 'A core precautionary principle' (2006) 14 *Journal of Political Philosophy* 33, 35.

[7] Andrew Jordan, 'The precautionary principle in the European Union' in Tim O'Riordan (ed), *Reinterpreting the precautionary principle* (Cameron May, 2001) 145.

[8] Principle 15.

[9] Owen McIntyre and Thomas Mosedale, 'The precautionary principle as a norm of customary international law' (1997) 9 *Journal of Environmental Law* 221; OW Pedersen, 'From abundance to indeterminancy: The precautionary principle and its two camps of custom' (2014) 3 *Transnational Environmental Law* 1, 17.

[10] Kenisha Garnett and David J Parsons, 'Multi-case review of the application of the precautionary principle in European Union Law and case law' (2017) 37 *Risk Analysis* 502, 513.

[11] Elizabeth Fisher, 'Precaution, precaution everywhere: developing a 'common understanding' of the precautionary principle in the European Community' (2002) 9 *Maastricht Journal of European and Comparative Law* 7, 17.

[12] This version is rare, see Geert Van Calster, 'Repeat after me: the precautionary principle does not imply reversal of the burden of proof. Neither does it mean "when in doubt, opt-out"' (GAVC LAW, 21 February 2018), available at www.gavclaw.com/2018/02/21.

[13] Cass R Sunstein, *Laws of Fear: Beyond the Precautionary Principle* (Cambridge University Press, 2005) 18–19.

[14] Garnett and Parsons (n 10) 505.

The European Court of Justice (ECJ) has qualified the precautionary principle as a general principle of Union law. In its definition, the Court points out that the principle can create either obligations or possibilities for public authorities:[15]

> [I]t follows that the precautionary principle can be defined as a general principle of Community law *requiring* the competent authorities *to take appropriate measures to prevent specific potential risks to public health, safety and the environment*, by giving precedence to the requirements related to the protection of those interests over economic interests … It is settled case-law that, in the field of public health, the precautionary principle implies that where there is *uncertainty* as to the existence or extent of risks to human health, the institutions *may take precautionary measures* without having to wait until the reality and seriousness of those risks become fully apparent.

Member States thus often invoke the principle themselves, in cases brought before the ECJ, as a basis for restricting for instance the free movement of potentially harmful goods. The principle then operates in a justifying manner rather than as a constraint.[16] But there are also examples of case law where the Union or the Member States are explicitly *required* by the Court to take precaution in the face of scientific uncertainty.[17]

In the ECJ definition, the wording 'appropriate measures' indicates a proportionality analysis, which means the Court generally opts for a weak form of the precautionary principle.

B. European Precautionary Principle and Animal Welfare

It is not just European environmental policy that must respect the precautionary principle. To ensure a high level of protection of health, consumers and the environment, the ECJ applies the principle to all Union policies.[18] Animal welfare too is a policy area which can contribute to the European protection of health and environment, since according to the World Organization for Animal Health, it is strongly linked to 'animal health, human health and welfare and the sustainability of socio-economic and ecological systems'.[19] In ECJ case law, the 'hazard' to be identified in the precautionary risk assessment is commonly used in a broader

[15] See eg, Case C-269/13 *Acino v Commission* ECLI:EU:C:2014:255 [2014], [57]; Case T-429/13 and T-451/13, *Bayer Crop Science AG and Others v Commission* ECLI:EU:T:2018:280 [2018], [110] (emphasis added).

[16] See eg, Case C-343/09, *Aftond Chemical Limitd v Secretary of State for Transport* ECLI:EU:C:2010:419, [2010] ECR I – 7062, [49]; Christoph Sobotta, 'Recent applications of the precautionary principle in the jurisprudence of the CJEU – a new yardstick in EU environmental decision making?' (2021) 21 *ERA Forum* 723, 732.

[17] See eg, Case C-616/17, *Mathieu Blaise and others* ECLI:EU:C:2019:800 [2019], [42].

[18] Case T-74/00, *Artegodan GmbH and Others v Commission* ECLI:EU:T:2002:283, [2002] ECR II-04945, [184].

[19] OIE, 'OIE Global Animal Welfare Strategy' (May 2017) 3, available at www.woah.org/app/uploads/2021/03/en-oie-aw-strategy.pdf.

sense and describes any product or process capable of having an adverse effect on human health or *any other interest safeguarded by the legal order.*[20]

Even though there is no explicit basis for it, the EU legal order does safeguard animal welfare: Article 13 TFEU in primary EU law is supplemented by a significant amount of secondary European legislation on animal welfare.

The European precautionary principle may therefore apply to animal welfare matters, even though the ECJ has not yet explicitly done so. This is also supported by the European Commission's view on the scope of the precautionary principle, according to which the application of precaution additionally depends on the development of case law, reflecting the social and political values prevailing in society.[21] In the case law of the ECJ, animal welfare plays an ever-increasing role. The Court has repeatedly accepted animal welfare protection, which it considers to be an EU value,[22] as a restriction on human freedoms.[23] The judgment on the Flemish decree requiring prior stunning even in the case of ritual slaughter[24] is a leading case in that respect. According to the Court, this decree did not violate the freedom of religion, given, amongst others, the value of animal welfare in contemporary democratic societies.[25] In this judgment, Article 13 TFEU even seems to be transforming into a general principle of Union law.[26]

Furthermore, the ECJ adds that whether a public authority should apply the precautionary principle in cases of scientific uncertainty depends on the level of protection chosen by the competent authority in the exercise of its discretion.[27] For animal welfare, European authorities have chosen a high level of protection, which can generally be derived from Article 13 TFEU, with additional indications in secondary legislation. For instance, under the Council Regulation on the protection of animals at the time of killing,[28] the Union seeks to promote *high*

[20] Joined cases T-429/13 and T-451/13, *Bayer Crop Science AG v Commission* ECLI:EU:T:2018:280 [2018], [121]; Case T-719/17, *FMC Corporation v Commission* ECLI:EU:T:2021:143 [2021], [74].

[21] Commission, 'Communication from the Commission on the precautionary principle' COM(2000) 1 final, 9.

[22] Case C-336/19, *Centraal Israëlitisch Consistorie van België and Others* ECLI:EU:C:2020:1031 [2020], [41]–[42].

[23] See eg, on ritual slaughter: Case C-426/16, *Liga van Moskeeën en Islamitische Organisaties Provincie Antwerpen, VZW and Others v Vlaams Gewest* ECLI:EU:C:2018:335 [2018], or on French glue hunting: Case C-900/19, *Association One Voice and Ligue pour la protection des oiseaux v Ministre de la Transition écologique et solidaire*, ECLI:EU:C:2021:211 [2021].

[24] Art 3 Decreet van 7 juli 2017 houdende wijziging van de wet van 14 augustus 1986 betreffende de bescherming en het welzijn der dieren, wat de toegelaten methodes voor het slachten van dieren betreft, (freely translated: *Art 3 Decree of July 7, 2017 amending the law of August 14, 1986 on the protection and welfare of animals, as regards authorized methods for slaughtering animals*), *BS* 18 juli 2017.

[25] Case C-336/19, *Centraal Israëlitisch Consistorie*, [77].

[26] The Court stated that, 'where several *fundamental rights and principles* enshrined in the Treaties are at issue, such as, in the present case, the right guaranteed in Article 10 of the Charter and *animal welfare* enshrined in Article 13 TFEU, the assessment of observance of the principle of proportionality must be carried out in accordance with the need to reconcile the requirements of the protection of those various rights and principles at issue, striking a fair balance between them' [emphasis added]; ibid, [65].

[27] Case T-74/00, *Artegodan*, [184] and [186].

[28] Council Regulation (EC) 1099/2009 of 24 September 2009 on the protection of animals at the time of killing (Regulation on Killing of Animals) [2009] OJ L303/1.

welfare standards in livestock populations worldwide, particularly in relation to trade.[29] Regarding the treatment of animals in slaughterhouses and in scientific procedures, legislation literally mentions a 'high level of protection' for animals.[30]

Not only does animal welfare seem to meet the main conditions of application of the precautionary principle (link with human health and environment, interest protected by the EU legal order, importance in case law and high level of protection), the ECJ already applied the principle in policy areas closely related to animal welfare, like animal health and biodiversity.

In *Andibel*, the ECJ had to decide on the legality of the Belgian 'positive list' of animals[31] in light of the free movement of goods (Article 36 TFEU). This list enumerates the species of mammals that are allowed to be kept by humans in Belgium, and thus restricts the trade of companion animals across European borders, which in principle goes against EU internal market rules. Firstly, the Court stressed that the protection of animal *welfare* and the fundamental requirements of *health* and *life* of animals may justify a restriction on the free movement of goods.[32] According to the ECJ, the authorities can only refuse a new species on the positive list on the basis of a scientifically established danger to these legitimate interests.[33] The Court subsequently relied on the precautionary principle and stated that:

> Where it proves impossible to determine with certainty the existence or extent of the risk envisaged[34] because of the insufficiency, inconclusiveness or imprecision of the results of the studies conducted, but the likelihood of real harm to human or animal health or to the environment persists should the risk materialize, the precautionary principle justifies the adoption of restrictive measures.[35]

Note that the Court still refers to the envisaged risk (being the risk to animal welfare, animal health or the environment referred to in the previous paragraphs of the judgment) in the first part of the sentence, but only mentions animal health and the environment in the last part.

In *Commission v Belgium*, the Court reiterated its position where it examined the Royal Decree on the protection of birds in the Flemish Region,[36] which restricted the import, keeping and sale of wild bird species bred in captivity. That restriction too was potentially contrary to the free movement of goods. As in *Andibel*, the Court first recognised both the protection of animal welfare and

[29] Recital 37.

[30] Recital 44 Regulation on Killing of Animals and Recital 10 Directive 2010/63/EU of the European Parliament and of the Council of 22 September 2010 on the protection of animals used for scientific purposes (Laboratory Animals Directive) [2010] OJ L 276/33.

[31] Royal Decree of 7 December 2001 establishing the list of animals that may be kept, *BS* 14 februari 2002, 5479.

[32] Case C-219/07, *Nationale Raad van Dierenkwekers en Liefhebbers VZW and Andibel VZW v Belgische staat* ECLI:EU:C:2008:353, [2008] ECR I-04475, [27]–[28].

[33] ibid, [28].

[34] Being the danger to animal welfare, animal health or the environment referred to in the previous paragraphs of the judgment.

[35] Case C-219/07, *Andibel*, [38].

[36] *BS* ('*Belgian official journal*') 31 oktober 1981.

animal health as legitimate public interest objectives. But again, when applying the precautionary principle, it only mentioned scientific uncertainty about harm to animal health, not welfare.[37]

The question is whether, in both judgments, the Court deliberately wanted to limit the scope of the precautionary principle to animal health, to the exclusion of animal welfare. Given the above-mentioned broad definition and conditions of the precautionary principle, that would make little sense. Especially given the undeniably strong relation between animal welfare and the policy areas of animal health, human health and the environment, which are explicitly mentioned in the ECJ's definitions and applications of the precautionary principle. Also, the Belgian positive list from *Andibel* was based on the Belgian Animal Welfare Act, and clearly resulted mainly from animal welfare considerations, not animal health.[38] In any case, in the statutory translation of *Andibel*, the Belgian authorities included both animal health and welfare in the scope of the precautionary principle. Thus, the current version of the positive list explicitly asks the Government to give the benefit of the doubt to the animal in general: in case of conflicting data or information on whether a species can be kept, it is considered that one or more of the criteria have not been met.[39]

In these decisions on animal health, the precautionary principle worked to *justify* a state measure, whereas in the realm of biodiversity, the ECJ has also already imposed *obligations* on Member States based on the precautionary principle, leaving limited policy discretion for public authorities. In a 2019 judgment, the Court had to rule whether Finnish wolf hunting was in line with the Habitats Directive.[40] With reference to the precautionary principle, the ECJ did not allow a Member State to grant a hunting exception if there remains uncertainty as to whether or not a derogation will be detrimental to the maintenance or restoration of populations of an endangered species at a favourable conservation status.[41] So the least amount of uncertainty obliges the Government to ban the practice, which points to a strong form of the precautionary principle (see description in section A).

The Court again invoked the precautionary principle in a ruling on Finnish spring hunting of the eider duck. That practice falls within the scope of the Birds Directive,[42] which the Court interprets as strictly as the Habitats Directive.[43]

[37] Case C-100/08, *Commission v Kingdom of Belgium* ECLI:EU:C:2009:537, [2009] ECR I-00140, [102].

[38] Explanatory memorandum on the draft law amending the law of 14 August 1986 on the protection and welfare of animals, *Parl St* Senaat 1993–94, 972-1, 2.

[39] Art 2 Royal Decree of 16 July 2009 establishing the list of mammals not kept for production purposes that may be kept, *BS* 24 August 2009.

[40] Arts 12(1)(a) and Art 16(1)(e) Council Directive 92/43/EEC of 21 May 1992 on the conservation of natural habitats and of wild fauna and flora [1992], OJ L206/7.

[41] Case C-674/17, *Luonnonsuojeluyhdistys Tapiola Pohjois-Savo and Others* ECLI:EU:C:2019:851, [2019] OJ C 63, [66].

[42] Directive 2009/147/EC of the European Parliament and of the Council of 30 November 2009 on the conservation of wild birds [2009], OJ L20/7.

[43] Case C-217/19, *European Commission v Republic of Finland* ECLI:EU:C:2020:291, [2020] OJ C 172, [84].

Article 9(1)(c) of the Directive allows Member States to exceptionally 'authorize the use' of certain birds in small quantities. According to the Court, the calculation of those small quantities must be done with due regard to the precautionary principle. Overestimation of the number of birds available must be avoided.[44]

Why is the strong application of the precautionary principle in biodiversity relevant for the possible future application of precaution to animal welfare? On the European level, the boundaries between nature conservation and animal welfare are slowly blurring. Biodiversity law also pays more and more attention to the welfare of the individual animal.[45] The ECJ ruling on the French tradition of glue hunting is a striking illustration of this. With this hunting technique, birds which are caught on branches smeared with glue serve as decoys for other bird species. When testing this practice against the Bird Directive, the ECJ opted for a rather animal- and individual-oriented interpretation of the Directive. The Court focused on the method of hunting, the resulting by-catch and 'its possible impact on the species caught in terms of injuries sustained by the birds caught'.[46] It considered it very likely that the glued birds would suffer irreparable injuries, as the glue can damage their feathers.[47] The practice was considered illegal. This was the first judgment in which the ECJ used Article 13 TFEU (animal welfare) as a tool to interpret nature conservation law.[48]

Animal welfare and species protection are clearly inextricably linked, which means precaution in the treatment of individual animals, can also contribute to the Union's biodiversity objectives. The significance of the European precautionary principle for biodiversity may thus at some point trickle down to the domain of animal welfare.

III. Precautionary Reasoning: Err on the Side of Sentience

A. Why should we Err on the Side of Sentience?

So the European precautionary principle *may* apply to animal welfare, but why *should* it apply? Precautionary reasoning aims to prevent potential serious damage. But should this concern only direct damage to humans or the environment, or by extension to animals? There is a need to apply the precautionary principle in

[44] ibid, [91].

[45] Hendrik Schoukens and Elien Verniers, 'Natuurbescherming en dierenwelzijn, twee zijden van dezelfde Medaille: de rechtspraak inzake de Franse lijmjacht als keerpunt?' (2021) 24 *Rechtskundig Weekblad* 931, 945.

[46] Case C-900/19, *Association One Voice and Ligue pour la protection des oiseaux v Ministre de la Transition écologique et solidaire* ECLI:EU:C:2021:211, [2021] OJ C 54, [62].

[47] ibid, [67].

[48] Schoukens and Verniers (n 45) 939.

animal law, particularly in the determination of the scope of welfare law, for five reasons.

First of all, sentience is crucial to European animal welfare protection.[49] Article 13 TFEU, which is part of primary, foundational EU law agreed upon by all Member States, obliges Member States and the Union to pay full regard to animal welfare *since* animals are sentient beings. In secondary legislation adopted by the EU institutions,[50] the Regulation on killing of animals also takes sentience as its basis: 'There is sufficient scientific evidence to demonstrate that vertebrate animals are sentient beings which should therefore fall within the scope of this Regulation'.[51] Similarly, recital[52] 20 states that 'many killing methods are painful for animals. Stunning is therefore necessary to induce a lack of consciousness and sensibility before, or at the same time as, the animals are killed'. Sentience is also emphasised in the Laboratory Animals Directive, as a reason to improve the welfare of animals used in scientific procedures.[53] The Directive even mandates using, as far as possible, animals with the lowest capacity to experience pain, suffering, distress or lasting harm.[54]

In addition, many European Member States recently explicitly recognised animals as sentient beings, and for that reason, distinguished them from objects under private law.[55] Sentience is thus an essential attribute in animal welfare law.

But secondly, at the same time, chances are that certain aspects of animal consciousness and sentience remain unfathomable to science. Inferences about animal sentience are inevitably based on indications, not evidence (see description in section IV). There are for instance scientific indications of pain in several species of fish, which give rise to a high probability of sentience,[56] but not to scientific certainty.[57] Scientific certainty on the matter is actually unattainable, since sentience is a subjective experience and one can never directly measure subjective experiences in other living beings (even humans).[58] Doubt is thus inherent to research on sentience.

[49] Charlotte E Blattner, 'The recognition of animal sentience by the law' (2019) 8 *Journal of Animal Ethics* 121, 122.

[50] Proposal by the EU Commission, adoption by EU Parliament and Council.

[51] Recital 19.

[52] A recital sets out the reasons for and the reasoning behind EU regulatory instruments, they do not have the same binding force as the instrument itself, but are an important interpretative tool.

[53] Recitals 6, 12 and 13.

[54] Art 13(2)(b).

[55] See eg, Art 3.38 Belgian Civil Code (BW); s 285a Austrian Civil Code (AGBG); Art 2a Dutch Civil Code (BW); S 90a German Civil Code (BGB); Art 333bis Spanish Civil Code; Art 1302 Portugese Civil Code.

[56] Kristopher P Chandroo, Ian James Heatly Duncan and Richard D Moccia, 'Can fish suffer?: perspectives on sentience, pain, fear and stress' (2004) 86 *Applied Animal Behaviour Science* 225, 250.

[57] James D Rose, Robert Arlinghaus, Steven J Cooke, Ben K Diggles, William Sawynok, ED Stevens and CDL Wynne, 'Can fish really feel pain?' (2014) 15 *Fish and Fisheries* 97, 97.

[58] Lynne U Sneddon, Robert W Elwood, SA Adamo and MC Leach, 'Defining and assessing animal pain' (2014) 97 *Animal Behaviour* 201, 202.

Thirdly, the legal qualification of an animal species as sentient (or not) immediately affects a very large number of animals.[59] Under European law, fish do not (yet) receive the welfare protection that sentient terrestrial animals enjoy.[60] Fishing, and the limited legal protection of fish, affects trillions of animals annually.[61] When doubt does not play in the animal's favour, the law may be allowing and facilitating animal suffering on an enormous scale. This is exactly the kind of potential serious harm that calls for precautionary reasoning.[62]

Fourthly, such mass suffering of sensitive animals is also what animal welfare laws are trying to prevent.[63] Sensitive animals have an interest in being protected from harmful human interventions; it is one of the ethical premises of animal law.[64] If legislators continue to wait for (unreachable) scientific certainty, they risk ignoring the interest in welfare protection for a large part of the animal kingdom for too long.

Lastly, humans also benefit from applying precaution when dealing with animals: 'systematic inflicting of what we assume to be pain and suffering on other beings (or seeing it happen) can make people callous'.[65] The regulation of risk is 'very much an exercise in deciding how as a democratic community "we wish to live"'.[66] That includes a choice in our attitude towards animals.

B. How would we Err on the Side of Sentience?

Birch does point out that science and the law need to clearly define exactly what evidence of sentience in an animal is then sufficient to activate the precautionary principle and lead to welfare protection.[67] He argues for a specific definition of the precautionary principle for animals, by analogy with the definition in the Rio Declaration.[68]

A strong application of the precautionary principle for animal welfare would assume that an animal is a sentient being until proven otherwise.[69] This would lead to unworkable results. First, it makes the burden of proof for animal welfare

[59] Jonathan Birch, 'Animal sentience and the precautionary principle' (2017) 16 *Animal Sentience* 4; Richard H Bradshaw, 'Laboratory animal consciousness and feelings: adopting the precautionary principle' (1999) 27 *Alternatives to Laboratory Animals* 791, 793.

[60] Recitals 6, 11 and Art 1(1) Regulation on killing of animals.

[61] Birch (n 59) 4.

[62] ibid, 5.

[63] Florence Arnaud, 'La gastronomie: le défi de l'éthique (humains, environnement, animaux)' in A Quiquerez (ed), *Gastronomie et droit. Entre droit culturel et droit économique* (Bruylant, 2022) 176.

[64] Birch et al (n 3) 14.

[65] Jennifer A Mather, 'Animal suffering: an invertebrate perspective' (2001) 4 *Journal of Applied Animal Welfare Science* 151, 153.

[66] Elizabeth Fisher, 'Is the precautionary principle justiciable?' (2001) 13 *Journal of Environmental Law* 315, 317.

[67] Birch (n 59) 2.

[68] ibid, 3.

[69] ibid, 5.

science too heavy, because how would one prove that an animal is not sentient?[70] Second, it shifts the discussion to the definition of 'animal'. Would that include fruit flies?[71] Birch suggests instead a moderate application. An order of animal species (eg decapod crustaceans) should be legally protected, if there is substantial scientific evidence for at least one reliable indication of sentience, in at least one animal species of that order (eg the lobster).[72]

Evidence of sentience in one species (eg the lobster) thus, in his definition, has immediate implications for the entire order (eg decapod crustaceans). Indeed, Birch considers it practically unfeasible, and contrary to the *ratio legis* of the precautionary principle, to first examine each species of the order for sentience.[73] The choice for a particular species as a research object is mainly practical in nature. It concerns for instance only those species that can be kept in a laboratory.[74] Legal protection of animals should not depend on how suitable animals are for scientific research: otherwise, researchers' preferences would seep into the law.[75]

He leaves it to animal welfare science to draw up a list of sentience indications.[76] Proof of one reliable indication suffices for him, otherwise welfare progress takes too long.[77] Yet it is precisely the combination of indications that leads scientists to a well-founded, widely supported conclusion.[78] Other authors therefore raise the bar for legal protection and call for at least two independent indications of sentience.[79]

In any case, given legal precaution was born out of scientific precaution, the development of the precautionary principle in animal welfare science should guide the application of the principle in animal welfare law.

Once the scientific burden of proof of sentience is met, the law should offer protection to the relevant order of species in a proportionate manner.[80] The European precautionary principle demands taking *appropriate* measures (see definition in section II.A), which implies a certain margin of discretion for authorities in weighing the requirements of the precautionary principle with other interests. Thus, in deciding where to draw the line, the law will be guided by scientific information as well as the principle of proportionality.

[70] Birch (n 59) 5; Brian Key, 'Falsifying the null hypothesis that "fish do not feel pain"' (2016) 3 *Animal Sentience* 39–43.

[71] Birch (n 59) 5.

[72] ibid; HI Browman et al, 'Quo Vadis. Welfare of aquatic animals: where things are, where they are going, and what it means for research, aquaculture, recreational angling and commercial fishing' (2019) 76 *ICES Journal of Marine Science* 82, 86.

[73] Birch (n 59) 6.

[74] Birch et al (n 3) 81.

[75] ibid.

[76] ibid, 7.

[77] ibid.

[78] Sneddon et al (n 58) 209.

[79] Jon Mallatt, 'Shoring up the precautionary BAR' (2017) 16 *Animal Sentience* 1, 3; Michael L Woodruff, 'Scientific uncertainty and the animal sentience precautionary principle' (2017) 16 *Animal Sentience* 1, 1.

[80] Birch (n 59) 8.

Because of this proportionality aspect, the precautionary principle never creates unrealistic expectations for legislators. In the case of animal welfare, it merely obliges a legislator to fairly and rationally consider the interests of beings who are most probably sentient. In this sense, the principle protects animals from unscientific human prejudice.

IV. European Precautionary Principle and Protection of Invertebrates

A. Science on Invertebrates: The Example of Decapods

Once we assume the applicability of the precautionary principle to animal welfare, what are the implications for the legal protection of invertebrates in European law?[81]

Whereas vertebrates have a traditional central nervous system (the brain and spine), invertebrates lack a vertebral column; their neuroanatomy is very different.[82] Within the invertebrate group, there is a huge variety of species, biological characteristics and nervous systems, as more than 90 per cent of animal species are invertebrates.[83]

Humans usually regard invertebrates as an 'inferior' group of species. The animals' low moral status is even embodied in our language, as in the saying 'lacking a backbone'.[84] Invertebrates' appearance and behaviour is very strange to us, so they elicit empathy from few.[85] Animal welfare science too has long showed little interest in invertebrates[86] and assumed that these animals were not able to feel pain and were not sentient.[87]

Yet recent studies show strong scientific indications of sentience for certain invertebrate species. By way of illustration, this section looks at some of the evidence of pain in the order of decapod crustaceans (eg lobsters).

Pain is a subjective negative experience and thus an aspect of sentience.[88] It goes beyond a mere reflexive reaction (in scientific terms: nociception[89]) to a

[81] Of course, the precautionary principle would also have implications for the welfare protection of fish (vertebrate animals), although their exclusion from EU animal welfare regulation currently seems to be mainly motivated by economic and proportionality considerations rather than their lack of sentience.

[82] Pierre Le Neindre et al, 'Animal consciousness' (2017) 14 *EFSA* 2, 73.

[83] www.britannica.com/animal/invertebrate.

[84] Paul LR Andrews, 'Laboratory invertebrates: only spineless, or spineless and painless?' (2011) 52 *ILAR Journal* 121, 121.

[85] Steve Nash, 'Desperately Seeking Charisma: Improving the Status of Invertebrates' (2004) 54 *BioScience* 487, 494.

[86] Andrews (n 84) 121.

[87] Mather (n 65) 151.

[88] Sneddon et al (n 58) 202.

[89] Lynne U Sneddon, 'Evolution of nociception in vertebrates: Comparative analysis of lower vertebrates' (2004) 46 *Brain Research Reviews* 123, 124 and 127.

stimulus and also includes an emotional component: the processing of stimuli into a subjective, conscious experience of negative feelings (eg fear).[90]

Given pain cannot be measured directly, science uses indirect evidence, such as behavioural, physiological and neurological indicators.[91]

Behavioural research on the shore crab and the red crayfish (both decapod crustaceans) for instance shows that once these animals have experienced an electric shock, they show a long-term increased motivation to avoid it.[92] The motivation to avoid pain points to a learning process, which helps the animals in preventing future damage.[93] Experiments on the red crayfish also indicate behaviour meeting the criteria of fear.[94]

Decapods, like vertebrates, also 'groom' a negatively stimulated area on their bodies for longer.[95] After administration of local anaesthetic, certain research again noticed a decrease in that targeted grooming.[96] These are indications of pain.[97] For instance, the common sturgeon shrimp started to 'polish' the antennae on which researchers applied a caustic agent more and rub it against the wall of the tank.[98] The animal can thus precisely localise the impact of the noxious stimulus, which is not the case with a general reflex reaction.[99] Brown crabs of which scissors were twisted off, as happens during fishing, tended the wound, protecting it from conspecifics with their other scissors.[100]

Edible crabs (*Cancer pagurus*) of which researchers forcibly removed scissors showed a prolonged physiological stress response.[101] That response does not occur when the animals amputate their scissors themselves without wounding, which, incidentally, is a remarkable talent of the species.[102]

[90] ibid.

[91] RC Jones, 'Fish sentience and the precautionary principle' (2016) 3 *Animal Sentience* 3.

[92] N Kawai, R Kono and S Sugimoto, 'Avoidance learning in the crayfish (Procambarus clarkii) depends on the predatory imminence of the unconditioned stimulus: A behavior systems approach to learning in invertebrates'(2004) 150 *Behavioural Brain Research* 229; B Magee and RW Elwood, 'Shock avoidance by discrimination learning in the shore crab (Carcinus maenas) is consistent with a key criterion for pain' (2013) 216 *Journal of Experimental Biology* 353.

[93] Annamaria Passantino, Robert W Elwood and Paolo Coluccio, 'Why protect decapod crustaceans used as models in biomedical research and in ecotoxicology ? Ethical and legislative considerations' (2021) 11 *Animals* 73, 76.

[94] See eg, Pascal Fossat et al, 'Anxiety-like behavior in crayfish is controlled by serotonin' (2014) 6189 *Science* 1293.

[95] See eg, for shore crabs: Robert Elwood, Natasha Dalton and Gillian Riddell, 'Aversive responses by shore crabs to acetic acid but not to capsaicin' (2017) 140 *Behavioural Processes* 1.

[96] Sneddon et al (n 58) 203.

[97] Daniel M Weary, Lee Niel, Frances C Flower and David Fraser, 'Identifying and preventing pain in animals' (2006) 100 *Applied Animal Behaviour Science* 64.

[98] Lynne U Sneddon, 'Pain in Aquatic Animals' (2015) 218 *Journal of experimental biology* 967, 974.

[99] Passantino et al (n 93) 75.

[100] Claire McCambridge, Jaimie TA Dick and Robert W Elwood, 'Effects of autotomy compared to manual declawing on contests between males for females in the edible crab cancer pagurus: Implications for fishery practice and animal welfare' (2016) 35 *Journal of Shellfish Research* 1037.

[101] Lynsey Patterson, Jaimie TA Dick and Robert W Elwood, 'Physiological stress responses in the edible crab, Cancer Pagurus, to the fishery practice of declawing' (2007) 152 *Marine Biology* 265.

[102] ibid.

Such *individual* indications are of course not conclusive evidence for pain in decapod crustacean, but their *combination* does show a complex response to pain stimuli that goes beyond a pure reflex.[103]

However, particularly as regards neurological indications, not everything is yet known about the anatomy of the nervous system of invertebrates.[104] The functions of their different nerve centres have not been fully researched. So in invertebrates, scientific doubt about pain, and more generally sentience, is mainly situated at the level of the neural anatomy.[105]

B. Legal Protection of Invertebrates Globally

Nevertheless, some countries explicitly added invertebrates to the scope of animal welfare regulations. The choice in protected orders and species varies.

All cephalopods (eg octopuses) fall within the scope of Swiss[106] and Austrian[107] animal welfare legislation. In New Zealand[108] and Norway,[109] within that order of species, only octopuses and squids are protected. Based on a new scientific report by Birch et al, the UK recently qualified cephalopods as sentient animals in the new Sentience Act.[110]

Decapod crustaceans are subject to some welfare protection for the entire order in Austria,[111] Norway[112] and in several Australian states.[113] For instance, New South Wales in Australia protects crustaceans, but only if they are in a building or place (such as a restaurant) where food is prepared or offered for consumption.[114] Based on this legislation, in 2007, the company Nicholas Seafoods was fined AUD 1,500, because an employee of the company was filmed dissecting a live lobster with a band saw. The court considered this unnecessary suffering, in breach of the NSW Prevention of Cruelty to Animals Act.[115]

[103] Sneddon et al (n 58) 209.

[104] Pierre Le Neindre et al, 'Animal consciousness' (2017) 14 *EFSA Journal* 2, 73.

[105] ibid, 141.

[106] Arts 1 ('les céphalopodes (*Cephalopoda*)'), 2, 23, 178 and 178a Ordonnance sur la protection des animaux du 23 avril 2008, (freely translated: *Ordinance on the Protection of Animals of April 23, 2008*), *RO* 2008, 2985.

[107] §3(2) and §32(1) Bundesgesetz über den Schutz der Tiere (freely translated: '*Federal law on the protection of animals*'), BGBL I Nr 118/2004.

[108] Animal Welfare Act (1999), s 2(1)(a)(vi): 'any octopus, squid, crab, lobster, or crayfish (including freshwater crayfish'.

[109] Kapittel I, §2 en §12 Lov om Dyrevelferd, 19 juni 2009, kl 16.45, English translation available at www.regjeringen.no/en/dokumenter/animal-welfare-act/id571188.

[110] The Sentience Act was enacted on 28 April 2022; Animal (Welfare) Sentience Act 2022, s 5(1)(b); Birch et al (n 3) 79.

[111] n 107.

[112] Kapittel I, §2 and §12 Lov om Dyrevelferd, 19 juni 2009, kl 16.45.

[113] More specifically in ACT, New South Wales, Victoria and The Northern Territory: RSPCA, 'Are crustaceans protected by animal welfare legislation?' (RSPCA Knowledge Base, 10 December 2021), available at kb.rspca.org.au/knowledge-base.

[114] New South Wales Prevention of Cruelty to Animals Act (1979), s 4(1)(b).

[115] That conviction came from Sydney's Downing Centre Local Court, upheld on appeal by the District Court; RSPCA NSW, 'Crimes Against Crustaceans: Nicholas Seafood Still In Hot Water As

The New Zealand Animal Welfare Act[116] applies within the order of decapod crustaceans only to crabs, lobsters and crayfish. Swiss law opts for the same species but via the description 'walking decapod crustaceans', excluding the infra-orders *Stenopodidea* (boxer shrimp) and *Caridea* (true shrimp).[117] The above-mentioned new Sentience Act in the UK also recognises decapod crustaceans as sentient animals.[118] For now, it remains unclear what the concrete (legal) consequences of this Act will be, for example for the cooking alive of lobsters.[119]

In Italy, neither the Criminal Code nor the overarching Animal Welfare Act[120] provides any further definition of the term 'animal'. But in 2017, Italy's Corte di Cassazione upheld a criminal conviction of a restaurant under Article 727 of the Italian Criminal Code for chilling lobsters in ice before cooking them alive.[121] The Italian court weighed animal welfare against economic considerations. According to the court, the chilling causes unnecessary suffering and is an unusual practice, unlike live cooking itself.

A few jurisdictions have a specific ban on cooking lobsters alive. This protection against live cooking the lobster enjoys only indisputably in Switzerland,[122] Norway,[123] New Zealand[124] and some Italian regions.[125] In Austria, protection of lobsters at the time of killing is more legally uncertain. The law there prohibits the slaughter of animals without anaesthesia.[126] Slaughter is defined as killing an animal by bleeding and evisceration, for the purpose of meat production.[127] It is not entirely clear whether this includes, for example, boiling a lobster alive. Next, the executive Austrian Tierschutz-Schlachtverordnung states that crustaceans and

"Severity" Appeal Fails For Cruelty To Lobster'(1 August 2017), available at www.rspcansw.org.au/blog/media-releases.

116 s 2(1)(a)(vi).

117 Arts 1 and 2(w) ('les décapodes marcheurs (*Reptantia*)'), 2, 23, 178 and 178a Ordonnance sur la protection des animaux du 23 avril 2008 (freely translated: *Ordinance on the Protection of Animals of April 23, 2008), RO* 2008, 2985.

118 Animal Welfare (Sentience) Act 2022, s 5(1)(c).

119 For now, the Animals (Scientific Procedures) Act 1986, the Animal Welfare Act 2006 and the Welfare at the Time of Killing Regulations (England) 2015 (SI 2005/1782) have not yet been amended; the Welfare of Animals (Transport) (England) Order (SI 2006/3260) already applied to all cold-blooded invertebrates (reg 3).

120 Legge 20 luglio 2004, n 189.

121 Corte di Cassazione Sezione III 16 giugno 2017 (freely translated: *Court of Cassation Section III June 16, 2017*), n 30177, available at www.ambientediritto.it/giurisprudenza/corte-di-cassazione-penale-sez-3-16-06-2017-sentenza-n-30177.

122 Arts 177–178 Ordonnance sur la protection des animaux, modification du 10 janvier 2018 (freely translated: *Ordinance on the protection of animals, amendment of January 10, 2018*), *RO* 2018, 573.

123 Kapittel I, §12 Lov om Dyrevelferd, 19 juni 2009, kl 16.45.

124 Art 11(1) Animal Welfare (Care and Procedures) Regulations 2018; See also Minimum standard nr 22 a, b, c, d and e Code of Welfare: Commercial Slaughter (2018).

125 The regions Parma, Ferrara, Monza and Foggia; Gaetano Liuzzo et al, 'Analysis of provincial and municipal regulations governing crustacean welfare in Italy' (2017) 6 *Italian Journal of Food Safety* 54, 56.

126 n 107.

127 'Art §4, 13: '*Das Töten eines Tieres durch Blutentzug und nachfolgende Ausweidung zum Zweck der Fleischgewinnung*'.

shellfish may only be killed in water that boils strongly.[128] This seems to imply that prior stunning is not a requirement. But the paragraph then closes with: crustaceans must be stunned before they are killed.

In Australia, there is no case law yet on live cooking of crustaceans. Federal government guidelines do strongly advise against it.[129]

Legal welfare protection for invertebrates is thus not as unfeasible or unenforceable as some lawmakers claim it to be.[130] Multiple jurisdictions deliberately chose to grant these animals at least a minimum form of welfare protection. So why not the EU?

C. The Way Forward for Invertebrates in European Law

In 2003, during the revision of the Laboratory Animals Directive, the European legislator considered adding invertebrates to its scope. According to the Technical Expert Working Group, the precautionary principle had to be taken into account when making that decision.[131] The European Commission subsequently requested a study by the European Food Safety Authority (EFSA), which recommended, on the basis of scientific research, to extend the protection of the directive to decapod crustaceans, cephalopods (eg octopuses) and cyclostomes (non-vertebrate fish).[132] That advice was translated into a 2008 draft directive, but only cephalopods made it into the final Directive.[133] Some attribute this to heavy resistance from the biomedical research sector, others to the uncertainties still apparent in the EFSA study.[134]

Invertebrates are also excluded from the scope of application of the Regulation on killing of animals.[135] However, the European Commission has highlighted that Member States can take additional protective measures if they wish.[136] As part of

[128] Anhang B, (8) Verordnung der Bundesministerin für Gesundheit über den Schutz von Tieren bei der Schlachtung oder Tötung (Tierschutz-Schlachtverordnung), BGBl II, Nr 312/2015.

[129] C Johnston and P Jungalwalla, 'Aquatic Animal Welfare Guidelines: Guidelines on Welfare of Fish and Crustaceans in Aquaculture and/or in Live Holding Systems for Human Consumption' (2000), available at www.ais.sa.edu.au/wp-content.

[130] eg in Belgium, these practical considerations are enough reason for the Flemish Minister for Animal Welfare to keep on excluding invertebrates, see *Vr en Antw* Vl Parl, Vr nr 131, 5 November 2020 (ELS STERCKX, antw B WEYTS).

[131] Technical Expert Working Group for the revision of Directive 86/609/EEC on the protection of animals used for experimental and other scientific purposes, Final Report Sub-Group Scope (11 November 2003) 6, available at ec.europa.eu/environment/chemicals/lab_animals/pdf/finalreport-scope.pdf.

[132] EFSA (European Food Safety Authority), 'Opinion on the aspects of the biology and welfare of animals used for experimental and other scientific purposes' (2005) 292 *EFSA Journal* 1.

[133] Art 1(3)(b); Birch (n 59) 9.

[134] Passantino et al (n 93) 74.

[135] Art (2)(c).

[136] Answer given by Ms Kyriakides on behalf of the European Commission to question from Aurelia Beigneux (ID), 16 September 2021, nr E-003646/2021, available at www.europarl.europa.eu/doceo/document/E-9-2021-003646-ASW_EN.html.

the Farm-to-Fork-strategy, the Commission is reviewing EU farm animal regulations, based on recent scientific insights. It has, however, made clear that this review does not extend to invertebrates.[137]

In my view, reading Article 13 TFEU in conjunction with the European precautionary principle leads to the conclusion that the limited scientific uncertainty about the sentience of certain invertebrate species no longer justifies the lack of legal protection for these animals.[138]

The absence of invertebrate protection in European law is twofold: invertebrates usually do not fall within the scope of existing secondary regulation (such as the Regulation on the killing of animals), and there is also no species-specific regulation for these species (similar to, eg, the Pigs Directive[139]). De Sadeleer believes that the precautionary principle generally comes into play mainly in the first situation: it is especially relevant for the legality of already existing EU regulations, and less so for the total lack of such regulations.[140] In this respect, an appeal to the precautionary principle is more likely to succeed if it asks the Union legislator to supplement and amend existing animal welfare regulations and directives. For invertebrates, a broader scope for existing legal instruments is thus a more realistic demand than a new 'Lobster Directive'.

Currently, European lawmakers apply the precautionary principle inconsistently, resulting in strange legal contradictions. For instance, recital 6 of the Laboratory Animals Directive stresses that its content should be updated according to new scientific knowledge on the sensory capacity of animals:

> [N]ew scientific knowledge is available in respect of factors influencing animal welfare as well as the capacity of animals to sense and express pain, suffering, distress and lasting harm. It is therefore necessary to improve the welfare of animals used in scientific procedures by raising the minimum standards for their protection in line with the latest scientific developments.

In line with this, cephalopods (eg octopuses) were included within the scope of the Directive because there is scientific evidence that they may experience pain, suffering, distress and lasting harm.[141] But given the same scientific evidence exists for decapod crustaceans, the limited broadening of the scope of the Directive is unscientific and insufficient.

Moreover, if the EU is committed to translating science on sentience into the Laboratory Animals Directive, it is unreasonable not to do the same in the Regulation on the killing of animals. Cephalopods now receive protection under the former, but not under the latter, which leads to notable discrepancies: for

[137] ibid.

[138] Passantino et al (n 93) 81.

[139] Directive 2008/120/EC of the European Parliament and of the Council of 18 December 2008 laying down minimum standards for the protection of pigs (Pigs Directive) [2008] OJ L 47/5.

[140] Nicolas De Sadeleer, *Environmental principles: from political slogans to legal rules* (Oxford University Press, 2020) 474.

[141] Recital 8.

instance, killing an octopus used as laboratory animal must be done according to the strict rules of the Laboratory Animals Directive, while killing other octopuses is not subject to any welfare regulations.

When adding decapods to the scope of the Regulation on the killing of animals, it is best that the legislator also, as a first necessary step in light of the precautionary principle, immediately provides for a clear ban on the practice of cooking lobsters (and other decapod crustaceans) alive, given the major welfare hazards of this killing method.[142] A lobster can still be safely cooked and eaten two to three hours after its death,[143] so it does not necessarily pose a food safety hazard to cook a dead rather than a live lobster.

The Regulation could either require stunning prior to slaughter, or only allow killing methods which ensure a much quicker, painless death. Such methods are already in place: Crustastun® has been validated as a stunning and killing device for lobsters. It administers an electric shock sufficient to causes the animals to lose consciousness within a second, killing them within 10 seconds.[144] The device costs about €3,000.

Of course, this is a significant cost for individuals or restaurants. But if lobsters are sentient, it could prevent the suffering of a large number of animals in many kitchens. Given the increasing legal importance of animal welfare in democratic societies, this one-off investment does not therefore seem a disproportionate measure. Live cooking is clearly rather a matter of custom and tradition, not of economic necessity. Besides, to spare vertebrate animals unnecessary suffering, society is prepared to make much larger investments, in the form of separate slaughterhouses, with accompanying infrastructure and staff. A lobster differs from vertebrate farm animals in many ways, but probably not in terms of pain experience.

Horizontal splitting (eg decapitation), live dissection and immersion in fresh water are not suitable slaughter methods for decapod crustaceans like lobsters.[145]

In summary, the Regulation on the killing of animals and the Laboratory Animals Directive are legal instruments that seek to prevent unnecessary suffering in animals; it is highly likely that certain orders of invertebrates, such as decapod crustaceans, are able to suffer; and the European precautionary principle requires taking appropriate measures to prevent potential risks for interests protected by the European legal order. It is therefore time for European authorities to add (more) invertebrates to the scope of those instruments, granting them protection in a proportionate and consistent manner.

[142] See research under heading A of this chapter and G Rotllant et al, 'Methods to Induce Analgesia and Anesthesia in Crustaceans: A Supportive Decision Tool' (2023) 12 *Biology* 387, 417.

[143] survivalfreedom.com/is-it-safe-to-cook-dead-lobster-crabs-and-crawfish.

[144] Douglas Neil, 'The effect of the Crustastun ™ on nerve activity in two commercially important decapod crustaceans: the edible brown Cancer pagurus and the European lobster Homarus gammarus' (University of Glasgow, 2012), available at eprints.gla.ac.uk/81430/1/81430.pdf.

[145] Birch et al (n 3) 83.

Enforcement of welfare regulations for invertebrates would be undeniably challenging. Nevertheless, while our dealings with companion and farm animals are also mainly private, the law does grant these animals extensive legal protection, despite the difficult enforceability of the legislation. And if protecting crustaceans' welfare is indeed unfeasible, why do some countries choose to do so?

V. Conclusion

Animal welfare law is in need of precautionary reasoning for five reasons. First, sentience determines animals' eligibility for legal welfare protection; second, scientific doubt is inherent to research on sentience; third, a wrong decision affects a very large number of animals; fourth, precautionary reasoning stems from the *ratio legis* of animal welfare regulation; and finally, humans also benefit from precaution in animal welfare.

In European law, Article 13 TFEU, combined with the broad definition of the European precautionary principle, provide a legal basis for precaution in animal welfare. Moreover, the ECJ already applied the precautionary principle in relation to animal health, and opted for a strict interpretation of the principle in policy areas closely related to animal welfare, such as species protection.

Certain invertebrate species, according to the current state of science, probably feel pain. An application of the precautionary principle implies that the inevitable scientific doubt on the matter cannot be a permanent excuse for the European legislator to exclude all invertebrates from legal welfare safeguards. The scope of application of existing animal welfare regulations and directives should be proportionately broadened to certain orders of invertebrates, such as decapods and cephalopods. At the very least, the high-risk practice of boiling lobsters alive should be banned.

Not cuddliness or human empathy, but *sentience* should, in light of Article 13 TFEU, form the basis for European animal welfare protection. Sentience is a scientific criterion that law must apply consistently, even where it clashes with human preferences. Rational and careful animal welfare law acts with precaution and also protects very different but no less valuable species.

The legal divide between vertebrates and invertebrates is no longer scientifically sound and rationally justifiable. This realisation is growing in various legal systems; European law should not lag behind.

16

Animal Sentience Recognition and Theoretical Connotations: Possible Implications for Animals in Research

JANE KOTZMANN AND HOPE FERDOWSIAN*

I. Introduction

While numerous jurisdictions have banned the testing of cosmetics on animals[1] and progress in advancing non-animal methods of toxicity testing has been achieved[2] in recent decades, the use of animals in research remains widespread. Increasing knowledge of animal sentience and development of technologies enabling the replacement of animals in research might suggest a decline in the use of animals in these settings. However, this has not been the case. Instead, the best available data suggests an increasing trajectory in the overall numbers of animals used in research. It is conservatively estimated that approximately 192 million animals were used in laboratories in 2015, representing an increase from approximately 127 million animals used in 2005.[3]

* Thank you to Ashleigh Best and Morgan Stonebridge for their research assistance that contributed to this chapter, and to Ashleigh Best for her ideas that influenced the development of the chapter.

[1] Regulation (EC) 1223/2009 of the European Parliament and of the Council of 30 November 2009 on cosmetic products [2009] OJ L342/59; The Cosmetic Products Enforcement Regulations 2013 (UK); Prevention of Cruelty to Animals Law (Experiments on Animals) 5754 (Israel); Drugs and Cosmetics (Fifth Amendment) Rules 2014, 135-B (India); Animal Welfare Act 1999 (NZ); Humane Cosmetics Act, HR 2858, 114th Cong (2015) (US); Cosmetics Regulation, Law No 25823, 2005 (*Kozmetik Yönetmeliği*) (Turkey); Cosmetic Hygiene and Safety Act 2018 (Taiwan); Federal Act on Foodstuffs and Utility Articles (Foodstuffs Act, FSA) of 20 June 2014 (Switzerland) Industrial Chemicals Act 2019 (Cth) (Australia).

[2] Kathrin Herrmann, 'Refinement on the Way Towards Replacement: Are We Doing What We Can?' in Kathrin Herrmann and Kimberley Jayne (eds), *Animal Experimentation: Working Towards a Paradigm Change* (Brill, 2019) 29.

[3] Katy Taylor and Laura Rego Alvarez, 'An Estimate of the Number of Animals Used for Scientific Purposes Worldwide in 2015' (2019) 47 *Alternatives to Laboratory Animals* 196, 196; Andrew Knight, 'Estimates of Worldwide Laboratory Animal Use' (2008) 36 *Alternatives to Laboratory Animals* 494, 494; Katy Taylor et al, 'Estimates for Worldwide Laboratory Animal Use in 2005' (2008) 36 *Alternatives to Laboratory Animals* 327, 327; 'Facts and Figures on Animal Testing' (Cruelty Free International),

Research involving animals has historically been justified by reference to the Cartesian conception of animals as unfeeling automata.[4] In modern times, however, regulation of the use of animals in research has long been (at least implicitly) informed by a concern for animal sentience, which refers to the capacity to subjectively experience positive and negative states.[5] Attorney Katrina Sharman identifies sentience as a principle for the use of animals in research emerging from 'international, regional and national legislative instruments and guidelines'.[6] Yet while animal research is generally conducted pursuant to the 3Rs framework (replacement, reduction and refinement),[7] animals routinely endure pain and suffering because of their experiences in research.[8] These experiences should not be overlooked. As Sharman describes, 'laws and policies continue to be used as shields by those who gas, burn, confine, clone, infect, mutilate, force-feed, starve, poison and kill healthy animals in nations everywhere'.[9]

In this context, this chapter considers whether and how the express legal acknowledgement of animal sentience might transform decisions about the use of animals in scientific research. This research builds upon the work of philosophers Heather Browning and Walter Veit who recently explored the impact of sentience recognition on animal research from a philosophical perspective.[10] In further investigating the potential for legal sentience recognition to change decisions about the use of animals in research, this chapter employs legal doctrinal methods, the principle of equality and concepts of vulnerability and relationality. These theories may be particularly useful in this context to help move beyond the focus on a single capacity (sentience) to justify attribution of moral status to a being, an approach which 'reduces living creatures to being regarded as a bundle of capacities'.[11]

available at www.crueltyfreeinternational.org/about-animal-testing/facts-and-figures-animal-testing. It is difficult to obtain accurate global figures of the number of animals used in research as only a small percentage of countries report data in relation to due animals in research, and differences in the recording and reporting of research involving animals are common. For more detailed information see 'Worldwide Animal Research Statistics' (Speaking of Research), available at www.speakingofresearch.com/facts/animal-research-statistics; 'About Animal Testing' (Humane Society), available at www.hsi.org/news-media/about. See also Elizabeth Ellis, *Australian Animal Law: Context and Critique* (Sydney University Press, 2022) 265.

[4] Andrew Knight, 'Scientific and Educational Animal Use' in Andrew Knight, Clive Phillips, Paula Sparks (eds), *Routledge Handbook of Animal Welfare* (Routledge, 2022) 162.

[5] Lori Marino, 'Sentience', *Encyclopedia of Animal Behavior* (Academic Press, 2010), available at www.sciencedirect.com/science/article/abs/pii/B9780080453378000991.

[6] Katrina Sharman, 'Opening the Laboratory Door: National and International Legal Responsibilities for the Use of Animals in Scientific Research – an Australian Perspective' (2006) 2 *Journal of Animal Law* 67, 78.

[7] For a brief discussion, see Alex Bruce, *Animal Law in Australia: An Integrated Approach*, 2nd edn (Butterworths, 2017) 256–57.

[8] Sharman (n 6) 68.

[9] ibid.

[10] Heather Browning and Walter Veit, 'The Sentience Shift in Animal Research' (2022) 28 *The New Bioethics* 299.

[11] See Jane Johnson, 'Our (Bio)ethical Relations with Nonhuman Animals' in Wendy A Rogers et al (eds), *The Routledge Handbook of Feminist Bioethics* (Routledge, 2022) 538.

As has been asserted in the context of animal welfare laws, it could be argued that express recognition of animal sentience in this context is superfluous – that the relevant legislation is underpinned by an inherent recognition of sentience and thus nothing can be gained by express recognition.[12] However, in the processes of statutory interpretation words have consequences, both intended and unintended. Further, even where express recognition is only intended to be symbolic,[13] express reference to sentience carries connotations that may lead to changes in the public perception of animals, with the potential for those changes to influence human conduct in relation to animals, including with respect to research.[14]

On this basis, this chapter argues that the legal recognition of animal sentience has the potential to refocus attention away from what constitutes tolerable cruelty by and for humans, towards the impact of research on the subjective experience of animals and resulting ethical and legal implications. In the shorter term, this may create the possibility of increasing the threshold benefit to risk ratio required to be obtained from animal research for it to be approved. In the longer term, the assumption that animals are appropriate subjects for human research may itself come to be invalidated.

In relation to the progression of this chapter, section II will survey contemporary international practice in relation to the use of animals in research and will introduce some of the ethical concerns which flow from this. Section III will provide some background to the legal recognition of animal sentience. This will be followed by Section IV, which will explore some of the potential connotations of the term 'sentience' and their implications for how people think about animals. Section V will explore how these potential changes in how people think about animals might impact decisions about the use of animals in research.

II. The Use of Animals in Research

The contemporary approach to decisions about the use of animals in research is underpinned by the 3Rs framework, which is embedded in regulation in most countries.[15] This framework was developed by William MS Russell and Rex L Burch and set out in their text, *The Principles of Humane Experimental Technique*.[16]

12 Similar arguments were expressed by the Social Policy Scrutiny Committee of the Northern Territory Parliament after having considered several submissions supporting the legal recognition of animal sentience in Northern Territory legislation: see Social Policy Scrutiny Committee, Parliament of the Northern Territory, 'Inquiry into the Animal Protection Bill 2018' (Report, May 2018) 20 [3.12].

13 See MB Rodriguez Ferrere, 'The (Symbolic) Legislative Recognition of Animal Sentience' (2022) 28 *Animal Law* 119.

14 See Browning and Veit (n 10) for a similar argument.

15 Knight (n 4) 167; Jane Johnson, 'Vulnerable Subjects? The Case of Nonhuman Animals in Experimentation' (2013) 10 *Bioethical Inquiry* 497, 497; Browning and Veit (n 10) 303-304.

16 William MS Russell and Rex L Burch, *The Principles of Humane Experimental Technique* (Methuen, 1959).

In essence, this approach focuses on reducing the harm suffered by animals in research. It seeks to do this by replacing animals in research with non-animal methods or by using animals regarded as being 'less sentient', reducing the number of animals used in research, and refining research techniques to minimise the pain and suffering of animals in research.[17]

While these principles are focused on the reduction of pain and suffering in animals, they are problematic for several reasons. First, the principles can themselves be difficult to employ.[18] Moreover, they presume that animal research is necessary and that human interests are more important than animal interests.[19] Perhaps because of this assumption, animal ethics committees may be perceived as focusing on the level of cruelty that is tolerable for humans rather than on the impact of research on the animals themselves.[20] In this respect, proper consideration has not been given to the extent of the pain and suffering experienced by animals in research – from their births to their deaths.[21] The principles also fail to provide a framework against which to assess the ethical validity of proposed research.[22] While various jurisdictions have made recent changes to policies regulating the use of animals in research, including total or partial bans on the use of particular species,[23] this lack of an ethical framework remains an ongoing problem.

In this context, animals are being used in research in increasing numbers in countries across the world. According to Humane Society International, the most used animals in research are mice, rats, guinea pigs, rabbits, fish, birds, farmed animals (cows, sheep, pigs, chickens), mini-pigs, cats, dogs and non-human primates.[24] Scientific research has demonstrated that all of these animals are sentient.[25] In terms of which countries undertake the most research on animals, Cruelty Free International estimates that the top animal-testing countries are (in order): China, Japan, the United States, Canada, Australia, South Korea, the United Kingdom, Brazil, Germany and France.[26]

[17] Tom L Beauchamp and David DeGrazia, *Principles of Animal Research Ethics* (Oxford University Press, 2020) 21; Holly Kantin and David Wendler, 'Is There a Role for Assent or Dissent in Animal Research?' (2015) 24 *Cambridge Quarterly of Healthcare Ethics* 459, 459.

[18] Johnson (n 11) 536.

[19] Hope Ferdowsian et al, 'A Belmont Report for Animals?' (2020) 29 *Cambridge Quarterly of Healthcare Ethics* 19, 21.

[20] See, for example, Johnson (n 15) 500–03.

[21] Hope Ferdowsian et al, 'Toward an Anti-Maleficent Research Agenda' (2022) 31 *Cambridge Quarterly of Healthcare Ethics* 31, 54.

[22] Ferdowsian (n 19) 21.

[23] ibid.

[24] 'About Animal Testing' (Humane Society), available at www.hsi.org/news-media/about.

[25] See Jane Kotzmann and Morgan Stonebridge, 'There is Value in Stating the Obvious: Why United States Legislatures Should Explicitly Recognize Animal Sentience in Their Laws' (2021) 30 *Cornell Journal of Law and Public Policy* 425, 430–40; Donald M Broom, 'Considering Animals' Feelings' (2016) 5 *Animal Sentience* 1, 2.

[26] 'Facts and Figures on Animal Testing' (Cruelty Free International), available at www.crueltyfreeinternational.org/about-animal-testing/facts-and-figures-animal-testing. See also Matej Mikulic, 'Number of Animals Used in Research and Testing Worldwide 2020 by Country' (Statista, 17 February 2023), available at www.statista.com/statistics/639954/animals-used-in-research-experiments-worldwide.

III. Background to the Legal Recognition of Animal Sentience

A. Growing Understanding and Legal Recognition of Animal Sentience

While a precise definition of sentience is the subject of debate,[27] sentience is generally defined as the capacity to sense or feel.[28] Scientific knowledge in relation to animal sentience has been accelerating over the last few decades. Scientists have determined that vertebrate animals are sentient.[29] More recent research has identified that many cephalopods, including octopods, squids and cuttlefish, are sentient.[30] Tellingly, where researchers are not able to establish a likelihood of sentience in a particular animal, it is 'invariably because of a lack of positive evidence, rather than because of clear evidence that the animals fail the criterion'.[31] Lack of evidence of sentience in particular animals may be due to a lack of scientific attention to those animals.[32] Inherent cognitive limitations in humans also impact our understanding of other animals' capacities.

The increasing human knowledge of other animals' sentience has been gradually incorporated into human laws and policies. It could be argued that the first animal welfare laws had little to do with ensuring animal welfare and more to do with protecting human property interests[33] and conserving public morality.[34] Increased awareness and concern for animals, however, have motivated legislators to amend such laws so that they have at least a minimal focus on animal experiences.[35] Moreover, concern for animal welfare over the last few decades has prompted legislatures in various jurisdictions to enact laws that expressly recognise animal sentience.[36]

[27] Rodriguez Ferrere (n 13).

[28] www.merriam-webster.com/dictionary/sentient.

[29] See, eg, Jaak Panksepp, 'Affective Consciousness: Core Emotional Feelings in Animals and Humans' (2005) 14 *Consciousness and Cognition* 30, 43–56; Helen Proctor, 'Animal Sentience: Where are We and Where are We Heading?' (2012) 2 *Animals* 628, 632–34; Jacky Turner, *Stop – Look – Listen: Recognising the Sentience of Farm Animals* (Report, Compassion in World Farming Trust, 2006) 11–26.

[30] Jonathan Birch et al, 'Review of the Evidence of Sentience in Cephalopod Molluscs and Decapod Crustaceans' (Report, LSE Consulting, London, 2021) 7–8.

[31] ibid, 8.

[32] ibid.

[33] See, for example, Joseph D Eisenstadt, 'The Law of Humanity: Tracing the History of Animal Welfare Law in Massachusetts, and Anticipating the Next Step' (2010) 92 *Massachusetts Law Review* 184, 185.

[34] David Favre and Vivien Tsang, 'The Development of Anti-Cruelty Laws during the 1800s' (1993) 1 *Detroit College of Law Review* 1, 11.

[35] For example, Eisenstadt (n 32).

[36] See, for example, Consolidated Version on the Treaty on the Functioning of the European Union [2012] OJ C326/01, Art 13; Code Rural et de la Peche Maritime (Rural and Maritime Fisheries Code) (France) Art L214–1; Bill 54, An Act to Improve the Legal Situation of Animals, 1st session, 41st Leg, Quebec, 2015, s 1; Ley No 1774 de 2016 (Colombia), Art 1, 665.

This context gives rise to the question considered in this paper: whether the express legal recognition of animal sentience is likely to confer any benefit for animals, including in decisions about their use in research. As noted above, sentience has been a key principle in the regulation of animal research for decades.[37] Further, sentience is already implied within the 3Rs framework.[38] In this context, can the express recognition of animal sentience in animal welfare legislation have any additional impact on the lives of animals in the context of research?

B. Legal Impact of Sentience Recognition on Animals in Research

In purely legal terms,[39] express recognition of animal sentience in animal welfare legislation is unlikely to help animals in research where those animals are excluded from general legal protections. For example, in 2015 the National Assembly of Quebec amended the Civil Code of Quebec to declare that animals are 'sentient beings with biological needs'.[40] Sections 5 and 6 of the Animal Welfare and Safety Act (AWSA) 'set up the concrete legal protection of animal sentience'[41] by placing obligations on humans to care for animals and prohibiting certain conduct in relation to animals.[42] Section 7 of the AWSA, however, explicitly states that animals used in scientific research pursuant to 'generally recognized rules' are not protected by sections 5 and 6.[43] While section 12 of AWSA requires that slaughtering or euthanising animals used in research must be done in a way that causes minimal pain and suffering, on the face of it this would not seem to require anything more than the 3Rs framework already commands.

Similarly, the Australian Capital Territory Parliament passed legislation recognising animal sentience in 2019.[44] Pursuant to section 4A(1)(a) of the Animal Welfare Act, 'animals are sentient beings that are able to subjectively feel and perceive the world around them'.[45] While the Act imposes obligations on humans caring for animals, and prohibits particular human conduct in relation to animals,[46] section 20 provides an exception to these provisions for conduct in

[37] Sharman (n 6) 67.

[38] It has been explicitly referenced within the New Zealand 3Rs framework since 1999: Animal Welfare Act 1999 (NZ), ss 80(2)(b)(iii)–(iv), 100(1)(fa)(i)–(ii).

[39] Notwithstanding the arguments below.

[40] Civil Code of Québec, CQLR, c CCQ-1991, Art 898.1 (Canada); Michaël Lessard, 'Can Sentience Recognition Protect Animals? Lessons from Quebec's Animal Law Reform' (2021) 27 *Animal Law* 57, 58.

[41] Animal Welfare and Safety Act, CQLR 2016, c B-3.1, ss 5–6; Lessard (ibid) 27 65.

[42] ibid, s 5.

[43] ibid, s 7.

[44] Animal Welfare Act 1992 (ACT), s 4A(1)(a).

[45] ibid.

[46] Animal Welfare Act 1992 (ACT), Part 2.

accordance with an approved or mandatory code of practice.[47] In this respect, the Animal Welfare (Australian Code for the Care and Use of Animals for Scientific Purposes) Code of Practice 2014 (No 1) was approved under section 22 of the Act. The Code is extensive, underpinned by the 3Rs framework and recognises, at least to some extent, that animals are sentient.[48] Thus, the express recognition of sentience in the Animal Welfare Act is unlikely to have any additional impact on animals used in research in Australia.

Where animals used in research *are* covered by general legal protections, the impact of express legal recognition of animal sentience is less clear. The potential impact, if any, is that recognition of animal sentience may influence the statutory interpretation of general cruelty prohibitions. For example, animals are recognised as sentient beings with intrinsic value pursuant to Article 1.3(1)–(2) of the Animals Act 2011 (Netherlands). Animals used in research are included within the scope of the general prohibition in Article 2.1(1) on causing an animal pain or injury without reasonable purpose or surpassing what is required to achieve a reasonable purpose.[49] Interpretation of the words 'reasonable purpose' may change considering the sentience recognition provision in Article 1.3(1)–(2). In particular, a higher threshold for 'reasonableness' might be required in light of an understanding of animals as being sentient.

A similar argument could be made in relation to the Tanzanian Animal Welfare Act (2008).[50] Section 4(b)(i) recognises that 'an animal is a sentient being', and sentient is defined in section 3 as a capacity to be 'aware of sensations, emotions, feeling pain, suffering and enjoying their species specific needs'.[51] General cruelty prohibitions are set out in section 59(1) and include proscriptions on taking or carrying an animal in a way that causes 'unnecessary suffering',[52] administering a poisonous drug or substance to an animal without 'reasonable' excuse,[53] and operating on an animal without 'due care and humanity'.[54] Here, recognising that animals are capable of their own subjective feelings may alter the interpretation of the legislative words of qualification. For example, the threshold for what constitutes 'necessary' suffering might be raised while what counts as a 'reasonable' excuse may be limited because of sentience recognition. The impact of the legal recognition of animal sentience on animals in research that are covered by general anti-cruelty provisions is thus largely unclear.

[47] ibid, s 20.

[48] For example, one of the governing principles for use of animals in research is 'avoiding or minimising harm, including pain and distress, to those animals': Animal Welfare (Australian Code for the Care and Use of Animals for Scientific Purposes) Code of Practice 2014 (No 1) 8th edn (NHMRC, 2013) 1.1(iii).

[49] Wet dieren 2011 (Animals Act) (Netherlands), Art 2.1(1), (7). Note that the Wet op de dierproeven 1977 (Experiments on Animals Act) (Netherlands), art 1a also recognises animals as having 'intrinsic value' and applies specifically to animals used in research.

[50] Animal Welfare Act 2008 (Tanzania).

[51] ibid, ss 3, 4(b)(i).

[52] ibid, s 59(1)(c).

[53] ibid, s 59(1)(f).

[54] ibid, s 59(1)(g).

IV. Sentience Recognition and its Theoretical Connotations

While the above discussion suggests some ways that sentience recognition might influence the statutory interpretation of general cruelty prohibitions, it can be difficult to predict the way judges will interpret the law. It is evident, however, that judges would consider the meaning of the word 'sentient' when seeking to interpret it. Similarly, awareness of animal sentience amongst the public is likely to initiate some reflection on what it means to be sentient. In this respect, contemplating the meaning of sentience may provide some indication as to its potential for changing practices. The next section will explore some likely theoretical connotations of the term 'sentient', and how they might change the way that humans perceive animals.

A. Sentience and Vulnerability

Sentience can be considered a proxy term to assign moral status to beings.[55] In this respect, to recognise that another being is sentient involves recognising that their interests should be considered in moral decision-making. Sentient beings have interests in their own well-being, for example, having enough food and water, having access to shelter, and not being harmed by others. Some sentient beings also have agency-based interests, which might include individual values or beliefs.[56]

A sentient being that has the capacities referred to above is inherently vulnerable to harm caused by the actions of others. Recognising that an animal is sentient may therefore give rise to a view that the animal is or may become vulnerable.[57] While these uses of the term 'vulnerability' are broad, vulnerability theory can assist in better understanding the meaning and implications of the word, as well as how it relates to the concept of sentience.[58] At the outset, however, it is worth observing that while animals used in research would instinctively seem to be vulnerable, the concept of vulnerability is not generally used in relation to animals in that context.[59]

Although different conceptions of vulnerability exist in the literature, two broad themes can be identified.[60] First, vulnerability can be conceived of as a universal

[55] Angela K Martin, 'Animal Vulnerability and its Ethical Implications: An Exploration' (2021) 38 *Journal of Applied Philosophy* 196, 197.

[56] ibid, 202.

[57] See generally, Maneesha Deckha, *Animals as Legal Beings: Contesting Anthropocentric Legal Orders* (University of Toronto Press, 2021) 130–37.

[58] While the term 'vulnerability' may also be used in relation to non-sentient entities, this is a different use of the term and beyond the scope of this discussion. See Martin (n 55) 198.

[59] Johnson (n 15) 497.

[60] This analysis draws on the taxonomy developed by Catriona Mackenzie, Wendy Rogers and Susan Dodds: Catriona Mackenzie, Wendy Rogers and Susan Dodds, 'Introduction: What is Vulnerability and Why Should it Matter for Moral Theory?' in Catriona Mackenzie, Wendy Rogers and Susan Dodds

condition. In this respect, all human beings are vulnerable, a condition that arises from embodiment, through which a person may be subject to pain or suffering.[61] Animals can also be understood as vulnerable in this sense.[62] Like humans, their vulnerability originates from their embodied sentience. As a result of sentience, all animals are subject to an ongoing possibility of pain and suffering resulting from their own biology (for example, disease), external events (for example, bushfires) or other beings (for example, humans).[63]

Second, vulnerability can also be understood as being context- or circumstance-dependent. In this conception, a person's vulnerability arises from some aspect of their situation, for example, from their environment or from their economic context.[64] In relation to animals, it could be argued that some animals are vulnerable in particular settings, such as in research, or for specific reasons, for example, their dependence on humans,[65] their lack of language capacity, or the failure of human laws and institutions to recognise their agency and protect them from harm.[66] In this respect, animals used in research can be seen as vulnerable as a result of their dependence on humans to protect their interests and needs.[67]

Pathogenic vulnerability is a subcategory of context- or circumstance-dependent vulnerability and can arise in two situations. First, relationships that are ethically dysfunctional can give rise to vulnerability.[68] This might occur, for example, where relationships involve discrimination or injustice.[69] Second, vulnerability can arise where efforts to ameliorate or fix prevailing vulnerabilities instead serve to exacerbate them.[70] As philosopher Jane Johnson explains, animals in research may be conceived as being pathogenically vulnerable as a result of human prejudice in relation to animals (speciesism) which underpins their current use in research in the first place, together with the manner in which Animal Ethics Committees operate.[71]

Express recognition of animals as sentient may raise human awareness of animal vulnerability. Sentience shifts focus to the embodied physical experience, and in the theory discussed here, it is the physical body that gives rise to vulnerability. As a result of this connection between the concepts of sentience and

(eds), *Vulnerability: New Essays in Ethics and Feminist Philosophy* (Oxford University Press, 2013). See also Johnson (n 15) 498–99.

[61] Martha Albertson Fineman, 'The Vulnerable Subject: Anchoring Equality in the Human Condition' (2008) 20 *Yale Journal of Law and Feminism* 1, 9.

[62] Ani B Satz, 'Animals as Vulnerable Subjects: Beyond Interest-Convergence, Hierarchy, and Property' (2010) 16 *Animal Law* 65, 79–80. See also Martin (n 55) 197; Johnson (n 15) 499.

[63] See Albertson Fineman (n 60) 9; Satz (n 62).

[64] Johnson (n 15) 499.

[65] Satz (n 62) 79-80.

[66] Martin (n 55) 197.

[67] Johnson (n 15) 500.

[68] ibid.

[69] ibid.

[70] ibid.

[71] Johnson (n 15) 500–03.

vulnerability, sentience recognition has the potential to shift the human focus to the impact of human actions on the animal. Within current regulatory frameworks, the focus for animal ethics committees has become determining what level of cruelty is tolerable for humans.[72] Conceiving of animals as sentient and thus potentially vulnerable may lead to greater emphasis being placed on the potential subjective and cumulative experiences of animals. This may serve to highlight the similarity of human and animal experiences and potentially contribute to transformative change.

B. Sentience and Relationality

Sentience also gives rise to a capacity to have relationships with others. That most animals have the capacity to have relationships with other animals and with humans is well documented.[73] For example, primatologist Jane Goodall's often-quoted story of a chimpanzee called Flint grieving following the death of another chimpanzee called Flo is suggestive of the very close bonds between the animals.[74] The close bonds between humans and their animal companions are personally experienced by many humans.

Thinking about animals as being relational in this way may have an impact on how animals are viewed and treated in the context of research. To use animals in research, researchers often feel the need to 'cast animals as strangers'.[75] Distancing themselves from the animals enables researchers to maintain their perception of 'scientific objectivity'.[76] Conversely, viewing animals as sentient, relational beings, combined with observation of individual animal needs and personalities, may result in a re-envisioning of the conduct of research involving animals. As social scientist Pru Hobson-West and veterinary surgeon Ashley Davies observe, 'the perceived sentience or capacities of individual animals can matter in practice. This suggests a more relational approach is operating.'[77] This shift in approach could

[72] See, for example, ibid.

[73] See generally, Deckha (n 57) 128–30; Ashleigh PA Best, 'Material Vulnerabilities and Interspecies Relationalities: A Critical Appraisal of the Legal Status of Animals in Disasters' (2022) 31 *Griffith Law Review* 287; Lisa S Freund et al (eds), *The Social Neuroscience of Human-Animal Interaction* (American Psychological Association, 2016); Yizheng Zhao, Pinyu Chen and Xiang Kong, 'More than Human Consumption Space: Human-Animal Encounters and Relationships in Cat Cafes in Shanghai' (2023) *Social & Cultural Geography*; Maja Pasaric and Graeme Warren, 'Interactions of Care and Control: Human-animal Relationships in Hunter-gatherer Communities in Near-contemporary Eastern Siberia and the Mesolithic of Northwest Europe' (2019) 29 *Cambridge Archaeological Journal* 465; Niloofar Solhjoo, '"I Can Tell He is in a Good Mood." Embodied Aspects of Information in Human-Animal Relationship' (2022) 27(Special Issue) *Information Research – An International Electronic Journal.*

[74] Jane Goodall, *Through A Window: My Thirty Years with the Chimpanzees of Gombe* (Mariner Books, 1990) 224–25.

[75] Johnson (n 11) 543.

[76] ibid.

[77] Pru Hobson-West and Ashley Davies, 'Societal Sentience: Constructions of the Public in Animal Research policy and Practice' (2018) 43 *Science, Technology and Human Values* 671, 681.

potentially provide a source of protection for animals, if those relationships were reimagined. For example, viewing 'animals as patients', similar to the conduct of human clinical research, could result in significant changes in perceptions regarding the permissibility of certain types of research.[78]

C. Sentience and Equality

A continued focus on the meaning of 'sentience' might also suggest that the similar capacities of sentient beings (human and nonhuman) should merit equal or similar protection. In this respect, scientific literature indicates not only that many animals are sentient, but that they are sentient in a similar manner to humans.[79] While similarity to humans is not and should not be the moral yardstick for animal protection, the shared and equal capacities of sentient humans and animals to experience life subjectively, including to experience negative states of pain and suffering, suggests that some equality of protection from these states is appropriate. If this premise were accepted, it may have radical implications for the way humans treat animals. In particular, general protections that apply in relation to research involving humans could extend to research involving animals.[80]

Recognising that animals are sentient, and that sentience is the justification for animal welfare laws, also exposes the inconsistency within and weakens existing animal welfare laws. Animal sentience is rightly posited as the reason that animal welfare matters and as a baseline for legal protection.[81] At the same time, however, whole groups of sentient animals are routinely excluded from welfare protections, including animals used in research.[82] Further, while laws frequently prohibit the infliction of 'unnecessary suffering' on animals, what is necessary is interpreted by reference to human interests rather than animal interests.[83] Thus, animals with the same capacity for suffering, even of the same species, can be treated very differently depending on the way they are being used by humans. This approach obscures the purpose of animal protection laws. As legal scholar Ani Satz states, 'When animals with similar abilities are treated differently, the use of animal capacities as a relevant baseline for legal protection is undermined.'[84] Because the justification for animal welfare laws is undermined, the 'precedential value of animal law' is

[78] Ferdowsian (n 19) 32.

[79] For a detailed discussion, see Kotzmann and Stonebridge (n 25) 430–40.

[80] For a proposal in this respect, see Ferdowsian (n 19) 21. See also Satz's similar proposal for Equal Protection of Animals, which she argues would require the end of laboratory experimentation on animals: Satz (n 62) 115.

[81] See Jane Kotzmann and Gisela Nip, 'Bringing Animal Protection Legislation into Line With its Purported Purposes: A Proposal for Equality Amongst Non-Human Animals' (2020) 37 *Pace Environmental Law Review*, 247, 285.

[82] See discussion at section III.B above.

[83] Jane Kotzmann, 'Recognising the Sentience of Animals in Law: A Justification and Framework for Australian States and Territories' (2020) 42 *Sydney Law Review* 281, 284.

[84] Satz (n 62) 92.

in turn damaged.[85] Further, because of this 'legal gerrymandering',[86] the ability of animal welfare laws to achieve their purpose is impeded.[87]

V. Potential Implications of Sentience Recognition for Animals in the Context of Research

Legal recognition of animal sentience is unlikely to immediately end the use of animals in research. Recognising that animals are sentient does not necessarily change their legal status as property. Nevertheless, sentience recognition may still have some, albeit insufficient, implications for animals now and in the future, as discussed in this section.

A. Possible Decrease in Number of Animals Used in Research

Viewing animals as sentient, with that word's associations of vulnerability and relationality, has the potential to impact the decisions made by animal ethics committees. As noted above, animals used in research are often excluded from general animal welfare protections. In relation to these animals, animal ethics committees[88] are commonly responsible for deciding what levels of cruelty to animals in research are justified by specified human interests.[89] Although usually required to consider this question from the perspective of the 3Rs, there is frequently a lack of transparency in relation to the decisions of animal ethics committees,[90] and their decisions involve the application of some discretion.

In this respect, sentience recognition has the potential to raise the bar in terms of what is required to justify the use of animals in research. Recognising that an animal is sentient implies understanding that the animal has an 'increased scope for harm'.[91] As an animal is more susceptible to physical, psychological and physiological harm, researchers may need to provide greater justification for the research question and methods. In this case, researchers that come to empathise with animals may show an increased reluctance to engage in research using animals. They may also have difficulty reaching the increased justification threshold.[92]

[85] ibid.
[86] 'Legal gerrymandering is when the natural baseline for the legal protection of animals – premised on their inherent capacities – is redrawn to facilitate human use of animals': ibid, 70.
[87] Kotzmann and Nip (n 81) 247.
[88] Or an analogous body.
[89] See, for example, Johnson (n 15) 500–03.
[90] See ibid, 502; Jessica Eisen, 'Beyond Rights and Welfare: Democracy, Dialogue, and the Animal Welfare Act' (2018) 51 *University of Michigan Journal of Law Reform* 469, 480.
[91] Browning and Veit (n 10) 310.
[92] ibid.

In this case, the possible result would be a reduction in the number of research projects using animals and thus a reduction in the number of animals used in research.

B. Possibility of Better, Maybe Differential, Treatment in Research

Following the above argument, recognition of animal sentience may also lead to better, and perhaps differential, treatment of sentient animals in research. Although sentience recognition cannot ensure adequate welfare for animals used in research, it has the potential to raise the moral status of such animals, which may contribute to a view that animals deserve better treatment. In this respect, increased awareness of animals' physical and psychological complexities and needs has led to legal recognition of animal sentience; this recognition in turn may highlight the embodied vulnerability and relationality of animals, and possibly motivate humans to ensure better standards in research. For example, in the United States and in many other countries, concerns about the sentience of chimpanzees eventually led to a phase out of their use in biomedical research.[93] Since then, others have argued that similar protections should be extended to other nonhuman primates[94] and to other sentient animals.[95]

C. Possible Implications for Animals for whom Sentience is Unclear

While laws to date have sought to regulate the use of animals in research based on arbitrary species categories, increased focus on sentience may usefully shift the regulatory focus to the subjective experience of animals. Focusing on sentience may pose an ethical problem, however, to the extent that the sentience of some animals remains unclear to humans. This is highlighted in Birch et al's recent report.[96] The authors note that in the cases where they were not able to establish at least high confidence that a criterion indicating sentience was met, it was 'invariably because of a lack of positive evidence rather than because of clear evidence that the animals fail the criterion'.[97] A regulatory system for animals that is focused

[93] Tom L Beauchamp, Hope Ferdowsian and John Gluck, 'Where Are We in the Justification of Research Involving Chimpanzees?' (2012) 22 *Kennedy Institute of Ethics Journal* 211, 213.

[94] Maria Padrell, Miquel Llorente and Federica Amici, 'Invasive Research on Non-Human Primates – Time to Turn the Page' (2021) 11 *Animals* 2999, 2999.

[95] Jane Kotzmann and Nick Pendergrast, 'Animal Rights: Time to Start Unpacking What Rights and for Whom' (2019) 46 *Mitchell Hamline Law Review* 157, 160.

[96] Birch et al (n 30).

[97] ibid, 8.

on sentience may struggle to provide guidelines in relation to how to ethically treat such animals.

As this issue arises to a lesser extent in the context of the 3Rs framework, some jurisdictions have already addressed the situation. For example, the Australian Code for the care and use of animals for scientific purposes[98] does not cover decapod crustaceans.[99] However, the Code indicates that research institutions must decide when the use of an animal species that falls outside of the Code requires approval from an animal ethics committee, 'taking into account emerging evidence of sentience and ability to experience pain and distress'.[100] Thus, this approach leaves the responsibility for deciding whether and how animals for whom the research as to sentience is unclear can be used in research with animal ethics committees.

A preferable approach to waiting for some level of scientific certainty or entrusting animal ethics committees with such decisions would be to adopt a precautionary principle in these contexts.[101] A precautionary principle would essentially provide that where it is unclear whether an animal is sentient, one should only proceed on the assumption that they are.[102] While a precautionary principle might limit researchers, it would prevent the possibility of unknowingly inflicting harm on sentient animals and thus would be more in keeping with the focus on respecting animal sentience.

D. Potential Contribution to an 'Evolving Ethic'

One of the curious aspects of sentience recognition as a legal reform is that it cannot necessarily be categorised as either a rights or welfare-based reform.[103] It may be, nonetheless, that legal recognition of animal sentience has the potential to contribute to public consideration of the lived experiences of animals and public debate about the ethics that can and should underpin human/animal relationships. In this respect, animal sentience recognition may fall within the 'evolving ethic' approach advocated by Jessica Eisen.[104] While the concept of sentience itself may be accused of being abstract in a similar manner to concepts like welfare,[105] it

[98] Animal Welfare (Australian Code for the Care and Use of Animals for Scientific Purposes) Code of Practice 2014 (No 1) 8th edn (NHMRC, 2013).

[99] ibid, 3; Anthony Rowe, 'Should Scientific Research Involving Decapod Crustaceans Require Ethical Review?' (2018) 31 *Journal of Agricultural and Environmental Ethics* 625, 627.

[100] n 98, 1.

[101] Browning and Veit (n 10) 304–06; Sharman (n 6) 79–80.

[102] In relation to what level of uncertainty is required, Birch suggests 'statistically significant evidence, obtained by experiments that meet normal scientific standards, of the presence of at least one credible indicator of sentience in at least one species of that order': Johnathan Birch, 'Animal Sentience and the Precautionary Principle' (2017) 16 *Animal Sentience* 1, 5. See also Browning and Veit (n 10) 305.

[103] Kotzmann (n 83) 285.

[104] Eisen (n 90) 495–530.

[105] In a similar manner to rights are welfare, which are critiqued by Eisen on this basis: see ibid, 494.

may nevertheless 'generate space for public consideration of concrete cases'[106] in a way that other concepts do not.[107] If so, recognition of sentience may be more than symbolic. As Eisen states,

> Critical analyses of law are united by their acknowledgment that every social justice struggle inscribed in rights and law has demonstrated this quality of shifting and disputed substantive justice goals arrived at through *deliberation* and *social context*.[108]

The potential of sentience recognition to contribute to public consideration of the situation of animals in the context of research in particular is worth considering. As noted, there is a lack of transparency in relation to how and when animals are used in research. This necessarily operates to prevent public consideration of the lived experiences of these animals. Recognising that animals are sentient, with that term's accompanying theoretical connotations, may serve to increase public awareness and discussion of animals' subjective embodied experiences.[109]

VI. Conclusion

Sentient animals continue to be used in scientific research in increasing numbers. In research contexts they are frequently subject to pain, suffering and death. The harm that animals suffer in these contexts is commonly regulated by reference to the 3Rs. This requires researchers to seek to undertake research without animals where deemed possible, and where not deemed possible, to reduce the number of animals used in research and adopt methods that minimise potential pain and distress to animals. This approach is premised on the 'presumption of animal use for human interest'[110] and undermined by a lack of transparency[111] and accountability.[112]

As research using animals has long been informed by a concern for animal sentience, it is unclear whether there will be any legal implications of sentience recognition for animals. Many animals used in research are exempted from general cruelty prohibitions and consequently, in a legal sense, are unlikely to experience any change. In relation to animals that are protected by general cruelty

[106] Eisen (n 90) 536.

[107] This suggestion is speculative only. There is a need for research in relation to how sentience is influencing public discussion.

[108] Eisen (n 90) 518 (emphasis added).

[109] Perhaps similarly, the escape of three baboons from captivity in Sydney in 2020 led to advocacy for transparency in animal research: Rachel Clun, 'Baboon Escape Sparks Calls for Transparency in Animal Medical Research' (*The Sydney Morning Herald*, 26 February 2020), available at www.smh.com.au/national/baboon-escape-sparks-calls-for-transparency-in-animal-medical-research-20200226-p544kl.html.

[110] Satz (n 62) 109.

[111] Johnson (n 15) 502; Eisen (n 90) 480.

[112] See Eisen (n 90) 486–87.

prohibitions, the interpretation of those provisions may become more favourable to animals when read in the context of sentience recognition.

Nevertheless, sentience recognition may have less tangible impact by virtue of its theoretical connotations and the influence that they may have on the way humans perceive other animals. Conceiving of other animals as sentient may serve to highlight their vulnerability in research settings, their capacity for relationships with other animals and with humans, and the equality of their interests in avoiding pain and suffering with other animals and humans. Rather than viewing animals in research as 'research subjects', the focus may shift to the subjective and embodied experiences of the animals themselves.

If sentience recognition were to influence the human perception of animals in this way, it is likely that it would have positive consequences for animals in the context of research. Sentience recognition may create space for more professional and public debate, grounded in real cases, about the ethics of using animals in research.

This chapter cannot conclude that sentience recognition will 'provide a radical and much needed shift' in how humans view and treat animals and 'strongly impact the care and use of animals in research', at least in the short term.[113] If humans are serious about protecting sentient animals, then much greater changes are needed in the research context. The paradigm must change from one of a presumption of animal use for human interest to one where the presumption is *against* animal use. Legal recognition of sentience could help expedite such a paradigm change.

[113] Browning and Veit (n 10) 311.

17

The Utility (or Otherwise) of Symbolic Legislation

MB RODRIGUEZ FERRERE

I. Introduction

Often, the recognition of animal sentience in legislative instruments is labelled as symbolic, broadly meaning that such recognition was not intended to have any direct legal consequences. This chapter will test whether this label is an accurate one, and if so, outline the advantages, disadvantages and overall utility of the symbolic legislative recognition of animal sentience. It will do so in five sections. First, it will assess the various definitions of symbolic legislation, before looking to circumstances where the legislative recognition of animal sentience is accurately characterised as symbolic. The chapter will then identify the advantages of symbolism in legislation, including the potential to establish communicative and educative frameworks (ie the beginning a societal conversation about a concept or initiative), the potential for setting international benchmarks and the power of including purely rhetorical ideals within the legislative context. It will also look to the pitfalls of the use of symbolic legislation, including the potential for unintended consequences and the capacity of symbolic legislation to forestall more meaningful progress. Finally, the chapter assesses the overall utility of the legal recognition of animal sentience, concluding that while symbolic recognition has the real potential to change narratives and begin a paradigm shift in the way we think about our relationship with non-human animals, such recognition is not without its dangers.

II. Definitions of Symbolic Legislation

The terms 'symbolic legislation' or 'symbolic law' are both oft-used and reasonably understood, and usually with a pejorative connotation: legislative provisions that sound and look good, but do little, if anything, in practice. Symbolic legislation is 'never intended to have any effect' or expresses 'goals that we wish we could achieve, rather than what we can realistically achieve'.[1] While these vague parameters are accurate, it is important to traverse the various definitions of symbolic legislation in order to properly understand its advantages and disadvantages.

At its broadest, some have argued that law by its very nature is symbolic; a signal that 'shapes how people think about and react to social and political problems'[2] and a 'cultural system of meaning as well as a system of instrumental controls'.[3] As Joseph Gusfield noted, the symbolic aspects of law:

> [D]o not depend for their effect on enforcement. They are symbolic in a sense close to that used in literary analysis. The symbolic act 'invites consideration rather than overt action.' […] In analyzing law as symbolic we are oriented less to its behavioral consequences than to its meaning as an act or gesture important in itself, as a symbol.[4]

There is however, a distinction 'between the policy-oriented concept of *symbolic legislation* and the concept of *legal symbolism* as a more general concept describing the symbolic function of the system of positive law'.[5] This chapter focuses on the more specific 'symbolic legislation', because we are concerned more generally in this volume about the effectiveness of the recognition of animal sentience, and that recognition most often takes place within a statutory framework. However, while there might be consensus around the general parameters about what is meant by symbolic legislation, in terms of a singular, specific definition 'there is no consensus what the term stands for'.[6]

Mark Tushnet and Larry Yackle attempt to provide some contours to the definition by contrasting symbolic legislation with other types of legislation.[7] Their tripartite categorisation is differentiated by the targets of the legislation, the targets' values and preferences, and how the legislature is attempting to modify the targets' behaviour:

- *Instrumental statutes* assume the targets' preferences and values as given but alter the costs and benefits associated with courses of action taken pursuant to those preferences and values. For example, increasing penalties for an existing

[1] Mark Tushnet and Larry Yackle, 'Symbolic Statutes and Real Laws: The Pathologies of the Antiterrorism and Effective Death Penalty Act and the Prison Litigation Reform Act (1997) 47 *Duke Law Journal* 1, fn 362, citing Robert W Gordon, 'The Independence of Lawyers' (1988) 68 *Boston University Law Review* 1, 72 and Carolyn McNiven, 'Using Severability Clauses to Solve the Attainment Deadline Dilemma in Environmental Statutes' (1992) 80 *California Law Review* 1255, 1295.

[2] Monica Williams et al, 'The Politics of Symbolic Laws: State Resistance to the Allure of Sex Offender Residence Restrictions' (2020) *Law and Policy* 209, 220, citing Stuart A Scheingold, *The Politics of Rights: Lawyers, Public Policy, and Political Change* (University of Michigan Press, 2004) and Murray Edelman, *The Symbolic Uses of Politics* (University of Illinois Press, 1985).

[3] Mauricio García-Villegas, *The Powers of Law: A Comparative Analysis of Sociopolitical Legal Studies* (Cambridge University Press, 2004) 20, 23.

[4] Joseph R Gusfield, 'On Legislating Morals: The Symbolic Process of Designating Deviance' (1968) 56 *California Law Review* 54, 57.

[5] Jiří Přibáň, 'On Legal Symbolism in Symbolic Legislation: A Systems Theoretical Perspective' in Bart van Klink et al (eds) *Symbolic Legislation Theory and Developments in Biolaw* (Springer, 2016) 106.

[6] Angelika Siehr, 'Symbolic Legislation and the Need for Legislative Jurisprudence: The Example of the Federal Republic of Germany' (2008) 2 *Legisprudence* 271, 279.

[7] Tushnet and Yackle (n 1) 74–76.

crime is not attempting to change preferences or values of the criminal, but is trying to increase the costs of acting on those values in order to dissuade them from doing so.

- *Expressive statutes* also attempt to alter costs and benefits but simultaneously also attempt to change their targets' values and preferences. For example, the creation of a new offence will attempt to dissuade people from behaving (or continuing to behave) in a particular way by increasing the costs of doing so. However, the creation of a new offence also sends a signal of social disapproval, and that mere signal may suffice to change the values of society at large.
- *Symbolic statutes*, in contrast, 'simply make a statement. They do not have targets as instrumental and expressive statutes do. Instead, they define for the public what its own values and preferences are.'[8] They are not aiming to change behaviour, either through changing values or the cost-benefit analysis for those seeking to breach the statute. Instead, it is the very act of legislating and sending the message of societal approval/disapproval that is the reason for its enactment.

Witteveen and Van Klink use similar terminology and make similar distinctions. If the traditional 'instrumental' style of legislation attempts to guide behaviour through command and punishment for disobedience, then 'communicative' styles of legislation attempt to guide behaviour through persuasion.[9] Such communicative legislation 'can be called "symbolic" in the positive sense, if a law has acquired an extraordinary meaning within the legal and political community. The law is not merely a set of rules, but it is also a symbol for something higher, more valuable.'[10]

As Tushnet and Yackle acknowledge, the categories are not sharply distinguishable, and any one statute will have provisions from each category.[11] Adding to that fuzziness, the reality is that legislators will seldom know the difference between each type of legislation, and given the pejorative connotations of symbolic legislation, will hardly clamour to affix such a label to an initiative. Instead, symbolic legislation is often drafted by political accident rather than design. As John Dwyer notes, using environmental legislation as an example, such legislation will often provide lofty goals, with little in the way of mechanisms to achieve them:[12]

> By enacting this type of statute, legislators reap the political benefits … and successfully sidestep the difficult policy choices that must be made in regulating public health and the environment. The actual regulatory program takes shape only after additional legislative, administrative, or judicial developments that transform symbolic guarantees into enforceable standards.[13]

[8] ibid, 75.
[9] Willem Witteveen, and Bart van Klink, 'Why is soft law really law? A communicative approach to legislation' (1999) 14 *Regelmaat* 126, 126.
[10] Bart van Klink, 'Symbolic Legislation: An Essentially Political Concept' in Bart van Klink et al (eds), *Symbolic Legislation Theory and Developments in Biolaw* (Springer, 2016) 23.
[11] Tushnet and Yackle (n 1) 76.
[12] John Dwyer, 'The Pathology of Symbolic Legislation' (1990) 17 *Ecology Law Quarterly* 233.
[13] ibid, 233.

However, symbolic legislation is not (necessarily) the result of pure political cynicism. Some legislators will be committed to the symbol itself. Thus, even if they would accept that a goal is unattainable, there is value in having a government publicly commit to the values that underlie that goal.[14]

Thus the legislative intention becomes as important as the text of the legislation itself when determining whether it is truly symbolic. Like John Dwyer, Jens Newig has analysed when it is possible to categorise environmental legislation as symbolic.[15] Newig places the intention and design at the heart of his analysis: there is a distinction between legislation that – despite drafters' best intentions – proves legally ineffective ex post, and that which was *designed* to be legally ineffective, *ex ante*.[16] It is only the latter that has the capacity to be symbolic legislation: it might be effective in communicating or entrenching higher values and ideals, but it will not have any direct substantive effect, ie, a direct effect on people's legal rights, duties or statuses.[17]

This helps us differentiate between law that is ineffective or unenforced, which is also often labelled symbolic: legislation sincerely drafted to solve a problem or effect some substantive change is not truly symbolic, even if it fails to achieve those goals.[18] Instead, symbolic legislation is drafted with a political or strategic intention to achieve something other than a substantive change in the law.[19] Of course, legislative intention, and how to discern it (if it is even possible to do so) is obviously a matter of rich debate,[20] and not one we can properly discuss here. The key idea is that the legislature, through its statements and actions, does not *expect* symbolic legislation to have a direct substantive effect.

The foregoing gives us a little more certainty as to the parameters of symbolic legislation. It is any legislation intended by its drafters and the legislature not to have any direct substantive effect. It may well be effective in many other ways – signalling a government commitment to particular values, starting a conversation and shifting the political needle, quelling agitation from lobby or pressure groups, and/or improving the image and fortunes of its drafters – but in failing to effect direct substantive change, it remains symbolic.[21]

[14] ibid, 248–49.

[15] Jens Newig, 'Symbolic Environmental Legislation and Societal Self-Deception' (2007) 16 *Environmental Politics* 276. Newig's own analysis is based primarily on the work of Peter Noll, 'Symbolische Gesetzgebung' (1981) *Zeitschrift für Schweizerisches* 347; Harald Kindermann, 'Symbolische Gesetzgebung' (1988) 13 *Jahrbuch für Rechtssoziologie und Rechtstheorie* 222; and Dwyer (n 12).

[16] ibid, 278–79; Marcelo B Rodriguez Ferrere, 'The (Symbolic) Legislative Recognition of Animal Sentience' (2022) 28 *Animal Law* 117, 136.

[17] ibid, 279.

[18] ibid, 279.

[19] ibid, 280.

[20] For example, Richard Ekins argues that 'the well-formed legislature exercises rational agency in legislating, forming and acting on complex intentions to convey certain meanings and to change the law in the chosen way, for the common good' (*The Nature of Legislative Intent* (OUP, 2012) 14), *cf* Ronald Dworkin's argument that legislative intent is a fiction (*Law's Empire* (Belknap Press, 1986) 335–56).

[21] Rodriguez Ferrere (n 16) 136.

III. When Does the Legislative Recognition of Sentience Become Symbolic?

The European Union was the first jurisdiction to recognise animal sentience. This first took the form of a declaration annexed to the Maastricht Treaty in 1992,[22] before the same declaration was annexed to the Treaty of Amsterdam in 1997 as a legally binding protocol.[23] That protocol's recognition of sentience was brief and simple, with its preamble including the following: 'DESIRING to ensure improved protection and respect for the welfare of animals as sentient beings' before requiring member states to pay 'full regard' to the welfare requirements of animals.[24]

Since the European Union's recognition in 1997, dozens of jurisdictions have recognised animal sentience, often taking the form and content of the European Union. For example:

- In the Australian Capital Territory, one of the objects of the Animal Welfare Act 1992 (as amended in 2019) is to recognise that 'animals are sentient beings that are able to subjectively feel and perceive the world around them'.[25]
- Chile's Law 20.380 on the Protection of Animals of 2009 states that animals are 'respected and protected as living sentient beings that are part of nature'.[26]
- The French Civil Code (amended in 2014) recognises that 'Animals are living beings gifted with sentience. Subject to the laws that protect animals, they are subjected to the regime of goods'.[27]
- The long title (a type of preamble) to New Zealand's Animal Welfare Act 1999 (as amended in 2015) recognises that 'animals are sentient'.'[28]
- Oregon recognises in its legislative finding – a sort of preamble to the animal welfare chapter of its revised statutes – by stating that: 'Animals are sentient beings capable of experiencing pain, stress and fear'.[29]
- Québec recognises in the preamble to its Animal Welfare and Safety Act that 'Animals are not things. They are sentient beings with biological needs.'[30]
- One of the fundamental principles in Tanzania's Animal Welfare Act 2008 is to recognise that 'an animal as a sentient being' with 'sentient' defined as

[22] Treaty on the European Union 1992.

[23] Treaty of Amsterdam amending the Treaty on European Union 1997.

[24] ibid;.

[25] Animal Welfare Act 1992 (ACT), s 4A(1)(a).

[26] Ley N° 20.380 – Ley sobre protección de animales (Chile), Art 2: 'El proceso educativo, en sus niveles básico y medio, debera inculcar el sentido de respeto y protección a los animales, como seres vivientes y sensibles que forman parte de la naturaleza.'

[27] Code Civil, Art 515-4 'Les animaux sont des êtres vivants doués de sensibilité. Sous réserve des lois qui les protègent, les animaux sont soumis au régime des biens.'

[28] Animal Welfare Act 1999 (NZ), long title.

[29] ORS § 167.330; 167.325.

[30] Animal Welfare and Safety Act 2015 b-31(Que).

> 'capability of an animal to be aware of sensations, emotions, feeling pain, suffering and enjoying their species' specific needs'.[31]

Many other examples exist throughout the world, either following the European's minimal approach – simply acknowledging animals as sentient – or something a little more substantial, such as Oregon and Tanzania, which provide a definition for sentience alongside its recognition. The commonality, however, is that the recognition of sentience is simply that: recognising animals are sentient beings.

Unless that legislative recognition is contextualised – for example, indicating the sentience of animals is the motivating reason behind enacting an animal welfare protection system – the consequences or implications of such bare recognition are indeterminate: a strong indicator that the recognition is symbolic. This seems to fit within Tushnet and Yackle's definition of 'simply making a statement', and without articulating the implications of such recognition, lack any target. Certainly, the consistent placement of such recognition in the preambles of statutes is a strong indicator of symbolism. As Kent Roach notes, preambles are often 'used to provide a symbolic concession to values that are not really advanced by the legislation and thus provide an attempt to assuage those who may be concerned about the [legislation]'.[32]

Nevertheless, if we take Newig's definition, then we need to know more about the legislators' intentions and expectations when drafting such provisions. That is beyond the scope of this chapter (but not this volume), although generally, recognition does seem to be part of an international trend.[33] If a core motivation to recognise animal sentience is to 'keep up' with similar jurisdictions, then this would certainly provide evidence that there is no intention to effect substantive change.

Were those investigations into legislative intent to find that there was no expectation of substantive legislative change, then it is worth noting that that the recognition of sentience is perhaps exactly the type of provision where symbolism is justified. Witteveen and van Klink argue that there are three situations where symbolic legislation is appropriate:

> (i) the legislator possesses insufficient technical knowledge to formulate clear and distinct rules;
> (ii) the matter at hand is too complex conceptually to be regulated in detail; and/or
> (iii) the matter has strong ideological implications.[34]

Recognition of animal sentience arguably falls within all three situations. Charlotte Blattner has noted that, 'despite the widespread avowal to sentience, the function and operability of the legal recognition of animal sentience are nebulous and lack

[31] Animal Welfare Act 2008 (Tanz), ss 3 and 4(b)(i).

[32] Kent Roach, 'The Uses and Audiences of Preambles in Legislation' (2001) 47 *McGill Law Journal* 129, 149.

[33] Marc Bekoff, 'Spain Joins Other Nations in Declaring Animals Are Sentient' Psychology Today, 8 December 2021, available at www.psychologytoday.com/ca/blog/animal-emotions/202112/spain-joins-other-nations-in-declaring-animals-are-sentient.

[34] Witteveen and van Klink (n 9) 138.

scholarly conceptualisation'.[35] If this is the case, it makes it unlikely that a drafter will possess the technical knowledge to operationalise animal sentience. Animal sentience is a conceptually complex idea, which might make symbolic recognition of the concept appropriate. Moreover, as Witteveen and van Klink note:

> If the legislator does not possess sufficient knowledge about the matter to be regulated or if the scientific insights on the matter are constantly changing … she simply has no other choice than to use general clauses like aspirational norms which have to be filled in case-by-case in accordance with current insights.[36]

This allows us to take a more sympathetic view of the legislator; even if the recognition of animal sentience was symbolic, the aspirational nature of the concept and its complexity means that not only was such symbolism appropriate, it might have been the only option.

As we will discuss, however, even if symbolic recognition of animal sentience is the only appropriate option for its inclusion in legislation, that does not mean that the legislature should take it. Moreover, the United Kingdom's recent passage of the Animal Welfare (Sentience) Act 2022 *does* show that there is an alternative.[37] This Act directs the establishment of an Animal Sentience Committee whose task will be to assess any government policy, and determine whether 'the government is having, or has had, all due regard to the ways in which the policy might have an adverse effect on the welfare of animals as sentient beings'.[38]

While such a model might meet Dwyer's definition of symbolic legislation – it side-steps actual policy choices and instead delegates power to a committee to implement change and oversight – there is no doubt that it is substantially and substantively different to the other recognitions of sentience identified above in that it could lead to real and substantial legal implications. In this way, the United Kingdom's model is proof that an alternative model to simple recognition of animal sentience is possible, and only strengthening the conclusion that other jurisdictions' recognitions are mere exercises in symbolism. The desirability of that type of legislation will be the focus of the next parts of this chapter.

IV. The Advantages of Symbolic Legislation

The main driver behind symbolic legislation is optics: the political advantage a drafter gains for publicly committing to legislation that represents a set of

[35] Charlotte E Blattner, 'The Recognition of Animal Sentience by the Law' (2019) 9 *Journal of Animal Ethics* 121, 122.

[36] ibid.

[37] Other alternatives exist, including the Animal Welfare Ombudsman in Austria, or an Independent Office for Animal Welfare and Animal Welfare Commissioner proposed in Australia and New Zealand, respectively: see Jane Kotzmann et al, 'Evolving Conceptions of Legal Personhood: What Might Recent Legal Developments Herald for Non-Human Animals in Australia?' (2023) 46 *University of New South Wales Law Journal* 347, 372.

[38] Animal Welfare (Sentience) Act 2022 (UK), ss 1(1), 2(2).

values, even if the legislation does not realise those values through substantive change. This means that the core advantage behind symbolic legislation is the personal political gain for its drafters. Beyond this particular advantage, however, there are broader advantages behind symbolic legislation that deserve greater examination.

A. Interpretative Guidance

As noted above, often legislative recognition of sentience will occur in the preambles of legislation; parts of legislation that express the purpose, object or intent of the enactment. While this might indicate an intent for symbolism – by recognising sentience merely as a throat-clearing statement, it ensures it will not cause direct substantive change – this does not mean such recognition is becomes meaningless. As Roach notes: 'the symbolic, aspirational, and expressive ordering that occurs in preambles can be an important instrument of governance and in itself a form of legal pluralism that complements the usual instrumental ambitions of legislation.'[39]

Preambular statements about the purpose, object and intent behind an enactment are also powerful tools in statutory interpretation: 'by spelling out the assumptions *the legislature* takes to be true, the policies and principles *it* wants to advance and the values to which *it* is committed, the preamble offers interpreters an authoritative form of guidance'.[40] Of course, by their nature, preambles are not directory; they cannot force a particular outcome. Thus, although 'preambles may be used to provide courts with guidance about how they should interpret statutes, there is no guarantee that courts will follow this guidance'.[41]

Moreover, generally, common law courts have given limited weight to preambles in practice.[42] There need not be an 'exact correspondence between a preamble and enactment' and an enactment 'may go beyond, or it may fall short of the indications that may be gathered from the preamble'.[43] As Roach notes, 'courts are alive to the danger that preambles can oversell the fine print of the legislation' and resistant to any less-than-explicit attempt by the legislature to direct the interpretative task.[44] However, where legislative references to sentience are accompanied by definitions, or indications of the expected effect, the interpretative power and prominence increases.

[39] Roach (n 32) 151.

[40] ibid, 153, citing R Sullivan (ed), *Driedger on the Construction of Statutes*, 3rd edn (Butterworths, 1994) 261 (original emphasis).

[41] ibid.

[42] *Desnoyers Estate v Desnoyers* (2020) ABQB 120, [40]–[41].

[43] *Attorney General v Prince Ernest Augustus of Hanover* (1956), [1957] AC 436 (HL), at 476, cited by *Desnoyers Estate v Desnoyers* (2020) ABQB 120, [40]–[41].

[44] Roach (n 32) 153.

B. Communicative Frameworks

Relatedly, Witteveen and Van Klink's reference to symbolic legislation as 'communicative' legislation indicates the power of symbolic legislation to introduce and broadcast new ideas to the public at large. In this way, 'a communicative law offers a vocabulary' and gives 'voice to the central values of a community'.[45] In later work, van Klink built on this idea, arguing that it is this framework and the vocabulary it provides which can affect the way an interpretative community – judges, for instance – perceive reality and the law.[46]

This means symbolic legislation's reliance on amorphous or vague language – 'aspirational norms' – is not a negative attribute: 'aspirational norms have no fixed meaning and have to be developed in an ongoing interaction between various legal, political and social actors'.[47] The inclusion of those norms begins a dialogue about their meaning and importance. Seanna Shiffrin has similarly championed the haziness of opaque legal standards and the purpose they can serve.[48] The uncertainty of a legal standard can prompt citizens to pay greater attention to their behaviour and how they can comply, and that deliberative impact is a positive outcome.[49]

This means that legislative recognition that animals are sentient is thus powerful in two interconnected ways. First, it changes the reality for those applying and interpreting the legislation. Even if judges do not take interpretative guidance from the recognition of animal sentience, they now *know* that animals are sentient. Second, the amorphousness of the term 'sentience' forces a dialogue amongst that interpretative community as to what – if anything the implications of that recognition means in practice. These twin effects are what Nancy Marion has highlighted as the moral educative function of symbolic legislation.[50] The inclusion of sentience in animal welfare regulatory systems makes it relevant, and those who participate within those systems have an obligation to discuss with their peers and educate themselves, as to what sentience could and should mean, and how it might change the way they view animals. In other words, it is precisely the vagueness and symbolism of sentience that forces citizens to think about what it means, how it applies in a particular instance. Symbolic legislation thus has the power to communicate, educate and persuade.

[45] Witteveen and Van Klink (n 9) 128–29.

[46] van Klink (n 10) 25.

[47] ibid, 23.

[48] Seanna Shiffrin, 'Inducing Moral Deliberation: On the Occasional Virtues of the Fog' (2010) 123 *Harvard Law Review* 1214.

[49] ibid, 1220.

[50] European Council Convention on Cybercrime 2001; Nancy Marion, 'The Council of Europe's Cyber Crime Treaty: An exercise in Symbolic Legislation' (2010) *International Journal of Cyber Criminology* 699.

C. Trendsetting

Marion also refers to the function of symbolic legislation as serving as a model for other states to follow.[51] Indeed, it is the amorphousness and vagueness of sentience that presents itself as perfect for dispersal into all legal systems throughout the globe. Regardless of the form of the legal system, each state has the capacity to recognise the sentience of the animals within its jurisdiction. There does not need to be any jurisdiction-specific amendment if the recognition is kept at a level of generality. Moreover, given the lack of substantive legal effect there are few disincentives to recognise sentience, and considerable incentive to do so: not being left behind as other similar jurisdictions recognise sentience in their own legislation.

This cost–benefit analysis could explain why we have seen the proliferation of the legislative recognition of sentience. The European Union's legislative recognition of animal sentience in 1997 appears to be the start of a trend.[52] The European Union's recognition of sentience was, as discussed above, brief and simple, allowing jurisdictions to emulate that approach taken by the European Union, both in terms of placement within a preamble, and a lack of definition as to what sentience means. This is an indication that the European Union set a new standard by recognising sentience; one that other likeminded jurisdictions have been quick to follow.

It is the very nature of symbolic legislation and its aspirational power that makes it an easy export and benchmark for other countries to import and meet. That global proliferation strengthens the first advantage outlined above: if more jurisdictions recognise sentience, then the language of sentience becomes more commonplace, as do dialogues about its place, power and potential (as evidenced by this volume).

D. The Inherent Power of Symbolism

As we will discuss in the next section, the pejorative connotation of symbolic legislation is that it is a sham, allowing legislators to *appear* progressive whilst simultaneously avoiding taking more concrete action to effect substantive change. There is, however, a risk that such political opportunism backfires.

EP Thompson has shown how law that serves to mask and further entrench a power imbalance in the status quo can have the opposite effect.[53] If legislators really wish to simply preserve the status quo and the unjust imbalance between the interests of human and nonhuman animals, then they must be careful not to

[51] Marion (ibid) 706.

[52] Consolidated Version of the Treaty Establishing the European Community, Part D: Annexed Protocols, Protocol (No 33) on protection and welfare of animals (1997) OJ C 321E/314.

[53] Edward Thompson, *Whigs and Hunters: The Origins of the Black Act* (Allen Lane, 1975). A text that among other things, examines the passage of the Black Act 1723 (9 Geo 1 c 22) and its part in creating the working class.

present the recognition of animal sentience as an empty gesture. If they do, then it will mask nothing, and will not quell the agitation for change.[54] This is why the legislative recognition of animal sentience is often lauded by those legislators as anything but an empty gesture.

However, even when bad faith legislators have their fingers crossed behind their backs when they extol the virtues of such recognition, safe in the knowledge that in reality it is an exercise in rhetoric, they nevertheless have indeed recognised the sentience of animals, and perhaps bound themselves in doing so. The aspirational norms contained within symbolic legislation are such that it is very difficult to repeal them once enacted. That means these jurisdictions are essentially (at least, politically) permanently committed to their recognition that animals are sentient, and in doing so, may have unwittingly curbed their power:

> The rhetoric and rules of a society are something a great deal more than a sham … They may disguise the true realities of power, but, at the same time, they may curb that power and check its intrusions. And it is often from within that very rhetoric that a radical critique of the practice of the society is developed.[55]

Recognition of sentience does not evaporate the power imbalance between humans and non-humans. However, it may represent an irreparable chink in the armour of humans' legal dominance over animals.[56] 'Why, if legislation recognises animals as sentient, does the common law continue to categorise them as non-sentient property?' seems a very reasonable question to ask in the wake of such legislative recognition, and indeed, *has* been asked by courts. For example, New Zealand's preambular recognition of sentience is simple and lacks a definition.[57] Despite this, a court juxtaposed it against other legislation that provided for the 'destruction' of dogs:

> Such wording reflects the fact that animals have historically been classed as personal property that can be 'destroyed'. Of course, most New Zealanders would not classify their dog as an inanimate object that can be 'destroyed'. But neither does the Animal Welfare Act, which recognises animals are sentient.[58]

If legislators intend a simple and undefined recognition of animal sentience to go unnoticed, they will be sorely disappointed. The recognition will raise questions, and legislators only have themselves to blame for their asking. The idea of sentience has caused small pieces of grit to lodge in the common law, and like the making of a pearl, although it may take decades, the process might eventually see something far more powerful eventuate. Legislatures have shackled themselves to the language of sentience, and if coopted in the right way, this might lead to results

[54] ibid, 263.
[55] ibid, 265.
[56] Rodriguez Ferrere (n 16) 142.
[57] Above n 28.
[58] *Haenga v Porirua City Council* [2021] NZHC 1549, [35]; see ch 9 of this volume.

that are the direct opposite of their intention to mollify agitators for change.[59] Thus, while it is easy to attack the seeming empty rhetoric of symbolic recognitions of sentience, forgoing such recognition also prevents using that rhetoric to its full potential.

There are advantages to symbolic legislation. It can act as a powerful interpretative tool for courts, or provide new vocabulary to advance existing conversations in the wider community. It can set benchmarks to which other jurisdictions will seek to meet, and even the most cynical legislator cannot prevent the use of what was intended as empty rhetoric to achieve powerful ends.

V. The Disadvantages of Symbolic Legislation

However, there is a reason why most connotations of symbolic legislation tend to be pejorative. In this section, we will attempt to locate the cause of that cynicism.

A. Ineffectiveness

The most obvious concern with symbolic legislation is that it is ineffective. As we now know, by definition, symbolic legislation is not intended to reach particular targets or lead to substantive change. However, there is a risk that it is ineffective in its symbolism, too. As Tushnet and Yackle note,

> the larger the symbolic content, the more problematic the statute is likely to be when it is implemented as a real law. The difficulty with symbolic statutes is captured by the Hollywood quip about movies with a message: 'If you want to send a message, use Western Union.'[60]

Assuming drafters of symbolic legislation are acting in good faith – that they are attempting to send a message through the use of symbolism – then it is crucial that the message is clear. That clarity is often lacking with legislative recognition of sentience. To take the example of European Union – which many other jurisdictions have followed as a model – its recognition of sentience is notable for its vagueness, and when in read in context within the protocol in which it features, it is so abstract and caveated that it becomes close to meaningless.[61] As noted above, the European Union's recognition of sentience became a model that many other

[59] Rodriguez Ferrere (n 16) 141.
[60] Tushnet and Yackle (n 1)76.
[61] Above n 23. The full protocol reads as follows: 'In formulating and implementing the Community's agriculture, transport, internal market and research policies, the Community and the Member States shall pay full regard to the welfare requirements of animals, while respecting the legislative or administrative provisions and customs of the Member States relating in particular to religious rites, cultural traditions and regional heritage.'

jurisdictions followed: preambular, contextless and undefined recognition that animals are sentient. Those bare recognitions of animal sentience depend on other actors – the interpretative community – giving life, meaning and impact to the term. While such an iterative process of definition is not inherently problematic, it does mean that the interpretative community lacks the clear guidance it should expect from authoritative legislative pronouncements.

Moreover, absent an alternate authority within the interpretative community providing a definitive pronouncement on the definition of sentience there is no reason to presume that this iterative process will be a successful one, and overall this lack of clarity arguably undermines the rule of law.[62] Both Lon Fuller and Joseph Raz argue that clarity is a requirement of the rule of law,[63] and applied here, that means that symbolic legislation – and especially an amorphous term like 'sentience' – poses a problem: it is not capable of guiding the behaviour of citizens.[64] It simply is not sufficiently self-evident to the community at large what sentience is and how its recognition impacts the animals (and their owners) within that community. Thus, while symbolic legislation has the positive potential to represent a signal of the values a polity upholds, when the value itself is unclear, so too becomes the signal. That potential is never realised, and potentially undermines the tenets of good law-making.

B. Deception

The ineffectiveness of symbolic legislation to signal particular values assumes good-faith drafters. Much of our discussion, however, has involved the assumption of bad-faith drafters: those who are using symbolic legislation with the intention to avoid taking more substantive action. Newig describes this as the dilemma that faces politicians.[65] Where the community demands a solution to a problem, but the cost of an effective solution is so significant that it will harm the popularity of the politician that promotes it, what is the politician to do? Symbolic legislation provides an answer: 'a merely symbolic "solution" has, from the perspective of the politicians involved, the double advantage that it demonstrates that action is being taken whilst at the same time the costs any substantive solution would incur are avoided.'[66]

The performative act of legislating as a solution to the dilemma becomes the focus of the drafter, instead of trying to find a solution to the original problem, and the symbolic legislation that results 'either deliberately misleads the public,

[62] Timothy Endicott, *Vagueness in Law* (OUP, 2000) 185.
[63] ibid.
[64] Joseph Raz, *The Authority of Law: Essays on Law and Morality* (Clarendon Press, 1979) 214–18, cited in Endicott (n 62).
[65] Newig (n 15) 282.
[66] ibid.

or amounts to self-deception by politicians who are, perhaps, divided between a desire to support a cause and concerns about its financial cost'.[67] Without wishing to be a Pollyanna, drafters ought to focus on providing substantive solutions to problems, and symbolic legislation in providing an option to the drafter to avoid finding that solution, whilst also deceiving the community into thinking that they are taking substantive action, amounts to a worrying moral hazard.

C. Unexpected Consequences

As Tushnet and Yackle note: 'Symbolic statutes can have undesirable effects.'[68] The problem comes when judges must reconcile and integrate symbolic legislation with instrumental statutes, sometimes leading to peculiar results.[69] We saw such an effect with the New Zealand example above: a judge forced to reconcile the symbolic recognition of sentience with another piece of legislation that appeared to deny it. While this example illustrated the power of symbolic legislation, it also illustrates its unpredictability.

If symbolic legislation is that which drafters intend to be legally ineffective *ex ante*, what happens when – despite those intentions – it leads to substantive legal change? Vaughan Black has argued there are legitimacy issues with the unintended change that results.[70] Black derides symbolic legislation for the wasted time spent in enacting it, but also because 'we cannot be confident that such statutes will in future be confined to the symbolic role that their progenitors and proponents claim for them'.[71] Since they were explicitly promoted as symbolic, such legislation 'may not be subject to the degree of legislative or committee scrutiny that a substantive statute attracts, thus increasing the possibility of unanticipated effects'.[72]

Of course, in common law systems, legislation is not, and should not, be the only source of law. But there is a general judicial reluctance to adjudicate upon what Fuller called 'polycentric problems', namely those decisions with indeterminate and unforeseen repercussions far beyond the decision at hand because a judge 'is inadequately informed and cannot determine the complex repercussions' of substantive legal change.[73] Given that unpredictability and the legitimacy gap, few judges will be prepared to effect major substantive change on the basis of a weak legislative signal often in the form of a preambular and abstract recognition of animal sentience. That means, as Tushnet and Yackle identify, that while a handful

[67] Tamara Walsh, 'Homelessness Legislation for Australia: A missed opportunity' (2014) 37 *UNSW Law Journal* 820, 838.
[68] Tushnet and Yackle (n 1) 84.
[69] ibid.
[70] Vaughan Black, 'Rights Gone Wild' (2005) 54 *University of New Brunswick Law Journal* 3.
[71] ibid, 25.
[72] ibid, 26.
[73] John Allison, 'Fuller's Analysis of Polycentric Disputes and the Limits of Adjudication' (1994) 53 *Cambridge Law Journal* 367, 369–70.

of judges might use symbolic legislation to (perhaps illegitimately) justify substantive legal change, most will simply condemn symbolic statutes to ineffectiveness, and 'the result will be that the statutes will occasionally have essentially random adverse effects, serving no discernible public purpose'.[74]

Given the judicial reluctance to use symbolic legislation as the basis to effect major change, the most likely outcome is that the drafters' intent is realised, and it is largely ignored. Nevertheless, such legislation could still have significant negative effects, for as Black notes 'such statutes stand as an effective road-block to any fundamental legislative reform'.[75] This is, of course, fulfilling the intent of drafters who enact symbolic legislation for the very purpose of avoiding more substantive and effective legal change.

In accepting the symbolic recognition of animal sentience, groups pushing for the reform of animal welfare legislation or a change in the legal status of animals may have unwittingly forestalled more meaningful progress. Indeed, given the nature of legislative inertia, and the scarcity of resources, the time and political spent on achieving this legal victory might be at the expense of that progress: putting it more out of reach than had the symbolic recognition of sentience not occurred. Drafters could – somewhat reasonably – respond to those agitating for further change that they have already accepted their demands; a political compromise was reached and further action is unnecessary. Interests opposing the improvement in the status of animals and animal welfare regulation may in fact welcome the symbolic recognition of animal sentience: while there is a risk that it might lead to unpredictable outcomes, there is a greater certainty that it might prevent larger, more costly change, and is therefore worth the bargain.

VI. The Overall Utility of Symbolic Legislative Recognition of Animal Sentience

There are many advantages to symbolic legislation. Even if, by design, it does not achieve substantive legal change in the short term, by providing a communicative framework it can persuade a community and shift the Overton window, which is crucial to effecting substantive change in the long term. Per Witteveen and van Klink's rationale, the complexity of the term 'sentience' makes it more than appropriate candidate for symbolic legislation. Moreover, the introduction of the term 'sentience' into the vocabulary of mainstream animal welfare discourse might have intangible but crucial impacts that go far beyond drafters' imaginations.

The foregoing analysis has shown, however, that enactment of symbolic legislation is not a risk-free proposition. While it *might* lead to overall change in the

[74] Tushnet and Yackle (n 1) 84.
[75] Black (n 70) 27.

long term, there is a greater likelihood that it is a damp squib. This is especially so when the recognition of animal sentience is in its minimal form. A bare statement that animals are sentient – preambular, undefined and uncontextualised – is not aspirational. It does not stipulate the desires of that legislative recognition, eg that owners of animals must now ensure and enhance the positive experiences of their animals. Instead, recognition of sentience in its minimal form is simply a statement of fact and accepted scientific consensus. It is important that the law has caught up with science, but it does not represent a great leap forward. Without effectively articulating its aspirations, the potential for symbolic legislation to create communicative framework to reach those aspirations is minimal.

That ineffectiveness of symbolic legislation is accompanied by attendant dangers. It is not overly cynical to assume the proliferation of various jurisdictions recognising sentience is due to the ease of the process. Meaningful legal change is difficult. There is dissent. There is robust debate. In other words, there is a proper legislative process. While the recognition of animal sentience has formal legitimacy – it was enacted according to the appropriate processes – the vagueness of those minimal forms of recognition lacks the clarity that the rule of law arguably demands. Moreover, while that vagueness means that courts are unlikely to use it as the basis of substantive legal change, any unexpected substantive legal change that *does* eventuate will lack the appropriate scrutiny and debate that ought to have occurred during the legislative process.

This all comes with the opportunity cost of not pursuing the more meaningful change. The United Kingdom's creation of a sentience committee has shown that there is an alternative to minimalist recognition of animal sentience. Although obviously it is not a fait accompli, the committee stands a significantly higher chance of effecting real and substantial change to improve the lives of animals precisely because it is not a merely symbolic gesture.[76] The likelihood, however, of jurisdictions which have already recognised sentience following the United Kingdom's lead by establishing such a committee is potentially lower because of that recognition: it gives those opposed to more substantive change licence to argue that they have already 'done enough' and need not go any further.

This volume indicates that the symbolic recognition of animal sentience has most certainly initiated dialogue about how people around the world think about animals. That dialogue has created momentum, encouraging other jurisdictions to follow the suit of those which have already recognised sentience, which will in turn create further conversations. However, the counterfactual is using the political capital and time expended on recognising sentience to instead effect smaller but more substantial legal change that might have seen greater impact on the lives of animals. Certainly, this volume indicates that the effect of recognising sentience does not have a direct and clear correlation to improvements in the welfare of animals. We may not be able to detect those improvements because the recognition

[76] See Rachel Dunn and Joshua Jowitt's contribution to this volume.

of sentience will shift paradigms only gradually. Perhaps in the long term, it will be seen as the catalyst for major change; we can but only hope so. While holding out that hope, however, it is important to be wary, and question whether it has been the best use of finite political resources, and whether in fact it might, ironically, prevent other changes from occurring. Only with this realistic perspective can we accurately determine the overall utility of recognising animal sentience.

VII. Conclusion

This chapter has advanced the proposition that the legal recognition of animal sentience often amounts to an exercise in enacting symbolic legislation. It has done so by first defining symbolic legislation – that which drafters expect will not lead to substantive legal change – and assessing various jurisdictions' recognition of sentience fall within this category. It has then assessed the advantages and disadvantages of symbolic legislation, before concluding that while there are concrete advantages to symbolic recognitions of sentience, there are also dangers. We can all agree that the symbolic legislative recognition of animal sentience is not a silver bullet. Whether it ultimately leads to a net-positive improvement in the status and lives of animals remains to be seen: we can hope that it does so, but given the dangers of symbolic legislation, it is not a foregone conclusion.

INDEX

www.ingramcontent.com/pod-product-compliance
Ingram Content Group UK Ltd.
Pitfield, Milton Keynes, MK11 3LW, UK
UKHW020235290926
15470UKWH00002B/567

9 781509 970452